SAFETY AND RISK IN SOCIETY

VICTIMS OF VIOLENCE

SUPPORT, CHALLENGES
AND OUTCOMES

SAFETY AND RISK IN SOCIETY

Additional books and e-books in this series can be found on Nova's
website under the Series tab.

SOCIAL ISSUES, JUSTICE AND STATUS

Additional books and e-books in this series can be found on Nova's
website under the Series tab.

SAFETY AND RISK IN SOCIETY

VICTIMS OF VIOLENCE

SUPPORT, CHALLENGES AND OUTCOMES

MATHIAS L. KNUDSEN
EDITOR

Copyright © 2020 by Nova Science Publishers, Inc.

All rights reserved. No part of this book may be reproduced, stored in a retrieval system or transmitted in any form or by any means: electronic, electrostatic, magnetic, tape, mechanical photocopying, recording or otherwise without the written permission of the Publisher.

We have partnered with Copyright Clearance Center to make it easy for you to obtain permissions to reuse content from this publication. Simply navigate to this publication's page on Nova's website and locate the "Get Permission" button below the title description. This button is linked directly to the title's permission page on copyright.com. Alternatively, you can visit copyright.com and search by title, ISBN, or ISSN.

For further questions about using the service on copyright.com, please contact:
Copyright Clearance Center
Phone: +1-(978) 750-8400   Fax: +1-(978) 750-4470   E-mail: info@copyright.com.

NOTICE TO THE READER

The Publisher has taken reasonable care in the preparation of this book, but makes no expressed or implied warranty of any kind and assumes no responsibility for any errors or omissions. No liability is assumed for incidental or consequential damages in connection with or arising out of information contained in this book. The Publisher shall not be liable for any special, consequential, or exemplary damages resulting, in whole or in part, from the readers' use of, or reliance upon, this material. Any parts of this book based on government reports are so indicated and copyright is claimed for those parts to the extent applicable to compilations of such works.

Independent verification should be sought for any data, advice or recommendations contained in this book. In addition, no responsibility is assumed by the Publisher for any injury and/or damage to persons or property arising from any methods, products, instructions, ideas or otherwise contained in this publication.

This publication is designed to provide accurate and authoritative information with regard to the subject matter covered herein. It is sold with the clear understanding that the Publisher is not engaged in rendering legal or any other professional services. If legal or any other expert assistance is required, the services of a competent person should be sought. FROM A DECLARATION OF PARTICIPANTS JOINTLY ADOPTED BY A COMMITTEE OF THE AMERICAN BAR ASSOCIATION AND A COMMITTEE OF PUBLISHERS.

Additional color graphics may be available in the e-book version of this book.

Library of Congress Cataloging-in-Publication Data

ISBN: 978-1-53617-140-2

Published by Nova Science Publishers, Inc. † *New York*

CONTENTS

Preface		ix
Chapter 1	Intimate Partner Violence and Risk Assessment by the Police	1
	Ana Sani, Cátia Rodrigues and Paulo Vieira Pinto	
Chapter 2	Police Attitudes toward Victims of Domestic Violence: Proposal of an Assessment Questionnaire	23
	Sónia Caridade and Maria Alzira Pimenta Dinis	
Chapter 3	Intimate Partner Violence Victimization and Help-Seeking among College Students: Comparisons of Three Measures	39
	Hyunkag Cho, Jisuk Seon and Ilan Kwon	
Chapter 4	Psychopathological Symptomatology in Victims of Intimate Partner Violence	61
	Ana Sani, Ana Isabel Lopes and Cristina Soeiro	
Chapter 5	Forensic Implications in the Management of Sexual Violence in Hospitals	79
	Sarah Gino and Luciana Caenazzo	

Contents

Chapter 6   Working with Victims/Survivors of
Intimate Partner Violence:
The 'Self' in the Therapeutic Relationship   **99**
*Madalena Grobbelaar, Yolanda Strauss and
Marika Guggisberg*

Chapter 7   Supporting Victims of Trauma through the
Human Animal Bond:
Crisis Center North's Paws for
Empowerment Program   **131**
Grace A. Coleman

Chapter 8   Maternal Parenting of Victims of
Domestic Violence   **161**
Ana Sani, Ana Catarina Vieira and Dora Pereira

Chapter 9   Indonesian Women 'Breaking the Silence' of
Domestic Violence through the Domestic
Violence Act 2004: Between The Law 'on the
Books' and the Law 'on the Ground'   **179**
Rika Saraswati

Chapter 10   An Examination of Circumstances Related to
Forced Marriage among Culturally and
Linguistically Diverse Women in Australia   **205**
Marika Guggisberg and Madalena Grobbelaar

Chapter 11   Cyber Dating Abuse Victimization and
Association with Offline Dating Violence   **231**
*Sónia Caridade, Isa Ataíde and
Maria Alzira Pimenta Dinis*

Chapter 12   Multiple Victimization of Children
and Adolescents: Developmental Impact
and Psychological Intervention   **251**
*Ana Sani, Daniela Bastos
and Maria Alzira Pimenta Dinis*

Chapter 13	Youth Victims of Community Violence: Developmental Outcomes and Prevention Challenges *Sónia Caridade, Ana Sani, Laura M. Nunes and Maria Alzira Pimenta Dinis*	**279**
Chapter 14	Violence in Urban Community: Diagnosis of Local Security and Victimization *Ana Sani, Laura M. Nunes, Sónia Caridade and Vanessa Azevedo*	**291**
Chapter 15	Safety and Island Life *Lori K. Sudderth*	**315**
Index		**333**
Related Nova Publications		**341**

PREFACE

Victims of Violence: Support, Challenges and Outcomes critically exposes some of the factors used in the risk determination of intimate partner violence, alongside an analysis on the definition and management of the risk of recidivism.

Traditional beliefs and gender stereotypes underlying police attitudes associated with domestic violence are explored. The authors provide considerations for domestic violence prevention and intervention programs, highlighting the importance of adopting proactive and supportive attitudes in response to victims.

Researchers have measured intimate partner violence and survivors' help-seeking through a variety of different instruments, making it difficult to paint a consistent picture of intimate partner violence. As such, this collection includes the results of a study comparing three measures so as to examine whether a certain measure produces a discernible pattern of results.

A subsequent study analyzes the relationship between psychopathological symptomatology and intimate partner violence in a sample of 122 Portuguese women participants, 61 with a judiciary victim status and 61 without this status.

To avoid discrepancies between medical reporting and the reconstruction of sex crimes, it is crucial to use strategies which focus not only on technical aspects of evidence collection, but also on the way the victim's story will be recorded.

Women most commonly experience violence victimisation by someone close to them. Therapeutic work with victims/survivors of intimate partner violence may range from immediate crisis intervention to long-term support.

The award winning PAWS FOR EMPOWERMENT program in Pittsburgh, Pennsylvania is discussed, as well as the successes and challenges the program has faced in rescuing and training shelter dogs to serve as canine advocates.

A qualitative study is presented which aims to further our understanding of how domestic violence between intimate partners can affect maternal parenting. The sample used comprised 15 mothers and victims of domestic violence, focusing on understanding how they conceive of their role as a parent.

The authors go on to explore the extent to which domestic violence is regulated in Indonesia, and the extent to which such regulation is implemented.

This compilation also examines how the practice of forced marriage arrangements creates vulnerabilities for girls and young women. Accordingly, a discussion is provided concerning differences and similarities between the concepts of arranged and forced marriage, and its relationship to sexual trafficking.

The authors summarize findings on the association between cyber dating abuse and offline dating violence in a sample of 145 Portuguese adolescents and young adults.

Additionally, a review of the literature on the phenomenon of multiple child and youth victimization is carried out, addressing the main risk factors, the implications for the development of children and young people, and guidelines for intervention.

The impact that community violence exposure has on youth is assessed, accompanied with practical proposals for prevention. The concept of community violence and the different types of violence and crimes that could be involved are examined, mapping the prevalence of youth affected by this type of violence.

Preface

Accordingly, to develop appropriate helpful responses to victims of violence and crime, it is particularly relevant to assess people's perceptions, to be aware of their victimization experiences and to identify their needs.

In closing, using Saint Lucia as an example, some of the challenges of supporting victims of intimate violence on an island are illustrated, discussing innovative policies and practices to best support victims in this context.

Chapter 1 - Intimate partner violence is a crime, typified as domestic violence in the Portuguese Penal Code, and has a great statistical expression among the total of crimes reported to the authorities, despite the dark figure of crime related to this phenomenon. Police authorities are often the first institution that victims of domestic violence choose to report the crime. Since 2014, the Police has had to carry out the risk assessment in all domestic violence situations, with the aid of a brief, simple and standardised instrument that has been created for that purpose. This instrument (RVD) is based on risk factors for re-victimization, corroborated in several scientific studies and that it is important to know. Therefore, the purpose of this chapter is to critically expose some of the factors used (e.g., presence or threat to use firearm, will of separation from the abusive relationship, forced sex, and abuse during pregnancy, substance abuse such as alcohol and/or drugs) in the risk determination, alongside an analysis that they have in definition and management of the risk of recidivism. In the application of a proficient risk assessment by the security forces in the protection of domestic violence victims, it is important, not only to know and collect the various risk factors that the literature identifies as necessary, but also had a critical judgement on the weight that which one of this risk factors has. Improving the protection of victims of violence and crime by the security forces largely depends on critical assessment and risk management of re-victimization.

Chapter 2 - Domestic violence (DV) is a problem of global concern, widely recognized as a public health issue. There are still many bias and gender stereotypes associated with this phenomenon, particularly when occurring between same-sex partners and against men. As the first official authorities answering to DV situations, police officers play a crucial role in the support for victims of DV. Police attitudes and their perceptions and responses to DV are very important in promoting a sense of security and well-being in victims seeking assistance and protection from DV. The police attitudes toward DV also determine the availability of the victims to seek help from this formal source. Regardless of all the DV studies available in literature, few studies have focused on the role of gender stereotypes affecting police attitudes in response to DV, either through the support provided to the victims or in relation to the victims' complaints. Knowledge of police attitudes in response to DV can contribute to better policymaking practice. This chapter aims to analyse and discuss the traditional beliefs and gender stereotypes underlying police attitudes associated with DV. An assessment questionnaire (POLICE DV) is proposed as a result. The chapter ends with considerations encompassing DV prevention and intervention programs, highlighting the importance of the police authorities in adopting proactive and supportive attitudes in assisting DV victims.

Chapter 3 - Researchers have measured intimate partner violence (IPV) and survivors' help-seeking through a variety of different instruments, which makes it difficult to paint a consistent picture of IPV. While it might be unrealistic to expect consistent estimates in the near future, there might be practical ways to help service providers to make better use of the available data. This study compares three measures so as to examine whether a certain measure produces a discernible pattern of results. This study used the results of three surveys from a Midwestern public university. Findings show that IPV prevalence rates varied across the three surveys, and that compared to males, females experienced more IPV, reported more negative consequences of IPV, sought more formal help, and found formal help-seeking more useful.

Chapter 4 - Intimate partner violence is one of the most significant risk factors for the development of psychopathological symptomatology. The negative impacts of violence, over both short and long time scales, can emerge in different ways. The authors present a study that analyzes the relationship between psychopathological symptomatology and intimate partner violence in a sample of 122 Portuguese women participants, 61 with a judiciary victim status - the forensic group - and 61 without this status and criminal lawsuit - the normative group. Both samples were assessed with a sociodemographic questionnaire, the Inventário de Violência Conjugal (IVC) and the Brief Symptom Inventory (BSI). The forensic group demonstrated a higher number of psychopathological disturbance indicators than the normative group. In the forensic group, the victims that maintained the relationship with the abusive partner and those that already terminated this relationship showed no differences in their psychopathological symptomatology indicators. The authors also found that psychopathological symptomatology had a stronger association with physical violence than with psychological violence. These results substantiate the need to perform a broader violence risk assessment that takes into account the psychological and physical well-being of the victim, as well as clinical and forensic psychological monitoring.

Chapter 5 - Sexual assault involves a broad spectrum of nonconsensual sexual activity, including events with and without vaginal and/or anal penetration and/or oral sex and events characterized by the use of physical force or psychological coercion.

Given the acute nature of sexual assault, emergency medicine providers are often the first clinicians to take care of the victim, and care of such patients differs from care of those presenting other kind of trauma or injuries.

The sexual assault examination poses many problems to health personnel that have a dual responsibility regarding the management of the victims of sexual assault. The first is to provide the victim with the required medical and psychological treatment, while the second is to assist the victims in their medico-legal proceedings by collecting evidence and performing good quality and thorough forensic medical examination and documentation.

Healthcare professionals treating victims of sexual assault admitted to Emergency Departments (ED) need a high level of professionalism, and the personnel involved in this process must perform their role in a scientific manner to effectively aid the administration of justice. They must listen and gather useful information for treatment as well as not just focusing on clinical intervention, but also on taking legal and forensic implications into account.

Despite the fact that indicators have been published in the literature, even today there is still a lack of consistency in how they are applied in some hospital settings. Sometimes the case histories collected from the victim in the ED are still inadequate or incomplete in determining how the case event should be reconstructed.

To avoid discrepancies between the medical reporting and the reconstruction of sex crimes, it is crucial to use strategies, which focus not only on technical aspects of evidence collection, but also on the way the victim's story will be recorded. Such efforts could lead to better management of sexual assault victims, and to securing their legal rights. Within this setting, the involvement of healthcare professionals specialized in the forensic field is paramount both for conducting accurate clinical examination for collecting a detailed documentation of physical injuries and for sampling biological evidence for forensic purposes.

Chapter 6 - Women most commonly experience violence victimisation by someone close to them. Therapeutic work with victim/survivors of Intimate Partner Violence (IPV) may range from immediate crisis intervention to long-term support. This includes therapists maintaining the ability to listen to their clients' agonising, sometimes unbearable experiences. Various therapeutic perspectives, commencing with psychodynamically informed ones such as Attachment Theory, recognise that the therapists' personal history and their relationships are relevant to therapeutic work.

Within the therapeutic domain of IPV, awareness of transference and countertransference dynamics, ubiquitous to all relationships, is particularly important as therapists can become drawn into certain positions vis-à-vis the client; a rescuer, a persecutor, or a victim/survivor themselves. Transference and countertransference issues can impact therapy through practices that interfere with the therapeutic process, such as therapist avoidance, misattunement, denial, dismissal or unconscious manifestations of prior interpersonal dynamics. Additionally, vicarious trauma or secondary stress, are typical therapeutic responses experienced as adverse psychological and physical effects of therapists' exposure to clients' trauma. Considerations for individual therapists comprise the need to assume responsibility for their

Preface

personal histories by attending to their own experiences of pain, trauma or loss, engage in meaning-making activities or relationships, and develop skills in mindfulness and self-care strategies. Organisations can counterbalance implications for therapists by providing appropriate supervision, adequate training and allowing increased time to debrief and discuss cases.

Chapter 7 - As a relatively new field, victim services continually seeks new and innovative methods to address trauma for survivors of domestic violence and their families. Recently, a limited number of programs have begun to experiment with the utilization canines on their advocacy teams, as a mechanism to address the impact of victimization. While little research exists on the effectiveness of utilizing working canines to address the impact of trauma, primarily due to limited research dollars nationally, practitioners can attest to the effectiveness of the approach. This chapter seeks to examine the award winning PAWS FOR EMPOWERMENT Program in Pittsburgh, Pennsylvania, and the successes and challenges the program has faced in rescuing and training shelter dogs to serve as "canine advocates." Further, the chapter explores how working canines transform the advocacy experience with their unique talents and skill sets, providing additional information for therapists and advocates alike to use in untangling the dynamics of trauma.

Chapter 8 - This chapter presents a qualitative study that aims to further our understanding of how domestic violence between intimate partners can affect maternal parenting. The sample comprised 15 women - mothers and victims of domestic violence – and the authors' focus was on understanding how they conceive their role as mothers and how they perceive their parenting skills. The authors used a semi-structured individual interview and the collected data were recorded and then transcribed for analysis. The results are organized into categories related to maternal experiences and domestic violence. The results reveal that an abusive relationship has negative effects on the mother-child relationship(s). Moreover, the authors find that the mothers try to maintain their abilities, motivations and skills in their role as parents, despite the abusive context. This qualitative study reinforces the need for the development of effective parenting interventions in support of victims of domestic violence.

Chapter 9 - 'Breaking the silence' is necessarily part of women being able to obtain their rights and resolve issues of violence in their lives. The Indonesian government's passage of the Domestic Violence Act in 2004 increased people's awareness of the issue of domestic violence (including women's awareness of domestic violence). The presence of such legislation correlates with the State's serious intention to deal with this matter; nevertheless, the law 'on the books' (i.e., present in theory) and the law 'on the ground' (i.e., present in fact) differ markedly. This paper will explore the extent to which domestic violence is regulated and the extent to which such regulation is implemented. While the law aims to protect women (and children), in reality the ability of the women victims to assert their rights vary for each woman. This is largely attributable to the varied understandings of the legal officers encountered and their consequent responses.

Chapter 10 - Forced marriage is a form of modern slavery considered a distinct form of sexual violence in Western countries. Forced marriage, which has been identified as the most prevalent form of modern slavery followed by commercial sexual exploitation and labour exploitation, was criminalized in Australia in 2013. Given that Australia's population is highly culturally diverse, it is unsurprising that increasing concerns are being raised in relation to forced marriage. This chapter examines how the practice of forced marriage arrangements creates vulnerabilities for girls and young women. Accordingly, the chapter presents a discussion concerning differences and similarities between the concepts of arranged and forced marriage, its relationship to sexual trafficking, along with challenges in relation to cultural practices, motivations and barriers for women's help-seeking behaviour. The chapter concludes by offering recommendations for future directions, such as raising awareness of the issue of forced marriage and professional development training for human service providers who are likely to come in contact with victims.

Chapter 11 - Despite the positive effects associated with information and communication technologies (ICTs) on youth socialization process (e.g.,

Preface

xvii

ability to exercise self-control, to promote tolerance and respect for others, to adequately express feelings, to exercise critical thinking, and to make decisions), negative effects have also been documented (e.g., cyberbullying or online risk behaviour), including cyber dating abuse (CDA). Some studies have been documenting that CDA is an extension of offline dating violence (ODV). Accordingly, this chapter summarizes the findings when analysing the association between CDA and ODV in a sample of 145 Portuguese adolescents and young adults, mostly female (89%), with a mean age of 23.54 years and standard deviation (SD) of 4.01 years. Results show that CDA and ODV are very prevalent among Portuguese youth involved in dating relationships and that both types of abuse are positively associated in terms of victimization and perpetration. The co-occurrence of CDA and ODV signals the importance of finding additional strategies to encourage a more cautious use of ICTs in order to prevent specific situations between dating partners, able to trigger abusive behaviour.

Chapter 12 - Children and adolescents are exposed to violence every day and in various contexts, either in the family, at school or in the community. Child and youth victimization is considered a serious public health problem. The lack of knowledge and understanding about it has serious consequences for the individual and for the society. International scientific literature has shown that in addition to life-long victimization, children and young people tend to experience multiple forms of victimization, so an evaluative and interventive approach focused on a single type of violence may be ineffective and inefficient. The study of the phenomenon of multiple victimization is crucial to understand the impact on the adjustment of children and adolescents, as well as for the development of intervention strategies better suited to the needs assessed in this population. In this chapter, a review of the literature on the phenomenon of child and youth multiple victimization will be carried out, addressing the main risk factors, the implications for the development of children and young people, and subsequently suggesting guidelines for intervention. Awareness of the phenomenon of child and youth multiple victimization is of particular importance for the prevention of violence at all developmental stages.

xviii   *Mathias L. Knudsen*

Chapter 13 - Community violence (CV) is recognized as a complex problem, with multiple origins and expressed in variable ways, encompassing different types of violence and crimes (e.g., assault, rape, robbery), as a result of circumstances that are related to the characteristics of the environment. Due to socialization and independence processes that are part of youth developmental pathways, young people tend to spend more time away from home and on the street, becoming more exposed to violence and thus also contributing to repeated victimization processes. Different studies have shown that distinct situations may promote numerous victimization processes, with a particular impact on the developmental outcomes of youth and causing great suffering. It has been reported that exposure to violence in the community is associated with mental health issues, i.e., post-traumatic stress disorder (PTSD), anxiety, depression, poor academic performance, aggressive and antisocial behaviours, alcohol and substance abuse, along with multiple adverse health risk behaviours, suicidal ideation, and also resulting in subsequent homelessness in adulthood. With this review chapter, it is intended to analyse and discuss the impact that CV exposure has on youth, accompanied with practical proposals to prevent it. The concept of CV and the different types of violence and crimes that could be involved are examined, mapping the prevalence of youth affected by this form of violence, analysing the effects of exposure to CV, and concluding with initiatives aimed to contribute to the prevention against this sort of violence, and to minimize the consequences and suffering involved.

Chapter 14 - Community violence is one of the phenomena that most affects perceptions of security. Moreover, when it is associated with violent or criminal victimization (both direct and indirect), it can deeply impact a population's level of security and fear of crime within a specific geographical context. Accordingly, to develop appropriate helpful responses to victims of violence and crime, it is particularly relevant to assess people's perceptions, to be aware of their victimization experiences and to identify their needs. The Diagnosis of Local Security (DLS) is a community assessment measure that allows for not only the gathering of information about criminal occurrences in a specific geographical area but also the collection of data on experiences of victimization and feelings of

Preface

(in)security. The DLS became an internationally well-known procedure that empirically supports the development of community interventions. In this regard, based on a study that the authors are conducting through the community project "LookCrim," in this chapter, the authors propose to analyze the DLS's potential to assess perceptions of (in)security with respect to the experience of victimization to discuss the challenges of and the responses to the phenomenon of community violence.

Chapter 15 - Island communities in the Caribbean experience high levels of gender-based violence and low levels of reporting. Victim advocates in these settings assist survivors within a complicated context of individual and structural violence that includes high levels of poverty and marginalization in communities with little anonymity and limited options for escape. The geographic isolation of islands demands both a creative and informed response from the criminal justice system and an intentional campaign to carve out safe space for survivors of intimate violence; moreover, it is important to invest in prevention campaigns to create communities that not only support victims, but no longer tolerate intimate violence within their boundaries. Using Saint Lucia as an example, this chapter illustrates some of the challenges of supporting victims of intimate violence on an island and discusses innovative policies and practices to best support victims in this context.

In: Victims of Violence
Editor: Mathias L. Knudsen

ISBN: 978-1-53617-140-2
© 2020 Nova Science Publishers, Inc.

Chapter 1

INTIMATE PARTNER VIOLENCE AND RISK ASSESSMENT BY THE POLICE

Ana Sani[1,2,3,], Cátia Rodrigues[1] and Paulo Vieira Pinto[4,5,6]*

[1]University Fernando Pessoa (UFP), Porto, Portugal
[2]Permanent Observatory Violence and Crime (OPVC),
University Fernando Pessoa (UFP), Porto, Portugal
[3]Research Center on Child Studies (CIEC),
University of Minho (UM), Braga, Portugal
[4]Faculty of Medicine, University of Santiago de Compostela, Spain
[5]IINFACTS - Institute of Research and Advanced Training in
Health Sciences, Department of Sciences, CESPU,
University Institute of Health Sciences (IUCS), Gandra, Portugal
[6]Guarda Nacional Republicana (GNR), Porto, Portugal

ABSTRACT

Intimate partner violence is a crime, typified as domestic violence in the Portuguese Penal Code, and has a great statistical expression among

---

[*] Corresponding Author's E-mail: anasani@ufp.edu.pt.

the total of crimes reported to the authorities, despite the dark figure of crime related to this phenomenon. Police authorities are often the first institution that victims of domestic violence choose to report the crime. Since 2014, the Police has had to carry out the risk assessment in all domestic violence situations, with the aid of a brief, simple and standardised instrument that has been created for that purpose. This instrument (RVD) is based on risk factors for re-victimization, corroborated in several scientific studies and that it is important to know. Therefore, the purpose of this chapter is to critically expose some of the factors used (e.g., presence or threat to use firearm, will of separation from the abusive relationship, forced sex, and abuse during pregnancy, substance abuse such as alcohol and/or drugs) in the risk determination, alongside an analysis that they have in definition and management of the risk of recidivism. In the application of a proficient risk assessment by the security forces in the protection of domestic violence victims, it is important, not only to know and collect the various risk factors that the literature identifies as necessary, but also had a critical judgement on the weight that which one of this risk factors has. Improving the protection of victims of violence and crime by the security forces largely depends on critical assessment and risk management of re-victimization.

Keywords: police, risk assessment, domestic violence

INTRODUCTION

In Portugal, combating domestic violence is one of the priority social problems, and there are a number of legally based instruments that underpin domestic violence prevention plans, actions and strategies (Faro & Sani, 2014). Included in this set of instruments are regulations addressed to formal social control entities such as the police, as it is determined that combating this phenomenon should "ensure swift and effective police and judicial protection for victims of domestic violence" (Law no. 129/2015).

Police are often among the first agencies to respond in domestic violence situations, which is why some police squads have police officers with special training in domestic violence response, in order to provide the best support, information and referral to victims (Sani & Lopes, 2018). In addition to police reports and other specific actions carried out in such crimes, the police must also fill in a risk assessment, taking into account the risk factors that may help determine them (Law No. 112/2009). Thus, since 2014 the police have to assess the risk in all domestic violence cases using for that purpose an instrument called Domestic Violence Risk (RVD) (Quaresma, 2012).

Based on the items that were used in the design of the risk assessment instrument, in use by all the Portuguese police, this chapter aims to discuss the main conclusions drawn from the literature on the factors that may contribute to (re)victimization by domestic violence, including marital homicide risk.

A DOMESTIC VIOLENCE RISK ASSESSMENT (RVD) INSTRUMENT

Among the measures taken by Portugal to ensure a rapid and more effective response to domestic violence situations is the preparation of police officers to respond to this problem is one of them. For that agents received specialized training focused on the problem and learned to apply to any victim of domestic violence an instrument (RVD) which allows the risk assessment. Such assessment is based on the positive indicators of a checklist of factors that the literature holds as potentially increasing the risk of homicide and serious offenses to the victim's physical integrity (Quaresma, 2012). This standardized, objective and structured instrument allows police officers to provide a homogeneous risk assessment, supporting their professional decision making. RVD is part of the set of actuarial and statistical instruments (Cunha, 2016; Grove & Meehl, 1996), and once the 20 items are added, by the presence or absence of the risk factors, it is possible to classify in three levels the degree of risk that the victim is exposed to, therefore assisting a longitudinal and dynamic analysis of this phenomenon (Quaresma, 2012).

RVD comes in two versions: RVD-1L, to be used by first-line responders, in all reports of domestic violence or in the event of a relapse, based on available information provided by the victim or others; RVD-2L, to be used in a second-line, focused in risk reassessment, which may occur within 60 days, 30 or 3 to 7 days, depending on the previous conclusions to whether the risk was low, medium or high (Paulino & Rodrigues, 2016; Quaresma, 2012).

Briefly, Table 1 presents the topics existing in the RVD-1L risk assessment instrument, whose items refer to a set of risk factors for severe violence in domestic violence, which are later debated based on the literature on the subject.

Table 1. Risk factors for spousal violence or homicide

• Type of violence (verbal, physical, sexual) • Firearms access • Personal perception of risk by the victim • Violence or threat to domestic animals • Jealousy and possessiveness • Stalking and Threats • Mental disorders/mental health problems • Substance use: excessive alcohol/drugs • Background or criminal record • (Un) employment • Separation/attempted separation/divorce • Pregnancy

Risk Factors for Domestic Violence

Risk assessment is a process that aims to predict the likelihood that a particular behavior or event may occur, its frequency and the impact it may cause (Richards, Letchford, & Stratton, 2008). This is a dynamic process, as the degree of risk may increase or decrease depending on the situation or moment. The risk assessment process involves identifying risk factors (predictors), whose presence means a higher probability of an episode of violence (Neves, 2016). Identifying and assessing risk does not mean eliminating or accurately predicting recurrence of violence, but its assessment is fundamental in decreasing the likelihood of a new episode of victimization or escalation of violence (Matos, 2011).

Most of the factors presented in risk assessment instruments have been identified and studied by the international scientific community (Harne & Radford, 2008). Such factors may be static in nature (not subject to change, characteristic of the individual or his past that are not changeable) or dynamic (characteristics that are subject to change and may be transformed throughout the life of the individual) (Almeida & Soeiro, 2010; Borum, Fein, Vossekuil, & Berglund, 1999; Cunha, 2016).

Thus, we would begin by exposing some of the main factors that the literature states for the risk of intimate partner violence, not excluding the risk of homicide (Aldridge & Browne, 2003) as the extreme end of continued violence (Puente & Cohen, 2003). According to the literature on the subject, about 75% of marital homicide cases were preceded by domestic violence (Campbell, Webster, & Glass, 2009; Campbell et al., 2003). Therefore, it is important to understand now how difficult it is to distinguish severe and lethal violence from non-severe or moderate violence (Echeburúa, Fernández-Montalvo, Corral & López-Goñi, 2009).

Types of Violence (Verbal, Physical, Sexual)

International literature (e.g., Bennett, Goodman, & Dutton, 2000) points out that psychological and verbal violence are often predictors of physical violence. Psychological violence is followed by physical and subsequently sexual violence (Davins-Pujols, Salamero, Aznar-Martinez, Aramburu-Alegret, & Pérez-Testor, 2014). However, there is no consensus in literature as to whether the dynamics of violence is always like this and that the typologies of violence correspond fully to the degree of risk.

In a study by Sugarman, Aldarondo, and Boney-McCoy (1996), victims who considered themselves to be the target of "low moderate" violence reported 99% verbal abuse. On the other hand, within the group that reported being the target of severe violence about 80% also reported verbal aggression by the offender. Thus, according to this study, verbal violence is not considered a discriminating typology of the degree of risk, emerging across the various degrees of risk.

Coker, Smith, McKeown, and King (2000) report that women who suffered physical and sexual violence were at high risk on two scales: Physical Spouse Abuse Scale and Female Experience with Battering Scale. These results are consistent with those found in other studies such as by Aldridge and Browne (2003), in which victims of homicide in intimate relationships had been violently assaulted before they died. In the study by Campbell et al., (2003), the authors also concluded that 70% of marital homicide victims had been beaten before death and that physical violence is, therefore, the first risk factor for marital homicide.

Intimate partner sexual violence is one of the control strategies used by the aggressor and in some cases tends to last for several years (Devries et al., 2013). According to Campbell et al., (2003) is also a high-risk factor for the occurrence of marital homicide.

Firearms Access

Access to firearms, including previous gun threats, are both predictors of high risk, including for marital homicide (Campbell et al., 2003; Campbell et al., 2004).

Several studies on this matter refer to the differentiated use of an instrument for intimate partner aggression in different countries. So, for example, in the United Kingdom the use of cold weapons (e.g., knives) or strangulation are the most common methods of intimate partner homicide, while in the United States the use of the firearm is more typical in this type of crime (Aldridge & Browne 2003). Wiebe (2003) concluded that having a firearm at home in the United States is a risk factor for homicide or suicide. A recent study by Robinson, Pinchevsky, and Guthrie (2016) compared the risk factors that British and American police perceived to be most relevant at the time of risk assessment and concluded that threat or use of a firearm was one of greatest risk factors for marital homicide.

From Sorenson's (2017) perspective, gun use is primarily intended to intimidate, threaten and coerce victims of intimate partner violence, rather than causing physical harm. However, in a study by Folkes, Hilton, and Harris (2013) from a sample of 1421 men with criminal records for intimate partner violence, only 6% used an object as weapon during the violent episode and 8% knew they had access to fire gun. Although the literature points to firearm access/use as a factor associated with the risk of marital homicide, in their study the authors concluded that this factor was of little significance in predicting the occurrence or severity of domestic violence (Folkes et al., 2013).

Personal Perception of Risk by the Victim

Several studies have focused on the victim's own perception of risk of revictimization, stating that the victim can usually perceive, identify and anticipate the risk as the intimate partner prepares to assault her (Campbell et al, 2009; Cattaneo, 2007; Davins-Pujols et al., 2014; Myhill & Hohl, 2016; Sherrill, Bell, & Wyngarden, 2016).

From the perspective of Sherrill et al., (2016), the risk factors referred by the victims as predictors of aggression are: excessive alcohol or drug consumption; verbal behaviour (e.g., tone of voice) and offender's method (e.g., throwing objects); and the sudden increase in the tendency for possessiveness and jealousy. In this line, Gondolf and Heckert (2003) add that the victim makes his risk assessment taking into account practically only the last violent episode: if the partner has been constantly drunk or has increased alcohol consumption in recent years; if the partner has already been married; if the partner has been controlling behavior for the past 3 months; and if both are not living together.

On the other hand, there are some studies referring that approximately half of the women who were victims of attempted murder by their intimate partners reported being completely surprised by the attack (Campbell et al., 2004), which may be related to the normalization of violence within the relationship (Nicolaidis et al., 2003). Repeated and constant aggressions and threats may develop, in many victims of domestic violence, high levels of pain tolerance, which leads to the devaluation of the acts of violence that they consider less serious (Manita, Ribeiro, & Peixoto, 2009) and therefore may not be able to assess the severity of their situation.

Violence or Threat to Domestic Animals

Several studies (e.g., Ascione, 1997; Plant, Schaik, Gullone, & Flynn, 2016) corroborate that domestic violence is significantly associated with violence against animals, including pets. About 71% of victims with domestic animals mentioned that their partner had already threatened to hurt or kill and/or had already hurt or killed their pets (Ascione, 1997). A systematic review study states that, in virtually all articles reviewed, violence against animals is not only related to domestic violence, but it is also associated with childhood abuse and criminal record and, therefore, may be an indicator of other types of violent behaviour (Monsalve, Ferreira, & Garcia, 2017).

Jealousy and Possessiveness

Violent possessiveness, extreme jealousy and constant threats, ideas of victim's unfaithfulness and social isolation are problems of control and power present in most violent relationships and are intertwined with violence and significantly related to the risk of recidivism of spousal homicide (Aldridge & Browne, 2003; Campbell et al., 2003; Messing, Campbell, Wilson, Brown & Patchell, 2017; Myhill & Hohl, 2016; Nicolaidis et al., 2003; Serran & Firestone, 2004; Wilson & Daly, 1993).

Morbid jealousy can be considered as a form of illusion, an overrated idea or a combination of both (Kingham & Gordon, 2004). For the authors, alcohol abuse is a significant ally and any substance abuse should be treated as a priority. Unhealthy jealousy has the potential to cause high stress to both intimate partners and therefore becomes a serious risk factor for violence.

Stalking and Threats

Stalking is a risk factor closely associated with a high risk of violence (Melton, 2007; Sheridan & Davies, 2001), including marital homicide (Campbell et al., 2003).

McFarlane et al., (1999) indicate that there is a significant association between stalking and intimate partner physical violence, as well as between stalking and homicide or attempted spousal homicide. Therefore, if the victim of marital homicide had been physically assaulted before the homicide, there was a high likelihood of having been stalked. Among the victims who were the target of attempted spousal homicide, the authors explain that there is also a significant relationship between physical violence and stalking. The study also states that there is a higher incidence of stalking after the separation of the victim from the offender, both in homicide victims (76%) and in victims of attempted homicide (85%).

In a study by Tjaden and Thoennes (1998), the authors concluded that most victims of physical violence (81%) had already been persecuted by their current offenders or former offenders. The same study indicated that half of the women persecuted by their former partners reported that stalking began before the relationship had ended and 43% after the relationship had ended, while 36% reported being stalked in both cases, i.e., before and after the relationship was over.

Mental Disorders/Mental Health Problems

Myhill and Hohl (2016) claim that there is a significant positive association between some mental disorders and the risk of domestic violence. There seems to be some consensus in the literature regarding the existence of a moderate but significant relationship between violence and schizophrenia (Angermeyer, 2000). The results of the study by Sugarman et al., (1996) showed that depressive symptomatology alone is a risk factor for victims of domestic violence. However, Aldridge and Browne (2003) point to the offender's mental disorders as one of the most relevant factors to consider when assessing the risk of marital homicide.

Juodis, Starzomski, Porter, and Woodworth (2014) compared homicide in the context of domestic violence with homicide in general, concluding that psychopathy was a more common feature in non-marital homicides. However, the authors explained that this evidence does not imply that psychopathology was irrelevant in marital homicides. Nonetheless, reactive emotion was more commonly characterized in marital homicide, rather than homicide in general, which usually commit the crime in the expectation of obtaining some external gain (e.g., money, drugs, etc.). Only one homicide risk factor was less frequently present for perpetrators of domestic violence homicide with psychopathic characteristics - the offender threatened or attempted suicide.

Substance Use: Excess Alcohol/Drugs

Several studies suggest that excessive alcohol or drug use are risk factors for the occurrence of domestic violence (Juodis et al., 2014; Myhill & Hohl, 2016; Sherrill et al., 2016), regardless of whether the victim is also a consumer or not (Coker et al., 2000; Macy, Renz, & Pelino, 2013).

Other studies (e.g., Fanslow, Gulliver, Dixon, & Ayallo, 2015; Sugarman et al., 1996) further emphasize that excessive alcohol consumption was a considerable risk factor for the possible occurrence of domestic violence. The authors add that victims too may resort to alcohol consumption as a temporary refuge for what is their violent reality (Sugarman et al., 1996). In turn, Macy et al., (2013) suggest that the same can happen with drug abuse by victims. However, neither excessive alcohol consumption nor drug use by the victim are factors that, even considered in isolation, are associated with the risk of marital homicide (Aldridge & Browne 2003; Campbell et al., 2003).

Background or Criminal Record

Bennett et al., (2000) in a study on risk assessment among offenders with a domestic violence criminal record found that approximately half of the offenders (45.2%), had a previous criminal record for domestic violence, with 92% of victims reporting that they had been the target of severe physical violence. Some studies indicate that penalties for domestic violence do not deter re-arrest (Sloan, Platt, Chepke, & Blevins, 2013) and that a criminal record or background is a high-risk factor, including spousal homicide (Aldridge & Browne, 2003; Campbell et al., 2003).

(Un)Employment

Unemployment is considered one of the most significant sociodemographic risk factors for domestic violence (Campbell et al., 2003). Employed individuals were less likely to report intimate partner violence (Song, Wenzel, Kim, & Nam, 2017). The unemployment factor associated with alcohol or drug abuse contributes to the increase of financial problems between the couple which, in turn, can cause stress and thus increase the risk of domestic violence (Slabbert, 2016). According to Coker et al., (2000), unemployment seems to be associated with physical and sexual violence, typologies of violence strongly associated with more severe violence.

As for victims, in a study by Brown, Trangsrud, and Linnemeyer (2009) it is reported that female victims explained that the control tactics used by their abusive partners contributed to the difficulty of keeping a job. At the same time, other difficulties are the lack of funding to pursue the desired career, physical and mental health problems that interfered with job security and maintenance, among others.

Separation/Attempted Separation/Divorce

While coercive violence and credible threats from the offending partner are intended to intimidate the victim and contradict their views, these factors also tend to trigger incentives for the victim to leave the violent relationship, which may result in an escalation of violence (Myhill & Hohl, 2016; Wilson & Daly, 1993). Given these factors, the offender may be motivated to act, especially in this way, when he realizes that the victim expresses intentions to leave him (Wilson & Daly, 1993). In this sense, separation or attempted separation by the victim is strongly associated with the escalation of violence and high risk, including the risk of spousal homicide (Campbell et al., 2003; Messing et al., 2017; Myhill & Hohl, 2016; Nicolaidis et al., 2003; Serran & Firestone, 2004; Wilson & Daly, 1993).

Wilson and Daly (1993) demonstrated that women run a greater risk of being killed by their partners within a period of 2 months to 1 year after separation. The period immediately after separation (the first 2 months) is of particularly high risk (Cattaneo, 2007), suggesting therefore that the threats by the partners or ex-partners are generally true.

According to Campbell et al., (2003), the offender's high controlling behavior and verbal violence, together with the victim's separation from the offender, are significantly related to high risk for the occurrence of spousal homicide. However, the same does not seem to happen when apart from the offender's controlling behavior and verbal violence there is no attempted separation. Aldridge and Browne (2003) also report that the victims are more likely to be killed by their intimate partners when they threaten to separate.

Pregnancy

Domestic violence can begin or escalate during pregnancy (Mezey & Bewley 1997; Stewart & Cecutti 1993). However, the average to high risk appears to increase in the postpartum period (Gielen, O'Campo, Faden, Kass & Xue, 1994; Mezey & Bewley, 1997).

Victims of domestic violence during pregnancy are more likely to have experienced all forms/types of violence, particularly the most severe forms of violence. Women who are victims of violence during pregnancy are more likely to be victims of severe violence than women who have not experienced violence during pregnancy. These characterize the offender's behavior as a patriarchal dominator (Brownridge et al., 2011).

CONCLUSION

Assessing risk in cases of domestic violence using a standardized and empirically validated instrument becomes an important aid to all professionals, including police working daily with domestic violence victims and offenders (Nicolaidis et al., 2003; Robinson, 2004). These instruments were developed to help these professionals make empirically guided decisions (Robinson & Howarth, 2012). Although these instruments are important guides to the work of professionals, they should not be absolute and deterministic means of assessing the degree of risk in a given situation. Each case is unique and, despite having similar dynamics, must be analyzed and evaluated individually, because the instrument is not infallible (Campbell et al., 2004; Richards et al., 2008).

The literature also warns that the risk factors should not have the same weight in determining the risk, that is, some factors are more strongly suggestive to the occurrence of violence and thus more determinant for the victim's safety. In order to avoid this absolutist determination of the risk level, which is provided by the instruments, it might be relevant to consider for different risk factors, different weights. Within those already selected by the instrument, risk factors should have different ponderations, as similarly suggested by Echeburúa et al., (2009) in the development of the Severe Intimate Violence Partner Risk Prediction Scale instrument.

Among the factors analyzed in this chapter, separation/attempted separation/divorce, victim's pregnancy or postpartum period, easy access to firearms, and unemployment are solid risk factors, where the various scientific studies have had greater consensus. On the other hand, factors such as excessive alcohol and drug use, mental disorders, or the victim's ability to assess their own risk generate some controversy in the international literature.

In addition to the police, several other entities should develop risk assessment so they can be part of an important coordinated community response, a network and multidisciplinary support to fight the domestic violence phenomenon. Advocacy for work in tune to increase the safety of women and children and thus improving lines of communication, taking

14   *Ana Sani, Cátia Rodrigues and Paulo Vieira Pinto*

appropriate action and monitoring results (Campbell et al., 2009; Echeburúa et al., 2009; Harne & Radford, 2008; Messing et al., 2017; Lent, 2012; Richards et al., 2008; Robinson, 2004) is a matter of growing consensus in the literature..

ACKNOWLEDGMENTS

This work was financed by National Funds through FCT (Foundation for Science and Technology) under the project LookCrim - Looking at Crime: Communities and Physical Spaces - PTDC/DIR-DCP/28120/2017 and within the framework of the CIEC (Research Center for Child Studies of the University of Minho) project under the reference UID/CED/00317/2019.

REFERENCES

Aldridge, M. L., & Browne, K. D. (2003). Perpetrators of spousal homicide: A review. *Trauma, Violence & Abuse, 4*(3), 265-276. https://doi.org/10.1177/1524838003004003005
Almeida, I., & Soeiro, C. (2010). Avaliação de risco de violência conjugal: Versão para polícias [Risk Assessment of Marital Violence: Police Version] (SARA-PV). *Análise Psicológica, 28*(1), 179-192. https://doi.org/10.14417/ap.263.
Angermeyer, C. (2000). Schizophrenia and violence. *Acta Psychiatrica Scandinavica, 102*(s407), 63-67. .https://doi.org/10.1034/j.1600-0447. 2000.00012.x.
Ascione, F. R. (1997). Battered women's reports of their partners' and their children's cruelty to animals. *Journal of Emotional Abuse, 1*(1), 119-133. https://doi.org/10.1300/J135v01n01_06.
Bennett, L., Goodman, L., & Dutton, M. A. (2000). Risk assessment among batterers arrested for domestic assault: The salience of psychological

abuse. *Violence Against Women*, *6*(11), 1190-1203. https://doi.org/10.1177/10778010022183596.

Borum, R., Fein R., Vossekuil, B. & Berglund, J. (1999). Threat assessment: Defining an approach to assessing risk for targeted violence. *Behavioral Sciences & the Law*, *17*(3), 323-337. https://doi.org/10.1002/(SICI) 1099-0798(199907/09)17:3<323::AID-BSL349>3.0.CO;2-G.

Brown, C., Trangsrud, H. B., & Linnemeyer, R. M. (2009). Battered women's process of leaving: A 2-year follow-up. *Journal of Career Assessment*, *17*(4), 439-456. https://doi.org/10.1177/1069072 709334244.

Brownridge, D. A., Taillieu, T. L., Tyler, K. A., Tiwari, A., Ko Ling, C., & Santos, S. C. (2011). Pregnancy and intimate partner violence: Risk factors, severity, and health effects. *Violence Against Women*, *17*(7), 858-881. .https://doi.org/10.1177/1077801211412547

Campbell, J. C., Koziol-McLain, J., Webster, D., Block, C. R., Campbell, D., Curry, M. A., Manganello, J. (2004). Researcher results from a national study of intimate partner femicide: The danger assessment instrument. *Violence Against Women and Family Violence: Developments in Research, Practice, and Policy*. Retrieved from: https://www.ncjrs.gov/pdffiles1/nij/199710.pdf.

Campbell, J. C., Webster, D. W., & Glass, N. (2009). The danger assessment: Validation of a lethality risk assessment instrument for intimate partner femicide. *Journal of Interpersonal Violence*, *24*(4), 653-674. https://doi.org/10.1177/0886260508317180.

Campbell, J. C., Webster, D., Koziol-McLain, J., Block, C., Campbell, D., Curry, M. A., Sharps, P. (2003). Risk factors for femicide in abusive relationships: Results from a multisite case control study. *American Journal of Public Health*, *93*(7), 1089-1097. https://doi.org/ 10.2105/AJPH.93.7.1089.

Cattaneo, L. B. (2007). Contributors to assessments of risk in intimate partner violence: How victims and professionals differ. *Journal of Community Psychology*, *35*(1), 57-75. https://doi.org/10.1007/s10896-007-9097-8.

Coker, A. L., Smith, P. H., McKeown, R. E., & King, M. J. (2000). Frequency and correlates of intimate partner violence by type: Physical, sexual, and psychological battering. *American Journal of Public Health, 90*(4), 553-559. https://doi.org/10.2105/AJPH.90.4.553.

Cunha, O. S. (2016). Fator protetor [Protective factor]. In R. Maia, L. Nunes, S. Caridade, A. Sani, A., R. Estrada, C. Nogueira, H. Fernandes, & L. Afonso (Coord.), *Dicionário Crime, Justiça e Sociedade [Crime, Justice and Society Dictionary]* (pp. 213-215). Lisboa: Edições Sílabo.

Davins-Pujols, M., Salamero, M., Aznar-Martínez, B., Aramburu-Alegret, I., & Pérez-Testor, C. (2014). Acts of intimate partner violence and feelings of danger in battered women seeking help in a Spanish specialized care unit. *Journal of Family Violence, 29*(7), 703-712. doi: 10.1007/s10896-014-9626-1.https://doi.org/10.1007/s10896-014-9626-1.

Devries, K. M., Mak, J. Y., Garcia-Moreno, C., Petzold, M., Child, J. C., Falder, G., Pallitto, C. (2013). The global prevalence of intimate partner violence against women. *Science, 340*(6140), 1527-1528. https://doi.org/10.1126/science.1240937.

Echeburúa, E., Fernández-Montalvo, J., Corral, P., & López-Goñi, J. J. (2009). Assessing risk markers in intimate partner femicide and severe violence: A new assessment instrument. *Journal of Interpersonal Violence, 24*(6), 925-939. https://doi.org/10.1177/0886260508319370.

Fanslow, J. L., Gulliver, P., Dixon, R., & Ayallo, I. (2015). Women's initiation of physical violence against an abusive partner outside of a violent episode. *Journal of Interpersonal Violence, 30*(15), 2659-2682. https://doi.org/10.1177/0886260514553632.

Faro, P., & Sani, A. (2014). Reconhecimento social da violência doméstica como um problema a combater [Social recognition of domestic violence as a problem to combat]. In A. Sani, & L. Nunes (Eds.), *Crime, Justiça e Sociedade. Desafios emergentes e propostas multidisciplinares [Crime, Justice and Society. Emerging challenges and multidisciplinary proposals]* (pp. 35-49) Porto: Edições CRIAP.

Folkes, S. E., Hilton, N. Z., & Harris, G. T. (2013). Weapon use increases the severity of domestic violence but neither weapon use nor firearm

Intimate Partner Violence and Risk Assessment by the Police 17

access increases the risk or severity of recidivism. *Journal of Interpersonal Violence, 28*(6), 1143-1156. https://doi.org/10.1177/0886260512468232.

Gielen, A. C., O'Campo, P. J., Faden, R. R., Kass, N. E., & Xue, X. (1994). Interpersonal conflict and physical violence during the childbearing year. *Social science & medicine, 39*(6), 781-787. https://doi.org/10.1016/0277-9536(94)90039-6.

Gondolf, E. W., & Heckert, D. A. (2003). Determinants of women's perceptions of risk in battering relationships. *Violence and Victims, 18*(4), 371-386. https://doi.org/10.1891/vivi.2003.18.4.371.

Grove, W. M., & Meehl, P. E. (1996). Comparative efficiency of informal (subjective, impressionistic) and formal (mechanical, algorithmic) prediction procedures: The clinical–statistical controversy. *Psychology, Public Policy, and Law, 2,* 293-323. https://doi.org/10.1037/1076-8971.2.2.293.

Harne, L., & Radford, J. (2008). *Tackling domestic violence: Theories, policies and practice.* United Kingdom: McGraw-Hill Education.

Juodis, M., Starzomski, A., Porter, S., & Woodworth, M. (2014). A comparison of domestic and non-domestic homicides: Further evidence for distinct dynamics and heterogeneity of domestic homicide perpetrators. *Journal of Family Violence, 29*(3), 299-313. https://doi.org/10.1007/s10896-014-9583-8.

Kingham, M., & Gordon, H. (2004). Aspects of morbid jealousy. *Advances in Psychiatric Treatment, 10*(3), 207-215. https://doi.org/10.1192/apt.10.3.207.

Lei nº. 112/2009. Estabelece o regime jurídico aplicável à prevenção da violência doméstica, à protecção e à assistência das suas vítimas [Establishes the legal regime applicable to the prevention of domestic violence, the protection and assistance of its victims]. *Diário da República, 1ª serie A, nº189* – 16 de setembro de 2009. https://dre.pt/application/dir/pdf1s/2009/09/18000/0655006561.pdf.

Lei nº. 129/2015. Terceira alteração à Lei n.º 112/2009, de 16 de setembro. *Diário da República n.º 172/2015, Série I - 03 de setembro de 2015.*

https://dre.pt/web/guest/home/-/dre/70179158/details/maximized? p_auth=SS3I3dTa.

Macy, R. J., Renz, C., & Pelino, E. (2013). Partner violence and substance abuse are intertwined: Women's perceptions of violence-substance connections. *Violence Against Women, 19*(7), 881-902. https://doi.org/ 10.1177/1077801213498208.

Manita, C., Ribeiro, C. & Peixoto, C. (2009). Violência doméstica: Compreender para intervir: Guia de boas práticas para profissionais das forças de segurança [Domestic Violence: Understanding to Act: Best Practice Guide for Security Forces Professionals]. Lisboa: Comissão para a Cidadania e Igualdade de Género.

Matos, M. (2011). Avaliação psicológica de vítimas de violência doméstica [Psychological assessment of victims of domestic violence]. In M. Matos, R. A. Gonçalves, & C. Machado (coord.) *Manual de Psicologia Forense: Contextos, práticas e desafios [Handbook of Forensic Psychology: Contexts, Practices and Challenges]*. (1ªed., pp. 175-197). Lisboa: Psiquilibrios Edições.

McFarlane, J. M., Campbell, J. C., Wilt, S., Sachs, C. J., Ulrich, Y., & Xu, X. (1999). Stalking and intimate partner femicide. *Homicide Studies, 3*(4), 300-316. https://doi.org/10.1177/1088767999003004003.

Melton, H. C. (2007). Predicting the occurrence of stalking in relationships characterized by domestic violence. *Journal of Interpersonal Violence, 22*(1), 3-25. https://doi.org/10.1177/0886260506294994.

Messing, J. T., Campbell, J., Wilson, J., S., Brown, S., & Patchell, B. (2017). The lethality screen: The predictive validity of an intimate partner violence risk assessment for use by first responders. *Journal of Interpersonal Violence, 32*(2), 205-226. https://doi.org/10.1177/0886 260515585540.

Mezey, G. C., & Bewley, S. (1997). Domestic violence and pregnancy. *BJOG: An International Journal of Obstetrics & Gynaecology, 104*(5), 528-531. https://doi.org/10.1111/j.1471-0528.1997.tb11526.x.

Monsalve, S., Ferreira, F., & Garcia, R. (2017). The connection between animal abuse and interpersonal violence: A review from the veterinary perspective. *Research in veterinary science, 114*, 18-26. https://doi.org/10.1016/j.rvsc.2017.02.025.

Myhill, A., & Hohl, K. (2016). The "Golden Thread": Coercive control and risk assessment for domestic violence. *Journal of Interpersonal Violence.* Advance online publication. doi: 10.1177/0886260516675464.

Neves, A. C. (2016). Factor de risco [Risk factor]. In R. Maia, L. Nunes, S. Caridade, A. Sani, A., R. Estrada, C. Nogueira, H. Fernandes, & L. Afonso (Coord.), *Dicionário Crime, Justiça e Sociedade [Crime, Justice and Society Dictionary]* (pp. 211-213). Lisboa: Edições Sílabo.

Nicolaidis, C., Curry, M. A., Ulrich, Y., Sharps, P., McFarlane, J., Campbell, D., ... Campbell, J. (2003). Could we have known: A qualitative analysis of data from women who survived an attempted homicide by an intimate partner. *Journal of General Internal Medicine, 18*(10), 788-794. https://doi.org/10.1046/j.1525-1497.2003.21202.x.

Paulino, M. & Rodrigues, M. (2016). *Violência Doméstica: Identificar, avaliar, intervir [Domestic violence: Identify, evaluate, intervene]*. Lisboa: Prime Books.

Plant, M., van Schaik, P., Gullone, E., & Flynn, C. (2016). "It's a Dog's Life": Culture, empathy, gender, and domestic violence predict animal abuse in adolescents: Implications for societal health. *Journal of Interpersonal Violence.* Advance online publication. https://doi.org/10.1177/0886260516659655.

Puente, S., & Cohen, D. (2003). Jealousy and the meaning (or nonmeaning) of violence. *Personality and Social Psychology Bulletin, 29*(4), 449-460. https://doi.org/10.1177/0146167202250912.

Quaresma, C. (2012). *Violência Doméstica: Da participação da ocorrência à investigação criminal [Domestic violence: From occurrence reporting to criminal investigation]*. https://cedis.fd.unl.pt/blog/project/violencia-domestica-da-participacao-da-ocorrencia-a-investigacao-criminal/.

Richards, L., Letchford, S., & Stratton, S. (2008). *Policing domestic violence*. United Kingdom: Oxford University Press.

Robinson, A. L. (2004). Domestic Violence MARACs (Multi-Agency Risk Assessment Conferences) for very high-risk victims in Cardiff, Wales: A Process and outcome evaluation. http://citeseerx.ist.psu.edu/viewdoc/download?doi=10.1.1.485.3056&rep=rep1&type=pdf.

Robinson, A. L., & Howarth, E. (2012). Judging risk: Key determinants in British domestic violence cases. *Journal of Interpersonal Violence*, *27*(8), 1489-1518. https://doi.org/10.1177/0886260511425792.

Robinson, A. L., Pinchevsky, G. M., & Guthrie, J. A. (2016). A small constellation: Risk factors informing police perceptions of domestic abuse. *Policing and Society*, 1-16. https://doi.org/10.1080/10439463.2016.1151881.

Sani A., & Lopes, A. I. (2018). Police intervention in cases of violence against women and their exposed children. In M. Guggisberg & Henricksen (Eds.), *Violence against women: Global perspectives, challenges and issues of 21st century* (pp. 211-235). New York: Nova Science Publishers, Inc.

Serran, G., & Firestone, P. (2004). Intimate partner homicide: A review of the male proprietariness and the self-defense theories. *Aggression and Violent Behavior*, *9*(1), 1-15. https://doi.org/10.1016/S1359-1789(02)00107-6.

Sheridan, L., & Davies, G. M. (2001). Violence and the prior victim-stalker relationship. *Criminal Behaviour and Mental Health*, *11*(2), 102-116. https://doi.org/10.1002/cbm.375.

Sherrill, A. M., Bell, K. M., & Wyngarden, N. (2016). A qualitative examination of situational risk recognition among female victims of physical intimate partner violence. *Violence Against Women*, *22*(8), 966-985. https://doi.org/10.1177/1077801215616706.

Slabbert, I. (2016). Domestic Violence and poverty: Some women's experiences. *Research on social work practice, 27(2)*, 223-230. https://doi.org/10.1177/1049731516662321.

Sloan, F. A., Platt, A. C., Chepke, L. M., & Blevins, C. E. (2013). Deterring domestic violence: Do criminal sanctions reduce repeat offenses? *Journal of risk and uncertainty*, *46*(1), 51-80. https://doi.org/10.1007/s11166-012-9159-z.

Song, A., Wenzel, S. L., Kim, J. Y., & Nam, B. (2017). Experience of domestic violence during childhood, intimate partner violence, and the deterrent effect of awareness of legal consequences. *Journal of Interpersonal Violence, 32*(3), 357-372. https://doi.org/10.1177/0886260515586359.

Sorenson, S. B. (2017). Guns in intimate partner violence: Comparing incidents by type of weapon. *Journal of women's health, 26*(3), 249-258. https://doi.org/10.1089/jwh.2016.5832.

Stewart, D. E., & Cecutti, A. (1993). Physical abuse in pregnancy.*CMAJ: Canadian Medical Association Journal, 149*(9), 1257.

Sugarman, D. B., Aldarondo, E. & Boney-McCoy, S. (1996). Risk marker analysis of husband-to-wife violence: A continuum of aggression. *Journal of Applied Social Psychology, 26*(4), 313-337. https://doi.org/10.1111/j.1559-1816.1996.tb01852.x.

Tjaden, P. G., & Thoennes, N. (1998). Stalking in America: Findings from the national violence against women survey. *National Institute of Justice,* 1-20. https://doi.org/10.1037/e521072006-001.

Wiebe, D. J. (2003). Homicide and suicide risks associated with firearms in the home: A national case-control study. *Annals of emergency medicine, 41*(6), 771-782. https://doi.org/10.1067/mem.2003.187.

Wilson, M., & Daly, M. (1993). Spousal homicide risk and estrangement. *Violence and Victims, 8*(1), 3-16.

In: Victims of Violence
Editor: Mathias L. Knudsen

ISBN: 978-1-53617-140-2
© 2020 Nova Science Publishers, Inc.

Chapter 2

POLICE ATTITUDES TOWARD VICTIMS OF DOMESTIC VIOLENCE: PROPOSAL OF AN ASSESSMENT QUESTIONNAIRE

Sónia Caridade[1,2,3,] and Maria Alzira Pimenta Dinis[1,2,4]*
[1]University Fernando Pessoa (UFP), Porto, Portugal
[2]Permanent Observatory Violence and Crime (OPVC),
University Fernando Pessoa (UFP), Porto, Portugal
[3]Behaviour and Social Sciences Research Center (FP-B2S),
University Fernando Pessoa (UFP), Porto, Portugal
[4]UFP Energy, Environment and Health Research Unit (FP-ENAS),
University Fernando Pessoa (UFP), Porto, Portugal

ABSTRACT

Domestic violence (DV) is a problem of global concern, widely recognized as a public health issue. There are still many bias and gender stereotypes associated with this phenomenon, particularly when occurring between same-sex partners and against men. As the first official authorities

---

[*] Corresponding Author's E-mail: soniac@ufp.edu.pt.

answering to DV situations, police officers play a crucial role in the support for victims of DV. Police attitudes and their perceptions and responses to DV are very important in promoting a sense of security and well-being in victims seeking assistance and protection from DV. The police attitudes toward DV also determine the availability of the victims to seek help from this formal source. Regardless of all the DV studies available in literature, few studies have focused on the role of gender stereotypes affecting police attitudes in response to DV, either through the support provided to the victims or in relation to the victims' complaints. Knowledge of police attitudes in response to DV can contribute to better policymaking practice. This chapter aims to analyse and discuss the traditional beliefs and gender stereotypes underlying police attitudes associated with DV. An assessment questionnaire (POLICE DV) is proposed as a result. The chapter ends with considerations encompassing DV prevention and intervention programs, highlighting the importance of the police authorities in adopting proactive and supportive attitudes in assisting DV victims.

Keywords: domestic violence (DV), police attitudes, assessment questionnaire (POLICE DV)

INTRODUCTION

Domestic violence (DV) is widely recognized as a serious social problem and a public health issue. In this chapter, the definition of DV encompasses it as a psychological, sexual and physical abuse of one partner involved in a relationship with other, sometimes also nominated as intimate partner violence (IPV) (Sigurdsson, 2019). The World Health Organization (WHO) (WHO, 2015) estimates that 35% of women worldwide have already been victims of physical and/or sexual IPV. A European study on violence against women (FRA, 2014), developed with 42,000 women in 28 European countries, has also demonstrated the disturbing dimension of the phenomenon, reinforcing the need to develop more and better responses to fight this problem. DV is transversal to the whole society, regardless of age, sex, ethnicity, sexual orientation, social class or geographic location (Cardoso & Quaresma, 2012). It can occur within heterosexual or homosexual relationships (Messinger, 2011; Stiles-Shields & Carroll, 2014). Initially considered as a women-only problem (e.g., Dobash & Dobash,

2004), studies have now shown that men are also victims of DV (e.g., Archer, 2000) and that is also a relevant social problem (e.g., Randle & Graham, 2011). Male violence is often unnoticed, as men are less likely to report such incidents, out of shame and fear of ridicule, as well as due to a lack of support services (e.g., Shuler, 2010). Consequently, as DV victims, men are not as well studied as women in the same context (e.g., Shuler, 2010). Nevertheless, there are already studies documenting that both men and women may be perpetrating IPV (e.g., Archer, 2000, Hines & Douglas, 2010). Despite the assumptions that DV is primarily a heterosexual issue, a critical overview of the literature (Stiles-Shields & Carroll, 2014) regarding DV in same-sex relationships found that the current prevalence rates of same-sex DV are considered similar or slightly higher than other sex DV rates. Compared to violence against women in heterosexual relationships, DV in lesbian and homosexual relationships tends to be less reported to authorities and less likely to be prosecuted within the legal system (Brown, 2008; Turell, 2000).

Recognized by WHO as a serious human rights and public health problem (Cardoso & Quaresma 2012), DV could result in a diversity of consequences and damage to the victims, e.g., physical, sexual and emotional, resulting in psychological and social isolation and/or economic deprivation (Manita, Ribeiro, & Peixoto, 2009). However, victims of DV may present diverse reactions and respond differently, depending on how they define and conceptualize the abusive situation (Matos, Machado, Santos & Machado, 2012). This fact tends to influence the decision to seek help or disclosing DV incidents from informal and formal sources of support, particularly when involving the police authorities. As the first official authorities answering to DV situations, the performance of the police officers and their reactions and responses in this first contact will determine the effectiveness in the resolution of situations, as well as the perception of safety and insecurity by the victims (Dichter & Gelles, 2012). In addition, the responses of police officers are also influenced by prior knowledge and beliefs about DV (cf., Russel, 2017), as well as by other individual, social, institutional (Buzawa & Buzawa, 2017; Gracia, García, & Lila, 2008, 2009; Hagemann-White, 2017) or legal (e.g., visible injury and use of weapons) and extralegal factors (e.g., police beliefs and attitudes towards DV) (cf. Lee et al., 2013; Wang, Hayes, & Zhang, 2019), that need to be considered in order to better improve police performance. Traditional beliefs and gender-based stereotypes underlying police attitudes associated with DV are analysed and discussed in this chapter. As a result, an assessment questionnaire focusing police officers' attitudes is proposed. DV prevention and intervention strategies are discussed at the end, highlighting the role of the police authorities in adopting proactive and supportive attitudes in response to the DV victims.

POLICING DOMESTIC VIOLENCE: TRADITIONAL BELIEFS AND GENDER STEREOTYPES

DV is strongly associated with violence in the context of heterosexual relations and certain beliefs and gender roles are assumed, making it difficult to recognize abuse in other relational contexts (e.g., same-sex relationships) and against men (Russell & Kraus, 2016).

Historically, the social image of women has always been linked to a multiplicity of stereotypes (e.g., weak, passive, vulnerable, maternal, etc.) (Matos & Machado, 2012; Mellor & Deering, 2010), making them almost incompatible with the role of aggressor, and contributing to identifying them primarily as victims (Russel, 2017). In addition, the frequent association between transgression, violence and masculinity seems to promote gender stereotypes that conceal the possibility of men and women to experience and use violence for different reasons, circumstances, and as a result of distinct histories and contexts of gender belonging (Duarte, 2012). In this sense, a situation involving a woman attacked by a man is perceived as involving greater danger to the victim. This differentiated risk assessment seems to be determined by two important dimensions: physical differences between victims and offenders, such as size and strength, and personality dynamics and relationship proximity (Hamby & Jackson, 2010). This greater focus on man as an aggressor and more susceptible to inflict injury often leads to the ridicule of man when assuming aggression by his female partner (Douglas & Hines, 2011). The less serious perception of male victimization interferes with the situations that are reported to the authorities, leading to the lowest reporting rates of this cases. There is also a fear that men will be perceived as aggressors and consequently detained by security forces (Russell & Kraus, 2016), and that their victimization reports will not be validated (Ristock & Timbang, 2005).

Concomitantly, the society expresses situations of discrimination and impose stressors directed to those who are not part of the dominant cultural group, being marginalized as a sexual minority, as it is the case of same-sex DV victims (Stiles-Shields & Caroll, 2014). This also tends to interfere with the disclosure of DV situations by the victims involved in same-sex relationships, who choose not to seek help, fearing a possible discrimination and disbelief (Ristock & Timbang, 2005; Stiles-Shields & Caroll, 2014).

Being a woman and being a homosexual constitute two social statutes perceived as minorities that tend to interfere with the recognition of DV. It is common to fail to recognize lesbian DV aggressors due to the social perception that women are less aggressive and violent than men. Although lesbian experience the same threats that heterosexual victims do, they also fear the exposure relating their sexual orientation and/or aggression, leading to greater social isolation (Brown, 2008; Stiles-Shields & Caroll, 2014).

Effectively, it has been argued that attitudes about violence could significantly interfere with the victims' responses to victimization experiences (e.g., attributions of responsability reporting to authorities, psychological effects), as well as with community and institutional responses (Gracia, 2014), particularly by the police authorities (e.g., Belknap, 1995; Lila, Gracia, & Gracia, 2013). According to this, two different groups of police officers responses to DV (Chu & Sun, 2014; Sun, Su & Wu, 2014) may be identified: i) the traditional attitude, characterized by non-support behaviours and passive responses to DV; in addition, police officers tend to relativize and/or minimize the effect of police interventions in DV cases, considering that this is a problem that must be addressed by other professionals, such as social workers, rather than police officers; ii) the proactive attitude, involving supportive behaviours toward aggressive DV interventions; in this case, DV is identified as an important part of police work, considering the importance of police officers to be open-minded and receptive towards DV victims, as well as encouraging the request for victims to seek help.

At the same time, police response to a hypothetical DV incident can be influenced not only by legal factors, but also by extralegal factors (Lee et al., 2013). Among the different legal factors (e.g., seriousness of offense, visibility of injury, use of weapon, property damage and presence or not of witnesses) pointed out by the literature as being able to interfere in the decision-making of the police in a DV situation, the seriousness of the offense emerge as the main indicator of arrest among police officers in response to DV incidents, according to Wang et al. (2019). The same authors identify four types of extralegal factors: i) situational (e.g., presence of a suspect when the police officers arrive at the scene), ii) community (e.g., differentiated response of the police, depending on the status of those involved, iii) individual (e.g., police officers' age, gender, race, length of service and past experience may influence an officer's attribution of responsibility), iv) police officers beliefs and attitudes (e.g., gender roles, victim-offender behaviours, attributions of responsibility, and attitudes towards DV).

The impact of gender roles and the power dynamics underlying abusive relationships are thus two important variables to consider when working with the DV victims, particularly in same-sex relationships (Brown, 2008) and when involving male victims. Thus, DV against heterosexual men and homosexual individuals challenges traditional and gender stereotypes about abuse, which leads to this aggression against heterosexual female to be considered more serious than in any other scenario (Russell & Kraus, 2016). This is because police consider them as scenarios that do not fit the traditional DV perspective and, as such, do not deserve legal intervention (Younglove, Kerr, & Vitello, 2002). It is therefore important to know and assess the police attitudes towards DV victims, in order to contribute to improve the performance of actions to be carried out by the police.

POLICE ATTITUDES TOWARD DOMESTIC VIOLENCE: AN ASSESSMENT QUESTIONNAIRE – POLICE DV

As the first official authorities answering to DV situations, police attitudes deserve special attention and analysis in the context of DV studies, given that they are essential at different levels: attitudes of the police i) can determine the assessment and response of the police to a particular DV incident (Belknap, 1995), ii) may interfere with a sense of security and well-being in victims seeking assistance and protection, when exposed to DV situations (Lila, Gracia, & Gracia, 2010); iii) may determine the availability of the DV victims to seek help from this formal source; iv) or may even directly affect, facilitate or inhibit the access of DV cases into the legal system (Jordan, 2004). Accordingly, a questionnaire instrument (POLICE DV) to examine the influence of traditional beliefs and gender stereotypes on police attitudes toward DV, is proposed. It has been suggested that the police action is frequently sustained by beliefs and gender stereotypes that reinforce conservative and corporate trend behaviours (cf. Lockwood & Prohaska, 2015), as well as beliefs about the legitimacy of interfering in couple's relationships, and the notion of danger (Sun et al., 2011). Logan, Shannon & Walker (2006) reported that police attitudes towards the DV phenomenon were different from those in other crimes, which may influence police enforcement practices (e.g., DV perceived as an interpersonal problem, rather than a violent crime). In addition, it is important to remember that attitudes legitimating IPV (e.g., tolerance, acceptability, victim-blaming and partner violence as a private matter) by the different professionals involved in DV incidents (e.g., law enforcement or health services personnel) and by the diverse individualsintegrating the social environment surrounding the victim (e.g., family, neighbours and friends), tend to inhibit victims from disclosing the DV violence or leaving the relationship (Fagan, 1989 as cited by Gracia, 2014).

In the proposed POLICE DV, extralegal factors, namely some police beliefs and attitudes, are be focused. Accordingly, three variables that could interfere with the attitudes regarding DV among police officers, are considered and analysed: type of violence, gender of victim and offender, and same-sex relationships. Several studies (e.g., Jordan, 2004; Lila et al., 2010) have found that the perception of the relationship between the victim and aggressor, social gender stereotypes, domestic space privacy or attitudes towards the victim's complaints, may influence the intervention by police officers in DV situations. Other authors (Rhatigan et al., 2011; Russell & Kraus, 2016) report that violence perpetrated by a woman, when compared to the male aggressor, tends to be seen as less problematic criminally and thus detrimental to the victims, since the responsibility of the female aggressor tends to be diminished (Harris & Cook, 2004). In turn, Lila et al. (2013) found that benevolent sexism (e.g., the need for men to protect women) is a facilitator of certain attitudes legitimizing violence against women, particularly when they do not comply with the roles and standards of conducts traditionally assigned to both men and women. However, in Russel's (2017) study, police officers similarly classified perpetrators into different variables i.e., guilt, responsibility, intention to physically harm the partner and present danger to other family members, notwithstanding gender and sexual orientation.

The proposed POLICE DV questionnaire comprises two sections. A first part in which sociodemographic data are collected from the interviewed police officers (i.e., sex, age, schooling, etc.), as well as information about the functions and extension of service in the police institution, and experience in dealing with DV situations. A second part intends to assess perceptions about DV, involving ten items about legitimating beliefs of DV (e.g., "*In DV situations, the victim is assaulted because he/she deserves or allows*"; "*Domestic violence in same-sex couples is a rare phenomenon*"), using a five-point Likert scale, i.e., 1 - Totally disagree to 5 - Totally agree, and four hypothetical scenarios involving DV incidents that police officers can find in their daily work, developed considering other works (e.g., Lila et al. 2013; Russel, 2017). The four hypothetical scenarios were developed with the intention to analyse if the response of police officers differs when considering distinct variables: type of violence involved in the incident, gender of the victim and offender and sexual orientation of the couple involved. The first scenario involves a typical and traditional DV situation, with a heterosexual relationship encompassing psychological DV and a female victim. In the second scenario, only the sex of the victim changes, thus involving a male. The third scenario involves situation of psychological DV between two women. Finally, the fourth and last scenario involves psychological DV between two males. Based on a Likert type scale of 0 (definitely no) to 7 (definitely yes), and for each hypothetical scenario, the police officers will have to assess the following: the responsibility of the victim and aggressor; motivations for the use of violence; the possibility of recurrence of abusive situation; the credibility of the testimony of the intervenients involved. Cronbach's alpha for the scale is 0.85.

CONCLUSION

Interventions in DV must assume it as a public and complex problem, transversal to the various social, educational and cultural levels, with the inherent subjectively experienced by each victim. Police play an important role in repressive response to DV incidents and the police attitudes have a crucial impact on responses to DV victimization (e.g., well-being and seeking help). Therefore, this chapter emphasizes the importance of assessing police attitudes towards DV phenomenon, particularly in what relates traditional beliefs and gender stereotypes, constituting critical aspects, both in understanding and, thus, also contributing to, the prevention of this serious and generalized social problem.

An appropriate and effective approach to DV requires specialized training to be provided to police officers in order to increase their awareness, knowledge and skills to improve positive performance in DV incidents. Specifically, it is important to deconstruct and challenge traditional, gender-based beliefs and sexist perspectives about the DV phenomenon. All these aspects can interfere with victims and police safety. It is also necessary to analyse and discuss how DV victims are affected by police responses, promoting the development of proactive attitudes through a sensitive and empathic policing, and to encourage intolerance towards the DV phenomenon, considering it as serious as other types of crimes. Authors as

Logan et al. (2006) have even suggested that at the recruitment of police officers, strategies to disregard fundamental beliefs about crimes and sanctions, should be implemented.

This chapter may also constitute an important basis for other empirical studies in the area of the policing actions involved in the DV phenomenon. Further research is also necessary to better understand the police responses to DV, considering other personal and contextual factors, either relating the offenders (e.g., responsibility, substance use or personality traits) or the victims (e.g., credibility, culpability and impact), together with other situational DV incidents (e.g., imminent threat of danger, past and future harm or tolerance to certain DV incidents). The development of both comparative studies, on how police officers respond to offenders committing other types of crime, and also longitudinal studies, analysing how attitudes and beliefs developed or maintained over time influence the police performance, are also necessary.

REFERENCES

Archer (2000). Sex differences in aggression between heterosexual partners: A meta-analytic review. *Psychological Bulletin*, 126(5), 651-680. https://doi.org/10.1037/0033-2909.126.5.651

Belknap, J. (1995). Law enforcement officers' attitudes about the appropriate responses to woman battering. *International Review of Victimology*, 4, 47-62. https://doi.org/10.1177/026975809500400104

Brown, C. (2008). Gender-role implications on same-sex intimate partner abuse. *Journal of Family Violence*, 23(6), 457-462. https://doi.org/10.1007/s10896-008-9172-9

Buzawa, E. S., & Buzawa, C. G. (2017). *Global responses to domestic violence*. Cham, Switzerland: Springer. https://doi.org/10.1007/978-3-319-56721-1

Cardoso, A., & Quaresma, C. 2012. *Violência doméstica: Da participação da ocorrência à investigação criminal* [Domestic violence: From

Police Attitudes toward Victims of Domestic Violence   33

participation to criminal investigation]. Direção Geral da Administração Interna (Org.). Lisboa: Cadernos da Administração Interna.

Chu, D. C., & Sun, I. Y. (2014). Reactive versus proactive attitudes toward domestic violence: A comparison of Taiwanese male and female police officers. *Crime and Delinquency*, 60(2), 216-237. https://doi.org/10.1177/001112 8710372192

Dichter, M. E., & Gelles, R. J. (2012). Women's perceptions of safety and risk following police intervention for intimate partner violence. *Violence against Women*, 18(1), 44-63. https://doi.org/10.1177/10778012124370 16

Dobash, R., & Dobash, E. (2004). Women's violence to men in intimate relationships: Working on a puzzle. *British Journal Criminology*, 44, 324-349. https://doi.org/10.1093/crimin/azh026

Douglas, E. M., & Hines, D. A. (2011). The helpseeking experiences of men who sustain intimate partner violence: An overlooked population and implications for practice. *Journal of Family Violence*, 26(6), 473-485. https://doi.org/10.1007/s10896-011-9382-4

Duarte, V. (2012). *Discursos e percursos na delinquência juvenil feminina* [Discourses and pathways in female juvenile delinquency]. Lisboa: Húmus.

European Union Agency for Fundamental Rights - FRA (2014). *Violence against women: An EUwide survey* - Results at a glance. Luxembourg: Publications Office of the European Union. Retrieved from Http://fra.europa.eu/en/publication/2014/violene-against-women-eu-widesurvey-main-results-report.

Gracia, E. (2014). Public attitudes toward partner violence against women. In: A. C. Michalos (Ed.), *Encyclopedia of quality of life and well-being research* (vol. 9, pp. 5192-5195). Dordrecht, Netherlands: Springer. https://doi.org/10.1007/978-94-007-0753-5_2317

Gracia, E., García, F., & Lila, M. (2008). Police involvement in cases of intimate partner violence against women: The influence of perceived severity and personal responsibility. *Violence against Women*, 14, 697-714. https://doi.org/10.1177/1077801208317288

Gracia, E., García, F., & Lila, M. (2009). Public responses to intimate partner violence against women: The influence of perceived severity and personal responsibility. *The Spanish Journal of Psychology*, 12(2), 648-656. https://doi.org/10.1017/S1138741600002018

Gracia, E., García, F., & Lila, M. (2011). Police attitudes towards policing partner violence against women: Do they correspond to different psychosocial profiles? *Journal of Interpersonal Violence*, 26(1), 189-207. https://doi.org/10.1177/0886260510362892

Hagemann-White, C. (2017). Responses to domestic violence in Germany in a European context. In: E. S. Buzawa & C. G. Buzawa (Eds.), *Global responses to domestic violence* (pp. 87-105). Cham, Switzerland: Springer. https://doi.org/10.1007/978-3-319-56721-1_5

Hamby, S., & Jackson, A. (2010). Size does matter: The effects of gender on perceptions of dating violence. *Sex Roles*, 63(5-6), 324-331. https://doi.org/10.1007/s11199-010-9816-0

Harris, R. J., & Cook, C. A. (1994). Attributions about spouse abuse: It matters who the batterers and victims are. *Sex Roles, 30*(7), 553-565. https://doi.org/10.1007/bf01420802

Hines, D., & Douglas, E. (2010). Intimate terrorism by women towards men: Does it exist? *Journal of Aggression Conflict and Peace Research*, 2, 36-56. https://doi.org/10.5042/jacpr.2010.0335

Jordan, C. (2004). Intimate partner violence and the justice system: An examination of the interface. *Journal of Interpersonal Violence*, 19, 1412-1434. https://doi.org/10.1177/0886260504269697

Lee, J., Zhang, Y., & Hoover, L. T. (2013). Police response to domestic violence: Multilevel factors of arrest decision. Policing: *An International Journal of Policing Strategies and Management*, 36, 157-174. https://doi.org/10.1108/ 13639511311302524

Liang, B., Goodman, L., Tummala-Narra, P., & Weintraub, S. (2005). A theoretical framework for understanding help-seeking processes among survivors of intimate partner violence. *American journal of community psychology*, 36(1-2), 71-84. https://doi.org/10.1007/s 10464-005-6233-6

Lila, M., Gracia, E., & García, F. (2010). Actitudes de la policía ante la intervención en casos de violencia contra la mujer en las relaciones de pareja: Influencia del sexismo y la empatía [Police attitudes toward intervention in cases of partner violence against women: The influence of sexism and empathy]. *Revista de Psicología Social*, 25(3), 313-323. https://doi.org/10.1174/021347410792675570

Lila, M., Gracia, E., & García, F. (2013). Ambivalent sexism, empathy and law enforcement attitudes towards partner violence against women among male police officers. *Psychology, Crime & Law*, 19(10), 907-919. https://doi.org/1080/1068316X.2012.719619

Lockwood, D., & Prohaska, A. (2015). Police officer gender and attitudes toward intimate partner violence: How policy can eliminate stereotypes. *International Journal of Criminal Justice Sciences*, 10(1), 77-90.

Logan, T., Shannon, L., & Walker, R. (2006). Police attitudes toward domestic violence offenders. *Journal of Interpersonal Violence*, 21(10), 1365-1373. https://doi.org/10.1177/0886260506291653

Manita, C., Ribeiro, C., & Peixoto, C. (2009). *Violência doméstica: Compreender para Intervir: Guia de Boas Práticas para Profissionais de Saúde* [Domestic Violence: Understanding to intervene. A guide to best practices for health professionals] Lisboa: Comissão para a Cidadania e Igualdade de Género.

Matos, M., Machado, A., Santos, A., & Machado, C. (2012). Intervenção em grupo com vítimas de violência doméstica: Uma revisão da sua eficácia [Group intervention with victims of domestic violence: A review of their effectiveness]. *Análise Psicológica*, 1, 79-91. https:// doi.org/10.14417/ ap.534

Matos, R. & Machado, C. (2012). Criminalidade feminina e construção do género: emergência e consolidação das perspectivas feministas na criminologia [Female crime and gender construction: emergence and consolidation of feminist perspectives in criminology]. *Análise Psicológica*, 30(1-2), 33-47, 2012. https://doi.org/10.14417/ap.529

Mellor, D., & Deering, R. (2010). Professional response and attitudes toward female-perpetrated child sexual abuse: a study of psychologists, psychiatrists, probationary, psychologists and child protection workers.

Psychology, Crime & Law, 5(16), 415-438. https://doi.org/10.1080/106831 60902776850.

Messinger, A. M. (2011). Invisible victims: Same-sex IPV in the national violence against women survey. *Journal of interpersonal Violence,* 26(11), 2228-2243. https://doi.org/10.1177/0886260510383023

Randle, A., & Graham, C. (2011). A Review of the evidence on the effects of intimate partner violence on men. *Psychology of Men & Masculinity,* 12(2), 97-111. https://doi.org/10.1037/a0021944

Rhatigan, D. L., Stewart, C., & Moore, T. M. (2011). Effects of gender and confrontation on attributions of female-perpetrated intimate partner violence. *Sex Roles,* 64(11-12), 875. https://doi.org/10.1007/s11199-011-9951-2

Ristock, J., & Timbang, N. (2005). Relationship violence in lesbian/gay/bisexual/transgender/queer [LGBTQ] communities. *Minnesota Center against Violence and Abuse.*

Russell, B. (2017). Police perceptions in intimate partner violence cases: the influence of gender and sexual. *Journal of Crime and Justice,* 1-13. https://doi.org/10.1080/0735648x.2017.1282378

Russell, B., & Kraus, S. (2016). Perceptions of Partner Violence: How Aggressor Gender, Masculinity/Femininity, and Victim Gender Influence Criminal Justice Decisions. *Deviant Behavior,* 37(6), 679-691. https://doi.org/10.1080/01639625.2015.1060815

Shuler, C. (2010). Male victims of intimate partner violence in the United States: An examination of the review of literature through the critical theoretical perspective. *International Journal of Criminal Justice Sciences,* 5(1), 163-173.

Sigurdsson, E. L. (2019): Domestic violence-are we up to the task? *Scandinavian Journal of Primary Health Care,* Online publication. https://doi.org/10.1080/02813432.2019.1608638

Stiles-Shields, C., & Carroll, R. (2014). Same-sex domestic violence: Prevalence, unique aspects, and clinical Implications. *Journal of Sex & Marital Therapy,* Online Publication https://doi.org/10.1080/0092623X.2014.958792

Sun, I., Su, M. & Wu, Y. (2011). Attitudes toward police response to domestic violence: A comparison of Chinese and American college students. *Journal of Interpersonal Violence*, 26(16), 3289-3315. https://doi.org/10.1177/0886260510393008

Turell, S. (2000). A descriptive analysis of same-sex relationship violence for a diverse sample. *Journal of Family Violence*, 15(3), 281-293. https://doi.org/10.1023/a:1007505619577

Wang, X., Hayes, B., & Zhang, H. (2019). Correlates of Chinese police officer decision-making in cases of domestic violence. *Crime & Delinquency*, 1-23. https://doi:10.1177/0011128719850502

Younglove, J. A., Kerr, M. G., & Vitello, C. J. (2002). Law enforcement officers' perceptions of same sex domestic violence: Reason for cautious optimism. *Journal of Interpersonal Violence*, 17(7), 760-772. https://doi.org/10.1177/0886260502017007004

In: Victims of Violence
Editor: Mathias L. Knudsen

ISBN: 978-1-53617-140-2
© 2020 Nova Science Publishers, Inc.

Chapter 3

INTIMATE PARTNER VIOLENCE VICTIMIZATION AND HELP-SEEKING AMONG COLLEGE STUDENTS: COMPARISONS OF THREE MEASURES

Hyunkag Cho[1,*], PhD, Jisuk Seon[2], PhD and Ilan Kwon[1], PhD

[1]School of Social Work, Michigan State University,
East Lansing, MI, US
[2]Center for Innovation in Child Maltreatment Policy,
Research and Training, Washington University,
St. Louis, MO, US

ABSTRACT

Researchers have measured intimate partner violence (IPV) and survivors' help-seeking through a variety of different instruments, which makes it difficult to paint a consistent picture of IPV. While it might be

---

[*] Corresponding Author's E-mail: chohyu12@msu.edu.

unrealistic to expect consistent estimates in the near future, there might be practical ways to help service providers to make better use of the available data. This study compares three measures so as to examine whether a certain measure produces a discernible pattern of results. This study used the results of three surveys from a Midwestern public university. Findings show that IPV prevalence rates varied across the three surveys, and that compared to males, females experienced more IPV, reported more negative consequences of IPV, sought more formal help, and found formal help-seeking more useful.

Keywords: intimate partner violence, help-seeking, prevalence, formal, informal, service, gender

INTRODUCTION

Intimate partner violence (IPV) is a serious social problem among college students, and results in numerous negative health and behavioral problems (Ackard & Neumark-Sztainer, 2002; Callahan, Tolman, & Saunders, 2003; Gover, Kaukinen, & Fox, 2008). Survivors may seek help from a variety of sources on campus, including police, the student health clinic, the counseling center, and shelters (Amstadter et al., 2010; Cho & Huang, 2017). On-campus student service providers strive to meet the survivors' various needs, improving their well-being and safety. It is critical for the providers to be knowledgeable about how many students experience IPV and how many of them actually seek help. This would help them to plan and organize their services based on an estimate of how many students would visit them for help, but the study results are not consistent (Stoner & Cramer, 2017; Perkins & Warner, 2017). Service providers may evaluate and improve their services based on their interactions with clients, but these changes would not include those who do not seek help and may need to be reached out to by service providers. Researchers have measured IPV prevalence and incidences as well as survivors' help-seeking through a variety of different instruments, which makes it difficult to paint a comprehensive and consistent picture of IPV. While it might not be realistic to expect all researchers to adopt universal instruments and provide consistent estimates in the near future, there might be practical ways to help service providers to make better use of the available data. This study explores one way of doing this by comparing three measures related to IPV prevalence and survivors' help-seeking so as to examine whether a certain measure produces a discernible pattern of results. It will not only help service providers to use the available data in an educated and informed manner, it will also aid researchers in improving their measurements to better present their study results.

LITERATURE REVIEW

According to one of the most recent national surveys of adults in the US (National Intimate Partner and Sexual Violence Survey, NISVS), nearly one-third of females (33%) and males (28%) have experienced physical violence; almost half of all participants reported psychological violence; and one-in-five females (19%) and 2% of males were victimized by rape in their lifetime (Breiding, Chen, & Black, 2014). Survivors suffer from a broad range of consequences, including physical and mental health issues (Ackard & Neumark-Sztainer, 2002; Black et al., 2011; Breiding et al., 2014; Cisler et al., 2012; Plichta, 2004; Silverman, Rai, Mucci, & Hathaway, 2001). The NISVS showed that the majority of survivors experienced their first victimization at an early age; 71% of females and 58% of males were reported to have experienced some type of IPV before the age of 25 (Black et al., 2014). This implies that traditional college-aged students may be at an increased risk of IPV. A relatively small but growing number of studies have examined IPV among college students (Cho & Huang, 2017; Daley & Noland, 2001; Krebs, Lindquist, Warner, Fisher, & Martin, 2009; Scherer, Snyder, & Fisher, 2016). They consistently highlighted that college students are at substantial risk of IPV victimization. Among college students, psychological violence seems to be the most prevalent of several different types of IPV. With a wide variation in prevalence estimates across studies, psychological violence victimization ranges from 33.1% to 94.7%, with physical violence ranging from 10% to 65%, sexual violence about 10%, and technological violence about 10% (Cho & Huang, 2017; Daley & Noland, 2001; Krebs et al., 2009). These estimations of IPV among college students differ by gender (Daley & Noland, 2001; Gover et al., 2008; Saewyc et al., 2009). For example, Daley & Noland (2001) surveyed 528 college students and reported that while female students were victimized by physical violence (64.6%) more than psychological violence (58.5%), male students were victimized by psychological violence (34.0%) more than any other types of violence. Another survey of 2,542 students found a substantial gender difference in psychological victimization; female students were significantly more likely to experience psychological violence than male students (Gover et al., 2008). Saewyc et al. (2009) found that even if female and male students reported similar IPV prevalence rates (17% and 16%, respectively), females were more likely to report psychological violence victimization, with males reporting more physical violence victimization (Saewyc et al., 2009), which contradicts the findings of Daley & Noland (2001).

These inconsistencies in IPV prevalence and gender differences seem to be affected greatly by the different methodological approaches taken by the researchers. First of all, estimates vary in their operational definitions of violence (Gover et al., 2008). Some studies measured all types of violence together, not distinguishing the potential differences among them (e.g., Amar & Gennaro, 2005), while others examined each of them separately (e.g., Gover et al., 2008; Saewyc et al., 2009). The former is likely to report higher rates of IPV than the latter. Second, different survey reference periods may contribute to variations in estimates. Studies asking about lifetime IPV experiences tend to report higher rates of IPV (e.g., Garcia-Moreno, Jansen, Ellsberg, Heise, & Watts, 2006; Kilpatrick, Saunders, & Smith, 2000), compared to those asking about IPV experienced in the past 6 or 12 months (e.g., Daley & Noland, 2001; Sutherland, Fantasia, & Hutchinson, 2016). Third, study sites and demographic composition, such as gender and the age range of participants, may also affect prevalence estimates. Fourth, the utilization of different measures may result in inconsistent estimates of IPV victimization and perpetration between genders. The first national survey of IPV, the National Family Violence Survey in 1975, used the Conflict Tactics

Scales (CTS), which is one of the most frequently used measures of IPV, and reported that 12% of females and males had engaged in at least one action of physical aggression against their partners in the past year (Straus, 1979; Straus & Gelles, 1988). The equal rates in physical aggression between females and males prompted researchers to raise a question about whether the CTS adequately measures IPV prevalence, in that it does not include an assessment of sexual assault and does not consider contexts of violence (Archer, 2000; Hamby, 2005). While the CTS has been revised to address some of the critiques (Straus, Hamby, Boney-McCoy, & Sugarman, 1996), IPV measures have also been adapted by adding detailed information, such as frequency, patterns, and impacts of the violence experienced, which is likely to enable us to better recognize gender variations in motives, severity, chronicity, and the impacts of IPV (Breiding et al., 2014; Harned, 2001; Woodin, Sotskova, & O'Leary, 2013). Finally, individuals' perceptions of what constitutes IPV may have an impact on gender differences in IPV prevalence. For instance, a male may occasionally slap his partner's back hard, not considering it as violence but as a friendly gesture, while his partner interprets it as a violent and intimidating act. One such measure was developed and tested by Hamby (2016). With a hypothesis that gender parity in IPV prevalence could be attributed to self-reporting measures that involved false positives such as joking incidents, she compared the CTS physical victimization items to a revised CTS measure that reduced those false positives by adding phrases such as "not including horseplay or joking around" and "when my partner was angry." Two hundred fifty-one undergraduate students were randomly assigned to use either the original CTS measure or the revised CTS measure. As expected, female students reported more victimization than male students when they were asked about victimization using the new measure that reduced false positives. This result suggests the importance of contextualized IPV measures that can address different perceptions of IPV between genders.

In the adult population, IPV survivors are more likely to rely on informal help, such as friends and family, rather than reaching out for formal help, including police, hospital, or other social service agencies (Tsui, Cheung, & Leung, 2010). Studies focusing on college students have illustrated similar patterns of help-seeking, although only a few studies examined help-seeking among college students who have IPV victimization experience (e.g., Amar & Gennaro, 2005; Cho & Huang, 2017; Próspero & Vohra-Gupta, 2008). Próspero & Vohra-Gupta (2008) surveyed 200 college students and found that while 86% of students reported at least one type of IPV victimization, only 16% of them looked for mental health agencies. Similarly, Amar and Gennaro (2005) found that only 3% of college-student survivors had visited social service providers. Cho and Huang (2017) surveyed 351 college students and found that IPV survivors relied more on informal help (89%) than formal help (23%). There are studies pointing out several reasons that hinder college-student survivors from seeking formal and/or informal help, including fear, embarrassment, guilt, confidentiality issues, possible stigma, lack of knowledge of available campus resources, and perceptions of IPV as a private problem (Nasta et al., 2005; Próspero & Vohra-Gupta, 2008; Walsh, Banyard, Moynihan,Ward, & Cohn, 2010).

PRESENT STUDY

Although studies clearly show that college students are at high risk for experiencing IPV victimization, the IPV prevalence estimates and the nature of help-seeking vary across studies, partly due different measurements being utilized. This study addresses this limitation in the literature by comparing three recent surveys at a Midwestern public university in the U.S., which collected data from comparable samples, but using different measures. The research questions are two-fold: 1) How do different measures produce different estimates of IPV prevalence and survivors' help-seeking? and 2) How does gender affect different measures in their estimates of IPV prevalence and survivors' help-seeking?

METHODS

Study Data

We compared the descriptive results of three cross-sectional surveys on IPV among college students at a Midwestern public university: a Relationship Violence Survey collected by the authors in 2016 (RVS); a Campus Climate Survey on Sexual Assault and Sexual Misconduct in 2015 by the Association of American Universities (AAU); and the National College Health Assessment II in 2014 by the American College Health Association (ACHA). Each survey had a different focus. RVS mainly measured the prevalence of IPV and help-seeking behaviors; AAU, the prevalence of sexual assault and misconduct; and ACHA, health-related behaviors and perceptions. We obtained the descriptive reports of AAU and ACHA on this selected university from their websites (citations omitted for anonymity), and descriptive results of RVS through bivariate analyses of the data. This study has been reviewed by the Institutional Review Board at the authors' university.

Relationship Violence Survey

RVS included questions on IPV victimization and perpetration, IPV consequences, help-seeking behaviors, outcomes of help-seeking, and demographic information. RVS was reviewed and approved by the Institutional Review Board of the university where the study was conducted. An email survey was sent to 24,000 undergraduate students in the spring of 2016 through the Office of the Registrar at the university, with a total of 1,686 returned (7% response rate).

Campus Climate Survey on Sexual Assault and Sexual Misconduct

This survey was designed and conducted by the American Association for Universities (AAU) to examine the incidence of sexual assault and misconduct, and students' use of campus resources in 2015 (Cantor et al., 2015). The survey asked 63 questions, which included the topics of IPV and sexual violence victimization, IPV consequences, and help-seeking. An email survey was distributed to 49,896 undergraduate and graduate students at the selected university, with a total of 8,352 returned (18% response rate).

National College Health Assessment II

This is a national survey organized by the American College Health Association (ACHA) to assist college health service providers, health educators, counselors, and administrators by collecting data about students' health behaviors and other health topics (American College Health Association, 2014). It has collected data from more than 100 colleges and universities across the nation since 2000. A report on the 2014 survey for the selected university was used for this study. The survey questions include students' perceived health status, substance use, and IPV victimization. A total of 1,231 undergraduate and graduate students' responses were summarized in the report.

Measures

IPV Victimization and Consequences

RVS measured IPV and its consequences using a revised version of a standardized instrument known for its strong validity and reliability, the Partner Victimization Scale (Hamby, 2013). It included 10 questions to measure five types of lifetime IPV (i.e., physical, psychological, sexual, and technological violence, and threats, with citations omitted for anonymity), with four response options: never (0), just once (1), 2-3times (2), and 4 times and more (3). Exemplar items are: Not including horseplay or joking around, my partner pushed, grabbed, or shook me (physical), My partner put me down or called me names to make me feel bad (psychological), My partner made me do sexual things when I didn't want to (sexual), My partner sent emails or text messages to threaten, insult, or harass me (technological), Not including horseplay or joking around, my partner threatened to hurt me and I thought I might really get hurt (threat). The reliability of the scale is 0.78. IPV consequences were measured by asking those who reported IPV victimization whether they had physical hurts or daily routine problems.

AAU measured four types of IPV (technological violence not measured) in the past 12 months through modified survey items from the National Intimate Partner and Sexual Violence Survey (Black et al., 2011). AAU included victimization experiences committed by both intimate and non-intimate partners. It measured the consequences of victimization only for sexual violence, excluding other types of IPV victimization.

ACHA measured IPV with non-standardized questions, such as "Within the last 12 months, have you been in an intimate (coupled/partnered) relationship that was emotionally abusive/physically abusive/sexually abusive?" with "yes" or "no" response options. ACHA did not measure technological violence, threats and IPV consequences.

Help-Seeking

RVS measured help-seeking by asking those who reported any IPV victimization, "Have you talked about any of these incidents with the following agencies or persons?" A list of two types of help sources was provided for the respondents to answer dichotomously: seven formal (e.g., medical services, shelter, and police) and seven informal help sources (e.g., family, friends, and coworkers). Outcomes of help-seeking were asked of those who had reported using at least one help source—"Do you think the assistance you received was helpful?"—with the list of help sources for them to answer dichotomously. If the respondents did not seek any type of help, they were asked about their reasons for not doing so. Thirteen reasons that were drawn from the National Crime Victimization Survey were provided (Langton, Berzofsky, Krebs & Smiley-McDonald, 2012)

AAU measured help-seeking by asking, "Have you contacted at least one program or a person in the university list?" with "Yes" or "No" response options. A list of two types of help sources, which was specific to this selected university (but altered here for anonymity), was provided for the respondents to answer dichotomously: nine formal help sources (e.g., student health services, shelter, and police) and one informal help source (friends). Outcomes of help-seeking were only measured for formal help by asking "Thinking about the most recent time you contacted them, how useful was [Program] in helping you deal with the experience?" Of five response options, "very" and "extremely" were coded as being helpful, with "not at all," "a little," and "somewhat" as being not helpful. Respondents who did not contact any help were asked about their reasons, with a list of 11 reasons provided. ACHA did not measure help-seeking.

Demographic Characteristics

The three surveys measured demographic characteristics in different ways. While RVS included only undergraduate students, AAU and ACHA included both undergraduate and graduate students. RVS and AAU measured gender with 3 categories (female, male, or other), while ACHA provided two response options: female or male. RVS and ACHA asked respondents' race/ethnicity with one question, with response options such as White, Black or African American, Asian or Pacific Islander, Hispanic, American Indian/Alaskan Native/Native Hawaiian, Multiracial, and Other. AAU used two separate items asking race and Hispanic origin. In this report, we used the race/ethnicity format of RVS and ACHA.

Analysis

Descriptive analyses of RVS were conducted to examine IPV prevalence and health consequences, help-seeking after IPV, and its outcome by gender. Descriptive summary reports of AAU and ACHA were obtained from their websites to calculate comparable results with RVS. Comparisons of major study variables were made across the surveys.

RESULTS

Table 1 shows the comparisons of the results of the three surveys. The vast majority of respondents were White and in their early- to mid-twenties. In all three surveys, female students had more IPV victimization experiences than male students for all five types of violence. RVS reported a much higher prevalence of most types of IPV (25.3% to 62%), except sexual violence, than AAU (7% to 48%) and ACHA (0.7% to 8.2%); AAU found rates of sexual victimization (22.2% for males, 48% for females) that were similar to RVS (26.1% for males, 41.3% for females). Females reported higher levels of consequences of IPV (more physical injuries and more missed daily routines) than males; AAU reported higher rates than RVS. There were more female students who sought formal help (20.8% to 40%) than male students (10.7 to 11.3%) in both the RVS and AAU surveys. However, gender differences were not consistent for informal help-seeking. RVS showed fewer females seeking informal help than males (88.5% vs. 100%), while AAU reported the opposite (72.3% females vs. 51.6% males). Of those who sought help in RVS, more females found formal help-seeking useful than did males (74.5% vs. 66.7%) but fewer found informal help-seeking less useful than males (88.5% vs. 100%). Among the reasons for not seeking help, both female and male students who responded to the RVS thought of IPV as a private matter or as unlikely to be considered important by others. AAU students did not seek help because they did not think of IPV as being serious enough, or because it did not happen on campus.

DISCUSSION

The results show that IPV prevalence rates vary across the three surveys, with RVS respondents reporting the highest rates. As expected, prevalence was affected by the duration of the IPV experiences being measured. RVS measured life-time IPV, while AAU and ACHA measured IPV in the past 12 months. Similar results were seen in previous studies (e.g., Garcia-Moreno et al., 2006). Prevalence was also affected by how IPV was defined, presented, and measured. RVS measured IPV prevalence for five types; AAU four types; and ACHA three types. If respondents are provided with various types of IPV, with detailed examples of each, they are more likely to recognize, recall, and report what they experienced as IPV than when they are asked about IPV without specifics. The prevalence of technological violence, which was only measured by RVS, was as high as for other types of violence among college students. This demonstrates that technological violence needs to be included in IPV measures for young adults, either as a separate type of violence or as part of psychological violence or threats. Given that technological violence is a relatively recent phenomenon, future research needs to examine its nature and relationship with other types of violence. IPV prevalence was not only influenced by the duration and breadth of IPV, but also by the context in which questions are asked. Although RVS reported the highest prevalence of most types of IPV among the surveys, sexual violence was shown to be highest for females in AAU. AAU was clear in its purpose—a campus climate survey on sexual assault and sexual misconduct—and asked more detailed questions about sexual violence than other types of IPV. Thus, respondents were likely to be well aware of the intentions of the survey and pay more attention to sexual violence than other types of IPV. The lowest prevalence rates, seen in ACHA, might be similarly explained. ACHA focused on college students' health status and behaviors, with IPV questions asked within this health context. Respondents might only have reported IPV if it had impacted their health, such as physical injuries and depression, not reporting other incidents that were without apparent health consequences. These results suggest that IPV prevalence and incidence rates should be viewed in the context of survey administration, and that detailed questions for each type of IPV need to be used to help respondents to recall and report their occurrence (Kelly & Johnson, 2008; Taylor, Banyard, Grych, & Hamby, 2016).

Particularly interesting in this study is that gender differences in IPV prevalence, or that IPV is predominantly violence against women, was consistent across all IPV types. Compared to previous studies that indicated an inconsistent gender difference, depending on the types of violence (Gover et al., 2008; Saewyc et al., 2009), female college students in all three surveys in this study revealed higher IPV prevalence rates than male students, regardless of the IPV types. This result is comparable to Hamby (2009; 2016), which showed the IPV rates of female victimization as being much higher than male victimization when a false positive problem was recognized. The false positive problem indicates that item wording in a self-report survey includes some behaviors that do not map onto the legal or diagnostic criteria for violence. For example, Hamby's study (2016), which

Intimate Partner Violence Victimization and Help-Seeking ... 51

used an IPV questionnaire with the wording of "Not including horseplay or joking around" revealed that female students reported victimization more than twice as often as male students. The current study measured IPV using Hamby's questions, which contextualized IPV; the results confirm that the context really matters. Future research is strongly advised to consider the context of IPV, including the perpetrators' intention to use violence, when measuring IPV.

Gender differences were also found in help-seeking behaviors. Both RVS and AAU showed that female survivors sought formal help more than their male counterparts. Survivors are likely to use formal help sources, such as health clinics and police, if IPV is severe in its consequences or perceived by them as serious (Andersen, 1995). Female survivors in this study reported having more negative consequences from IPV than males. Female survivors might have sought formal help to address serious consequences. The use of informal help sources was not consistent between RVS and AAU. RVS reported that male survivors sought informal help more than females, consistent with previous studies (Amar & Gennaro, 2005; Cho & Huang, 2017; Próspero & Vohra-Gupta, 2008). However, AAU reported that male survivors used informal help less than females. This difference may be due to the different degree of specificity between the two surveys. RVS provided detailed examples of informal help, including family, friends, and co-workers, while AAU asked only about talking with friends. It may be that that male survivors do not talk with friends about IPV victimization experiences, perhaps because of shame and stigma, but do share with other informal helpers, such as family members. As with IPV prevalence, future research is encouraged to use detailed questions in measuring survivors' help-seeking; respondents are likely to recall and report better if questions are asked with detailed examples.

RVS is the only survey in this study to examine the outcome of help-seeking by gender, in which female survivors found formal help to be useful more than males, and males found informal help to be useful more than females. Formal help sources may not be as well-prepared to serve male survivors of IPV because of the bias that there are only a few males

Table 1. Comparisons of three measures of IPV among college students

	RVS		AAU**		ACHA**	
	Female (%)	Male (%)	Female (%)	Male (%)	Female (%)	Male (%)
Demographic characteristics						
Race/ Ethnicity						
White	84.4	82	79.6		78.7	
Black or African American	6.1	5.1	4.9		4.3	
Asian or Pacific Islander	8.9	7.6	11.4		12.2	
Hispanic	4.0	3.8	4.4		4.1	
American Indian, Alaskan Native or Native Hawaiian	1.5	2.3	-		1.6	
Multiracial	1.6	3.0	4.2		2.5	
Other	0.6	1.5	-		2.0	
Age*	20.01	21.13	18 ~ 25+		22.60	
Types of IPV victimization						
Physical violence	41.3	35.9	9.7	7.2	1.5	1.1
Psychological violence	62.0	59.7	15.1	9.9	8.2	4.9
Sexual violence	41.3	26.1	48.0	22.2	1.6	0.7
Technological violence	38.3	29.4	-	-		
Threats	33.9	25.3	10.1	7.0		
IPV victimization consequences						
Physically hurt	10.9	4.7	24.3	-		
Missed daily routines	14.3	7.3	23.8	16.9		
Help-seeking after IPV victimization						
Formal help	40.0	10.7	20.8	11.3		
Informal help	52.9	71.4	72.3	51.6		
Usefulness of help-seeking						
Formal help	74.5	66.7	46.1			
Informal help	88.5	100	-			
Reasons not to seek help*						
I thought this was private matter and took care of it myself	72.1	71.0				
They wouldn't think it's important nor want to be bothered.	17.4	11.5				
I didn't think it was serious enough to report.			56.2	68.4		
Incident was not on campus.			28.8	31.9		

* Mean or range of Age.
** AAU and ACHA reports did not provide gender break-downs for some variables; they did not collect data on some variables, which is shown blank.
*** Top two reasons per survey are shown.

victimized by it, which may make male survivors feel that visiting formal help sources is not particularly helpful. On the one hand, male survivors may feel a stronger sense of shame and stigma in seeking formal help than they do in seeking informal help, and may find sharing their victimization experiences with informal help sources useful. One the other hand, female survivors may be blamed for their victimization experiences even when talking with informal help sources, which may make them feel that informal help is not as useful. In this regard, the reasons for not seeking help did not show striking gender differences. Both men and women did not seek help mainly because they thought IPV was a private matter, not serious, or likely to be considered not important by help sources. Future research needs to examine what happens when survivors seek formal and informal help, which will provide information that may explain gender differences in survivors' perceived usefulness of help-seeking.

The findings of this study should be interpreted with several limitations taken into consideration. First, the three surveys measured IPV using different time frames. The RVS measure asked college students about lifetime experiences of IPV victimization, whereas ACHA and AAU measured IPV experiences in the past twelve months. The high prevalence of IPV experiences could be skewed toward lifetime IPV experiences more than experiences that occurred during a limited time period. Similarly, the types of IPV being measured varied across the surveys, so it was impossible to compare specific IPV types such as technological violence. In addition, the more types of IPV being measured, the higher the IPV prevalence. Compared to RVS, which provided an actual dataset to be analyzed, data from ACHA and AAU were limited only to summary reports. This made it impossible to conduct further statistical analyses, such as exploring the associations between IPV experiences, consequences, help-seeking, and gender differences. Another limitation is the variation of the study samples. RVS surveyed only undergraduate students, while the other two surveys contained both undergraduate and graduate students. Undergraduate students, who tend to be in a rapid transition from youth to young adulthood, may view IPV differently from graduate students. Finally, the vast majority of the samples were White students. For a generalization to the broader population, future research needs to use racially and ethnically inclusive and representative samples.

CONCLUSION

This study used three sets of survey results taken from a Midwest public university to examine the influences of different IPV measures on survivors' reporting of IPV victimization, help-seeking, and gender differences. The results provide implications for research, policy, and practice. Researchers are encouraged to strengthen their IPV measures by covering various types of IPV, including technological violence, with detailed examples, and considering the context of the IPV. Survivors' help-seeking needs to be measured with questions that provide detailed examples of help sources and ask about the detailed process of help-seeking, from visiting a specific help source to the outcomes. Colleges and universities need to strengthen IPV policies to develop and provide continuing education and training opportunities to faculty, staff, students, and service providers regarding the nature of IPV, such as gender differences in IPV prevalence and help-seeking. Service providers are recommended to interpret any results on IPV, such as prevalence, help-seeking patterns, and satisfaction with services, within the context of survey administration, and not impose any preconceptions of IPV onto their clients. They need to improve their services based on IPV being experienced by females more than males while still recognizing that males are also victimized at alarmingly high rates. Educational services need to be developed that are aimed at parents and the general student population so they can recognize, assist, and help IPV survivors who might not reveal their victimization experiences but desperately need help.

REFERENCES

Ackard, D. M. & Neumark-Sztainer, D. (2002). Date violence and date rape among adolescents: Associations with disordered eating behaviors and psychological health. *Child Abuse & Neglect, 26*, 455-473.

Amar, A. F. & Gennaro, S. (2005). Dating violence in college women: Associated physical injury, healthcare usage, and mental health symptoms. *Nursing research, 54*(4), 235-242.

American College Health Association (2014). *National college health assessment II: Michigan State University executive summary spring 2014.* Hanover, MD: American College Health Association.

Amstadter, A. B., Zinzow, H. M., McCauley, J. L., Strachan, M., Ruggiero, K. J., Resnick, H. S. & Kilpatrick, D. G. (2010). Prevalence and correlates of service utilization and help seeking in a national college sample of female rape victims. *Journal of Anxiety Disorders, 24*(8), 900-902.

Andersen, R. M. (1995). Revisiting the behavioral model and access to medical care: Does it matter? *Journal of Health and Social Behavior, 36*(1), 1-10.

Archer, J. (2000). Sex differences in aggression between heterosexual partners: A meta analytic review. *Psychological Bulletin, 126*(5), 651-680.

Black, M. C., Basile, K. C., Breiding, M. J., Smith, S. G., Walters, M. L., Merrick, M. T., Chen, J., & Stevens, M. R. (2011). *The national intimate partner and sexual violence survey (NISVS): 2010 Summary report.* Atlanta, GA: National Center for Injury Prevention and Control, Centers for Disease Control and Prevention.

Breiding, M. J., Chen J. & Black, M. C. (2014). *Intimate partner violence in the United States 2010.* Atlanta, GA: National Center for Injury Prevention and Control, Centers for Disease Control and Prevention.

Breiding, M. J., Chen J. & Black, M. C. (2014). *Intimate partner violence in the United States 2010.* Atlanta, GA: National Center for Injury Prevention and Control, Centers for Disease Control and Prevention.

Callahan, M. R., Tolman, R. M. & Saunders, D. G. (2003). Adolescent dating violence victimization and psychological well-being. *Journal of Adolescent Research, 18*(6), 664–681.

Cantor, D., Fisher, B., Chibnall, S. H., Townsend, R., Thomas, G. & Lee, H. (2015). *Report on the AAU campus climate survey on sexual assault and sexual misconduct-Michigan State University.* Rockville, MD: Westat.

Cho, H. (2012). Examining gender differences in the nature and context of intimate partner violence. *Journal of Interpersonal Violence, 27*(13), 2665-2684.

Cho, H. & Huang, L. (2017). Aspects of help seeking among collegiate victims of dating violence. *Journal of Family Violence, 32*(4), 409-417.

Cisler, J. M., Begle, A. M., Amstadter, A. B., Resnick, H. S., Danielson, C. K., Saunders, B. E. & Kilpatrick, D. G. (2012). Exposure to intimate partner violence and risk for PTSD, depression, delinquency, and binge drinking among adolescents: Data from the NSA-R. *Journal of Traumatic Stress, 25*(1), 33-40.

Daley, E. M. & Noland, V. J. (2001). Intimate partner violence in college students: A cross-cultural comparison. *International Electronic Journal of Health Education, 4*, 35-40.

Garcia-Moreno, C., Jansen, H. A., Ellsberg, M., Heise, L. & Watts, C. H. (2006). Prevalence of intimate partner violence: findings from the WHO multi-country study on women's health and domestic violence. *The lancet, 368*(9543), 1260-1269.

Gover, A. R., Kaukinen, C. & Fox, K. A. (2008). The relationship between violence in the family of origin and dating violence among college students. *Journal of Interpersonal Violence, 23*(12), 1667-1693.

Hamby, S. (2009). The gender debate about intimate partner violence: solutions and dead ends. *Psychological Trauma: Theory, Research, Practice, and Policy, 1*(1), 24.

Hamby, S. (2016). Self-report measures that do not produce gender parity in intimate partner violence: A multi-study investigation. *Psychology of Violence, 6*(2), 323.

Hamby, S. L. (2005). Measuring gender differences in partner violence: Implications from research on other forms of violent and socially undesirable behavior. *Sex Roles*, *52*(11), 725-742.

Harned, M. S. (2001). Abused women or abused men? An examination of the context and outcomes of dating violence. *Violence and Victims*, *16*(3), 269-285.

Hilton, N., Harris, G. T. & Rice, M. E. (2003). Correspondence between self-report measures of interpersonal aggression. *Journal of Interpersonal Violence*, *18*(3), 223-239.

Kelly, J. B. & Johnson, M. P. (2008). Differentiation among types of intimate partner violence: Research update and implications for interventions. *Family Court Review*, *46*(3), 476-499.

Kilpatrick, D. G., Saunders, B. E. & Smith, D. W. (2000). *Youth victimization: Prevalence and Implications*. Washington, DC: U.S. Department of Justice, Office of Justice Programs, National Institute of Justice. Retrieved from https://www .ncjrs.gov/pdffiles1/nij/ 194972.pdf.

Krebs, C. P., Lindquist, C. H., Warner, T. D., Fisher, B. S. & Martin, S. L. (2009). The differential risk factors of physically forced and alcohol-or other drug-enabled sexual assault among university women. *Violence and Victims*, *24*(3), 302-321.

Langhinrichsen-Rohling, J. (2010). Controversies involving gender and intimate partner violence in the United States. *Sex Roles*, *62*(3-4), 179-193.

Langton, L., Berzofsky, M., Krebs, C. P. & Smiley-McDonald, H. (2012). *Victimizations not reported to the police 2006-2010*. Washington, DC: US Department of Justice, Office of Justice Programs, Bureau of Justice Statistics.

Modified from Koss, M. P., Abbey, A., Campbell, R., Cook, S., Norris, J., Testa, M. ... & White, J. (2007). Revising the SES: A collaborative process to improve assessment of sexual aggression and victimization. *Psychology of Women Quarterly*, *31*(4), 357-370.

Krebs, C. P., Lindquist, C. H., Warner, T. D., Fisher, B. S. & Martin, S. L. (2007). *The campus sexual assault (CSA) study final report.*

Washington, DC: National Institute of Justice. Retrieved from https://www.ncjrs.gov/pdffiles1/nij/grants/221153.pdf.

Nasta, A., Shah, B., Brahmanandam, S., Richman, K., Wittels, K., Allsworth, J. & Boardman, L. (2005). Sexual victimization: Incidence, knowledge and resource use among a population of college women. *Journal of Pediatric and Adolescent Gynecology*, *18*, 91-96.

Plichta, S. B. (2004). Intimate partner violence and physical health consequences policy and practice implications. *Journal of Interpersonal Violence*, *19*(11), 1296-1323.

Perkins, W. & Warner, J. (2017). Sexual violence response and prevention: Studies of campus policies and practices. *Journal of School Violence*, *16*(3), 237-242.

Saewyc, E. M., Brown, D., Plane, M., Mundt, M. P., Zakletskaia, L., Wiegel, J. & Fleming, M. F. (2009). Gender differences in violence exposure among university students attending campus health clinics in the United States and Canada. *Journal of Adolescent Health*, *45*(6), 587-594.

Silverman, J. G., Rai, A., Mucci, L. A. & Hathaway, J. E. (2001). Dating violence against adolescent girls and associated substance use, unhealthy weight control, sexual risk behavior, pregnancy, and suicidality. *Journal of the American Medical Association*, *286*(5), 572-579.

Stoner, J. E. & Cramer, R. J. (2017). Sexual violence victimization among college females: A systematic review of rates, barriers, and facilitators of health service utilization on campus. *Trauma, Violence, & Abuse*, 1-14.

Straus, M. A. (1979). Measuring intrafamily conflict and violence: The Conflict Tactics (CT) Scales. *Journal of Marriage and the Family*, *41*, 75-88.

Straus, M. A. & Gelles, R. J. (1988). How violent are American families? Estimates from the National Family Violence Resurvey and other studies. In G. T. Hotaling, D. Finkelhor, J. T. Kirkpatrick, & M. A. Straus (Eds.), *Family abuse and its consequences: New directions in research* (pp. 14-36). Newbury Park, CA: Sage.

Straus, M. A., Hamby, S. L., Boney-McCoy, S. & Sugarman, D. B. (1996). The revised Conflict Tactics Scales (CTS2): Development and preliminary psychometric data. *Journal of Family Issues, 17*, 283-316.

Sutherland, M. A., Fantasia, H. C. & Hutchinson, M. K. (2016). Screening for intimate partner and sexual violence in college women: Missed opportunities. *Women's Health Issues, 26*(2), 217-224.

Taylor, E., Banyard, V., Grych, J. & Hamby, S. (2016). Not all behind closed doors: Examining bystander involvement in intimate partner violence. *Journal of Interpersonal Violence*, 1-21.

Tsui, V., Cheung, M. & Leung, P. (2010). Help-seeking among male victims of partner abuse: Men's hard times. *Journal of Community Psychology, 38*, 769-780.

Umana, J. E., Fawole, O. I. & Adeoye, I. A. (2014). Prevalence and correlates of intimate partner violence towards female students of the University of Ibadan, Nigeria. *BMC Women's Health, 14*(1), 131-139.

Walsh, W. A., Banyard, V. L., Moynihan, M. M., Ward, S. & Cohn, E. S. (2010). Disclosure and service use on a college campus after an unwanted sexual experience. *Journal of Trauma & Dissociation, 11*, 134-151.

Woodin, E. M., Sotskova, A. & O'Leary, K. D. (2013). Intimate partner violence assessment in an historical context: Divergent approaches and opportunities for progress. *Sex Roles, 69*(3-4), 120-130.

In: Victims of Violence
Editor: Mathias L. Knudsen

ISBN: 978-1-53617-140-2
© 2020 Nova Science Publishers, Inc.

Chapter 4

PSYCHOPATHOLOGICAL SYMPTOMATOLOGY IN VICTIMS OF INTIMATE PARTNER VIOLENCE

Ana Sani[1,2,3,*], Ana Isabel Lopes[1] and Cristina Soeiro[4]
[1]University Fernando Pessoa (UFP), Porto, Portugal
[2]Permanent Observatory Violence and Crime (OPVC),
University Fernando Pessoa (UFP), Porto, Portugal
[3]Research Center on Child Studies (CIEC),
University of Minho (UM), Braga, Portugal
[4]Superior Institute of Health Sciences Egas Moniz, Lisbon, Portugal

ABSTRACT

Intimate partner violence is one of the most significant risk factors for the development of psychopathological symptomatology. The negative impacts of violence, over both short and long time scales, can emerge in different ways. We present a study that analyzes the relationship between psychopathological symptomatology and intimate partner violence in a sample of 122 Portuguese women participants, 61 with a judiciary victim

---

[*] Corresponding Author's E-mail: anasani@ufp.edu.pt.

status - the forensic group - and 61 without this status and criminal lawsuit - the normative group. Both samples were assessed with a sociodemographic questionnaire, the Inventário de Violência Conjugal (IVC) and the Brief Symptom Inventory (BSI). The forensic group demonstrated a higher number of psychopathological disturbance indicators than the normative group. In the forensic group, the victims that maintained the relationship with the abusive partner and those that already terminated this relationship showed no differences in their psychopathological symptomatology indicators. We also found that psychopathological symptomatology had a stronger association with physical violence than with psychological violence. These results substantiate the need to perform a broader violence risk assessment that takes into account the psychological and physical well-being of the victim, as well as clinical and forensic psychological monitoring.

Keywords: victims, domestic violence, psychopathology, victimization

INTRODUCTION

Intimate partnerships including conjugality, dating and extramarital heterosexual/homosexual relationships (Almeida, 2012; BDJUR, 2013; Gonçalves, 2004) can involve violent behavior(s). Violence within intimate relationships can be psychological, economical, physical and sexual (Baldry & Roia, 2011) and can lead to psychopathological symptomatology. Alternatively, psychopathology can be considered to contribute to victimization, such as in psychological/dispositional theories of intimate partner violence (Bartholomew & Allison, 2006; Bartholomew, Cobb, & Dutton, 2015).

Psychopathology is the study of the nature and causes of mental disorders (Paulino & Godinho, 2009a). Mental disorders can develop as a result of several factors, for instance stressful situations (Harrison, Geddes, & Sharpe, 2002) or victimization, such as in the case of domestic violence. A diagnosis of mental disorders is established through the observation of the presence/absence of a group of associated symptoms, signs and behaviours (Harrison et al., 2002; Paulino & Godinho, 2009a).

This study intends to determine the existence of primary symptoms that develop during the normative functioning of the individual while in an abusive relationship (Paulino & Godinho, 2009a; Smits, Timmerman, Barelds, & Meijer, 2014) and are not directly related to diagnoses, nonetheless being able to maintain a strong relationship with these (Smits et al., 2014), like somatization, obsessions and compulsions, interpersonal sensitivity, depression, anxiety, phobic anxiety, psychoticism and hostility (Derogatis & Melisaratos, 1983; Derogatis & Spencer, 1982; Harrison et al., 2002; Paulino & Godinho, 2009b).

INTIMATE PARTNER VIOLENCE AND PSYCHOPATHOLOGICAL SYMPTOMATOLOGY

Victims of intimate partner violence are exposed to traumatic life events that can lead to the development of symptomatology, such as fear of closeness to others, containment of affection, inhibition of expression, hypervigilance and distrust, usually used as self-defense strategies (Torres et al., 2013). Several studies found depression as the most common psychopathological disorder in victims of intimate partner violence, whether using normative or forensic samples (Al-Modallal, 2012; Beck et al., 2010; Buesa & Calvete, 2013; Coker et al., 2002; Karakurt, Smith, & Whiting, 2014; Lagdon, Armour & Stringer, 2014; Maideen, Sidik, Rampal, & Mukhtar, 2014; Mechanic, Weaver, & Resick, 2008; Meekers, Pallin, & Hutchinson, 2002; Moreira, Pinto, Cloninger, Rodrigues, & Silva, 2019).

In comparative studies, victims of intimate partner violence generally reported worse mental health than non-victims (Maideen et al., 2014; Okuda et al., 2011; Ruiz-Pérez & Plazaole-Castaño, 2005; Temple, Weston, & Marshall, 2010; Vameghi, Akbari, Majd, Sajedi, & Sajjadi, 2018). Okuda and colaborators (2011) determined that around 22% of victims reported higher indices of psychopathological disorder, compared to 9.7% of non victims. The victims had a higher probability of presenting suicidal ideation and suicide attempts, as well as more severe depressive, anxious and traumatic symptoms (Pico-Alfonso et al., 2006; Blasco-Ros, Sánchez-Lorente, & Martinez, 2010; Okuda et al., 2011; Vameghi et al., 2018).

In a study in Portugal, Lisboa, Vicente and Barroso (2005) demonstrated that victims show higher indices of automutilation, suicide attempts, panic, delusional ideas, auditory and visual hallucinations, phobias and excessive fear, compared to a normative sample; amongst the range of symptomatology presented, lack of hope and solitude were highlighted (Lisboa et al., 2005). In parallel, Moreira and co-authors (2019) - applying the BSI tool used in this study - concluded that victims of intimate partner presented higher psycopathology indices, particularly depression.

In studying the impact of life events on psychopathological symptomatology, Pico-Alfonso and collaborators (2006) found contemporaneous experience of victimization to be important; however, one should also consider the emergence of psychopathology as a consequence of previous abuse. Cerulli et al. (2012) concluded that, even in situations where abuse has stopped, the offender seeks to continue to traumatize the victim by other means, such as regulating parental responsibilities and engaging in litigation, etc., Other studies (e.g., Anderson & Saunders, 2003; Ruiz-Pérez & Plazaola-Castaño, 2005; Temple et al., 2010) reported the continuity of symptoms long after the end of the relationship, corroborating the long-term impact on the mental health of victims.

Several studies of the type of violence suffered by victims and its impact on their psychopathological symptomatology suggest psychological violence makes a more significant contribution than physical violence particulary to depression (Coker et al., 2002; Lawrence, Yoon, Langer, & Ro, 2009; Mechanic et al., 2008; Pico-Alfonso et al., 2006; Taft et al., 2006); psychological violence has an erosive effect on self-esteem (Mechanic et al., 2008). However, Meekers and authors (2002) found mental health problems to be similar between victims of psychological or physical violence; victims of physical violence had a greater prevalence of depression, anxiety and psychotic disorders, as well as post-traumatic stress symptoms (Scott & Babcock, 2010).

This study analysed the relation between psychopathological symptomatology and intimate partner violence. Although there is a

Psychopathological Symptomatology in Victims ...

significant amount of international research on this topic, it has not previously been addressed in the Portuguese context.

- *The first objective* was to ascertain the presence of psychopathological symptomatology in normative and forensic samples. The hypothesis was that the forensic sample would present a higher number of indices of psychopathological disturbance (Blasco-Ros et al., 2010; Lisboa et al., 2005; Maideen et al., 2014; Moreira et al., 2019; Pico-Alfonso et al., 2006; Ruiz-Pérez & Plazaole-Castaño, 2005; Okuda et al., 2011; Temple et al., 2010; Vameghi et al., 2018).
- *The second objective* only concerned the forensic sample. Thus, the second hypothesis was that there are no differences in indices of psychopathological symptomatology between victims who terminated their relationship with the defendant and those that had not (Anderson & Saunders, 2003; Cerulli et al., 2012; Ruiz-Pérez & Plazaola-Castaño, 2005; Temple et al., 2010). The third hypothesis was that victimisation in cases of psychological violence is more strongly associated to psychopathological simptomatology than in cases of physical violence (Coker et al., 2002; Lawrence et al., 2009; Mechanic et al., 2008; Pico-Alfonso et al., 2006; Taft et al., 2006).

METHOD

Participants

This study aimed to analyse psychopathological symptomatology in victims of intimate partner violence, comparing a forensic group (of victims), and a normative group (of non-victims). In Portugal, domestic violence legislation (article 152 of the Penal Code) covers single or repeated acts of physical, psychological and sexual violence, as well as deprivation of liberty, that involve current or former partners, who may or may not be cohabitating (BDJUR, 2013).

Data for the forensic group were collected at the public prosecution and criminal investigation police station in Lisbon. Members of the normative group were - for convenience - also located in Lisbon.

The forensic group was composed of participants who were fluent in Portuguese, resident in Portugal and involved in a domestic violence criminal investigation. The sample of the study included 61 female participants, minimum age of 18 years old and maximum of 72 ($M = 36.61$; $DP = 11.05$).

The normative group was composed of 61 participants without victim legal status and involved in a romantic relationship. Although these participants were not involved in any criminal lawsuit, some participants identified victimisation and perpetration of physical and psychological violence. This group's minimum age was 18 years old and maximum of 60 ($M = 35.23$; $DP = 12.50$).

Other characteristics of the sample can be observed in Table 1.

In terms of relationship status at the time of the data collection, the number of participants of the forensic group maintaining the relationship with the abusive partner were 19 (31.1%); the number that had terminated it were 42 (68.9%). The relationship period for the forensic group varied between 1 month and 40 years, with an average of 10 years ($M = 121.67$; $DP = 120.34$). All members of the normative group had an intimate relationship; the minimum duration was 4 months and the maximum 37 years, with an average of 12 years ($M = 140.87$; $DP = 133.70$).

The forensic group reported psychological violence (6.6%), physical and psychological violence (9.8%), several types of violent behavior (4.9%) and the remaining participants did not report any violence (78.7%). In the normative group, 91.8% of the participants did not report any victimisation, compared to 6.6% that reported physical and psychological violence and 1.6% that did not report any psychological violence.

In the forensic sample, 24 victims (39.3%) chose to continue with their criminal lawsuit, and 35 (57.4%) chose not to; it was not possible to obtain this information from 2 participants.

Table 1. Biographical and relationship characteristics of the forensic group (victims) and normative group (non-victims)

	Forensic group		Normative group	
	n	%	*n*	%
Nationality				
Portuguese	53	86.9	61	100
Brazilian	6	9.8	-	-
Other	2	3.3	-	-
Qualifications				
Primary education	8	13.1	2	3.3
Lower secondary	28	45.9	1	1.6
High school	18	29.5	20	32.8
Degree	5	8.2	28	45.9
Master	1	1.6	8	13.1
Other	1	1.6	2	3.3
Relationship				
Non-marital partnership	25	41	9	14.8
Dating	19	31.1	26	42.6
Matrimony	16	26.2	26	42.6
Missing	1	1.6	-	-

Measures

In this study two self-report measures were used, the Marital Violence Inventory (I. V. C.: Matos, Machado & Gonçalves, 2006) and the Brief Symptom Inventory (B. S. I.: Derogatis, 1982, translated and validated by Canavarro, 2007).

The Marital Violence Inventory (IVC) assesses the level of perpetration and victimisation in intimate partner violence. This scale was created in Portugal by Machado and collaborators (2006). It comprises 21 items of self-report, 7 of which refer to emotionally abusive and intimidatory behaviour and 13 to physical violence. The valuation of this measure is qualitative. However, a sum of the items was also made so it would be possible to assess the frequency of violence.

The Brief Symptom Inventory (BSI), was created by Derogatis and Spencer (1982) in order to reflect patterns of psychopathological symptoms in assessing global indices of primary symptoms. These types of symptoms can occur in several disorders, even though they might be more strongly associated to one (Smits et al., 2014). This measure was translated and validated in the Portuguese population by Canavarro (2007); it encompasses 9 symptomatology dimensions and 3 global disorder indices assessed by 53 items of self-report (Derogatis & Melisaratos, 1983; Derogatis & Spencer, 1982). The dimensions are:

- *somatization*: sensation of ill-being in the respiratory, cardiovascular and gastrointestinal systems;
- *obsessions and compulsions*: cognitions and behaviours difficult to exert control over and behaviours which indicate general cognitive difficulties, e.g., related to memory and concentration;
- *interpersonal sensitivity*: feelings of personal inadequacy, low self-esteem and self-depreciation;
- *depression*: symptoms such as disforia, lack of motivation and interest in life;
- *anxiety*: triggering tension, panic attacks, etc.,
- *hostility*: cognitive, emotional and behavioural aspects of anger:
- *phobic anxiety*: desproportionate response in relation to the stimulus and situational context;
- *paranoid ideation*: suspicion, projective thinking, delusions and other symptoms; and
- *psychoticism*: hallucinations, schizoid lifestyle, amongst others.

There are also four additional dimensions that form part of the dimensions listed above and that contribute to the global scores (Derogatis & Spencer, 1982).

Of the 3 disorder indices, the index related to positive symptoms is an average of their individual intensities; the total positive symptoms represents the number of symptoms presented and the general index combines these two indicators to give an overall measure of symptomatology. The overall

Psychopathological Symptomatology in Victims ...   69

result is compared to the standard values for the normative population, allowing for a statistical method for determining the existence of psychopathological disorders indices. The original BSI had standard values covering men and women, hospitalized patients, non hospitalized and non patients; Canavarro's adaptation (2007) only has these values for the normative and emotionally disturbed population. In this study, we chose to use the values of the normative group, due to the absence of information on the psychiatric history of the participants.

In addition to the self-report measures, a sociodemographic questionnaire was used that was specifically designed to gather biographical and relationship data on the participants and their partners.

Application

Data collection took place from March to October 2014. In both forensic and normative groups, the individual tools were applied sequentially, following informed consent and the offer of help to clarify any questions or concerns; assistance was provided in cases of blindness and illiteracy. The Brief Symptom Inventory was applied first, followed by the Marital Violence Inventory, ending with the sociodemographic questionnaire.

RESULTS

For the first objective – the analysis of psychopathological symptomatology in the forensic and normative groups – it was assumed that the forensic group would present a higher number of psychopathological disorder indices than the normative group.

Significant differences in the dimensions of psychopathological disorders between the groups was found, with the highest indices being presented by the victims group (see Table 2).

Table 2. Characteristics of the Psychopathological disorder dimension indices for the two participant groups

	Type of participant					
	Forensic group		Normative group			
Disorder indicators	Yes	%	Yes	%	χ^2	p^*
Somatization	7	(11.5)	38	(62.3)	33.84	.000
Obsessions and compulsions	12	(19.7)	31	(50.8)	12.97	.000
Interpersonal sensitivity	19	(31.1)	35	(57.4)	8.51	.004
Depression	11	(18.0)	41	(67.2)	30.16	.000
Anxiety	8	(13.1)	36	(59.0)	27.87	.000
Hostility	14	(23.0)	35	(57.4)	15.04	.000
Phobic anxiety	6	(9.8)	33	(54.1)	27.48	.000
Paranoid ideation	19	(27.9)	37	(60.7)	13.29	.000
Psychoticism	8	(13.1)	38	(62.3)	31.41	.000

$^*p < .01.$

For the second objective – concerning the analyses of psychopathological symptomatology within the forensic sample – it was assumed, as a first hypothesis, that no difference would be found between the victims that terminated their intimate relationship with their abuser, and those that did not. No significant differences in the psychopathological symptomatology of the two groups was found, a result that is in line with former studies (performed outside of Portugal).

In the third hypothesis, it was proposed that victims of psychological violence would show higher indices of psychopathological symptomatology than victims of physical violence. The levels of physical violence victimization are positively and significantly correlated to the general index of symptoms ($r = .384$, $p = .003$), although the correlation is weak and not statistically significant. However, broadly speaking, the higher the level of physical violence victimization, the higher the general index of psychopathological symptomatology. The levels of psychological violence victimization are not significantly correlated to the general index of symptoms ($r = .256$, $p = .050$), therefore refuting the proposed hypothesis.

DISCUSSION

For the first objective, it was demonstrated that the forensic group presented a higher and more significant number of dimensions indicative of psychopathological symptomatology compared to the normative group; this confirmed the suggested hypothesis, corroborating the results of other studies (Blasco-Ros et al., 2010; Lisboa et al., 2005; Maideen et al., 2014; Moreira et al., 2019; Pico-Alfonso et al., 2006; Ruiz-Pérez & Plazaole-Castaño, 2005; Okuda et al., 2011; Temple et al., 2010; Vameghi et al., 2018). The dimensions identified were somatization, obsessions and compulsions, interpersonal sensitivity, depression, anxiety, hostility, phobic anxiety, paranoid ideation and psychoticism. The most frequent disorder indicators in the forensic group were depression (67.2%), somatization (62.3%), psychoticism (62.3%) and paranoid ideation (60.7%). Previous studies reported a predominence of depressive symptomatology in victims (Al-Modallal, 2012; Beck et al., 2010; Buesa & Calvete, 2013; Coker et al., 2002; Karakurt et al., 2014; Lagdon et al., 2014; Maideen et al., 2014; Mechanic et al., 2008; Meekers et al., 2002; Moreira et al., 2019); Lisboa and colaborators (2005) and Meekers and colleagues (2002) reported the presence of delusional ideas of ruin, hallucinations and psychotic disorders.

For the second objective, involving the analysis of the forensic group, no significant difference was found between the psychopathological symptomatology of victims that had and had not terminated their intimate relationship, supporting the proposed hypothesis. Thus, we add further evidence that consequences of abuse last longer than the (abusive) relationship (Anderson & Saunders, 2003; Cerulli et al., 2012; Ruiz-Pérez & Plazaola-Castaño, 2005; Temple et al., 2010), refuting the conclusions of Pico-Alfonso and colaborators (2006), in which the main factor to predict psychopathological symptomatology was the contemporaneous experience of violence. Cerulli and collaborators (2012) suggest that the offender is able to keep traumatizing the victim through means such as litigation and regulation of parental responsibilities, among others.

For the third hypothesis, the results of this study refute the conclusions of previous investigations (Coker et al., 2002; Lawrence et al., 2009;

Mechanic et al., 2008; Pico-Alfonso et al., 2006; Taft et al., 2006). We find that levels of physical violence victimization are correlated to the overall symptomatology index, whereas levels of psychological violence victimization are not. Thus, the higher the level of physical victimization, the higher the psychopathological symptomatology indices. Nonetheless, these results are congruent with the conclusions of Meekers and collaborators (2002) and Scott and Babcock (2010), which indicated that physical violence victimization is the largest contributor to depression, anxiety, psychotic disorders and post-traumatic stress disorders.

CONCLUSION

This study collected data on psychopathological symptomatology on Portuguese female victims of intimate partner violence, in comparison to a normative sample. The forensic group was identified as having a higher number of dimensions indicative of psychopathological symptomatology, with an emphasis on depression, suggesting that psychopathology acts as a risk factor or a consequence of victimization.

The second hypothesis, relating to the forensic sample, found no difference in the psychopathological symptomatology of victims still in an intimate relationship with the partner and those that had terminated it. This result, although not statistically significant, suggests that the consequences of violence in intimate relationships can be extended even after the removal of the abusive context.

The third hypotheses consisted in a stronger (and statistically significant) correlation between physical violence victimization and psychopathological symptomatology indicators, in contrast to psychological violence victimization. This result suggests that physical violence may have consequences for the psychological health of victims, in addition to the physical harm resulting from the violence itself.

Our detailed assessment of the impact of psychopathological symptomatology may assist the prevention, assessment and intervention on intimate partner violence. We hope that our study contributes to facilitating better support of victims by adjusting intervention programs, whether psychoeducation or psychotherapy, to an individual's characteristics, and therefore to greater success in victims' recovery and empowerment.

In terms of limitations of the study, our normative sample was one of convenience, and this may explain the disparity of the sociodemographic data between the two groups; the self-report measure might not be the most precise tool to analyse psychopathological symptomatology due to the subjectivity necessarily involved in self-assessing mental health.

For future studies, we suggest the same type of analyses on male victims, between victims and victims/defendants and also the use of an interview to complement the assessment of psychopathological symptomatology.

ACKNOWLEDGMENTS

This work is funded by National Funds through the FCT - Foundation for Science and Technology within the framework of the CIEC (Research Center for Child Studies of the University of Minho) project under the reference UID/CED/00317/2019.

REFERENCES

Almeida, I. (2012). *Avaliação de risco de femicídio: Poder e controlo das dinâmicas das relações íntimas* [Femicide risk assessment: power and control of intimate relations dynamics] (unpublished doctoral thesis). Instituto Superior de Ciências do Trabalho e da Empresa, Lisboa.

Al-Modallal, H. (2012). Psychological partner violence and women's vulnerability to depression, stress, and anxiety. *International Journal of Mental Health Nursing, 21*(6), 560-566. https://doi.org/10.1111/j.1447-0349.2012.00826.x.

Anderson, D., & Saunders, D. (2003). Leaving an abusive partner: An empirical review of predictors, the process of leaving, and psychological

74   *Ana Sani, Ana Isabel Lopes and Cristina Soeiro*

well-being. *Trauma, Violence & Abuse, 4*(2), 163-191. https://doi.org/10.1177/1524838002250769.

Baldry, A., & Roia, F. (2011). Strategie Efficaci per il Contrasto ai *Maltrattamenti e allo Stalking: Aspetti giuridici e criminologici* [Effective Strategies for Tackling Abuse and Stalking: Legal and Criminological Aspects]. Milão: FrancoAngeli.

Bartholomew, K., & Allison, C. (2006). An attachment perspective on abusive dynamics in intimate relationships. In M. Mikulincer, & G. Goodman (Eds.), *Dynamics of romantic love: Attachment, caregiving, and sex* (pp. 102-127). Nova Iorque: Guilford.

Bartholomew, K., Cobb, R., & Dutton, D. (2015). Established and emerging perspectives on violence in intimate relationships. In M. Mikulincer, P. R. Shaver, J. A. Simpson, & J. F. Dovidio (Eds.), *APA Handbook of Personality and Social Psychology* (Vol. III, pp. 605-630). Washington, DC: American Psychological Association

Beck, J., Clapp, J., Jacobs-Lentz, J., McNiff, J., Avery, M., & Olsen, S. (2014). The association of mental health conditions with employment, interpersonal, and subjective functioning after intimate partner violence. *Violence against Women, 20*(11), 1321-1337. https://doi.org/ 10.1177/1077801214552855.

BDJUR (2013). *Código Penal* [Penal Code]. Coimbra: Edições Almedina. Consultado no dia 22 de Janeiro de 2013 em http://bdjur.almedina.net/citem. php?field=item_id&value=1172736.

Blasco-Ros, C., Sánchez-Lorente, S., & Martinez, M. (2010). Recovery from depressive symptoms, state anxiety and post-traumatic stress disorder in women exposed to physical and psychological, but not to psychological intimate partner violence alone: A longitudinal study. *BMC Psychiatry, 10*(98). https://doi.org/10.1186/1471-244X-10-98.

Buesa, S., & Calvete, E. (2013). Violencia contra síntomas de depresión y estrés postraumático: El papel del apoyo social [Violence against symptoms of depression and post-traumatic stress: The role of social support]. *International Journal of Psychology and Psychological Therapy, 13*(1), 31-45.

Psychopathological Symptomatology in Victims ... 75

Canavarro, M. (2007). Inventário de sintomas psicopatológicos (BSI): Uma revisão crítica dos estudos realizados em Portugal [Inventory of psychopathological symptoms (BSI): A critical review of two studies carried out in Portugal]. In M. Simões, C. Machado, M. Gonçalves, & L. Almeida (Eds.), *Avaliação psicológica: Instrumentos validados para a população Portuguesa* (vol. III, pp. 305-331). Coimbra: Quarteto Editora.

Cerulli, C., Poleshuck, E., Raimondi, C., Veale, S., & Chin, N. (2012). "What Fresh Hell Is This?" Victims of intimate partner violence describe their experiences of abuse, pain, and depression. *Journal of Family Violence, 27*(8), 773-781. https://doi.org/10.1007/s10896- 012-9469-6.

Coker, A., Davis, K., Arias, I., Desai, S., Sanderson, M., & Smith, P. (2002). Physical and mental health effects of intimate partner violence for men and women. *American Journal of Preventive Medicine, 24*(4), 260-268. https://doi.org/10.1016/S0749-3797(02)00514-7.

Derogatis, L., & Melisaratos, N. (1983). The brief symptom inventory: An introductory report. *Psychological Medicine, 13*, 595-605. https://doi. org/10.1017/S0033291700048017.

Derogatis, L. R., & Spencer, M. S. (1982). *The Brief Symptom Inventory (BSI): Administration, scoring, and procedures manual-I.* Baltimore: Johns Hopkins University School of Medicine, Clinical Psychometrics Research Unit. https://doi.org/10.1037/t00789-000.

Gonçalves, R. A. (2004). Agressores conjugais: Investigar, avaliar e intervir na outra face da violência conjugal [Marital offenders: investigating, evaluating, and intervening on the other face of marital violence]. *Revista Portuguesa de Ciência Criminal, 14*(4), 541-558.

Harrison, P., Geddes, J., & Sharpe. M. (2002). *Introdução à Psiquiatria* [*Introduction to Psychiatry*]. Lisboa: Climepsi Editores.

Karakurt, G., Smith, D., & Whiting, J. (2014). Impact of intimate partner violence on women's mental health, *Journal of Family Violence, 29*, 693-702. https://doi.org/10.1007/s10896-014-9633-2.

Lagdon, S., Armour, C., & Stringer, M. (2014) Adult experience of mental health outcomes as a result of intimate partner violence victimisation: a systematic review. *European Journal of Psychotraumatology*, *5*(1). https://doi.org/10.3402/ejpt.v5.24794.

Lawrence, E., Yoon, J., Langer, A., & Ro, E. (2009). Is psychological aggression as detrimental as physical aggression? The independent effects of psychological aggression on depression and anxiety symptoms. *Violence and victims*, *24*(1). https://doi.org/10.1891/0886-6708.24.1.20.

Lisboa, M., Vicente, L., & Barroso, Z. (2005). *Saúde e violência contra as mulheres: Estudo sobre as relações existentes entre a saúde das mulheres e as várias dimensões de violência de que tenham sido vítimas* [Health and violence against women: Study on the relationship between women's health and the various dimensions of violence against women]. Lisboa: Direção-Geral da Saúde.

Machado, C., Matos, M., & Gonçalves, M. (2006). *Manual da escala de crenças sobre violência conjugal (E.C.V.C.) e do inventário de violência conjugal (I.V.C.): Escalas de avaliação e manual* [Manual on the Belief on Marital Violence Scale (E.C.V.C.) and Marital Violence Inventory (I.V.C.) Handbook: Rating Scales and Handbook]. Braga: Psiquilíbrios.

Maideen, S. F., Sidik, S. M., Rampal, L., & Mukhtar, F. (2014). Prevalence, associated factors and predictors of depression among adults in the community of Selangor, Malaysia. *PloS One*, *9*(4), e95395. https://doi.org/10.1371/journal.pone.0095395.

Mechanic, M., Weaver, T., & Resick, P. (2008). Mental health consequences of intimate partner abuse: A multidimensional assessment of four different forms of abuse. *Violence against Women*, *14*(6), 634-654. https://doi.org/10.1177/1077801208319383.

Meekers, D., Pallin, S. C., & Hutchinson, P. (2013). Intimate partner violence and mental health in Bolivia. *BMC Women's Health*, *13*(28), 1-16. https://doi.org/10.1186/1472-6874-13-28.

Moreira, P., Pinto, M., Cloninger, C. R., Rodrigues, D., & da Silva, C. F. (2019). Understanding the experience of psychopathology after intimate partner violence: the role of personality. *Peer J.*, *7*, e6647. https://doi.org/10.7717/peerj.6647.

Okuda, M., Olfson, M., Hasin, D., Grant, B. F., Lin, K. H., & Blanco, C. (2011). Mental health of victims of intimate partner violence: results from a national epidemiologic survey. *Psychiatric services*, *62*(8), 959-962. https://doi.org/10.1176/ps.62.8.pss6208_0959.

Pico-Alfonso, M., Garcia-Linares, M., Celda-Navarro, N., Blasco-Ros, C., Echeburúa, E., & Martinez, M. (2006). The impact of physical, psychological, and sexual intimate male partner violence on women's mental health: Depressive symptoms, posttraumatic stress disorder, state anxiety, and suicide. *Journal of Women's Health*, *15*(5), 599-611. https://doi.org/10.1089/jwh.2006.15.599.

Paulino, M., & Godinho, J. (2009a). Psicopatologia [Psychopathology] In J. Cordeiro, *Manual de Psiquiatria Clínica* (4ª Ed, pp. 429-436). Lisboa: Fundação Calouste Gulbenkian.

Paulino, M., & Godinho, J. (2009b). Semiologia [Semiology]. In J. Cordeiro, *Manual de Psiquiatria Clínica* (4ª Ed, pp. 409-428). Lisboa: Fundação Calouste Gulbenkian.

Ruiz-Pérez, I. & Plazaola-Castaño, J. (2005). Intimate partner violence and mental health consequences in women attending family practice in Spain. *Psychosomatic Medicine*, *67*, 791-797. https://doi.org/10.1097/01.psy.0000181269.11979.cd.

Scott, S., & Babcock, J. (2010). Attachment as a moderator between intimate partner violence and PTSD symptoms. *Journal of Family Violence*, *25*(1), 1-9. https://doi.org/10.1007/s10896-009-9264-1.

Smits, I., Timmerman, M., Barelds, D., & Meijer, R. (2014). The Dutch Symptom Checklist-90-Revised: Is the Use of the Subscales Justified? *European Journal of Psychological Assessment*. https://doi.org/10.1027/1015-5759/a000233.

Taft, C., O'Farrel, T., Torres, S., Panuzio, J., Monzon, C., & Murphy C. (2006). Examining the correlates of psychological aggression among a community sample of couples. *Journal of Family Psychology*, *20*(4), 581-588. https://doi.org/10.1037/0893-3200.20.4.581.

Temple, J., Weston, R., & Marshall, L. (2010). Long term mental health effects of partner violence patterns and relationship termination on low-income and ethnically diverse community women. *Partner Abuse*, *1*(4), 379-398. https://doi.org/10.1891/1946-6560-1.4.379.

Torres, A., Garcia-Esteve, L., Navarro, P., Tarragona, M. J., Imaz, M. L., & Martín-Santos, R. (2013). Relationship between intimate partner violence, depressive symptomatology, and personality traits. *Journal of Family Violence*, *28*(4), 369-379. https://doi.org/10.1007/s10896-013-9502-4.

Vameghi, R., Akbari, S., Majd, H., Sajedi, F. & Sajjadi, H. (2018). The comparison of socioeconomic status, perceived social support and mental status in women of reproductive age experiencing and not experiencing domestic violence in Iran. *Journal of Injury & Violence Research*, *10*(1), 35-44. https://doi.org/10.5249/jivr.v10i1.983.

In: Victims of Violence
Editor: Mathias L. Knudsen

ISBN: 978-1-53617-140-2
© 2020 Nova Science Publishers, Inc.

Chapter 5

FORENSIC IMPLICATIONS IN THE MANAGEMENT OF SEXUAL VIOLENCE IN HOSPITALS

Sarah Gino[1,] and Luciana Caenazzo[2]*
[1]Department of Health Sciences,
Università del Piemonte Orientale, Novara, Italy
[2]Department of Molecular Medicine,
University of Padova, Padova, Italy

ABSTRACT

Sexual assault involves a broad spectrum of nonconsensual sexual activity, including events with and without vaginal and/or anal penetration and/or oral sex and events characterized by the use of physical force or psychological coercion.

Given the acute nature of sexual assault, emergency medicine providers are often the first clinicians to take care of the victim, and care of such patients differs from care of those presenting other kind of trauma or injuries.

---

* Corresponding Author's E-mail: sarah.gino@uniupo.it.

The sexual assault examination poses many problems to health personnel that have a dual responsibility regarding the management of the victims of sexual assault. The first is to provide the victim with the required medical and psychological treatment, while the second is to assist the victims in their medico-legal proceedings by collecting evidence and performing good quality and thorough forensic medical examination and documentation.

Healthcare professionals treating victims of sexual assault admitted to Emergency Departments (ED) need a high level of professionalism, and the personnel involved in this process must perform their role in a scientific manner to effectively aid the administration of justice. They must listen and gather useful information for treatment as well as not just focusing on clinical intervention, but also on taking legal and forensic implications into account.

Despite the fact that indicators have been published in the literature, even today there is still a lack of consistency in how they are applied in some hospital settings. Sometimes the case histories collected from the victim in the ED are still inadequate or incomplete in determining how the case event should be reconstructed.

To avoid discrepancies between the medical reporting and the reconstruction of sex crimes, it is crucial to use strategies, which focus not only on technical aspects of evidence collection, but also on the way the victim's story will be recorded. Such efforts could lead to better management of sexual assault victims, and to securing their legal rights. Within this setting, the involvement of healthcare professionals specialized in the forensic field is paramount both for conducting accurate clinical examination for collecting a detailed documentation of physical injuries and for sampling biological evidence for forensic purposes.

Keywords: sexual violence, healthcare professional training

INTRODUCTION

The phenomenon of "gender violence" has its roots in the mists of time, although it has been identified and perceived as a problem only in relatively recent times.

The World Health Organization (WHO) defines violence as "the intentional use of physical force or power, threatened or actual, against oneself, another person, or against a group or community, that either results in or has a high likelihood of resulting in injury, death, psychological harm, maldevelopment or deprivation" [1]. In particular, the WHO highlights that sexual violence is "any sexual act, attempt to obtain a sexual act, unwanted sexual comments or advances, or acts to traffic, or otherwise directed, against a person's sexuality using coercion, by any person regardless of their relationship to the victim, in any setting, including but not limited to home and work" [2]. According to this definition, a very wide range of behaviours could be identified as an act of sexual violence.

Violence against women is a violation of human rights, crossing all cultures, classes, levels of education, earnings, ethnic and age groups. It has an important impact, not only on the justice and economy of every country in the world, but above all on women's health. It represents one of the main causes of mortality, disability and morbidity among female subjects, with an impact on health that goes well beyond the damage caused immediately by violent behaviour, also having important effects over the medium and long term.

The competence of health personnel who take care of abused subjects in conducting the examination and evidence collection is of fundamental importance, especially in cases of sexual and physical violence.

Indeed, healthcare professionals play a dual role in responding to the victims of sexual assault. The first is to provide the required medical treatment and psychological support. The second is to assist survivors in their medico-legal proceedings by collecting evidence and ensuring a good quality documentation. The problem is not in deciding what to ask and what to document, considering that most of the international recommendations give indications on these aspects. The main question is to consider that the task of health professionals is not to assess whether the victims tell the truth or whether they have been raped, but that of documenting and preparing a complete medical history in order to organise patient care, guide the clinical examination, document any injuries and collect evidence [3].

Indeed, in many countries the health sector has the duty to collect medical and legal evidence to corroborate the report of the victim and the circumstances of the assault, to help in identifying the perpetrator, but also to concern itself with the health consequences of the event.

In most countries, however, there is still a gap between the health care needs of victims of sexual abuse and the existing level of health services provided [4-7]: for instance, victims of sexual violence are not examined by a specially trained medico-legal examiner or health care provider, are subjected to multiple examinations in surroundings that do not meet minimum health standards. Moreover, until now, in many countries protocols or guidelines for health care professionals on the medical management of persons who have experienced sexual violence have not been widely available or if available they have been ignored.

THE IMPORTANCE OF GUIDELINES FOR A CLINICAL AND A FORENSIC APPROACH

The World Health Organization has drawn up guidelines for the clinical and medico-legal treatment of victims of violence, emphasising that victims' wellbeing is a priority and that the ideal organization should provide a single moment dedicated to medical care and forensic investigation [8]. Comprehensive protocols and guidelines for victims of sexual violence should include: recording a full description of the event, listing the medical history of the victim; documenting in a standard way the results of a full physical examination; assessment of the risk of pregnancy; testing for sexually transmitted diseases; providing psychological support; collecting biological evidence and performing toxicological analysis. In some countries, the protocol forms part of the procedure of a "sexual assault evidence kit" that includes instructions and containers for collecting evidence, appropriate legal forms and documents for recording histories [9].

The use of standard protocols and guidelines can significantly improve the quality of treatment and psychological support of victims, as well as of evidence collection [10]. Therefore, if the episode of sexual violence occurred shortly before the observation, an emergency medical intervention is of utmost importance, and it must take into account both the clinical aspects and the forensic implications [11]. Indeed, managing a proper clinical and forensic examination at the Emergency Department (ED) can allow a suspect or a crime scene to be identified, or to provide evidence as to which sexual acts have occurred. Furthermore, given that sexual assault is often associated with the consumption of alcohol and/or drugs, clinical forensic examination plays a special role when victims are unable to reliably remember what happened to them.

Sexually abused individuals should be offered a full medical-forensic examination involving an initial assessment, including obtaining informed consent; a medical history, including an account of the events described as sexual violence; a "head-to-toe" physical examination; a detailed genito-anal examination; recording, taking photos and classifying injuries; collecting and maintaining the chain of custody of forensic specimens; therapeutic opportunities; arranging follow-up care; storage of documentation; writing a medico-legal report.

MEDICAL AND FORENSIC EXAMINATION

Not in all hospitals with ED does the staff that first meets the victims include the forensic expert. In this case, it is important that the staff components have the consciouness and the ability to recognize the violence, expecially if it is not declared by the victims. In fact, there is even today a lack of consistency in how or if some hospital settings apply efficacy guidelines to the management of sexual assault. In this case, it happens that the case history collected from the victim in the ED is still sometimes inadequate or incomplete in determining how the case should be reconstructed.

To realize the right to health care for victims, healthcare professionals must be trained to respond appropriately to their needs, ensuring an approach based on empathy, understanding and a willingness to listen.

Both medical and forensic examination and medical and forensic specimens should be performed at the same time, in the same place and by the same personnel—so, in this way, the numbers of examination are reduced.

Informed Consent

Before a full medical examination of the patient can be conducted, it is essential that informed consent be obtained. Informed consent is a central issue in medico-legal matters. Examining a person without their consent could result in the medical officer in question being charged with the offences of assault, battery or trespass. In some jurisdictions, the results of an examination conducted without consent cannot be used in legal proceedings. The meaning of informed consent is an explanation of all aspects of the consultation to the patient. Particular emphasis should be placed on the matter of the release of information to other parties, including the police. This is especially important in settings where there is a legal obligation to report an episode of violence to the relevant authorities. It is crucial that patients understand the options open to them and are given sufficient information to enable them to make informed decisions about their care. To obtain an informed consent it is necessary to explain to patients that should they decide to pursue legal action against the perpetrator, any information they disclose in the course of the examination may become part of the public record. If mandatory reporting is required, it is very important that the patient understands this. The examiner must clearly explain each step of the examination process and the reasons for it. Moreover, the patient must be reminded of the option to refuse to undergo each part of the examination [8, 12].

In recent years, in many jurisdictions, victims of sexual assault have often reported an unclear story of what has happened to them. These reports can be associated with alcohol or drug consumption, or both (with awareness or a lack thereof). In these cases, one of the major challenges for healthcare providers lies in obtaining informed consent for examination and evidence collection. While it can be relatively easy for healthcare providers in dealing with a competent adult, problems do arise, however, when a patient is unconscious, intoxicated or underage, or, in any case, in a condition that impairs the ability to provide consent.

In general, the two conditions of adult and minor unconsciousness have to be treated differently. In the case of adults who are incompetent due to intoxication, it will be necessary to wait until the situation is resolved and then proceed with the request for informed consent. In the case of adult incapacitated patients, the request would be made to the guardian.

The case of minors, in which parental violence is suspected by the healthcare providers, the situation is different, because, they have to decide whether to give parents suspected of violence against their daughter/son any clinical information that might indirectly harm the child. In fact, they need to establish whether it is ethically acceptable to withhold information concerning medical investigations they conduct to support the diagnosis of violence. So, obtaining parental consent for tests is clearly likely to be difficult.

There are some legal exceptions to the rule of informed consent that enable healthcare professionals to proceed without obtaining any informed consent in the event of emergencies, incompetence and waiver. A controversial form of ethical exception to the need to provide information is the so-called 'therapeutic privilege,' according to which a healthcare professional may withhold information on the grounds that its disclosure could be harmful (as in the case of emotionally or clinically fragile, vulnerable, or unstable patients), generate anxiety and stress, or even endanger the patient's life by prompting irrational behavior.

In our opinion, in this situation, performing tests without informing the parents of their purpose and without obtaining their informed consent could be ethically justifiable under the provisions of therapeutic privilege. The reference to therapeutic privilege seems to be justified because some information is withheld from parents not only for their own good, but also for their child's (and here lies the difference vis-à-vis the typical definition of therapeutic privilege). What is important here is that the healthcare professional decides to withhold certain information because disclosing it would not place the parents in a position to make the most appropriate decisions in their child's interest - and this is what justifies our reference to therapeutic privilege. Providing detailed information might make parents suspicious, and induce them to alleviate or minimize their child's symptoms, take their child elsewhere, or otherwise potentially damage the victim.

If a diagnosis of parental violence has been confirmed, it is the doctor's duty to take action in the child's best interest, and protect the child from further injury or potential danger. It is therefore morally quite easy to justify the decision not to inform parents about the diagnostic process under these circumstances.

The difficulties arise, both in practice and from an ethical point of view, in doubtful cases, when any uncertainty regarding the diagnosis casts doubts on the best course of clinical action. Healthcare providers are morally bound to juggle their responsibilities in considering the following aspects.

They should run further (even invasive) tests to arrive at a certain diagnosis. They have to judge the pros and cons of any tools they use to ensure that the benefits exceed the risks, relying on the "first, do no harm" principle and causing the child the least possible harm.

They should ensure the clinical care of their young patient, which essentially means assessing the family setting and relations before and after the child's admission to hospital. In children where the violence is not clearly demonstrated, healthcare providers need to retain their relationship with the child's parents (who, in cases of a still uncertain diagnosis, may or may not be perpetrators); the child's 'best interest' should be sought and interpreted, striking the difficult balance between protecting them from further harm and preserving their original family context.

Healthcare providers should maintain a relationship with the parents because of the various possible scenarios: one or both parents may be involved in the violence, and one or both may be unaware of the child being abused by another member of the family or a person outside the family.

The decision not to inform parents about tests conducted to establish a diagnosis of violence may be taken without involving the law courts by giving precedence to the principle of non-maleficence so long as there is uncertainty in the diagnosis of abuse/violence [13].

Medical History and Account of the Event

To avoid discrepancies between the medical reporting and the reconstruction of sex crimes, it is crucial to use strategies, which focus not only on technical aspects of evidence collection, but also on the way the victim's story is recorded. Such efforts could lead to better management of sexual assault victims and to securing their legal rights. First of all, it is necessary to collect a medical history and an account of the inflicted violence.

The primary aim of taking a medical history is to obtain information that may aid in managing the medical examination of the patient or may help to explain subsequent findings, e.g., easy bruising or loss of consciousness or memory loss.

Concerning the account of the event, it is important to detect and track all acute injuries, to assess the risk of adverse consequences, to guide forensic examination and relevant specimen collection. It is important to report in the documentation what patients say, using their own words or expressions to avoid misinterpretation. The following details must be documented: date, time and location of the assault; the name (if known) and the number of the perpetrators; the nature of physical contacts; the use of weapons or restraints; the use of drugs, alcohol and medications; behaviour of the victims after the assault and before the medical examination (i.e., having washed themselves and / or changed their clothes). All these details will guide the sampling for laboratory tests, forensic genetics and forensic toxicology [13].

To achieve these objectives, many strategies have to be put in place to establish a good relationship with the victim. One example is what is reported by India's Ministry of Health and Family Welfare that, in the document providing guidelines for the victims of sexual assault, gives the following indications [3, 14]:

- never say or do anything to suggest disbelief regarding the incident;
- do not pass judgmental remarks or comments that might appear unsympathetic;
- appreciate the survivor's strength in coming to the hospital as it can serve to build a bond of trust;
- convey important messages such as: the survivor is not responsible for precipitating the act of rape by any of her actions or inaction;

- explain to the survivor that this is a crime/violence and not an act of lust or for sexual pleasure;
- emphasize that this is not a loss of honour, modesty or chastity but a violation of his/her rights and it is the perpetrator who should be ashamed;
- get help from a counselor, if required.

Medical and Forensic Examination

The right to health care requires that appropriate health services are available without discrimination and are accessible, acceptable and of good quality. This includes medical treatment for physical injuries, prophylaxis and testing for sexually-transmitted infections, emergency contraception, and psychosocial support. Recognizing the right of all persons to health, health care workers must obtain informed consent from the survivors/victims of sexual violence prior to conducting medical examinations or initiating medico-legal examinations that must respect the privacy and dignity of the victim.

As previously stated, the staff that first meet the victims in hospital emergency departments do not always include a forensic expert, so it is important that, in this case, the staff components have the competence to recognize and discover the violence. To realize this goal, healthcare professionals must be trained to respond appropriately to the victim's needs. It is obvious that health workers cannot refuse treatment or discriminate on the basis of gender, sexual orientation, disability, religion, language, marital status, occupation, political belief or other situations [14].

Before collecting the samples for clinical and forensic reasons, it is necessary to subject the patient to a complete examination (from head to toe) and, based on the collected history, to an oro-genito-anal examination. The timing of the physical examination is largely dictated by what is best for the patient (particularly where injury intervention is required) but for a number of reasons is best performed as soon as possible after the patient presents herself/himself. Delay in accessing services may result in lost therapeutic opportunities (e.g., provision of emergency contraception); changes to the physical evidence (e.g., healing of injuries); loss of forensic material (e.g., evidence of contact with assailant including blood and semen). In many instances, however, victims do not present themselves for treatment for considerable time after the assault.

Healthcare professionals must also record and classify the injuries by photographing or drawing them. When photography is performed, it is useful to take three images of each injury or group of injuries. The first should be taken from a distance to easily observe the body part where the injury is. The second one should be a close-up of the injury and the third should be a close-up with a ruler next to, but not covering, the injury [11]. These photographs may serve as evidence or may simply refresh the examiner's memory at the time of trial or other legal proceedings. The injury description or photography could be useful in answering the following questions: the age of injury; how the injury was produced (sustained in an accidental, assaultive or self-inflicted manner) and the consequences of them. It is important to highlight that not all women who allege sexual abuse have visible general and genital injuries. Indeed, in many cases, none are recognised.

The aim of an objective medical and forensic examination is to describe the health status of the person and to record the injuries and the consequences of these injuries. In the end, the expert tries to understand the mechanisms of the injuries and if these injuries are or are not consistent with the trauma history recounted by the person. For this, the expert needs to record not only the patient's account of the assault and all the injuries and their consequences, but also the previous medical history of the patient.

Collecting Evidence

It is recommendeded that samples be collected for forensic genetics and toxicological analysis as well as for medical purposes and disease diagnosis.

During examination, the collection of forensic evidence is essential in any sexual assault investigation because it can help in identifying a suspect or a crime scene, or in providing supporting evidence about what sexual acts have occurred. It may also identify possible series links or demonstrate repeat offending by the same suspect. Semen found on intimate swabs may have a more probative value than semen found on clothing or bedding because it only has a finite time for survival compared with dried stains on fabrics. If a sexual assault involves oral, digital or foreign object penetration, then it is useful for the examiner to be provided with as much detail as possible about the alleged offence to process the evidence most effectively. For example, when dealing with stains, it is important to identify which areas to target. Swabbing an assumed stain area that is smaller than the real deposition area could mean that some of the relevant sample goes uncollected. Alternatively, sampling a much larger area than that of the real deposit may mean that the sample is spread over a larger surface area and that overall less of a sample is collected or becomes diluted. Both practical approaches have the potential to give an inaccurate view of where the actual sample was located [15].

On the basis of the account of the assault and on the basis of the time elapsed between the event and the medical examination, the likelihood of collecting evidence decreases with the passing of time as shown in Table 1. The health personnel decide which specimens to collect for forensic genetics analysis. During collection, contamination must be avoided and, after collection, samples must be handled and stored appropriately and the chain of custody of specimens must be documented [8].

Alcohol or other drugs play an important role in many sexual assaults. Half of all sexual assaults involve drugs or alcohol, whether voluntarily ingested by the victim, surreptitiously given by the assailant, or ingested under force or coercion. The victim may complain of an impaired or lapse of consciousness with short segments of memory of a sexual act, genital pain, or may have no memory but are concerned that they may have been a victim of a possible sexual assault due to misplaced or missing undergarments or other concerns. Clinicians should use appropriate prudence in these cases and should consider performing a medical-forensic evaluation including toxicological investigation on the most appropriate matrix based on the time elapsed between the intake of the substance and the visit (Table 2) [11].

Table 1. The collection of evidence must be guided by the victim's story and the time elapsed between the event and the visit

Body area	Time elapsed between the event and the visit
Oral cavity	Within 48 hours
Anus and rectum	Within 5 days
Cervical canal fornix of the vagina	Within 7/10 days
External genitalia, skin and perineum	If the victim has not washed

Table 2. Depending on the time elapsed between the intake of the substance and the sampling, a different biological matrix must be chosen for toxicological analyses

Time elapsed between the event and the sampling	Biological matrix
Hours	Blood
Days	Urine
One/two months	Hair

THE POSITION OF HEALTH PERSONNEL

The care of the sexual assault patient begins with presentation to the ED and continues beyond disposition and discharge. A multifactorial, multidisciplinary approach will produce the most efficient and inclusive evaluation and management. Care should be taken to address a patient's psychosocial, medical, and forensic needs. This includes using victim advocacy services, treating associated injuries and medical conditions, collecting forensic evidence while maintaining proper chain of custody, and aptly administering emergency contraception, empirical treatment for sexual transmited infections (STIs), and pertinent postexposure prophylaxis. With the proper knowledge and preparation, appropriate and victim-centered care in the ED can provide the first step toward successful long-term healing after sexual assault [11].

The assistance provided by specialised healthcare personnel to victims of sexual violence cannot focus just on the clinical intervention appropriate for the injuries suffered by the patient, but must also take legal and forensic needs into account. Anamnestic data represents a crucial step towards the finding of forensic evidence. Collecting medical history is a crucial moment in dealing with the victim of violence, as this can decide the subsequent steps also geared at collecting evidence.

The health personnel's training and increased awareness are therefore essential in order to collect all relevant information to understand what happened and to identify perpetrators. Better training of health personnel could also allow for the identification of victims of violence, who use health services at least three times more than the rest of the population, as reported in the relevant literature [16–18]. Moreover, Gino and colleagues [19] suggests that, in parallel with the training of health personnel, a more in-depth training of judicial authorities is needed in order not to hinder the efforts that health professionals make during care and visits to victims of abuse (on average a visit in a dedicated centre takes 3–4 h).

It is necessary to recognise the great effort a woman exerts in undergoing the examination and evidence collection, often a short time after having suffered violence. Examinations of rape victims are by their nature extremely stressful not only for the woman but also for health personnel.

Training for health care professionals concerning sexual violence needs to be addressed in the training of all health service staff, including psychiatrists and counsellors, in basic training as well as in specialized postgraduate courses. Such training should give health care workers greater knowledge and awareness of sexual violence and make them more able to detect and handle cases of abuse in a sensitive effective way [2]. Furthermore, this training should allow these operators to correctly identify victims of violence, provide effective and temporally adequate responses and have intervention and treatment techniques of proven effectiveness. In fact, they have a unique opportunity and a great responsibility in screening all patients for sexual violence and, once identified, to provide competent and adequate assistance.

Violence against women is a problem of certain public health relevance and even if it is important to underline the extraordinary role played by associations, voluntary groups, individuals active in this field, the management of the health aspects of the problem must be actively managed by public health services, as much as for all other public health priorities.

A health worker is often the first contact for victims of sexual violence, and women who have experienced violence identify health professionals as the professionals they would most trust to reveal abuse to [20]. Regardless of the circumstances, health professionals who come into contact with women who have experienced violence must be able to recognize the signs, and respond to this problem adequately and safely. Individuals who have been exposed to violence require comprehensive, gender-sensitive health services that address the consequences for the physical and mental health of that experience and help overcome the traumatic event.

Documentation about injuries, medical reports and other problems arising from violence can be used as evidence in court by the abused woman, should she choose to take legal action. In addition to addressing the health consequences of violence, health workers are also in a favorable position to collect and document the evidence needed to better detail the circumstances of the reported abuses and to help identify the perpetrator.

Some studies have shown that women who have experienced violence are more likely than non-abused women to seek health care, even if they do not disclose the violence. A controversial aspect concerns the approach to identify these hidden cases of violence in health services. There are two different positions: that of universal screening, according to which, all women are routinely asked a question about violence, and that of "case-finding," according to which, this question is asked only to women who present risk factors or symptoms suggestive of violence. Some authors stress that there is no evidence that routine screening significantly improves the outcome. It must be said, however, that in such a complex situation, the doctor's question about violence, even when it represents an element of great importance, cannot by itself determine its outcome. Many other aspects come into play: the psychological and social characteristics of women, of violent men and their family environment, economic conditions, the answers of the forces of order and justice. Of course, when the health care professional asks this question, they send a message of great importance: the problem exists, it concerns so many women and it is relevant to health. It will then be up to the victim to decide if they want to talk about it immediately or on another occasion, or never. On the other hand, an important limitation of the case-finding is that the operator investigates a situation of violence above all or only when the woman corresponds to the stereotype of the victim: marginalized, belonging to a particular ethnic group, with an alcoholic partner with the result of further stigmatizing these women and ignoring the possibility of violence in those that do not correspond to the stereotype. The American Collage of Obstetricians and Gynecologists suggests providing screening to all women for a history of sexual abuse, especially women who report pelvic pain, dysmenorrhea, sexual disfunction or a history of drug/alcohol/medication use disorder [21].

The fundamental role that the health care system and health care professionals can play in terms of identification, assessment, treatment, crisis intervention, documentation, dispatch and follow-up, is poorly understood or accepted in the context of national health programs of various countries.

Health professionals should also be informed that they are also in a favorable position to collect and document the evidence needed to better detail the circumstances of the reported abuses and to help identify the perpetrator.

Healthcare professionals tend to view violence against women as a criminal justice problem. They are also poorly prepared to address the issue, as medical and nursing education in many countries does not address this issue. This situation can lead to unfamiliarity with the procedure; fear of becoming involved with a prolonged and difficult court case; the lengthy examination which interferes with emergency department activities; and the minimal payment for both the examination and time in court. Having already experienced tremendous trauma, these delays and the staff's reluctance add to the stress experienced by the victim [22].

In order for health professionals to play their role by mitigating the effects of violence and taking full responsibility, it is necessary to raise awareness of the problem and provide them with the information and tools needed to respond sensitively and effectively to the victims' needs.

CONCLUSION

Acute sexual assault is an all too common event, and emergency physicians, pediatricians, and family practitioners should be prepared to care for victims. However, given the acute nature of sexual assault, a great many victims are taken to the nearest hospital, so emergency medicine providers are often the first clinicians to care for a victim.

Healthcare providers caring for these patients should feel comfortable in obtaining an accurate history and in proceeding to a physical examination and then documenting and maintaining up-to-date knowledge about the most current recommendations. Furthermore, they should be familiar with legal mandates concerning reporting of abuse and consent for treatment and should seek to maintain confidentiality for the patient. By providing age-appropriate care in a thorough, systematic manner, including arranging an appropriate follow-up plan of care, providers can help victims of sexual assault begin the road to recovery.

Healthcare professionals treating victims of sexual assault admitted to Emergency Departments need to deal not only with clinical priorities, but also with the emotional suffering and anguish characterizing the experience of this type of patients. Therefore, it is important to ensure an approach based on empathy, understanding and a willingness to listen. Furthermore, they can then more effectively contribute to violence management by documenting injuries, and by collecting and sampling biological evidence for forensic purposes, including those of forensic interest to understand what happened and to identify perpetrators.

Even today, there is still a lack of consistency in how they are applied in some hospital settings. The case histories collected from the victim in the ED are still sometimes inadequate or incomplete in determining how the case should be reconstructed. There should be a standardized medical approach to such patients as much as possible, and the adoption of an appropriate protocol to collect details and samples that could be useful for forensic purposes.

It is also of paramount importance to provide specific training for healthcare professionals in this setting.

The final take-home message that the authors wish to highlight regarding all the aspects descibe above that have to be taken into consideration is that it is important to keep in mind that today's unsolved sexual assault investigations may well become the cold-case investigations of the future; as such, potential forensic evidence must be correctly collected, stored and examined with a competent approach in mind.

REFERENCES

[1] Violence: a public health priority. *WHO Global Consultation on Violence and Health.* 1996.

[2] World report on violence and health. Geneva, *World Health Organization*, 2002:149–181.

[3] *Guidelines and protocols Medico-legal care for survivors/victims of sexual violence.* Ministry of health & family Welfare Government of India. (2014). https://mohfw.gov.in/sites/default/files/953522324.pdf.

[4] South Africa: violence against women and the medico-legal system. New York, NY, *Human Rights Watch,* 1997. https://www.hrw.org/report/1997/08/01/south-africa-violence-against-women-and-medico-legal-system.

[5] Acosta M.L. (2002). Collecting evidence for domestic and sexual assault: highlighting violence against women in health care system intervention. *International Journal of Gynaecology and Obstetrics*, 78 (Suppl. 1): S99–S104.

[6] Cohen S., de Vos E., Newberger E. (1997). Barriers to physician identification and treatment of family violence: lessons from five communities. *Academic Medicine*, 72(Suppl. 1): S19–S25.

[7] Chaudhry S., Sangani B., Ojwang S. B., Khan K. S. (1995). Retrospective study of alleged sexual assault at the Aga Khan Hospital, Nairobi. *East African Medical Journal*, 72:200–202.

[8] Guidelines for medico-legal care for victims of sexual violence. Geneva, *World Health Organization*, 2003.

[9] Parnis D., Du Mont J. (2002). An exploratory study of postsexual assault professional practices: examining the standardised application of rape kits. *Health Care for Women International*, 23: 846-853.

[10] Harrison J. M., Murphy S. M. (1999). A care package for managing female sexual assault in genitourinary medicine. *International Journal of Sexually Transmitted. Diseases and AIDS*, 10:283–289.

[11] DeVore H. K., Sachs C. J. (2011). Sexual assault. *Emergency Medicine Clinics of North America*, 29(3):605-20.

[12] Ludes B., Geraut A., Väli M., Cusack D., Ferrara D., Keller E., Mangin P., Vieira D. N. (2018). Guidelines examination of victims of sexual assault harmonization of forensic and medico-legal examination of persons. *International Journal of Legal Medicine*, 132:1671–1674.

[13] Tozzo P., Picozzi M., Caenazzo L. (2018). Munchausen Syndrome by Proxy: Balancing ethical and clinical challenges for healthcare professionals ethical consideration in factitious disorders. *La Clinica Terapeutica*, 169(3):e129-e134.

[14] Tozzo P., Ponzano E., Spigarolo G., Nespeca P., Caenazzo L. (2018). Collecting sexual assault history and forensic evidence from adult women in the emergency department: a retrospective study. *BMC Health Services Research*, 29;18(1):383.

[15] Newton M. (2013). The forensic aspects of sexual violence. *Best Practice & Research: Clinical Obstetrics & Gynaecology*, 27(1):77-90.

[16] Ratner P. A. (1993). The incidence of wife abuse and mental health status in abused wives in Edmonton, Alberta. *Canadian Journal of Public Health*, 84:246–249.

[17] Davis J. W., Parks S. N., Kaups K. L., Bennink L. D., Bilello J. F. (2003). Victims of domestic violence on the trauma service: unrecognized and underrepoerted. *Journal of Trauma*, 54:352–355.

[18] Farchi S., Polo A., Asole S., Ruggieri M. P., Di Lallo D. (2013). Use of emergency department services by women victims of violence in Lazio region, Italy. *BMC Womens Health*, 13:31.

[19] Gino S., Canavese A., Pattarino B., Robino C., Omedei M., Albanese E., Castagna P. (2017) 58 cases of sexual violence bearing forensic interest: congruence between the victim's report and the data from laboratory analyses. *International Journal of Legal Medicine*, 131(5):1449-1453.

[20] Feder G. S., Hutson M., Ramsay J., Taket A. R. (2006). Women exposed to intimate partner violence: expectations and experiences when they encounter health care professionals: a meta-analysis of qualitative studies. *Archives of Internal Medicine*, 9;166(1):22-37.

[21] American Collage of Obstetricians and Gynecologists. *Giudelines for women's helath care: a resource manual. 4th ed.* Washington, DC: American Collage of Obstetricians and Gynecologists; 2014.

[22] Hargot L. A. (1985) The sexual assault examination. *Canadian Family Physician*, 31:775-80.

In: Victims of Violence
Editor: Mathias L. Knudsen

ISBN: 978-1-53617-140-2
© 2020 Nova Science Publishers, Inc.

Chapter 6

WORKING WITH VICTIMS/SURVIVORS OF INTIMATE PARTNER VIOLENCE: THE 'SELF' IN THE THERAPEUTIC RELATIONSHIP

Madalena Grobbelaar[1,], Yolanda Strauss[2] and Marika Guggisberg, PhD[3]*

[1]School of Arts and Humanities, Edith Cowan University,
Perth, Western Australia
[2]Domestic Violence Services: Women's Health and Family Services,
Perth, Western Australia
[3] School of Nursing Midwifery and Social Sciences,
CQUniversity, Australia and Queensland Centre for Domestic
and Family Violence Research, Perth, Western Australia

ABSTRACT

Women most commonly experience violence victimisation by someone close to them. Therapeutic work with victim/survivors of Intimate Partner Violence (IPV) may range from immediate crisis intervention to

---

[*] Corresponding Author's E-mail: m.grobbelaar@ecu.edu.au.

long-term support. This includes therapists maintaining the ability to listen to their clients' agonising, sometimes unbearable experiences. Various therapeutic perspectives, commencing with psychodynamically informed ones such as Attachment Theory, recognise that the therapists' personal history and their relationships are relevant to therapeutic work.

Within the therapeutic domain of IPV, awareness of transference and countertransference dynamics, ubiquitous to all relationships, is particularly important as therapists can become drawn into certain positions vis-à-vis the client; a rescuer, a persecutor, or a victim/survivor themselves. Transference and countertransference issues can impact therapy through practices that interfere with the therapeutic process, such as therapist avoidance, misattunement, denial, dismissal or unconscious manifestations of prior interpersonal dynamics. Additionally, vicarious trauma or secondary stress, are typical therapeutic responses experienced as adverse psychological and physical effects of therapists' exposure to clients' trauma. Considerations for individual therapists comprise the need to assume responsibility for their personal histories by attending to their own experiences of pain, trauma or loss, engage in meaning-making activities or relationships, and develop skills in mindfulness and self-care strategies. Organisations can counterbalance implications for therapists by providing appropriate supervision, adequate training and allowing increased time to debrief and discuss cases.

Keywords: IPV, therapist, transference and countertransference, vicarious trauma, victims/survivors

INTRODUCTION

This chapter briefly examines the prevalence and the nature of Intimate Partner Violence (IPV) from a feminist perspective and addresses some of the issues in working with victims/survivors of abuse. Following this examination an explanation of Attachment Theory is presented as a way of working with victims/survivors to highlight some of the unconscious issues that may arise in therapy when working with individuals who are experiencing IPV, with a particular focus on couples who both use violence. Finally, the typical responses experienced by therapists when working with this population group are discussed prior to concluding remarks

Working with Victims/Survivors of Intimate Partner Violence 101

Violence against women is a global problem and occurs most often within an intimate partner relationship (Guggisberg, 2010). The abuse and violent behaviour is overwhelmingly directed against female intimate partners, while it is acknowledged that men are also victims of IPV. IPV may include physical and/or sexual violence along with emotional, psychological, verbal, and economic abuse as well as stalking behaviours or wilfully damaging the victim's property and harming the family pet. Victimisation by IPV is a complex phenomenon that affects many victim/survivors from all walks of life.

While men most commonly experience violence at the hands of acquaintances or strangers who are primarily male, women most commonly experience violence victimisation by someone close to them (Guggisberg, 2010). National and international surveys indicate that approximately one in four women experience physical and or sexual violence by a current or former intimate partner at some stage in their life (Australian Institute of Health and Welfare, 2019; Devries et al., 2013). This victimisation is generally accompanied by controlling behaviour, which means that forms of violence are typically not mutually exclusive (Guggisberg, 2010). Many women experience non-physical forms of violence. However, if physical forms are part of the violence, controlling behaviour is almost always part of the victimisation profile. The effects of IPV include short-term and long-term consequences. Women and children are often the ones suffering the most adverse outcomes (Guggisberg, 2010; Stark, 2007).

Some researchers have argued that not all IPV is the same. Johnson (2008), for example, identified four types of IPV: coercive controlling violence, violent resistance, situational couple violence and separation instigated violence. Johnson argued that situational couple violence (SCV) is gender symmetrical IPV with no systematic power and control issues, and that, based on general population surveys, it is by far the most common form of IPV. Johnson (2008) further argued that the core distinction between coercive controlling violence (CCV) and SCV is that coercive controlling violence, being gender asymmetrical, has a clear pattern of power and control which is informed by the perpetrator's sense of male entitlement and his desire to achieve the victim's subordination and compliance. A fear of the perpetrator is a fundamental feature of this type of violence. By contrast, Johnson stipulated that SCV, being gender symmetrical, is the result of poor conflict resolution and communication skills, frustration and the desire to win an argument between two equal partners; a conflict which may be fuelled by alcohol and/or other drugs and involves the reciprocal use of aggression by both partners. Additionally, Johnson (2008; 2011) argued that other factors contributing to violence are the couple's level of education, and a history of IPV in the family of origin.

Unfortunately, Johnson's typology in relation to SCV is particularly attractive to statutory agencies (Meier, 2015) given that it is considered to be the most common type of IPV and 'extremely widespread' (O'Connell and DiFonzo, 2018, 30) in the family court process. In this regard, Meier (2015) observed that the remarkably quick adoption of Johnson's explanation of SCV has a detrimental effect on victim/survivors of IPV and their children when they are engaged in family court processes. Meier (2015, 8) stated that Johnson's typology of SCV has become "the new mantra in family law practice". Given the assumption that this type of IPV is "not terribly concerning" (Meier, 2015, 12), it is not surprising that most children exposed to IPV continue to remain in contact with the abusive parent (Jeffries et al., 2016). These ongoing issues may negatively impact on the women who are often affected by an everyday struggle to cope with the abuse.

The widespread nature of IPV in Australia and elsewhere means that there is a great demand for various kinds of victim services. While the quality and quantity of different services have improved since the women's movement in the late1960s in most Western nations (Stark, 2007), there is an underutilisation of service responses available to IPV victim/survivors. Similar to other forms of non-stranger violence, IPV is still significantly underreported and the circumstances constituting a barrier to victim/survivors' reporting their experiences vary considerably (Valor-Segura et al., 2018). A range of factors, including victim- and offender-characteristics, family make-up, victim-blaming social attitudes and other situational circumstances can influence the nature of victim/survivors' help-seeking decisions. In addition, factors such as the interplay of emotional attachment, shame, self-blame and the hope for change can also influence how victim/survivors respond to abuse by an intimate partner (Walker, 2017). Furthermore, the literature identified situational factors such as isolation and fear for the children's safety as barriers for reaching out and seeking help.

Victim/survivors' needs are complex and require a range of different services to ensure safety, protection and recovery, and may range from immediate crisis intervention to long-term support. De Lint and colleagues (2018, 23) argued that victim/survivors should be considered "power brokers". Consequently, interventions designed to address the needs of victim/survivors and children should follow a strength-based approach that supports victim/survivors' right to self-determination and informed decision-making without judgment. While the safety of women, and especially dependent children, needs to be assessed and made the number one priority, victim/survivors need to be given the opportunity to make active and informed choices throughout their help-seeking and recovery process (White and Sienkiewicz, 2018). This can be difficult for practitioners at times, especially when there are discrepancies in relation to perceptions regarding desirable outcomes, personal values or expectations. Importantly the ongoing focus should be on placing and examining the responsibility for IPV with the perpetrator and not the victim/survivor.

Unsurprisingly, therapeutic work with victim/survivors of IPV does not follow a straightforward path as therapists are required to negotiate between necessary practical tasks such as safety considerations, court processes, psychoeducation and emotional support. This includes therapists maintaining the ability to listen to their clients' agonising, sometimes unbearable experiences, which subsequently triggers and occasions an awareness of their own personal challenges and tragedies (Tummala-Narra, 2016). Various therapeutic perspectives, commencing with psychodynamically informed ones, have recognised that therapists' personal history, relationships, interests and passions are not only relevant to, but fundamentally guide the work with clients. Within the therapeutic domain of IPV, therapists' attachment styles in intimate relationships, as well as experiences of loss, trauma, and violence can have profound repercussions on the therapeutic relationship, the outcome of therapy and the therapist. Moreover, the work-related risks of providing services to a population that is increasingly traumatised due to violence exposure, is a public health issue which threatens stability in professionals' work life (Molnar et al., 2017). Consequently, this chapter aims to highlight some of the unconscious processes that may underlie the work with individuals experiencing IPV.

A PSYCHODYNAMIC PERSPECTIVE IN THERAPY

The relationship between one's past and present is a complex one; "We are formed through a variety of experiences, then and later, some remembered, some forgotten, some even misinterpreted, some of which makes us who we are now, some of which have left little apparent mark" (Jacobs 2012, 13). Implicit in a psychodynamic therapeutic approach is the notion that mental phenomena, such as thoughts and feelings, and the resultant behaviours, are the result of the interplay between opposing motivational forces; in other words, that a therapist will always listen out for the interaction between the client's conscious and unconscious thoughts and feelings (Auchincloss and Samberg 2012; Frederickson 1999). Consequently, the focus is on the client's movement between the different dynamic qualities of thoughts and feelings; therapists listen out for what the client is consciously aware of and what she/he is not aware of. All of this movement occurs in a mind, or an internal model of 'self and others' that has been shaped by one's past relationship experiences, affecting one's interactions with others, as well as the underlying assumptions that shape those interactions (Holmes and Slade 2018). Attachments are the inextricable connections one forms with those that care and protect us from the start of life.

Attachment Theory: An Example of Psychodynamic Theory

The work of John Bowlby and Mary Ainsworth contributed to the development of a theory of emotional bonding and emotion regulation (the ability to appraise and manage feelings) by combining significant insights from psychoanalysis, developmental and cognitive psychology and ethology; a theory which has been studied and tested in hundreds of ways in the last couple of decades (Shaver and Mikulincer 2005). From an attachment perspective, the basis of social life is underpinned by an affective exchange between individuals so that emotions are relational experiences (Holmes and Slade 2018). Infants are born into a world with countless threats and in seeking safety are motivated by internal, emotional states to seek proximity to a caregiver; thus, the infant-mother bond is conceptualised as crucial to the safety and protection of the infant. Bowlby remained true to his initial psychoanalytical thinking by considering threat as both internally derived, yet primarily arising from the external world (Holmes and Slade 2018; Shaver and Mikulincer 2005). Building on this conceptualisation, Schore (2003, 37) defined attachment theory "...as fundamentally a regulatory theory", as in the first year of life infants seek to create a secure bond or attachment with the primary caregiver. For a multitude of reasons, such as parental physical and mental illness, death, interpersonal violence, prolonged parental separations, or chaotic homes with drug and alcohol misuse, poverty, discrimination, trauma, etc. secure bonds are not always formed; instead insecure bonds may be the dominant form of attachment to a caregiver. There are also numerous individual differences in attachment system functioning that are mediated by the supportiveness, availability and responsiveness of the caregiver when infants are in need. Consequently, a three-category typology of attachment styles originating in infancy was developed, namely secure, anxious and, avoidant (both the latter are insecure); where attachment styles are "the systematic pattern of relational expectations, emotions, and behaviours that results from a particular history of attachment experiences" (Shaver and Mikulincer 2005, 27).

By virtue of the supportiveness, availability and responsiveness of the caregiver, individuals develop a set of maps that tell them about the world around them, as well as how they are in relation to the world; what Bowlby termed an 'internal working model' of self and others (Holmes 2010). The fundamental features of the internal working model concern the anticipated availability of the attachment figure as well as a complementary working model of the self, for example how acceptable or unacceptable the child feels in the eye of the attachment figure (Fonagy 2001, 12-13). Internal working models are considered representations of 'self and other' and this representational system underpins the attachment relationship. Within the secure-insecure typology of attachment styles, a secure attachment suggests an internal representation of the attachment figure as responsive when needed, whilst an insecure one suggests the child needs to adopt approaches to circumvent the unresponsiveness of the attachment figure. As Fonagy exemplified: "A child whose internal working model of the caregiver is focused on rejection is expected to evolve a complementary working model of the self as unlovable, unworthy and flawed" (2001, 12-13).

An additional and vital human capacity that underpins everyday interactions, developed within early attachment relationships, is mentalising: "the ability to understand actions by both other people and oneself in terms of thoughts, feelings, wishes, and desires" (Bateman and Fonagy 2016, 4). Mentalising is a non-conscious and reflexive recognition of others' intentions and is instrumental to our ability to understand others' behaviours, but similar to language acquisition it is modulated by our social environment (Asen and Fonagy 2017). A central concept is that internal states (i.e., thoughts, beliefs, wishes and feelings) are opaque so that individuals make inferences about them (Bateman and Fonagy 2016). A mentalising capacity may be temporarily lost in stress environments or emotionally charged interactions in family settings which may trigger a fight or flight mode (Asen and Fonagy 2017). In turn, an aroused state may inhibit mentalising (reflective assumptions about the self and others) and an automatic process of non-reflective mentalising is activated. Fonagy and Target (cited in Bateman and Fonagy 2016) suggested that mentalising is both an intergenerational and a transactional process, where social interactions, particularly with primary caregivers in early environments, have a direct bearing on the quality of one's capacity to mentalise. The more

Working with Victims/Survivors of Intimate Partner Violence 107

a parent can mirror a child's affect correctly, the more a child's capacity to emotionally regulate (including attention mechanisms and effortful control), and to mentalise is developed. Whilst psychodynamic observations regarding the mind have historically been speculative, neuroscience has currently been able to present a more realistic picture of how implicit mental processes, emotions, and emotion regulation work (Bateman and Fonagy 2016; Shaver and Mikulincer 2005).

Furthermore, in adult intimate relationships, corresponding attachment styles were conceptualised by Hazan and Shaver (1987, 523) as they noted that "…romantic love is a biological process designed by evolution to facilitate attachment between adult sexual partners who, at the time love evolved, were likely to become parents of an infant who would need reliable care". The previously discussed adult categories, and later a fourth (disorganised attachment), were derived from research exploring childhood memories of parental relationships and their effect on adult personality as identified by respondents (Feeney 2016). Thereafter, a four-style romantic adult attachment category was conceptualised, namely; secure, preoccupied, dismissing-avoidant, and fearful avoidant. Much research was devoted to establishing a link between the adult attachment categories and corresponding infant attachment styles, particularly through the use of measurement tools such as the Adult Attachment Interview (AAI) and the Strange Situation experimental method as devised by Ainsworth (Hesse 2016).

Contemporary insights into attachment models have recognised that what appears to be useful to understanding individual differences in how individuals attach are two major dimensions identified along the four-styles of attachment; that of 'avoidance' and of 'attachment anxiety' (Feeney 2016). The first dimension reflects the extent to which people distrust others' goodwill and strive to maintain emotional distance and remain independent from a relationship partner, while the second dimension reflects the degree to which people worry that a partner might not be available or act sufficiently supportive in times of need (Bartholomew 1990). In considering attachment insecurity and how it may contribute to relationship dissatisfaction and possibly violence, it is worth noting that research has identified that attachment security is directly correlated with marital satisfaction (Mikulincer, et al., 2004). Brassard and Johnson (2016, 813) stated that attachment theory identified that the "key issue in distressed relationships is the negative cycles that maintain disconnection and limited responsiveness to emotional signals and attachment cues". Thus, any therapeutic psychodynamic approach acknowledges the key role of emotion in human functioning and will consider how one's past traumatic experiences, particularly from attachment figures who were expected to be trustworthy and safe, affect the way current experiences are encoded and integrated, as well as whether this process leads to growth or dysfunction (Johnson 2019).

Working Therapeutically from an Attachment Model

Therapists recognise that individuals, including them, are often troubled by contradictory aspects of themselves which give rise to anxiety, and may be rejected consciously, even though feelings may remain at an unconscious level (Bateman, Brown, and Pedder 2010). Hence, one resorts to defence mechanisms to assist in denying or disowning parts of the self that are unacceptable. For example, from infancy onwards, any threat to the caregiver bond (attachment) is dangerous. Consequently children, and later as adults, develop strategies that minimise disruptions to the attachment bond, often suppressing their own thoughts, feelings, desires and wishes to maintain the attachment relationship (Holmes and Slade 2018). Children whose early overtures for comfort were rejected by a mother trying to cope with an intimate violent relationship, may learn to conceal their distress and hide it from others, potentially developing an internal model of the self as unworthy and of others as unreliable (Wallin 2007). Given that there is an interdisciplinary consensus that romantic and adult attachment bonds are shaped by the same mechanisms that regulate mother-infant bonds responsible for 'growing' a mind (Goldner 2014), understanding an individual's family of origin relationship dynamics is necessary to working with individuals who experience IPV; as Asen and Fonagy (2017, 6) asserted, "...the family can be thought of as more of a danger zone or

Working with Victims/Survivors of Intimate Partner Violence 109

"minefield" than a safe haven". As such, the goal of a psychodynamically informed therapy is to enhance awareness of the 'self', through exploring emotions, examining avoidances, identifying recurring patterns, discussing past experiences, focusing on relationships and examining the relationship between client and therapist (Shedler 2010). It is within the client-therapist relationship that transference and countertransference is manifested.

Transference and Countertransference in Therapy

Enactments in therapy refer to both the clients' and therapists' behavioural manifestations of "implicit relational knowings" whose origins date back to earlier attachment relationships, whereby unconscious thoughts and feelings are acted upon following the earliest attachment relationships (Wallin 2007, 122). Thus, the idea that one repeats rather than remembers past relationship dynamics is at the heart of transference. Transference denotes the displacement of thoughts, feelings and behaviours, which one experienced with early attachment figures, onto an individual in a current interpersonal relationship (Auchincloss and Samberg 2012). This process of displacement is largely unconscious; however, it is ubiquitous, occurring in a wide range of circumstances, and in a sense, we respond to any new relationship according to patterns from the past (Bateman et al., 2010). While transference has a general meaning in relationships, in a psychotherapeutic relationship it is used to explore the forgotten and suppressed past of attachment patterns. Clients may begin to experience feelings, attitudes and fantasies related to the therapist that do not befit that person, but rather are repetitions of unconscious reactions to earlier attachments. Likewise, rather than the notion that therapists are neutral, there is a mutual reciprocal influence on therapists, known as countertransference. This means that: either, unresolved past experiences may contaminate the therapy when they are enacted by the therapist; or the therapist's feelings are elicited, often unconsciously, and they become tuned into a client's conscious or unconscious communication, with a capacity to hold and tolerate the feelings a client cannot (Bateman et al. 2010). Wallin (2007) suggested that as early attachment relationships are constructed so too are psychotherapeutic ones (2007). However, the clinical challenge according to Goldner (2014, 409) is to "co-construct a way out while allowing oneself to be pulled in". Jacobs (2012, 18) referred to the connection between the past and present, between relationships within and outside of therapy, and relationships between the external and internal world, as the "triangle of insight", seen in Figure 1.

Accordingly, in working with victims/survivors of IPV, the assumption remains that the client will bring into therapy countless ways of relating to self, others and the world, and that therapists may be pulled into this dynamic. The therapeutic task is to tune in empathically, yet detach sufficiently to be able to reflect on the developing transference relationship; however, as violence can be so destructive, terrifying and shameful, there is a universal temptation to dissociate oneself from it, even as therapists (Goldner 1999). Importantly, therapists need to be able to tolerate uncertainty as well as manage and contain both their own and their clients' emotions, including anxiety, anger, and fear (Sanderson 2008). Moreover, even if therapists have not been exposed to abuse, they need to be aware of their own experience and understanding of power and control in relationships, including the therapeutic one, the role of shame in interpersonal violence, and their own way of relating to others, i.e., their attachment style and how this may intrude upon the therapeutic space (Sanderson 2009).

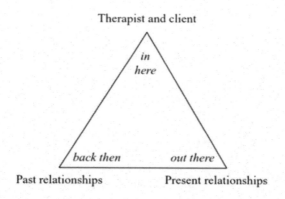

Figure 1. Triangle of insight.

VIOLENCE IN RELATIONSHIP: THERAPEUTIC CONSIDERATIONS

In this section, IPV is examined with the case of Alice and Jake to highlight some issues when considering the process of transference and countertransference. Some important caveats to bear in mind: focus of attention is placed on processes that are largely unconscious and particularly related to one's attachment style, thus the discussion is narrowly restricted to these aspects of therapy and does not cover other crucial influences on the development of the self and relationship dynamics, for example, the influences of gender and social norms, trauma and intergenerational abuse, personality disorders, psychopathology, mental health problems, social inequality, culture, political institutions, religion, and media. Accordingly, using a case study based on CCV, where motivations for violence, control tactics, fear of partner, and consequences of violence are important distinctions, would warrant a consideration of all these factors in therapy, both at a conscious and unconscious level, which is beyond the scope of the current chapter. Moreover, psychological modes of thinking, for example systemic or psychodynamic models, have been regarded as having the potential to blame the victim as they do not focus on the power inequality between the couple; meaning, psychological interdependence and individual responsibility become indistinguishable (Goldner 1998). As Goldner (1998, 2) asserted: "To argue that partners mutually participate in an interactional process does not mean they are mutually responsible for it, or for its catastrophic outcome", a point we wish to emphasise when there is unidirectional violence. Finally, conjoint therapy for individuals experiencing IPV remains controversial unless therapists are able to distinguish between types of IPV; accordingly, our discussion does not seek out to satisfy the controversy around assessment and differentiation of IPV for therapy (Karakurt et al., 2013; Karakurt et al., 2016; Slootmaeckers and Migerode 2019). The case study (a composite of clients using pseudonyms) describes a situation of bidirectional violence, yet it remains focused on the experience of Alice to note some therapeutic considerations.

An Attachment Perspective: Alice and Jake

Alice and Jake have been together for 10 years. Alice is a professional in an allied health field and describes a successful career, despite her misgivings about her competency at times. She recounts that when she first met Jake, he was one of the first men who she felt she could depend on and found him willing to "just be with me". She found Jake was able to "smooth things" for her, especially when she was feeling anxious with work or when she felt hurt by her mother's unpredictable interactions, often when her mother had been drinking. Alice's father left her mother when she was 3-years-old. She recounts that she and Jake "were mad for one another" and "I adored him", relating a satisfying sexual relationship. However, as time went by, Alice felt that Jake's willingness to be with her – to be intimate, loving, and patient - had diminished; her overtures for affection and intimacy, initially being subtle, became more demanding. The more demanding Alice became, the more she felt Jake ignored, dismissed and avoided her, until she would "freak out" and sometimes try to push him in sheer desperation for his attention and affection. Jake's response would be to push back, and he would "become mean", criticising her, laughing at her, infantilising her reactions as "pathetic" and withdrawing into his world, leaving Alice with a deep sense of shame. Through the years, the pushing and shoving had become more common, with Jake using more force, leading to Alice being hurt occasionally. Alice feels helpless to change her behaviour and their situation and decides to seek therapy as despite the conflict, they both want to remain together. Although she does not fear Jake, she does fear that their inability to resolve their issues will lead to further hurt and damage.

As therapists working with Alice, we commenced by hypothesising that the couple's attachment styles are based on a preoccupied attachment style (Alice) and a dismissing attachment style (Jake), two polar opposites on the dimensions of attachment anxiety and avoidance. This couple attachment pattern, which can be gender specific (i.e., high anxiety-attachment female and high avoidance-attachment male), appears to be supported by research (Belanger et al., 2015; Doumas et al., 2008), although these attachment styles are varied and can be non-gender specific. While the focus here is on

Working with Victims/Survivors of Intimate Partner Violence 113

the attachment pattern developed in childhood, others remind us that "relationship-specific attachment" needs to be taken into account too, specifically when considering a case of SCV such as that of Alice and Jake, i.e., when there is bidirectional violence (Slootmaeckers and Migerode 2019, 298).

Many clients in intimate relationships where violence may be a factor unsurprisingly experience fear, anxiety and anger given their interpersonal situation, however Alice's high level of distress, a characteristic that Alice consistently presents with in therapy, needs to be given a deeper and more unconscious consideration. Understood from an attachment perspective, Alice learnt early on that in order to secure attention from a caregiver, she needs to make her distress too obvious to ignore; what Wallin (2007, 225) referred to as "conspicuous insecurity" i.e., the most reliable method of obtaining attention from unreliable others. Research has found associations in victims/survivors of IPV of both elevated levels of attachment anxiety and avoidance, although this is an association and in no way a cause (Mikulincer and Shaver 2014). Alice is experienced by others, for example by Jake as well as the therapist, as 'merger hungry' due to her attempts at wanting to remain close to them (Goldbart and Wallin, cited in Wallin 2007, 225). Alice's biggest fears relate to abandonment, separation and loss and most of her energy is spent on amplifying a defensive strategy of hyperactivating which has prevented her from acquiring an ability to develop self-esteem, trust in self and others, and her own capacity to emotionally regulate. Alice's distress and demands to be responded to can be understood as an exaggerated protest against an unresponsive and unreliable Jake, and insecurity about the future of her relationship (Mikulincer and Shaver 2014).

Alice's style of attachment has given rise to a pattern of helplessness, a willingness to please, a fear of asserting herself and a reliance on the 'other', often experienced as an "other-directed" quality (Wallin 2007, 229). It is likely that at the beginning of the relationship, this pattern led to Alice idealising Jake, a pattern that is also likely to occur in therapy. Some research has indicated that avoidant individuals like Jake, have difficulty with conflict resolution due to hostility, and also have overt and grandiose narcissistic tendencies (Firestone 2017; Mikulincer and Shaver 2012). Jake was drawn in by Alice's idealisation, dependence and doting in the beginning however because he is avoidantly attached, his tendency is to deny attachment needs, avoid closeness and dependence by using deactivating strategies. "These strategies develop in relationships with attachment figures who disapprove of and punish closeness and expressions of need or vulnerability" (Mikulincer and Shaver 2012, 11). Consequently, Jake tends to use evasive communication and withdrawal strategies (Bonache, Gonzalez-Mendez, and Krahé 2019), whether directly or indirectly (for example, passive aggressive behaviour such as sarcasm, criticism, stalling, resisting, lying, contempt or sullen resentment), which can become violent when Jake and Alice get into a push-pull dynamic (demand-withdrawal); that is, the differing needs for closeness and distance between them (Doumas et al., 2008; Mikulincer and Shaver 2014). Although there are differing negative patterns of interactions, for example, pursuer/pursuer and withdrawer/withdrawer, the most common appears to be the push/pull of the pursuer/withdrawer pattern that we are describing (Slootmaeckers and Migerode 2019).

Alice, fearing rejection and hence being constantly concerned with Jake's distant responses to her attempts at proximity and closeness, may attempt to receive reassurance in a number of ways, for example: she may vacillate between escalating her distress (hyperactivating unconscious strategies pulling for intimacy) and being more ready to engage in conflict and becoming controlling (or aggressive, either directly or indirectly), whilst being helplessly unable to reject Jake's coercive or aggressive behaviour (often giving rise to using violence herself in response); in turn, Jake may become controlling, coercive or aggressive as he tries to avoid her intrusive and persistent demands (unconsciously pushing away from intimacy); she may give in to coerced unwanted sexual interactions for complex reasons, including because of her need for intimacy; or, she may interpret Jake's responses more negatively due to high attachment anxiety (Bonache et al., 2019; Mikulincer and Shaver 2014). In the current example, Alice's anger is understood as a consequence of an attachment loss, giving rise to the fear of abandonment, and activating her attachment system in a paradoxical attempt at seeking intimacy and closeness (Slootmaeckers and Migerode

Working with Victims/Survivors of Intimate Partner Violence 115

2019). Hence, the partner becomes both the cause and solution to one's attachment need – Alice's need may ignite Jake's unresolved/unsatisfactory attachment trauma and vice versa – a cycle of hurt and hurting continues (Goldner 2014).

Distinctions in Therapy When Working with IPV

An attachment focused view may also be helpful when considering the attachment patterns of individuals and/or couples who are experiencing coercive controlling violence (CCV); however, it is essential that this type of violence is differentiated and partners are seen for individual and not couple therapy given the risk to escalating violence and unethical consequences with CCV (Karakurt et al., 2013; Karakurt et al., 2016; Slootmaeckers and Migerode 2019). As a unidimensional phenomenon, CCV perpetrators appear to have insecure attachment styles too, and may demonstrate a similar preoccupation with the relationship, a constant and persistent desire for closeness, which can border on obsession, and exaggerated fears of abandonment and loss (Almeida et al., 2019; Dutton and White 2012). A violent perpetrator with an anxious attachment style facing a similar fear of abandonment and loss to Alice could in protest quickly escalate to rage and violence; or if they had an anxious avoidant attachment style like Jake, could use violence to distance themselves from the partner.

Seen from an attachment view, using inappropriate behaviour such as violence may be regarded as the individual's failure to mentalise. Individuals with emotionally poor or abusive and violent environments, who have not been 'mentalised' by others, in an attempt at communicating overwhelming and unmanageable affective states, appear to not perceive a victim/survivor as a feeling and thinking being; indeed, having had a balanced experience of mentalising by significant others, may make it very hard for an individual to hurt and abuse an 'other' (Asen and Fonagy 2017; Fonagy 1999; Goldner 1998; 1999; 2014; Slootmaeckers and Migerode 2019).

Transference and Countertransference

In therapy, Alice's need to be rescued manifested by her helplessness and her eagerness to engage (transference), the therapist's need to rescue or to be idealised as the good and helpful therapist, and the therapist's sense of vulnerability (countertransference) may strike at the core of therapist self-concepts (Sanderson 2009; Wallin 2007). If Alice's therapist remains focused only at the surface level reality, colluding with her defensive hyperactivating by being over-protective, without considering what may lie beneath Alice's defensive style, she may deny Alice "...the opportunity to grapple with the fear and distrust that make her compliance and pleasing feel so necessary" (Wallin 2007, 227). In considering countertransference, a therapist may feel a sense of powerlessness as well as helplessness and so may become invested in a particular outcome for Alice. For example, by constantly reassuring her, the therapist may unconsciously enact power over Alice, ratifying her sense of helplessness, which may be due to the therapist's own history of problematic romantic engagements, IPV victimisation, and/or trauma history, or the activation of a similar attachment style to Alice's. Goldner (2014, 403) suggested that clients or couples can often remind therapists of their own "shameful history of romantic loss and failure", whether conscious or not, and attempts to ward off aspects of selves that identify with this experience all too well. Alternatively, therapists that are preoccupied themselves may respond to Alice's dependency needs by becoming completely dependable, often going beyond the usual remit of their therapeutic practice and assuming full responsibility for Alice's situation, (for example, out of hours contact) and thwarting possibilities for promoting her autonomy and sense of competency (Slade 2016; Watson, Carthy and Becker 2017). Assuming responsibility for Alice's situation can contribute to a sense of one's therapeutic efficacy and self-belief, which is often the very quality a therapist with a preoccupied attachment style may not have developed. If therapists are not aware of what evokes in them a need for control to assuage their own feelings of helplessness, they are at risk of failing to relinquish control and restore this sense in a victim/survivor (Sanderson 2009).

Working with Victims/Survivors of Intimate Partner Violence 117

On the other hand, therapists who have insecure attachment styles, perhaps because of their own experiences of loss and trauma, and past punitive and dismissing caregivers, may feel a lack of empathy for Alice, consequently becoming withdrawn and controlling (for example, being prescriptive), and becoming focused on Alice's defensive interactions rather than on her desire to connect. Alice's dependency needs may evoke a fear-based intolerance to being regarded as too important, leading to rejection, dismissal or anger, a reaction to the feelings of dependent longing that the therapist is unable to tolerate given her own childhood losses (Slade 2016; Wallin 2007). Moreover, Alice's dependency may be experienced as intrusive when the therapists' ability to self-regulate is through distancing (Slootmaeckers and Migerode 2019). Similar to Alice's relationship experience with Jake, the therapist's defences and anxieties may easily be triggered to the point of inability to effectively self-regulate, leaving Alice with the same deep sense of shame at her inability to resolve her romantic crisis (Goldner 2014).

Typical Responses When Working with Violence in Relationships

> *"Milton Erickson used to say to his patients, "My voice will go with you." His voice did. What he did not say was that our clients' voices can also go with us. Their stories become part of us – part of our daily lives and our nightly dreams. Not all stories are negative - indeed, a good many are inspiring. The point is that they change us."* (Mahoney, cited in Macnamara, 2019, 4)

As illustrated in Alice's case study, violence in relationships can evoke fear and anxiety, leaving therapists to question their therapeutic ability and competence in the face of what seems a complex and hopeless situation; whether conscious or unconscious, they may doubt their own experience or knowledge base, and feel overwhelmed because they cannot 'fix' the situation (Karakurt et al., 2013; Watson et al., 2017). Therapists' own violent family of origin experiences can trigger fear and a sense of hopelessness resulting in the avoidance of exploring a client's full experience of feelings, wishes, desires, and expectations; in particular, the therapist's own unresolved and 'unthought of' traumatic attachment material can pose a barrier to confront Alice's past (Briere and Scott 2006; Brosi and Carolan 2006). In their study, Watson et al. (2017, 227) define helplessness as:

> *"...an absence of hope amongst participants in their confidence to work appropriately with women disclosing IPV. This is supported by the therapists' belief that the intervention offered would not have a positive impact on the patient. Therapists defined a positive impact as the patient leaving the abusive relationship. One participant spoke of her wish to "fix" a patient despite stating that she had no idea how to help."*

In the face of such raw and overwhelming emotions, therapists may also attempt to avoid, dissociate, minimise, or resort to the cognitive realm and impose rigid therapeutic models. Alternatively, they may vacillate between the desire to care-give and the desire to abdicate caregiving, as often happens in other relationships (Brosi and Carolan 2006; Goldner 2014).

For therapists working with CCV in particular, where the violence is unidirectional and visited by one person on another, the sense of hopelessness can become 'contagious' and therapists may experience fear of harm to themselves, become hypervigilant, not only at work but also in their personal lives, which may negatively impact their worldview (Beckerman, 2018) and result in them experiencing a number of effects, such as vicarious traumatisation (VT), secondary traumatic stress (STS) or compassion fatigue (CF). All three of these terms refer to the negative impact of clinical work with traumatised clients and even though there are some distinctions in terms of theoretical origin and symptom foci (Bride 2007) the terms recognise that counsellors who are exposed to their clients' trauma material can also be traumatised. In fact, in 2013 traumatisation resulting from secondary or vicarious exposure was formally recognised by the American Psychiatric Association (Brend, Krane, and Saunders, 2019). Morran (2008, 139) asserted that "the term 'vicarious' or 'secondary trauma' has been coined to describe a range of symptoms which impact negatively on professionals' emotions and core beliefs about themselves, their relationships with others and the nature of the world in general". Moreover, Morran (2008, 139) added that this includes "disruptions to feelings of intimacy and trust, self-esteem, safety, autonomy and personal agency, as well as debilitating intrusions such as flashbacks or lingering preoccupations with the painful experiences of others". In their article, Dunkley and Whelan (2006) pointed out that working with traumatised clients can lead some counsellors to experience anger, sadness and anxiety and even nightmares related to their clients' traumatic material.

Therapist Self-Care

Therapists working in the area of IPV can protect themselves from the negative impacts of working with traumatic material by ensuring they balance care for other with care for self. Therapist self-care strategies that are restorative, such as good diet and exercise, meditation and mindfulness, reading, monitoring their caseload and identifying clients' resilience and strengths appear to be most helpful in managing the stress resulting from working with clients experiencing IPV (Brend et al., 2019). Organisations on the other hand, are starting to recognise the inevitability of vicarious/secondary trauma and addressing the risk of vicarious traumatisation in their staff by providing appropriate supervision, adequate training and allowing increased time to debrief and discuss cases (Beckerman, 2018).

Moreover, Briere and Scott (2006, 84) propose that an additional intervention is personal therapy:

> It is an ironic fact that, at least in some environments, clinicians endorse the power of psychological treatment for others yet eschew it for themselves as somehow shameful or unlikely to help. This double standard is unfortunate, since having experienced psychotherapy is usually a good thing for therapists. Therapy is not only likely to reduce the clinician's trauma-related difficulties; it can also increase the richness of his or her

appreciation for human complexity, and can dramatically decrease the intrusion of his or her issues into the therapeutic process.

Although many therapists who have experienced attachment difficulties, loss, trauma and emotional pain may be more familiar and even comfortable with working with this population, unintegrated affect in therapists can negatively impact the work (Slade, 2016). Professional development should include not only supervision, with a focus on transference, countertransference and clinical process, but also separate personal therapy. Despite the risk to therapists of working with this population, a number of studies have also shown that this work could be enriching, with therapists describing a sense of privilege in sharing their clients' struggles or a sense of enjoyment in seeing their growth and change (Hogan et al., 2012; Iliffe & Steed, 2000).

CONCLUSION

This chapter discussed some of the issues that arise in therapeutic work with victims/survivors of IPV. Victimisation by IPV is a complex phenomenon that affects many individuals from every demographic background. While it is acknowledged that men are also victims of IPV, the abuse and violent behaviour is overwhelmingly directed against female intimate partners, and may include physical and/or sexual violence along with emotional, psychological, verbal, and economic abuse. An examination of typologies used to differentiate IPV was presented along with a qualification regarding the potential consequences of relying indiscriminately on these, namely, that certain types of IPV are minimised given that they occur all too commonly and are subsequently regarded as not that concerning. Following this discussion, Attachment Theory was presented as an explanation of how affective exchange between individuals forms the basis of social life, with an emphasis on emotions as relational experiences and therefore fundamental to one's capacity to mentalise, both self and others, in the quest to understand human behaviour. Additionally, working with victims/survivors of IPV and focusing on the conscious and unconscious dynamics in therapy, such as the attachment styles of both therapists and clients, was discussed through the use of a hypothetical case study. Though we acknowledge that IPV is a gendered phenomenon as females are the majority of victims/survivors of IPV, particularly through coercive and controlling tactics by intimate partners, the case study presented an example of a couple where both used violence, given the focus was primarily on highlighting attachment dynamics, rather than all the myriad factors to consider when couples present to therapy with IPV. Finally, the typical responses experienced by therapists when working with this population group were discussed.

The consequences for many victim/survivors of IPV are both extensive and severe, and therapists, like many first responders to traumatised and victimised individuals, are impacted by witnessing and hearing victims/survivors' stories and can be left vulnerable. The importance of self-awareness apropos one's own family and attachment dynamics and how these shape individuals, together with concerted efforts at balancing care for other with care for self, will contribute to the positive influences of working with this population group.

REFERENCES

Almeida, Iris, Ana, Ramalho, Maria, Belmira Fernandes. & Renata, Guarda. (2019). Adult attachment as a risk factor for intimate partner violence. *Annals of Medicine*, *51*, (sup1), 187-187. doi:10.1080/07853890. 2018.1562757.

Asen, Eia. & Peter, Fonagy. (2017). Mentalising family violence Part 1: Conceptual framework. *Family Process*, *56*, 6-21.

Auchincloss, Elizabeth L, Eslee, Samberg. & American Psychoanalytic Association. (2012). *Psychoanalytic Terms & Concepts*. Revised, expanded, and updated. New Haven: American Psychoanalytic Association.

Australian Institute of Health and Welfare. (2019). Family, domestic and sexual violence in Australia: Continuing the national story 2019. Cat. no. FDV 3. Canberra: *AIHW.* Accessed 8th October, 2019. https://www.aihw.gov.au/reports/domestic-violence/family-domestic-sexual-violence-australia-2019/contents/table-of-contents.

Bartholomew, Kim. (1990). "Avoidance of Intimacy: An Attachment Perspective." *Journal of Social and Personal Relationships, 7,* 147–78. doi:10.1177/0265407590072001.

Bateman, Anthony, Dennis, Brown. & Jonathan, Pedder. (2010). *Introduction to Psychotherapy: An Outline of Psychodynamic Principles and Practice,* Fourth Edition. Florence: Routledge. Accessed August 24, 2019. https://ebookcentral.proquest.com/lib/ecu/reader.action?docID=547326&ppg=20.

Bateman, Anthony. & Peter, Fonagy. (2016). *Mentalisation-Based Treatment for Personality Disorders: A Practical Guide*: Oxford University Press, Inc. Accessed 4th October, 2019. https://ebookcentral.proquest.com/lib/ecu/reader.action?docID=4413992&ppg=18.

Belanger, Claude, Cynthia, Mathieu, Caroline, Digal. & Catherine, Courchesne. (2015). The Impact of Attachment on Intimate Partner Violence Perpetrated by Women. *The American Journal of Family Therapy, 43,* 441–453. doi: 10.1080/01926187.2015.1080130.

Beckerman, Nancy L. & Danielle, F. Wozniak. (2018). Domestic violence counsellors and secondary traumatic stress (STS): A brief qualitative report and strategies for support, *Social Work in Mental Health, 16,* 470-490. doi.org 10.1080/15332985.2018.1425795.

Bonache, Helena, Rosaura, Gonzalez-Mendez. & Barbara, Krahe. (2019). Adult Attachment Styles, Destructive Conflict Resolution, and the Experience of Intimate Partner Violence *Journal of Interpersonal Violence, 34,* 287-309 doi: org/10.1177/0886260516640776.

Brassard, Audrey. & Susan, M. Johnson. (2016). Couple and family therapy: An attachment perspective. In *Handbook of Attachment, Third Edition: Theory, Research, and Clinical Applications,* edited Jude Cassidy, and Phillip R. Shaver, 805-823. New York: Guilford Publications. Accessed

September 1, 2019. https:// ebookcentral.proquest.com/lib/ecu/ reader.action?docID=4338858&ppg=464.

Brend, Denise M, Julia, Krane. & Sara, Saunders. (2019). Exposure to Trauma in Intimate Partner Violence Human Service Work: A Scoping Review. *Traumatology*. http://dx.doi.org/10.1037/trm0000199.

Bride, Brian E. (2007). Prevalence of secondary traumatic stress among social workers. *Social Work*, *53*, 63-70. doi.org/10.1093/sw/52.1.63.

Briere, John. & Catherine, Scott. (2006). *Principles of trauma therapy: A guide to symptoms, evaluation, and treatment*. Thousand Oaks, CA: Sage Publications.

Brosi, Matthew W. & Marsha, T. Carolan. (2006). Therapist response to clients' partner abuse: Implications for training and development of marriage and family therapists. *Contemporary Family Therapy*, *28*, 111-130. doi: 10.1007/s10591-006-9698-z.

DeKeseredy, Walter S. (2011). Feminist contributions to understanding woman abuse: Myths, controversies and realities. *Aggression and Violent behaviour*, *16*, 297-302.

DeKeseredy, Walter S. (2016). Understanding woman abuse in intimate heterosexual relationships: The enduring relevance of feminist ways of knowing. *Journal of Family Violence*, *31*, 1043-1046.

De Lint, Willem, Marinella, Marmo, Andrew, Groves. & Victoria, Laughton. (2018). Knowledge exchange: Collaborative reflexivity on self-medicated victims of crime. *Current Issues in Criminal Justice*, *30*, 19 – 34.

Devries, Karen, Joelle, Joelle, Claudia, Garcia-Moreno, Max, Petzold, Jennifer, Child, Gail, Falder, Stephen, Lim, et al. (2013). The global prevalence of intimate partner violence against women. *Science*, *340*, 1527-1528.

Doumas, Diana M, Christine, L. Pearson, Jenna, E. Egin. & Lisa, L. McKinley. (2008). Adult Attachment as a Risk Factor for Intimate Partner Violence The "Mispairing" of Partners' Attachment Styles. *Journal of Interpersonal Violence*, *23*, 616-634. doi: 10.1177/ 0886260507313526.

Dunkley, Jane. & Thomas, A. Whelan. (2006). Vicarious traumatisation: Current status and future directions. *British Journal of Guidance and Counselling, 34*, 107-116.

Dutton, Donald G. & Katherine, R. White. (2012). Attachment insecurity and intimate partner violence. *Aggression and Violent Behaviour, 17*, 475-481.

Feeney, Judith A. (2016). Adult romantic attachments: Developments in the study of couple relationships. In *Handbook of Attachment, Third Edition: Theory, Research, and Clinical Applications*, edited Jude Cassidy, and Phillip R. Shaver, 435-463. New York: Guilford Publications. Accessed September 1, 2019. https://ebookcentral.proquest.com/lib/ecu/reader.action?docID=4338858&ppg=464In

Firestone, Lisa. (2017). Is Narcissism Shaped by Attachment Style? There are two types of narcissists. How are they influenced by attachment style? *Psychology Today*. Accessed September 8, 2019. https://www.psychologytoday.com/au/blog/compassion-matters/201711/is-narcissism-shaped-attachment-style.

Fonagy, Peter. (2001). *Attachment theory and psychoanalysis*. New York: Other Press.

Fonagy, Peter. (1999). Male perpetrators of violence against women: An attachment theory perspective. *Journal of Applied Psychoanalytic Studies, 1*, 7-27.

Frederickson, Jon. (2013). *Psychodynamic Psychotherapy: Learning to Listen from Multiple Perspectives*. Hoboken: Taylor and Francis.

Goldner, Virginia. (1998). The treatment of violence and victimisation in intimate relationships. *Family Processes, 37*, 263-286.

Goldner, Virginia. (1999). Morality and multiplicity: Perspectives on the treatment of violence in intimate life. *Journal of Marital and Family Therapy, 25*, 325-336.

Goldner, Virginia. (2014). Romantic bonds, binds and ruptures: Couples on the brink. *Psychoanalytic Dialogues, 24*, 402-418.

Guggisberg, Marika. (2010). *Women, violence and comorbidity: The struggle with victimisation, mental health problems and substance use.* Saarbrücken, DE: Lambert Academic Publishing.

Hazan, Cindy. & Phillip, R. Shaver. (1987). Romantic love conceptualised as an attachment process. *Journal of Personality and Social Psychology, 52,* 511-524.

Hesse, Erik. (2016). The Adult Attachment Interview: Protocol, method of Analysis, and selected empirical studies: 1985-2015. In *Handbook of Attachment, Third Edition: Theory, Research, and Clinical Applications,* edited Jude Cassidy, and Phillip R. Shaver, 553-597. New York: Guilford Publications. Accessed September 1, 2019. https://ebookcentral.proquest.com/lib/ecu/reader.action?docID=433885 8&ppg=464.

Hogan, Kevin, John, R. Hegarty, Tony, Ward. & Lorna, Dodd. (2012). Counsellors' experiences of working with male victims of female perpetrated domestic abuse. *Counselling & Psychotherapy Research, 12,* 44-52. doi.org/10.1080/14733145.2011.630479.

Holmes, Jeremy. (1993). *John Bowlby and attachment theory.* London: Routledge.

Holmes, Jeremy. & Arietta, Slade. (2018). *Attachment in Therapeutic Practice.* Los Angeles: SAGE.

Iliffe, Gillian. & Lyndall, G. Steed. (2000). Exploring the counsellor's experience of working with perpetrators and survivors of domestic violence. *Journal of Interpersonal Violence, 15,* 393-412. doi.org/ 10.1177/088626000015004004.

Jacobs, Michael. (2012). *Presenting Past: The Core Of Psychodynamic Counselling And Therapy.* Maidenhead: McGraw-Hill Education.

Jeffries, Samantha, Rachael, Field, Helena, Menih. & Zoe, Rathus. (2016). Good evidence, safe outcomes in parenting matters involving domestic violence? Understanding family report writing practice from the perspective of professionals working in the family law system. *UNSW Law Journal, 39,* 1355-1388.

Johnson, Michael. (2008). *A typology of domestic violence: Intimate terrorism, violent resistance, and situational couple violence*. Boston, MA: University Press of New England.

Johnson, Michael. (2011). Gender and types of intimate partner violence: A response to an anti-feminist literature review. *Aggression and Violent Behaviour, 16*, 289-296.

Johnson, Susan M. (2019). *Attachment Theory in Practice: Emotionally Focused Therapy (EFT) with Individuals, Couples, and Families*. New York: Guilford Publications. Accessed September 1, 2019. https:// ebookcentral.proquest.com/lib/ecu/reader.action?docID=5604908&ppg =86.

Karakurt, Gunnur, Shannonn, Dial, Hannah, Korkow, Mansfield, Ty. & Alyssa, Banford. (2013). Experiences of Marriage and Family Therapists Working with Intimate Partner Violence. *Journal of Family Psychotherapy, 24*, 1-16. doi: 10.1080/08975353.2013.762864.

Karakurt, Gunnur, Kathleen, Whiting, Chantal, van Esch, Shari, D. Bolen. & Joseph, R. Calabrese. (2016). Couples therapy for intimate partner violence: A systemic review and meta-analysis. *Journal of Marital Family Therapy, 42*, 567-583. Doi: 10.1111/jmft.12178.

Macnamara, Noel. (2019). Practice Guide: Secondary traumatic stress and staff wellbeing: Understanding compassion fatigue and vicarious trauma in therapeutic care. *Centre for Excellence in Therapeutic Care*: Sydney NSW.

Meier, Joan. (2015). Johnson's differentiation theory: Is it really empirically supported? *Journal of Child Custody, 12*, 4-24. Accessed 10th October 2019. https://scholarship.law.gwu.edu/cgi/viewcontent.cgi?referer= https://www.google.com.au/&httpsredir=1&article=2420&context=fac ulty_publications.

Mikulincer, Mario, Victor, Florian, Phillip, A. Cowan. & Carolyn, Pape Cowan. (2004). Attachment security in couple relationships: A systematic model and its implications for family dynamics. *Family Process, 41*, 405-434.

Mikulincer, Mario. & Phillip, R. Shaver. (2014). *Attachment in Adulthood: Structure, dynamics and change*. Guilford Publications. (eBook).

Working with Victims/Survivors of Intimate Partner Violence 127

Accessed September 27, 2019. https://ebookcentral.proquest.com/lib/ecu/reader.action?docID=320570.

Mikulincer, Mario. & Phillip, R. Shaver. (2012). An attachment perspective on psychopathology. *World Psychiatry*, *11*, 11-15. Accessed September 30, 2019. https://www.ncbi.nlm.nih.gov/pmc/ articles/PMC3266769/.

Molnar, Beth. E., Ginny, Sprang, Kyle, D. Killian, Ruth, Gottfried, Vanessa, Emery & Brian, E. Bride. (2017). Advancing science and practice for vicarious traumatisation/secondary traumatic stress: A research agenda. *Traumatology*, *23*, 129-142.

Morran, David. (2008). Firing up and burning out: The personal and professional impact of working in domestic violence offender programmes. *The Journal of Community and Criminal Justice*, *55*, 139-152.

O'Connell, Mary. & Herbie, DiFonzo. (2018). Reprinted from Vol. 44, No. 4 in honour of Professor J. Herbie DiFonzo. The Family Law Education Reform Project final report. *Family Court Review*, *56*, 18-55.

Sanderson, Christiane. (2008). Working with survivors of domestic abuse. In *Counselling survivors of domestic abuse*, 85-109. London: Jessica Kingsley Publishers. Accessed September 8, 2019. https://ebookcentral.proquest.com/lib/ecu/reader.action?docID=581472&ppg =276.

Sanderson, Christiane. (2009). *Introduction to Counselling Survivors of Interpersonal Trauma*. London: Jessica Kingsley Publishers. Accessed September 7, 2019. Accessed September 8, 2019. https://ebookcentral.proquest.com/lib/ecu/reader.action?docID=581472&ppg =276.

Schore, Allan N. (2003). *Affect regulation and the repair of the self*. New York: W.W. Norton & Co.

Shaver, Phillip R. & Mario, Mikulincer. (2005). Attachment theory and research: Resurrection of the psychodynamic approach to personality. *Journal of Research in Personality*, *39*, 22–45.

Shedler, Jonathan. (2010). Getting to know me: Psychodynamic therapy has been caricatured as navel-gazing, but studies show powerful benefits. *Scientific American Mind*: New York: Nature Publishing Group.

Accessed August 25, 2019. https://jonathanshedler.com/PDFs/Shedler%20Scientific%20American.pdf.

Slade, Arietta. (2016). Attachment and adult psychotherapy: Theory, research and practice. In *Handbook of Attachment, Third Edition: Theory, Research, and Clinical Applications*, edited Jude Cassidy, and Phillip R. Shaver, 795-779. New York: Guilford Publications. Accessed September 27, 2019. https://ebookcentral.proquest.com/lib/ecu/reader.action?docID=4338858&ppg=464.

Slootmaechers, Jef. & Lieven, Migerode. (2019). Fighting for connection: Patterns of Intimate Partner Violence. *Journal of Couple & Relationship Therapy*, *17*, 294-312. doi:org/10.1080/ 15332691.2018.1433568.

Stark, Evan. (2007). *Coercive control: How men entrap women in personal life*. New York, NY: Oxford University Press.

Tummala-Narra, Patryusha. (2016). *Psychoanalytic theory and cultural competence in psychotherapy*. Washington, DC: American Psychological Association.

Valor-Segura, Immaculada, Gemma, Saez, Celia, Serrano-Montilla., Ana, Beltran-Morillas., Francisca, Exposito. & Gines, Navarro-Carrillo. (2018). Social psychological perspectives on violence against women. In *Violence against women in the 21st century: Challenges and future directions* edited by Marika Guggisberg and Jessamy Henricksen, 237-288. New York, NY: Nova Science Publishers.

Walker, Leonore. (2017). *The battered woman syndrome* (4th ed.). New York, NY: Springer Publishing LLC.

Wallin, David J. (2007). *Attachment in psychotherapy*. New York: The Guilford Press.

Watson, Carlie, Nikki, Carthy & Sue, Becker. (2017). Helpless helpers: primary care therapist self-efficacy working with intimate partner violence and ageing women. *Quality in Ageing and Older Adults*, *18*, 222-234. doi: 10.1108/QAOA-05-2017-0013.

White, Jacquelyn & Holly, Sienkiewicz. (2018). Victim empowerment, safety, and perpetrator accountability through collaboration: A crisis to transformation conceptual model. *Violence Against Women*, *24*, 1678 – 1696. doi.org/10.1177/1077801217743341.

AUTHOR BIOGRAPHIES

Madalena Grobbelaar, D. Psych, is an academic and a clinical psychologist in private practice. She is a lecturer in the Master of Counselling and Psychotherapy at Edith Cowan University, as well as the Master of Sexology at Curtin University, Perth. Dr. Grobbelaar's area of interest and research is in sexuality, intimate relationships, and interpersonal violence. Her work and therapeutic orientation is informed by the role of dysfunctional attachments in adult sexuality and intimacy, as well as the role of sexual socialisation, attitudes and beliefs and how these contribute to the intergenerational cycle of family violence.

Yolanda Strauss, MA Soc Sci, has worked for more than ten years in the field of interpersonal violence, both as a counsellor and coordinator for a large NGO in Perth, Western Australia. As a sessional staff member Ms Strauss, lectured in Interpersonal Violence at Edith Cowan University and is also in part-time practice. Her areas of interest include domestic and family violence and parenting, particularly in the context of histories of trauma and intergenerational transmission of violence.

In: Victims of Violence
Editor: Mathias L. Knudsen

ISBN: 978-1-53617-140-2
© 2020 Nova Science Publishers, Inc.

Chapter 7

SUPPORTING VICTIMS OF TRAUMA THROUGH THE HUMAN ANIMAL BOND: CRISIS CENTER NORTH'S PAWS FOR EMPOWERMENT PROGRAM

Grace A. Coleman[*]
Crisis Center North,
Pittsburgh, Pennsylvania, US

ABSTRACT

As a relatively new field, victim services continually seeks new and innovative methods to address trauma for survivors of domestic violence and their families. Recently, a limited number of programs have begun to experiment with the utilization canines on their advocacy teams, as a mechanism to address the impact of victimization. While little research exists on the effectiveness of utilizing working canines to address the impact of trauma, primarily due to limited research dollars nationally, practitioners can attest to the effectiveness of the approach. This chapter seeks to examine the award winning "Paws For Empowerment" Program

---

[*] Correponding Author's E-mail: ccncoleman@aol.com.

in Pittsburgh, Pennsylvania, and the successes and challenges the program has faced in rescuing and training shelter dogs to serve as "canine advocates." Further, the chapter explores how working canines transform the advocacy experience with their unique talents and skill sets, providing additional information for therapists and advocates alike to use in untangling the dynamics of trauma.

Keywords: animal assisted activities, animal assisted therapy, canine advocate, canine therapist, Crisis Center North, domestic violence, human animal bond, intuitive training, Paws for Empowerment

THE EMBRYO OF AN IDEA

Looking forlorn and districted, a young boy actively kicked at the pavement with the toe of his shoe, while his mother intently engaged with his counselor outside Crisis Center North (CCN), a domestic violence counseling and educational resource center in Pittsburgh, PA. Christopher (name changed for confidentiality) was less than enthusiastic about attending his counseling session that Fall day. As his mother continued speaking to his counselor, Christopher noticed a fluffy white spaniel enthusiastically bouncing around the corner of the Center. Running toward the playful spaniel mix, Christopher asked the Center's Director, if he could pet her. Penny, a border collie/spaniel mix was a frequent visitor at CCN and generally visited when the staff was facing intense deadlines for the submission of grant applications. Often labeled "The Center Muse," CCN's team recognized her ability to lower their stress levels, particularly around times of intense deadlines. As Christopher and Penny played together, Christopher's anxiety melted away. When the boy's Mother called him for his appointment, the Agency's Director quickly asked him, if he might be willing to take Penny to his counseling session. "Penny really had a tough week," she shared. Christopher delighted at the thought of giving his session away to his newly found canine friend, and beamed, as he slowly walked his new four legged friend to his appointment.

Supporting Victims of Trauma through the Human Animal Bond 133

Upon entering the session, Christopher sat cross legged on the floor. Penny responded by gently approaching him, laying her head on his lap. As events unfolded, Christopher's counselor disappeared in the backdrop, allowing Penny to organically take the lead in the session. Penny gazed at Christopher with her large cocoa brown eyes, while he slowly began telling Penny everything he had witnessed in his home. While Christopher's hands gently stroked the dog's feathery soft fur, the counselor was able to gather information that Christopher had not previously shared. Post his appointment, the counselor marveled at what had occurred, sharing that Christopher covered more ground in that one session than he had in six months. That session marked the first session that Christopher was willing to share his story and go into any depth regarding the violence he was witnessing in his home. Upon returning the dog to the Director, the counselor remarked, "You have to do something with this dog." It was on this day that the seeds for CCN's Paws for Empowerment Program found fertile soil.

GERMINATION

Canine History

During the 1960's the first formal presentation on Animal Assisted Therapy was given by Boris Levinson of Yeshiva University at the American Psychological Association in New York. While Levinson's presentation marked the first of its kind in North America, attendees report that Levinson was nearly laughed out of the room. Were it not for the discovery of Sigmund Freud's journals, shortly thereafter, validating the technique and Levinson's findings, the field may have taken a different turn away from the serious work of engaging animals as partners in the therapeutic settings (Coren 2011).

While the term animal assisted therapy is relatively new, the concept of humans working with dogs is as old as time. Consider the ancient legends from the Dombes region in France of the venerated canine saint, Guinefort,

134   *Grace A. Coleman*

who was considered the great protector of infants and is credited with healing sick children. As the legend goes, Guinefort, a greyhound, was owned by a wealthy knight. One day, the knight left his son in the care of a nurse for a hunting expedition, only to return to a nursery with an overturned crib and blood strewn everywhere around the room. Seeing the dog covered in blood and the carnage in the room, the knight believed his son to be killed and held the greyhound responsible for the damage. Drawing his sword, the knight swiftly killed the dog, only to hear his son's cries moments later. After seeing a mutilated serpent under his son's crib, the Knight understood that the dog had protected his son from the deadly poisonous snake. Feeling tremendous guilt, the Knight built a memorial to the greyhound, burying the dog in his well and planting a grove of trees around the dog's watery grave. The story of the brave canine, who protected his son, spread far and wide. For hundreds of years thereafter, pilgrims brought their children to Guinefort's grave until the Catholic Church attempted to end the pilgrimages by sending a friar to stop to the local tradition. To do so, the friar dug up the remains of the dog and burned down all the trees at the memorial site. Despite this, pilgrims still came to the site well after World War II and reportedly until the 1960's (Debenedette 2017).

Legends of healing power of dogs and their bravery have existed around the world and also include those closer to home. Sallie Ann Jarrett, an American Staffordshire Terrier, was the canine mascot of the 11th Pennsylvania Infantry during the Civil War. Sallie, as she was lovingly called by her unit, easily adapted to military life. The dog often marched with the unit's color guard and marched before President Abraham Lincoln on two separate occasions. President Lincoln was so impressed with the dog's contributions to the war, that he reportedly tipped his hat to the brave canine, during one of those occasions. Sallie's duties were not limited to the color guard. When leaving camp, her preferred position was next to her colonel and his horse at the front of the regimen. In battle, she joined the front lines, barking furiously at the enemy.

While engaging in many battles during the Civil War, she was remembered most for her bravery on the first day of the battle of Gettysburg in 1863. During the retreat to Cemetery Hill, Sallie was separated from her

Supporting Victims of Trauma through the Human Animal Bond 135

unit and presumed dead. Several days later, Sallie was found guarding the bodies of dead and wounded soldiers of her unit on Oak Ridge, where the 11th Infantry had begun the battle. This exceptional canine had not left the members of her unit behind. A monument is erected to Sallie and the soldiers she fought beside on the fields of Gettysburg in Gettysburg National Park (Stouffer and Cubbison 1998).

The Modern Canine

While not the battle fought on the fields of Gettysburg, on that Fall day in 2010, CCN's team inadvertently found a different kind of canine soldier, one adept at fighting the battle of domestic violence and addressing the wounds that trauma inflicts. Also tied to a Pennsylvania history, this little spaniel mix would be one who would ultimately change the landscape for victims of domestic violence in Pennsylvania through the development of canine advocacy services. To mobilize this concept, the Center's Director actively began researching an approach to develop an animal assisted therapy program to add to the Center's menu of already existing services. Research included understanding the history of animal assisted therapy and interviewing experts in the field; speaking to canine trainers; and extensive observation of other working canines.

Post the initial research phase, including both traditional and non-traditional research methods, programmatic roots were established to anchor the Paws for Empowerment Program moving forward. Planning for the fundamental underpinnings of the program, the team addressed such issues as:

- board authorization
- appropriate insurance coverage
- identifying potential liability concerns
- establishment of training standards for staff handlers
- creating organizational staff buy-in
- implementing client safety protocols

Grace A. Coleman

- establishing ethical standards for any working canines
- developing an underlying philosophical model for programming
- creating funding and financial sustainability for the program

CCN began utilizing canines in animal assisted activities (AAA's) and animal assisted therapy (AAT). AAA's refer to those interventions that do not have a consistent protocol, such as inclusion of animals in activities, while AAT refers to those interventions occurring in a therapeutic setting and which have specified goals (Fine 2019, 80).

Initial examples of AAA's included Penny joining client gatherings, such as the annual Christmas party (appearing as one of Santa's elves) and providing opportunities for selfies at the Canine Kissing Booth featured at the Center's signature fundraiser, Cocktails and Cuisine. During Halloween at the Center's Annual Witch's Ball, Penny dressed as "Zoltar the Fortune Telling Spaniel." In her specially made turban head gear, she joined her human fortune telling counterpart to the amazement of unbelieving guests. Though easy to underestimate, these activities led to increased community engagement with the Center. Repeatedly, the public welcomed the presence of a canine at events and felt more comfortable approaching and engaging with the advocates as domestic violence providers and community partners. The ease with which Penny interacted with the general public lead to greater community involvement, a natural marketing tool for agency services, a more welcoming experience for clients, and created an organizational image that was warmer and less institutional.

Later, as the program expanded into the realm of therapy, counselors utilized Penny in specific related goals for clients. Marie (name changed for confidentiality) was a client experiencing domestic violence who came to the Center for counseling. During session, she exhibited volatile behaviors, often raising her voice, and ultimately yelling in session. When she exhibited those behaviors, Penny would rapidly move away from her to the furthest corner of the room tucked away from Marie. Upon noticing the dog's behavior, Marie would call her, but the dog would not come to her when she was behaving in this manner. This disturbed Marie; and, she asked her counselor, "Why won't she come to me?" Marie loved animals and prided herself as being good with dogs. Her therapist astutely utilized the canine to help her realize the difference between how she felt about Penny inside, and what her outside behavior might be reflecting to Penny. She asked Marie to consider if this behavior might be pushing others away from her too, those important relationships beyond her abusive partner, who might be able to provide invaluable support while Marie was facing intimate partner violence. In this break through moment, Marie recognized the impact of her behavior on others through the use of a canine therapist and started making progress addressing her anger. CCN quickly realized that the power of a canine advocate was indispensable both in and outside therapeutic settings.

At the time, there were no other domestic violence programs in the state of Pennsylvania that were utilizing canine assisted therapy to address trauma in domestic violence victims, and the concept of utilizing rescued shelter dogs for work with victims was unknown. Nationally, the utilization of shelter dogs as working dogs was unconventional, but the program founder and Center's Executive Director, Grace Coleman, was motivated by what she experienced in childhood.

The daughter of a veterinarian, Coleman grew up in the Endless Mountains in Susquehanna County, Pennsylvania. Her father's experience with animals began on the family's dairy farm, established in 1918, a farm which is still in operation today. The farm is classified as a centennial farm in that it has been officially recognized as being continuously owned by a single family for more than 100 years. While obtaining a Veterinariae Medicinae Doctoris (VMD) from the University of Pennsylvania, Patrick B. Coleman served in the army during World War II, in part, caring for war horses. Post the war, Mr. Coleman established a large animal veterinary practice within miles of the farm he grew up on. He served the community for 59 years in his veterinary practice.

Mr. Coleman's experience with canines came from his work on the family's dairy farm, where they were used as working tools. Early on, he ingrained in his daughter that "a good dog is a dog with a job." As a part of his veterinary practice, she was occasionally asked by her father to train puppies to give to community members who had suffered loss as a means of breaking the isolation in an area where the nearest neighbor could be miles away. One such canine, "Starshine," went to a dairy farmer on Turkey Hill who recently lost his wife. Starshine helped his owner address the grief of losing his wife and the two became inseparable. Ultimately, the dog was responsible for saving his owner's life. While working in the fields alone, the owner's tractor flipped on a hill, trapping the owner beneath it. Starshine ran to the barn alerting those working there of the accident. When the men hurriedly followed the dog, they found its owner trapped under the oppressive weight of the farming equipment. Had the dog not responded quickly, the owner would have been crushed to death by the shear weight of the tractor.

Upon his death, Coleman's daughter wanted to commemorate her father's life by establishing a project that reflected his belief in the power of the human animal bond. Coleman spent her own career creating safety for women and children and wanted to use her domestic violence center to provide the same for shelter dogs in need of, not just safe homes, but meaningful work. She continues to believe in the power of shelter dogs and her father's philosophy that "a good dog is a dog with a job."

Many clients have responded to the approach. In speaking to Penny, one client remarked, "Penny, once, you were homeless like me. If you can find a loving home and a career, reinventing your life, well, maybe I can too." Clients at Crisis Center North continue to insist that the program focus on rescued shelter dogs, as opposed to dogs bred and sold for the work. Coleman believes that training the dogs as a team is essential, as there is a particular type of bond that develops between the dog and handlers that care for and work with the canine daily. The bond that is established with the animal and handler during the early weeks of its life and through ongoing training is pivotal. In the best of relationships, the canine and its handlers learn a unique unspoken language which becomes irreplaceable when doing work that, at times, can become dangerous. Though it requires years of work for each canine, Coleman believes something incredibly important, yet intangible, is lost when programs attempt to purchase already certified dogs. "Through the process of training, handlers learn the language of their partner and create their own beautiful dance while working in the field," states Coleman. While not a traditional choice, CCN has been recognized as an

Supporting Victims of Trauma through the Human Animal Bond   139

innovative domestic violence service provider, one that is willing to go outside the bounds traditional convention to bring unconventional tools to the field. Given the success of the Paws for Empowerment Program, it appears to have been the correct choice for both the canines and the human counterparts they serve.

AN IDEA GROWS

In 2010, the project began with the development of the team's recently discovered canine advocate, Penny. In October 2010, Penny received her American Kennel Club Canine Good Citizen certification and by November of the same year, she received a therapy dog certification. In 2011, Penny officially became a part of CCN's counseling team as a canine therapist.

In the initial phase of program development, Penny began working as a canine therapist with both the Center's children's counselor and later, the adult counselor. Several case studies demonstrate the efficacy of this work.

Case Study 1

A new client enters the Center for counseling services for the first time. As she walks toward the counseling room, Penny exits the consult room to greet the incoming client, per her normal practice. Upon seeing the client, Penny immediately freezes and swiftly drops to the ground, doing what can only be described as a military crawl across the floor toward the client. Penny's unusual response garners an immediate staff reaction. As her behavior was completely foreign, Center staff was uncertain if the dog is experiencing a medical emergency. The canine establishes no eye contact with the client and continues crawling across the floor on her belly, eyes downward, stopping only when she reaches the client's feet. The client watches the dog and ultimately drops to the floor, slowing embracing the dog in her arms. Responsively, Penny goes limp in the client's arms resembling a rag doll. The client begins sobbing, as she continues holding

140   *Grace A. Coleman*

the limp dog in her arms. She and Penny are still in the entry way to the counseling room, and before even reaching the consult room, her counseling session begins. Through tears, the client begins sharing with her counselor that she had been contemplating suicide that day.

The counseling team pieces together what their canine therapist, Penny, was attempting to communicate. By making herself as small as possible, she was attempt to make herself unintimidating, so as to not frighten a client in a very fragile state. It is well known that a dog's sense of smell is, on average, 100,000 times stronger than a human's. CCN's team believes that that client interaction was enhanced, due to Penny's ability to smell her client's distress and the underlying emotions affiliated with that distress. Through her unorthodox behavior, CCN's canine therapist was attempting to announce to her co-therapist that her new client was in a highly fragile state. This cue from the canine therapist resulted in immediate information for her human therapist's benefit, information that would have taken much longer to garner through any normal intake process. CCN's counselor believed that on that day the presence of a canine therapist saved a life. Perhaps more interestingly, it was the first time Penny had exhibited any untrained behavior in response to her role. Penny began the process of authoring her own job description, bringing more of her intuitive canine skills and abilities to augment her human handler's skill set. In this case, the canine therapist's ability to immediately recognize danger, saved her co-therapist valuable time. Time can save a life in a therapeutic setting. The client left the appointment stabilized, saying, "Maybe, what I really need is a dog." The staff responded, "We can help you with that!"

Case Study 2

Kathleen and Mary (names changed for confidentiality) came to the Center when Kathleen was approximately eight years old and Mary was five years old. The girls had the unfortunate experience of living in a domestically violent home. They were in counseling to address the issues resulting from the divorce of their parents and the confusion of living between two different homes.

lected as pilot sites, as, at the district magisterial offices, a victim of
omestic violence is presented as a plaintiff in a case where a defendant has
acted an assault and battery against them. These proceedings provide the
ctim and the offender the right to present their case via their respective
orneys. Unfortunately, for the victim, these proceedings are forced
teractions with their offender. In many instances, it is the first time a victim
s come in contact with their offender, since the violent incident occurred.
ften, this interaction is especially taxing for the victim and can result in re-
ctimization and re-traumatization. Not only is the victim required to meet
ce-to-face with the defendant; but also, she/he is recalling and describing,
great detail, the violent incident to a judge in a public forum.

At CCN, the canine advocate works in conjunction with our agency's
al advocate and is often utilized as a resource for the plaintiff/victim to
ctice re-telling her story, thus assisting the victim in becoming more
mfortable with recounting the incident to the judge and attorneys. CCN's
ws for Empowerment Program provides a greater opportunity for the
ocate to support the victim through on-site crisis counseling and
ngthen the referral process to CCN's network of services, including
nseling and case management. The canine advocacy team presents the
ed benefit of potentially lowering recidivism rates, by providing victims
h access to additional services at the Center or in the community, which
ritical in interrupting the cycle of violence.

By incorporating canine advocacy teams into court venues, victims are
vided with necessary emotional support prior to and during the
ceedings. These human/canine advocacy teams help improve a victim's
erstanding of the court process and provide emotional support to victims,
hey are better able to face their abusers while discussing their cases with
appropriate judicial parties. In the end, this powerful tool helps increase
ecution rates, as clients are more likely to appear for court hearings in
ies where programs promoting safety and sensitivity to trauma are
lable.

When originally coming to the Center, the children's counselor noted
the initial discomfort of the girls. As Kathleen responded to art therapy
techniques, CCN's children's counselor would often dedicate sessions using
this therapeutic modality. In one of those sessions, Kathleen drew a telling
image of herself in the counseling setting, which depicts her thoughts and
feelings on the presence of a canine therapist (Crisis Center North 2012).

The picture reflects Kathleen standing in the side of the counseling room
with Penny. Kathleen and Penny are small in comparison to the image of the
levitating counseling chair and the massive swirl of colors covering the
upper two thirds of the picture. Kathleen's choice of colors is interesting.
Most prominently featured in her drawing are various shades of purple and
green. In western culture, purple is thought to symbolize mourning,
transformation and enlightenment, while green represents nature, renewal,
and generosity. Turquoise often represents femininity and calm, while
yellow typically represents hope. All of these colors may indicate Kathleen's
long term hope about the therapeutic process, hope which she would be
unable to articulate as a young girl. Among the swirl of colors, Kathleen
depicts a block of red in the lower right of her drawing. The long red block
completely covers half the page and is directly above her head and that of
Penny, seemingly representing a barrier to the other colors. As red often
represents intensity and violence and is the closest color to Kathleen and
Penny, perhaps Kathleen is reflecting her need to address the larger issues
of violence in her home before reaching the state of transformation,
enlightenment, and renewal that the other colors in the upper portion of the
drawing represent.

Interestingly, she and Penny are depicted in a sea of brown within the
actual consult room. Brown typically represents reliability and stability,
perhaps the promise that the counseling room ultimately offers her on her
journey toward healing. Without doubt, the most prominent feature of the
drawing is the levitating counseling chair. What is clearly indicated in
Kathleen's drawing is a seeming fear of what sitting in the counseling seat
holds for her. The fact that the chair is levitating and that its seat is extremely
thick, seem to point toward Kathleen's fear of sitting in the chair. As
Kathleen approaches the chair, it is noteworthy that she is dressed in pink

colored dress, a color often representing acceptance and calm (Incredible Art Department n.d.). Seemingly, Kathleen's picture represents that she can face the chair in a calm and accepting manner, as long as she and Penny face it together.

Not surprisingly, not long after this drawing, the girls began to establish a strong therapeutic bond with their counselor and started to enjoy their visits to the Center. On the days when Penny was present, their counselor observed that the girls treated each other and their mother with more respect. They each took turns practicing commands with Penny giving her treats. This training time with Penny may have been the only area in their world where, when they said something, in this case, a spaniel, responded immediately to their request; thus, giving them a sense of empowerment which didn't exist anywhere else in their lives. Counseling sessions on these days were reportedly more successful, as the girls were able to relax with Penny, talking about their feelings, recent events in the family, and their concerns more openly.

Figure 1. "Kathleen's" original drawing reflects how CCN's canine therapist, Penny, eases the apprehension involved in individual counseling.

REPRODUCTION

While the Paws for Empowerment Program was originally de augment children's counseling at the Center, the program quickly to adults, due to the popular demand from individuals receiving c services. The program moved initially from serving children to a then, ultimately to the courtroom.

In July 2013, with the cooperation of the Allegheny Count Attorney Stephen Zappala; former President Judge Donna Jo McD the Honorable Anthony W. Saveikis, Penny became the first Allegheny County and the first shelter dog in the State to prov advocacy services to victims of domestic violence in court. The Anthony Saveikis offered his magisterial district court (MDC) i PA, as the first pilot site for CCN's Canine Court Program. Provi legal advocacy services in magisterial courts gives survivors advocates when navigating the unfamiliar and often intimid system.

The initial pilot to magisterial districts serving areas such a Oakdale; Coraopolis; and Findlay, all western Pennsylvania courts, ensures that victims living in remote areas of Allegheny afforded the same spectrum of resources as residents living in Residents in these communities, from which the first pilot site w are more likely to be underserved and less likely to know about exposed to services provided by CCN. Victims in these areas are at a disadvantage when navigating the courts or seeking res program later expanded into the former Judge Mary Murray Coraopolis. Most recently, Justice William K. Wagner, in W has incorporated Paws for Empowerment Program in his courtr

Canine coverage at these sites is particularly important, as of domestic violence enter the stream of judicial services, they at the height of their journey. Having escaped one or more abuse, victims are seeking justice. These court venues were

Supporting Victims of Trauma through the Human Animal Bond 145

Case Study 3

In the courts, Penny is seen as another working staff member. Her mornings in court begin with a greeting of court officials before taking her designated spot in the courtroom. On one particular morning, a victim and her perpetrator came to court for proceedings. Magisterial courts are often crowded, allowing for less space between the perpetrator and the victim, the primary reason CCN began its canine court program in such venues. On this particular court day, the perpetrator came running toward the victim. Noticing before anyone else, Penny quickly body blocked the victim, surprising the perpetrator and stopping him short of reaching her. While the advocate was working with the victim, Penny's keen eye and watchfulness provided an additional layer of safety on that day for both the victim and her handler. Her reaction allowed other court personnel to interrupt the interaction with the perpetrator. Perhaps most importantly, the victim was provided with additional safety. Were it not for the presence of a canine advocate, the day may have unfolded very differently for everyone in that courtroom.

Case Study 4

While in court with her advocate handler, Penny became focused on a man who was alone and preparing for his proceeding. The man was not a client of the Center. As the advocate prepared to leave court that day, Penny expressed the Border Collie side of her DNA and intently refused to budge. Her handler gently explained that this man was not one of CCN's clients. Still, the dog refused to move. Penny is known for communicating her professional desires clearly to her handlers, and often self selects clients to help. To date, she has never been wrong about identifying someone in the courtroom who is in need of emotional support. As the intuitive training method allows, the handler gently gave the dog a few more moments, trying to determine her fascination with this one particular man in the courtroom.

As the proceedings unfolded, Penny kept gently edging over, while remaining in the sit position, to be directly in front of the man testifying. As the testimony unfolded, it became clear that this man had been sexually assaulted. During the entire testimony, Penny did not take her eyes off him, nor did he ever break eye contact with her. Penny's human advocate and handler did not attempt to move her again, as Penny, had once again, identified a trauma victim in need of assistance. The man relayed his entire story, never breaking eye contact with the spaniel mix. After the proceeding, he made his way from the stand and came to CCN's advocate and Penny saying, "I don't know who you are or why you are in this courtroom with a dog today, but I would have never made it through those proceedings without looking into that dog's eyes." During this case, Penny was not interested in the artificial human constructs of which clients are and are not a part of CCN's case repertoire. This was not the first occasion where she helped a client who was not a victim of domestic violence. The judges have come to rely on the canine and her keen instincts, requesting use of her for cases that move beyond the bounds of domestic violence, a strong indicator that more trained canines are needed in the field to address the multiple layers of trauma that victimization presents.

From her canine perspective, it was clear that Penny has determined that the victims she works with are her responsibility, while in courtroom venues. Again, this behavior was not a trained response, but an intuitive canine one. This pattern of the PAWS canines evolving into and beyond their own job descriptions may be a direct result of CCN utilizing the intuitive training method. CCN's use of the intuitive method over basic obedience or task specific training highlights CCN's philosophical approach to using canines as respected partners. By utilizing an intuitive training method, the working canines are free to bring their own special talents to the table, creating a unique ability for canine skills to augment human ones. It also allows for the canines to think through unanticipated situations that they might not otherwise be able to train for. This specialized training approach makes the Paws for Empowerment Program rare in that it allows the canines to bring their distinct skill set, bred over thousands of years, to the table when addressing victims and their trauma.

Researching and Replication

In 2016, Penn State University students conducted a qualitative research study involving the impact of animal assisted therapy at Crisis Center North (Bandish and George 2016). The purpose of the study was to examine the benefits of animal-assisted therapy. The student led research team conducted in-depth phone interviews with victims of domestic violence who had utilized canine assisted services in counseling and in the courtroom. Victim advocates were also interviewed, during the course of the study. As CCN had only one canine advocate on staff at the time, the purpose of the study was to examine Penny's work and victims of domestic violence. The findings of the study reported:

- clients who engaged with the canine enjoyed her presence
- rates of attendance were higher when Penny was present
- clients reported feeling more relaxed when Penny was present
- her presence reduced the stress of sharing traumatic experiences
- clients preferred to have Penny in-session; and,
- Penny created a better work environment for advocates and handlers

Outside of the Center, in courtroom settings, the results were similar. In an independent evaluation of CCN services provided by Penn State University faculty in the 2018-2019 fiscal year, 271 evaluations were collected from Family court and magisterial settings. CCN's canine advocate and her handler worked with 65 of those clients in magisterial settings. The group surveyed was 87% female, 69% Euro-American, and 30% African-American. Participants ranged in age from 16-90 (Average = 37).

Survey results showed that 63% of participants felt more confident or comfortable with a dog present, and 49% said having the dog available would make them more likely to attend court. One hundred percent of the clients who worked with the canine advocate said they would use other CCN services, based on their experience with legal advocacy team (Chapin 2019, 3).

Regarding the program, Judge Saveikis stated, "Getting domestic violence victims to feel comfortable enough so they can tell their side of the story in front of strangers, in what can potentially feel like a threatening situation, is where Penny comes into the picture," (Hughey 2014, 40).

POLLINATION

Due to the success of the program, in 2016, CCN adopted its second rescue, Ari (pronounced "R-ee") from Action for Animals in Latrobe, PA., the same shelter that Penny was adopted from.

Ari is a Labrador Retriever/Australian Shepherd Mix with amber colored eyes and a dusty cinnamon colored coat accented with blonde markings. While Penny came to the Center with her name, Ari's owners wanted to baptize him with a significant name for his journey. Ari means "golden lion" in Hebrew, while in Hindi it means, "He who shows the right path." Ari brings a distinctly different skill set to CCN's Paws For Empowerment Program. Interestingly, unlike most dogs, Ari does not hesitate to stare deeply into clients' eyes, a rare trait in that most dogs avoid eye contact for prolonged periods of time. Ari has learned to gently nudge clients when they are in distress, redirecting their attention to his eyes.

Unlike Penny, who began her journey at the Center at age two, and by chance, Ari began his working journey at seven weeks old and with intention. Ari's training began with his owners, multiple handlers, and Center staff. A doggie play pen was rotated from office to office, so that he was exposed to new staff and new experiences on a daily basis. The team's goal was to acclimate him to human touch and in particular to touch areas such as his paws, in between his paws, and his ears, legs, and tail, areas that are often sensitive to a dog.

Team members collectively worked to expose Ari to a myriad of new experiences, including supply runs, meetings, intakes with clients, and the varied experiences typical of the robust environment that a domestic

Supporting Victims of Trauma through the Human Animal Bond 149

violence center provides. Once again, expanding the bounds of her job description, Penny began supervising Ari, ensuring that when clients come to the door, he greeted them appropriately. Often, she was faster at cuing Ari on key parts of his job than her human counterparts.

The Paws for Empowerment Program has established standards around the usage of the canines, including that all handlers must pass the Canine Good Citizen Test and the components therapy dog certification with their designated dog, even if the dog has passed that test many times with other handlers. Canines are given designated off duty areas to retreat to, during the working day, and are prohibited from working more than three hours at a time, without a break. Staff utilize lunch breaks to walk and play with the dogs, as the team is sensitive to the fact that canines absorb stress differently from their human counterparts. The Center's practice is to keep all working dogs in-house and in training until age three, when they are intellectually capable of the complexity and challenges of the work outside the Center.

After a year of exposure, going everywhere the team went and doing all that the team did, Ari began formal training for his canine counseling work. This time, the team opted to engage both dogs in private one-on-one training, realizing that therapy dog training alone was insufficient for the complexities of ongoing work with victims of trauma. Post-passage of both the American Kennel Club and Canine Good Citizen Test, canines and handlers receive ongoing private training in the intuitive training method with Cheri Herschell of Rebellion Kennels, a local kennel that has partnered with the PAWS Program, since its inception.

The intuitive training method is one in which the canine is encouraged to bring all of its innate skills and ability to the work situation. Rather than simple obedience training, where the dog performs cues on demand, intuitive training teaches a dog to think. For example, as a young dog, Penny often jolted out of her kennel when the door was lifted. When using the intuitive training method, handlers were encouraged to gently shut the door before she could get out, showing her that when she attempted to rush out of her kennel, the natural consequence was that the door would slowly close. This practice continued until the canine calmly sat and waited to be released. Once that occurred, the gate opened and the dog could leave. Eventually,

Penny learned that when she rushed the gate, the door closed. When she waited patiently, the door remained open, allowing her to meet her ultimate goal of leaving the kennel more expediently.

Ultimately, the PAWS team credits this method for how and why the dogs bring unique yet critically effective responses to their respective positions. The intuitive method allows human handlers to maximize the unique skill set that their canine co-workers bring to any therapeutic or courtroom setting. It is the philosophy of the Center that the dogs are joining their human handlers and providing skills in addressing trauma that their human counterparts are not capable of bringing. Training for the canines is continuous throughout the course of their careers.

In addition to training, the Center places a commitment on the health and well-being of the canines. As such, the dogs participate in other recreational classes such as swimming and scent dog certification classes. By doing so, the canine team has time with one another, and perhaps, more importantly, time to "just be dogs." It is imperative that working dogs be given down time given the extensive demands involved in working with trauma victims. As canines absorb stress differently than their human counterparts, the PAWS teams keeps a watchful eye on their canine colleagues. According to Nicholas H. Dodman, the director of the animal behavior clinic at the Cummings School of Veterinary Medicine at Tufts University, "PTSD in dogs can be managed, but never fully cured because 'dogs never forget," (Hickey 2015).

At age two, Ari was allowed admittance into select counseling sessions, where his behavior was observed over time to determine the efficacy of his work. By the end of his second year, he began going to counseling on a regular and consistent basis and he primarily works with an adult counselor on staff as her canine therapist.

Interestingly, like humans, the canines exhibit preferences for the type of work they perform; and, as was learned with Penny, that work changes over the landscape of time. Ari exhibits a strong preference for counseling work above court proceedings. His talent on the team lies in his ability to draw clients to the Center and its services as the following scenario illustrates.

Supporting Victims of Trauma through the Human Animal Bond 151

While taking his daily walk with his co-therapist on a warm summer day, a young woman spotted Ari from across the street. As soon as she laid eyes on him, she ran across the bustling Pittsburgh street for the opportunity to pet him. Immediately getting down on the sidewalk, she spent at least five minutes giving him hugs and telling him how beautiful he was. While petting the dog, she shared with our therapist that she was "three days old," quickly following that comment up with information that she was a very recent immigrant. To be with Ari longer, the young woman walked CCN's counselor back to the building, and, along the way, asked what work our agency did. Our therapist responded with the generic, "We offer counseling services." Sensing a trauma history within the young woman, CCN's counselor invited her into the Center. Once again, the young woman, sat on the floor petting Ari. While petting the canine therapist, her personal story of domestic and sexual abuse unfolded, which included the story of her flight from her native homeland. Tears flowed as she shared her story, which involved her perpetrator taking her child from her and constantly being at risk of homicide. Her interaction with a dog she met on the street that day literally led her to services. Much as Ari's name reflects, he did indeed show her the right path to services. Unfortunately, the young woman hasn't returned to the Center since that day, but staff is comforted by the knowledge that she knows where help is available when she is ready and would like to receive it.

Interestingly, Penny retired from counseling once Ari was fully in place, showing a preference for court work. Like many working dogs, her announcement into semi retirement was immediate and communicated by a refusal to walk into the main consult room of the counseling division, where she had worked for many years. From the day of her announcement forward, she has not gone back into the consult room and the team has accepted her decision to go to part-time, working several days a week in court, which, she still enthusiastically enjoys. It is our thought, that as an aging dog, the intensity of emotion in private sessions and within a closed space is too much for her. The team believes she has more than earned the right to engage in the work she loves during the final moments of her career.

SPREADING SEEDS

Since its inception in 2011, the Paws for Empowerment Program has established a national reputation, presenting at such conferences as the National Organization for Victim Assistance (NOVA); the Pennsylvania Commission on Crime and Delinquency's (PCCD) Pathway Conference; and serving as the keynote presentation at the New Challenges/New Solutions Conference for the Cape May and Cumberland County Prosecutors' Offices in New Jersey. CCN has also delivered a staff in-service to PCCD, a funding agency, on best practices in utilizing canines as a trauma informed approach with victims, helping to prepare funders for the anticipated growth of utilizing canines in the field of victim services.

In 2014, the PCCD selected CCN's canine work as one of the four most innovative practices within Pennsylvania's crime victim movement. Pennsylvania's four most innovative programs are featured in the annual report to the Office of Victims of Crime (OVC), which is housed within the Office of Justice Programs' in Washington, D.C. OVC shares this information at the national level as an innovative approach to service provision. OVC may utilize CCN's Paws for Empowerment Program when testifying to Congress and others about the importance of the availability of innovative services for victims through Victims of Crime Act Funding (VOCA). Often such testimony addresses how VOCA funding is being utilized at the state and county levels. Additionally, the information gathered about such innovations in the field is regularly cited at national conferences as an example of "up and coming" best practices within the field of victim services.

Locally, the canines have been recognized in their own right. In 2013, Pittsburgh Magazine awarded Penny the "4 with 4 Paws" award, the animal equivalent of the "40 under 40" award, which recognizes Pittsburgh's emerging young leaders. The "4 with 4 Paws" award recognizes the four most influential animals in Pittsburgh. Penny was recognized for her outstanding work with victims both in and out of the courtroom. Additionally, in 2016, the national publication, American Kennel Dog Magazine, featured Penny in Family Dog Magazine, labeling the article and

Supporting Victims of Trauma through the Human Animal Bond 153

the dog, "Penny from Heaven," (Donovan 2016, 8). In 2017, the Paws for Empowerment Program won a Governor's Victim Service Pathfinder Award for Program of the Year. The Governor's Victim Service Pathfinder Award is the most prestigious award that Pennsylvania gives to a victim service professional or program. The award is presented to one program and up to seven individuals who have made notable contributions to the program for which they work, the community they serve, or the field of victim services.

In 2016, CCN established a national advisory board to assist with the oversight of the program. The advisory board is composed of a wide variety of national experts including: Dr. Aubrey Fine, professor in the College of Education and Integrative Studies at California Polytechnic University and editor of *The Handbook on Animal Assisted Therapy: Theoretical Foundations for Guidelines for Practice, 5th edition*; Dora McQuaid, the internationally known award winning poet, activist, performer, teacher and author of *Scorched Earth;* Atiya Abdelmalik, MSN, RN, and founder of HCD Consulting and author of, *A Life Worth Saving: a nurse's journey from sickness to healing;* Dr. Donna Imhoff, president of the Western Campus and Brunswick University Center of Cuyahoga Community College (Tri-C), and the CCN board president responsible for supporting the launch of the award-winning program; and, last but not least, Lynn Shiner, award-winning author of *Stabbed In the Heart,* and current victim services consultant who served as the director of the PCCD's Office of Victims' Services. Lynn is the recipient of the National Crime Victim Service Award presented by John Ashcroft and the Visionary Voice Award by the National Sexual Violence Resource Center. Together, the advisory committee works with the PAWS program staff to guide and advance the program while providing innovative opportunities to advance this best practice program.

Believing community involvement is key, CCN has involved a group of children of various ages to help train the canines and sensitize them to the needs of children. CCN's "Canine Kids" program allows child volunteers to participate in training the canines by engaging in basic canine care, playing brain games with the canines, and hosting various fundraising events to support the development of the program. Quincy de las Alas, a nine-year-old "Canine Kid," created an illustration of Penny and Ari to express his own thoughts about his involvement in their training, and this illustration will soon be utilized in future funding and marketing meetings for the program (de las Alas 2019). It is often said that a picture is worth a thousand words.

Not unlike other domestic violence centers across the Country, CCN finds itself both understaffed and underfunded. The Paws for Empowerment Program provides assistance with both these problems. Through its programming, CCN has touched the lives of hundreds of domestic violence victims in both therapeutic and courtroom settings with the unique skill sets that only canines can bring to those experiencing trauma. Within CCN's program, client after client has reported that they would have never made it through their courtroom proceedings without a canine advocate accompanying them. These exceptional working canines have an inherent ability to transfer the love and loyalty most dogs show to only one human to complete strangers, many of whom they will not see again upon conclusion of services. Because of the uniquely innate skills these canines bring to court and therapeutic settings, primarily increased smell and acute hearing, they have provided a rich dimension to both those experiencing domestic violence and the staff who dedicates their lives to help them. Utilizing trained shelter dogs has allowed the program to maximize services; secure canine advocates more cost effectively; keep victims and advocates safer in the field; and, perhaps, equally touching, allow formerly homeless shelter dogs the opportunity to form lasting personal and professional bonds with the both the human handlers and clients who work with them. These canines and their handlers are responsible for impacting the field of domestic violence in unprecedented ways bringing healing to those who are who are most deserving, victims of trauma.

As the Paws for Empowerment Program looks to the future, it's setting its sights on training local veterinary clinics in recognizing the signs of domestic violence within families to provide a critically intersectional approach to the work. Given that "women residing at domestic violence shelters are nearly 11 times more likely to report that their partner had hurt or killed pets than those who had not experienced intimate violence," veterinarians are in a unique position to help identify domestic abuse prior to when the human counterparts in their family are experiencing it (Ascione, et al. 2007). By educating local veterinarians on the dynamics of domestic violence, the Center hopes to make the case of battered pet, thus interrupting the cycle of violence for victims (Yeoman 2008). The legacy of the Paws for Empowerment Program and, in particular, the legacy of one dedicated black and white shelter rescue named Penny is that the program and its original four-legged advocate have opened doors to healing for victims that will have an impact on the field of victim services for many years to come.

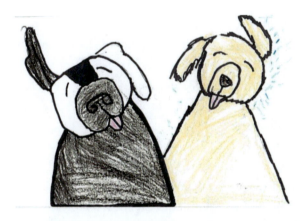

Figure 2. "Canine Kid" Quincy de las Alas, age 9, reflects his enthusiasm for working with canine advocates Penny and Ari as part of CCN's Paws for Empowerment Program.

REFERENCES

Ascione, Frank R., Weber, Claudia V., Thompson, Teresa M., Heath, John., Maruyama, Mika. and Hayashi, Kentaro. (2007). "Battered Pets and Domestic violence: Animal Abuse Reported by Women Experiencing Intimate Violence and by Nonabused Women." *Violence Against Women, 13* (4), doi:10.1177/1077801207299201.

Bandish, Marlee. & George, Ellie. (2016). "The Benefits of Animal Assisted Therapy." Pennsylvania State University.

Chapin, John. (2019). *PAWS Appendix Independent Evaluation of Crisis Center North Programs 2018 to 2019.* Internal Agency Report, Pittsburgh: Pennsylvania State University.

Coren, Stanley. (2011). "How Therapy Dogs Almost Never Came to Exist." *Psychology Today.* February 11. Accessed September 15, 2019. https://www.psychologytoday.com/us/blog/canine-corner/201302/how-therapy-dogs-almost-never-came-exist.

Crisis Center North. (2012). *Kathleen's Art Therapy Drawing.* Crisis Center North.

de las Alas, Quincy. (2019). *Penny and Ari.* Crisis Center North.

Debenedette, Valerie. (2017). "St. Guinefort, the Dog Venerated as a Saint." *Mental Floss.* August 22. Accessed September 15, 2019. http://mentalfloss.com/article/91855/st-guinefort-dog-venerated-saint.

Donovan, Liz. (2016). "Penny, From Heaven." *AKC Family Dog*, January/February, 8.

Fine, Aubrey H. ed. (2019). *Handbook on Animal-Assisted Therapy: Foundations and Guidelines for Animal-Assisted Interventions 5th Edition.* Cambridge: Academic Press.

Hickey, Lori. (2015). "12 Facts about Canine PTSD." *MSA Security.* July 9. Accessed September 15, 2019. http://www.msasecurity.net/security-and-counterterrorism-blog/12-facts-about-canine-ptsd.

Hughey, Doug. (2014). "Magistrate Awarded for Pilot Program Helping Domestic violence Victims." *Allegheny West Magazine*, June/July, 40.

Incredible Art Department. n.d. "Symbolism of Color: Using Color for Meaning." *Incredible Art Department/Art Education.* Accessed September 13, 2019. https://www.incredibleart.org/lessons/ middle/ color2.htm.

Stouffer, Cindy. and Cubbison, Shirley. (1998). *A Colonel, A Flag, And A Dog.* Gettysburg: Thomas Publications. Accessed September 15, 2019. https://en.wikipedia.org/wiki/Sallie_Ann_Jarrett.

Yeoman, Barry. (2008). "The Case of the Battered Pet." *Barry Yeoman Journalist.,* June 1. Accessed September 15, 2019. https://barryyeoman.com/2008/06/battered-pet/.

Biographical Sketch

Grace A. Coleman

Affiliation: Crisis Center North, Pittsburgh, PA, US

Education:
MA, Communication Studies, Bloomsburg University, PA, US
BA, English/Journalism, Bloomsburg University, PA, US

Business Address:
P.O. Box 101093 Pittsburgh, PA, US 15237

Grace Coleman has been the Executive Director of Crisis Center North (CCN), a domestic violence counseling and educational resource center in Pittsburgh, PA, from 1999 to present.

During her tenure as director, CCN has served approximately 40,000 victims of domestic violence. Coleman works daily to make the Pittsburgh community safer by lending her expertise to the Allegheny County Domestic Violence Task Force; the North Hills Non-Profit Consortium, as well as numerous other groups dedicated to addressing domestic violence in Southwestern PA. Grace has served as the Western Regional Vice President of the Pennsylvania Coalition Against Domestic Violence and was selected by the Pennsylvania Commission on Crime and Delinquency to serve as a core faculty member to the Pennsylvania Victim Assistance Academy, one of the nation's first comprehensive training academies for advocates.

In October 2010, Grace established CCN's Paws for Empowerment Program with her canine shelter rescue, Penny, in honor of Domestic violence Awareness Month. By 2013, she expanded her canine work by creating Allegheny County's First Canine Court Program. In 2014, the Pennsylvania Commission on Crime and Delinquency (PCCD) named the Paws for Empowerment Program as one of Pennsylvania's four most innovative practices, using stories from the program to testify before

Congress illustrating the importance of Victim of Crime Act funding. In 2017, the Paws Program was awarded a Governor's Victim Service Pathfinder Award as the program of the year. As the daughter of a veterinarian, Grace is passionate about what canines can bring to the field of victim services. She and Penny have been invited presenters at the National Organization of Victim Assistance Conference; the Pennsylvania Commission Against Crime and Delinquency Pathways Conference; and the New Challenges/New Solutions Conference in Cape May, NJ.

In addition to her work with canines, Grace has co-authored numerous research articles on violence prevention in journals such as *Adolescence*; *the Journal of School Violence*; *The Journal of Injury and Violence Research*; and *The Journal of Family Violence* among others. Most recently, in 2019, Grace contributed to a chapter in Dr. Aubrey Fine's *Handbook on Animal-Assisted Therapy: Foundations and Guidelines for Animal-Assisted Interventions, 5th Edition.*

Grace's work has been honored with the national Vita Wireless Samaritan Award from the Cellular Telecommunication and Internet Association in Washington, D.C; the Athena Award from the Northern Allegheny County Chamber of Commerce; and the Distinguished Service Award for Contributions to Humanity from the Bloomsburg University Alumni Association, and two Governor's Victim Service Pathfinder Program Awards, including the Governor's Victim Service Pathfinder Organizational Capacity Building Award and the Governor's Victim Service Program Award, among others.

When not at work, Grace enjoys rescuing shelter dogs, hiking, gardening, and teaching her grandsons, John Patrick and James Ernest to kayak.

Publications from the Last 3 Years:

Refereed Journal Articles
Chapin, John. And Coleman, Grace. (2017). "The cycle of cyberbullying: Some experience required." *The Social Science Journal, 54* (3), 314-318. doi:10.1016/j.soscij.2017.03.004.

Book Chapters
Chapin, John. and Coleman, Grace. (2018). "Anatomy of a bully." In *Gender, Sexuality, and Peace Education: Issues and Perspectives in Higher Education*, edited by Laura Finley. Charlotte: Information Age.

Content Contributions for a Book Chapter
Fine, Aubrey H. ed. (2019). *Handbook on Animal-Assisted Therapy: Foundations and Guidelines for Animal-Assisted Interventions 5th Edition*. Cambridge: Academic Press.

In: Victims of Violence
Editor: Mathias L. Knudsen

ISBN: 978-1-53617-140-2
© 2020 Nova Science Publishers, Inc.

Chapter 8

MATERNAL PARENTING OF VICTIMS OF DOMESTIC VIOLENCE

Ana Sani[1,2,3,], Ana Catarina Vieira[1] and Dora Pereira[4]*

[1]University Fernando Pessoa (UFP), Porto, Portugal
[2]Permanent Observatory Violence and Crime (OPVC), (UFP),
Porto, Portugal
[3]Research Center on Child Studies (CIEC),
University of Minho (UM), Braga, Portugal
[4]University of Madeira (UMa), Funchal, Portugal

ABSTRACT

This chapter presents a qualitative study that aims to further our understanding of how domestic violence between intimate partners can affect maternal parenting. The sample comprised 15 women - mothers and victims of domestic violence – and our focus was on understanding how they conceive their role as mothers and how they perceive their parenting skills. We used a semi-structured individual interview and the collected data were recorded and then transcribed for analysis. The results are

---

[*] Corresponding Author's E-mail: anasani@ufp.edu.pt.

organized into categories related to maternal experiences and domestic violence. The results reveal that an abusive relationship has negative effects on the mother-child relationship(s). Moreover, we find that the mothers try to maintain their abilities, motivations and skills in their role as parents, despite the abusive context. This qualitative study reinforces the need for the development of effective parenting interventions in support of victims of domestic violence.

Keywords: domestic violence, mothers, parenting, victims

INTRODUCTION

Domestic violence is a criminal issue of great concern in many societies that prioritize the defense of human rights and the search for social justice and equality. Portugal is one of those countries that, in the last two decades, have been developing many initiatives, mechanisms and strategies, across several organizations (e.g., police, courts, non governamental organization), in order to better understand domestic violence and to generate interventions that are aligned with the victims' needs (Sani & Lopes, 2018).

Domestic violence between intimate partners is a gendered phenomenon. In Portugal, as in many other countries, most victims are women, as shown by official data (78.6%) (Internal Security System - ISS, 2019) and data from victim support associations (86.3%) (Portuguese Association for Victim Support - APAV, 2019). Literature has highlighted violence against women (Guggisberg & Henricksen, 2018) in heterosexual relationships, although same-sex victimization is now increasingly recognized (Sani, Domingues, & Soi, 2016; Sani, Osorio, Dinis, & Soeiro, 2019).

There is a tendency for victims of domestic violence to belong to nuclear families with children (37.7%) (APAV, 2019) and the resulting exposure of children to parental violence (Sani & Lopes, 2019) leads to child victimization. Thus it is not uncommon for parenting to occur within a context of violent relationship dynamics, which in themselves negatively affect the quality of parenting (Levendosky & Graham-Bermann, 2001; Sani, 2008). Our aim is to explore the effect of domestic violence on the parenting practices of the victim. We study mothers who are victims of violence in heterosexual intimate relationships and who live with children fathered by the aggressor.

According to several studies, the experience of domestic violence between intimate partners tends to negatively affect the victim's physical and mental health (Walker, 2017) and to interfere with parenting (Sani, Pereira, & Dinis, *in press*), namely with the ability to manage relationships with children, e.g., in the quality of attachment, the level of adjustment of children, and the way mothers and fathers exercise parenting practices (Cecconello, De Antoni, & Koller, 2003; Levendosky, Huth-Bocks, Shapiro, & Semel, 2003; Sani & Cunha, 2011). Some studies on this theme have shown that violent families tend to be less supportive of their children compared to non-violent families (McCloskey, Figueredo, & Koss, 1995) and that these parents tend to use inappropriate educational practices more often when interacting with children (Sani & Cunha, 2011). However, studies also reveal that sometimes negative life experiences can lead to new learning and consolidate parenting skills, require greater resource mobilization to cope with violence in defense of their children, and provide structure to, or improve, relations with children (Levendosky, Lynch & Graham-Bermann, 2000; Van Horn & Lieberman, 2002). Additionally, some victims of violence seek to provide their children with reinforced support and affection in order to compensate for the negative environment caused by violence (Lapierre, 2010).

With the functional model of parenting behavior (Pereira, 2018, 2019) parenting is conceived as a process with three fundamental constituents: parenting capacity, mediating processes and parenting skills. Parenting capacity is conceived as the potential the parents have to develop and adapt their practices to the specific needs of their children throughout their development and according to the specific circumstances of their living contexts. It results from the interaction of the features of the psychic structure of parents, with the specific modifiers of context and relationships, including the specific contribution of the child. Parenting skills referes to the way parents perform their role, e.g., how they manage children'behavior, how they coomunicate or how they express afection, etc.. The mediating processes refers to cognitive and affective processes (as integration, recognition of responsibility or impulse control) determinant to make use of parenting capacity in parenting skills. To understand parenting behavior in specially challenging situations as domestic violence must be known the specific features of it's functioning, not just from the description of behaviors, but from a dinamic stance, that considers how differents constituents of parenting can contribute to the unique features of each situation. The perception of parents about their own behavior is specially relevant to decisions that can foster their engagement in social and psychological interventions with the victims of domestic violence (Platt, 2012).

In this chapter we present a qualitative, descriptive and exploratory study of women victims of domestic violence by their intimate partner, whose general objectives were to access their representations of maternity and to understand how their experiences of victimization influence their roles as mothers and their parenting skills. We focus our attention on three specific objectives:

1. To know the criteria associated with the exercise of the role of mother;
2. To understand how these mothers define themselves in the exercise of this role;
3. To characterize the contribution of domestic violence on maternal parenting.

METHODS

This study developed from a request for collaboration from a non-governmental organization that supports victims of domestic violence, who sought a better understanding of parenting in victims of domestic violence.

15 mothers, partners in heterosexual relationships who had direct personal experience of domestic violence by their intimate partner were interviewed. The sample, selected to be sufficiently heterogeneous to

Maternal Parenting of Victims of Domestic Violence 165

encompass a range of experiences (cf. Table 1), consisted of five married, five divorced, four single, and one widow women, aged 29-71 (M = 47.9; SD = 12.0). These mothers were residents of Oporto city (Portugal) and in terms of educational attainment have mostly (46.7%) the 1st cycle of basic education. Once the theoretical saturation of the sample was reached, it was closed (Fontanella, Ricas, & Turato, 2008).

**Table 1. Sociodemographic characterization
of the total sample (N = 15)**

Categories	Variables	n	%
	25 to 30	1	6.7
	31 to 40	3	20.0
	41 to 50	6	40.0
Age group (years)	51 to 60	2	13.3
	61 to 70	2	13.3
	71 to 80	1	6.7
	1st cycle (ISCED Level 1)	7	46.7
	2nd cycle (ISCED Level 1)	3	20.0
Educational level	3rd cycle (ISCED Level 2)	3	20.0
	Secondary (10th - 12th year)	1	6.7
	University: Bachelor's degree	1	6.7
	Single	4	26.7
Marital status	Married/Unmarried union	5	33.3
	Divorced/Separated	5	33.3
	Widow	1	6.7

For data collection, two instruments were used: (i) sociodemographic data sheet, for the collection of personal data (referred to above); ii) semi-structured interview script, built after a theoretical review around the theme and a in consultation with professional collaborators. This script contained nine questions, guided by the objectives of the study (e.g., What does it mean for you to be a mother?; How do you define your role as a mother?; Which aspects most influence the role of mother? How might violence have affected parental function in relation to the child?).

The preparation for this study required the formal request for institutional collaboration with a Victim Support Office (GAV), as well as the submission of the research project to the University Ethics Committee. Once all the conditions, authorizations and queries were met, the investigation began. The GAV informed its users of the study, its objectives and procedures, and those that were interested contacted us to participate. It should be noted that all data and information collected throughout the investigation were stored on a computer that remained on the GAV office, to which only one researcher had access through code provided by the entity. Interviews with subjects were made in the presence of a GAV psychologist during their planned appointments, limiting data collection solely through the instruments.

Prior to the semi-structured interview, participants were instructed on the purpose of the study, the importance of their participation and confidentiality measures; informed consent was signed by them. Interviews were audio recorded and lasted approximately 30 minutes. All interviews took place at the GAV facilities and were performed by one of the investigators.

Table 2. Analysis grid: Categories and subcategories

Categories	Subcategories
A. Perceptions about the concepts of motherhood	A1. Criteria that determine what is a "good mother"
	A2. Meanings about being a "good mother"
	A3. Personal fulfillment
B. Violence	B1. Acts of intimate partner violence
	B2. Acts of violence against children
C. Reasons for abusive relationship maintenance	C1. Being a "good woman"
	C2. Material dependence
D. Abandonment of abusive marital relationship	D1. Reasons that led to the abandonment
E. Impact of violence in motherhood	E1. Positive impact
	E2. Negative impact
	E3. No impact

After the information was collected through the sociodemographic questionnaire, it was entered into a database for statistical analysis,

Maternal Parenting of Victims of Domestic Violence   167

performed using the IBM Statistical Package for Social Sciences (SPSS) software, version 25.0. Qualitative data obtained through semi-structured interviews were subject to content analysis (Bardin, 2009). After full transcription of the interviews, we proceeded to the analysis in three phases (pre-analysis, exploration of materials and treatment of results, inference and interpretation) giving rise to several categories and subcategories of analysis (cf. Table 2). Taking into consideration our stated objectives, in this chapter we present the results and examples concerning the categories: A: perceptions about the concepts of motherhood; and E: Impact of violence in motherhood.

RESULTS

According to the participants there are a number of "criteria that determine what a' good mother" is (A1). One of these is the ability to provide for the child's needs (n = 6). Participants stress concern for their children in terms of their ability to meet their needs whenever possible, even if they face certain setbacks [I1-"I have always tried to give them the best, even in that life of slavery "; I3 -"Do everything possible for them and never miss them out on anything"; I8 -"To worry about the welfare of the child, try to suppress the needs of the child, not only emotional but material". This principle is associated with another, reported by several mothers, which is to *put the interests of their children above their own* (n = 8). Several participants report having gone through critical moments in their lives, yet have always tried not to overlook their priority, i.e., positively fulfilling all of their children's needs [I8- "He [child] is to me first. I often put my things aside to see what he needs, to meet his needs "; I12 - "I give up anything so that on that date I can be there, the sacrifices I make daily, the things I endure daily for her"].

Another important aspect is *affectivity* (n = 6). Mothers point out that cuddling their children, protecting them, and showing their love for them, whether by a more verbal or physical pathway, is crucial for these children to feel happy throughout their growth. [I4 –"Loving, protecting caring, treating as if we care of a part of ourselves, of our body "; I5 –"to be a mother to me is to be sweet to the children, to cherish them when they should be cherished"; I7 -"Love them, cherish them and protect them to the fullest"; I13 – "I am a loving and protective mother... I gained from her a love that has no explanation"].

Being a good mother also means *to educate the child* (n = 7). These mothers describe as essential the need to put limits on their child's behavior, i.e., to educate while transmitting social norms, in order to facilitate their social integration [I1- "Trying to explain both right and wrong... when it was needed to call attention to "; I5 - "Get attention when they should be called attention"; I9 - "I think a good mother, to be a good mother, has to be a little tough sometimes, imposing limits, not letting them do everything they want because then it ends up hurting them"].

At the same time, another fundamental criterion is to allow the *child's autonomy* (n = 2) so that children are independent as adults, which is one of the aspects [I8- "Try to encourage and teach them the best defenses to allow them to face the challenges of the world"; I14 - "I was able to give my daughter good values"].

As for the *meanings of being a 'good mother'* overall this is positive, although it can be improved. [I3 -" I think I am a mother who should perhaps be spending more time with my children; I should not stay with them so long at home "; I3 "There are things that I should do more work on in my relationship with them... many people tell me that I don't have much patience, that I should have more patience for my children"; I9 - "A good mother for me must impose limits, but I am a little weak in imposing limits on my children, I needed to be a bit tougher sometimes"].

Finally, the participants express feelings of *personal fulfillment* in the exercise of parenting [I1 – "It is a great joy, it has no explanation"; I5 – "I don't know, a lot of happiness, it's not easy to explain"; I9 – "I am very happy to have my little children, it feels very good, it is a good tiredness; I14 – "I was very happy in that role, I felt complete"; I15 – "It's not easy to explain, but it's a very good thing. Something that brings a lot of happiness"].

In the category E "Impact of violence in motherhood" there is a variability of experience that we coded into three simple subcategories: (E1) *positive impact*, (E2) *negative impact* and (E3) *absence of impact* (c.f. Table 2). The positive impact refers to changes caused by the experience of victimization that have positively reinforced other areas of the victim's life, namely in the exercise of her role as mother. Thus, despite the abusive situation in their homes, these participants report acting opposite to their lived experience, educating their children to non-violence (n = 2), seeing violence as something negative and condemnable, acting in order that their children do not become aggressors or victims [I4 - "The negative things that I went through also helped my children to look at my compromises and realize that no woman should give in to what I gave into and realize that many things must not happen. I am almost absolutely certain that they will never do to a woman what her mother has gone through "; I7 - "I want her [daughter] to be responsible... and if one day she goes through what I went through, she could get out of the relationship and at the same time I don't want my son to be like his father"].

Adversity also favored *emotional support in the relationship between mother and children* (n = 3), i.e., some mothers describe a closer relation between them and their children, which increased protection and security of both [I8 – "Maybe this made us closer to each other "; I4 - "In this respect, the love of my children has always been what completed me, even more in these times of vulnerability. Because I am their support, they have always been mine, no doubt "; I5 - "I think that directly affecting my relationship with my children but it did not affect. It only affected in my head. My daughter supported me, but my son not so much. But I understood, my son works with his father, he depended on him "].

Negative effects on the mother-child relationship were also reported (n = 3), caused by the abuser's manipulative behavior towards their children, intended to drive them away from the victim or to damage the mother-child relationship [I7 – "They were affected, especially my son, because the father turned him against me and today we have little connection"; I11 – "I had no patience and sometimes I was more impulsive with my son and I felt bad afterwards"].

Finally, some participants (n = 2) perceive a lack of impact, i.e., they consider that, despite all the violence they experienced, they did not change their behaviors and / or how they relate with their children [I3 – "I don't think it was affected. I always had little patience, I don't think it was because I went through this situation with my former partner that I changed"; I6 - "I was always the same with my daughter, I was always the same"; I14 - "Our relationship has always been solid, good, I always managed to make our relationship good, after all"].

DISCUSSION

Participants' perceptions of parenting focus on satisfying their children's needs and placing their interests above their own, even if they face certain setbacks. That is, the empathic capacity of mothers is seen as fundamental to their parenting practices. Empathy allows one to look at one's own emotional state to perceive others' and to organize oneself according to that perception, and is therefore fundamental to meet the child's needs, providing him/her with security and affection (Barudy & Dantagan, 2010; Siegel, 2013).

As stated by Lapierre (2010), sometimes, even in the face of adverse life circumstances, it is possible to sustain a positive approach, oriented to the well-being of children, even as a way to compensate them for the unfavorable environment in which they may live. From the participants' perspective, the care and well-being of their children are central elements of what constitutes the exercise of parenting in a given sociocultural context (Sarti, 2002). The wellbeing within the family should, according to the participants, be complemented with education and promotion of the child's autonomy, so that the child acquires principles and convictions in their personal development. Thus, as demonstrated in the studies by Baumrind (1971), one recognizes in these results a type of parenting that the author called "authoritative", which is characterized by the existence of educational practices by parents, sometimes controlling and sometimes supporting, that encourage the autonomy of their children. Even framed by a context of victimization, these mothers consider it possible that parenting and the attention and availability for their children should be accommodated (Montandon, 2005).

Regarding self-perception as mothers, the dominant expressions are satisfaction and contentment, although some participants consider that they should change and/or improve certain parenting behaviors in order to establish a stable and appropriate relationship with their children (Levendosky & Graham-Bermann, 2001; Sani, 2008).

The results also revealed that the participants recognize that the experience of victimization favored a closer approach and protection of their children, as well as greater emotional support. As supported by some studies (e.g., Levendosky et al., 2000; Van Horn & Lieberman, 2002) one of the effects that can result from this victimization experience is a positive attitude in other areas, e.g., the need for improved affection and emotional availability for children, as well as resourcefulness in defending their children against violence. As noted in this study, certain values become reinforced such as inculcating non-violence and promoting autonomy and equality in relationships. However, there were also participants who reported having less affection, greater withdrawal and lack of emotional in their relationship with their children as a result of the violence they suffered. The literature reveals that one of the effects of victimization is the possibility of more inconsistent parenting due to abuse (Hester, Pearson, & Harwin, 2002; Jaffe, Crooks, & Bala, 2006).

Finally, there were also participants who reported no significant changes in their relationship with their children (Levendosky et al., 2000), which suggests the response of victims to domestic violence is variable and that there is not a uniform knock-on affect on their parenting.

In summary, we find perceptions of mothers that refer to two fundamental constituents of parental behavior: parenting capacity and parenting skills (Pereira & Alarcão, 2014). Parenting capacity relates to the resources (psychic, contextual and relational) that these mothers have available and are able to use in their maternal role. Of these, the empathic capacity of mentalization (perceiving the needs of their children and understanding them as their own priorities) and the sense of self-efficacy stands out. Faced with a relational context marked by violence and which very often negatively affects conditions such as financial, housing and access to services, these psychological characteristics of mothers are essential resources that allow for the development and practice of appropriate parenting skills, namely (as mentioned by the participants) protection, emotional support, expression of affection, satisfaction of basic needs and the establishment of boundaries.

CONCLUSION

The literature has shown that domestic violence has an effect on the practice of parenting, which, in the concrete case of the victim, can translate into a very variable subjective experience. Understanding how the victimization experience can affect the parenting of the victim, in terms of cognitive and emotional factors, can be accessed from their narratives.

This qualitative study of mothers who are victims of domestic violence made it possible to draw out the dominant conceptions of their "parenting" in comparison to that of a 'good mother'; the notion of 'good mother' is based on concepts such as protection, affection, education and autonomy. According to the victims, the adjusted exercise in the parental role is to be able to choose such aspects as basic criteria for the care of children. This task can become harder depending on the needs of the children, e.g., in the case of their protection. The results reveal that this conception of parenting does not differ from that in families in a non-violent context. However, in a context of adversity it is possible that the exercise of parenting may change, as violence may or may not have an impact on family functioning, and consequently on parenting practices, communication and relationships between family members. There is no uniform and predictable negative impact, but there is a recognition that positive parenting becomes more difficult to exercise when there is adversity; the control, coercion, physical and psychological aggression experienced in the context of intimate relationships exert a negative force, that is not always easy to counteract. However, the study reinforces the possibility of redirecting and reinforcing

Maternal Parenting of Victims of Domestic Violence 173

key areas of the subjects' experience, specifically in relation to parenting, the reinforcement of their self-efficacy and their empathic capacity.

Further support for these conclusions will require more studies with different types of samples (number of participants, gender, cultural and other characteristics). In the case of this group of mothers, we see how some of them channel many of their efforts into what they value and to their own children. Victims of violence devise strategies, strengthen bonds and establish ways to ensure their safety and that of their children, thereby demonstrating that positive (re)building can take place despite the experience of victimization. Although not generalizable, we hope that this study makes a modest contribution to understanding the effects of domestic violence on the victim's parenting and thus to the development of more effective parenting interventions in support of victims of domestic violence.

REFERENCES

Associação Portuguesa de Apoio à Vítima – APAV. (2019). *Relatório de estatísticas da APAV 2016* [*APAV Statistics Report 2016*]. https://apav.pt/apav_v3/images/pdf/Estatisticas_APAV_Relatorio_Anual_201 8.pdf

Bardin, L. (2009). *Análise de conteúdo* [*Content analysis*] (Reimpressão da Edição revista e actualizada). Lisboa: Edições 70.

Barudy, J., & Dantagnan, M. (2010). *Los desafíos invisibles de ser madre o padre: manual de evaluación de las competencias y la resilencia parental* [*The invisible challenges of being a mother or father: manual of evaluation of competencies and parental resilience*]. Barcelona: Gedisa.

Cecconello, A., De Antoni, C., & Koller, S. (2003). Práticas educativas, estilos parentais e abuso físico no contexto familiar [Educational practices, parenting styles and physical abuse in the family context]. *Psicologia em Estudo, 8,* 45-54. https://doi.org/10.1590/S1413-73722003000300007

Fontanella, B. J., Ricas, J., & Turato, E. R. (2008). Amostragem por saturação em pesquisas qualitativas em saúde: contribuições teóricas [Saturation sampling in qualitative health research: theoretical contributions]. *Cadernos de Saúde Pública, 24*(1), 17-27. https://doi.org/10.1590/S0102-311X2008000100003

Guggisberg, M., & Henricksen, J. (2018). *Violence against women: Global perspectives, challenges and issues of 21st century.* New York: Nova Science Publishers, Inc..

Hester, M., Pearson, C., & Harwin, N. (2002). *Making an Impact: Children and Domestic Violence: A reade.* (3rd ed.). London: Jessica Kingsley Publishers.

Jaffe, P. G., & Juodis, M. (2006). Children as victims and witnesses of domestic homicide: Lessons learned from domestic violence death review committees. *Juvenile and Family Court Journal,* 13–28. https://doi.org/
10.1111/j.1755-6988.2006.tb00125.x.

Lapierre, S. (2010). *Striving to be 'good' mothers: Abused women's experiences of mothering.* Canada: School of Social Work, University of Ottawa. https://doi.org/10.1002/car.1113.

Levendosky, A., A., & Graham-Bermann, S. (2001). A parenting in battered women: The effects of domestic violence on women and their children. *Journal of Family Violence, 16,* 171-172. https://doi.org/
10.1023/A:1011111003373.

Levendosky, A. A., Huth-Bocks, A. C., Shapiro D. L., & Semel, M. A. (2003). The impact of domestic violence on the maternal–child relationship and preschool-age children's functioning. *Journal of Family Psychology, 17,* 275–287. https://doi.org/10.1037/0893-3200.17.3.275.

Levendosky, A. A., Lynch, S. M., & Graham-Berman, S. A. (2000). Mothers' perceptions of the impact of woman abuse on their parenting. *Violence Against Women, 6,* 247-271. https://doi.org/10.1177/10778010022181831.

Maternal Parenting of Victims of Domestic Violence 175

McCloskey, L. A., Figueredo, A. J., & Koss, M. P. (1995). The effects of systemic family violence on children's mental health. *Child Development, 66*, 1239-1261. https://doi.org/10.2307/1131645.

Montandon, C. (2005). As práticas educativas parentais e a experiência das crianças [Parenting practices and children's experience]. *Educ. Soc, 26*(91), 485-507. https://doi.org/10.1590/S0101-73302005000200010.

Pereira, D. (2018). Parenting and/or mental health? In J. G. Pereira, J. Gonçalves, & V. Bizzari (Eds). *The Neurobiology-psychotherapy-pharmacology intervention triangle: The need for common sense in 21st century mental health* (pp. 235-250). Delaware: Vernon Press.

Pereira, D. (2019). Parentalidade [Parenting]. In L. Nunes, C. Fonte, S. P. Alves, A. Sani, R. Estrada, & S. Caridade (Coords), *Comportamento e Saúde Mental: Dicionário Enciclopédico [Behavior and Mental Health: Encyclopedic Dictionary]* (pp. 57-59). Lisboa: Pactor.

Pereira, D., & Alarcão, M. (2014). Guia de Avaliação das Capacidades Parentais: estudo exploratório da fiabilidade em profissionais da proteção à infância [Parental Capabilities Assessment Guide: an exploratory study of reliability in child protection professionals]. In M. M. Calheiros, & M. V. Garrido (Eds.), *Crianças em Risco e Perigo [Children at Risk and Danger]* (Vol. 4, pp. 171-193.). Lisboa: Ed. Sílabo.

Platt, D. (2012). Understanding parental engagement with child welfare services: an integrated model. *Child & Family Social Work, 17*(2), 138-148. https://doi.org/10.1111/j.1365-2206.2012.00828.x.

Sani, A. I. (2008). Mulher e mãe no contexto de violência doméstica: A experiência de parentalidade [Woman and mother in the context of domestic violence: The experience of parenting]. *Ex-aequo – Revista da Associação Portuguesa de Estudos sobre as mulheres, 18*, 123-133.

Sani, A. I., & Cunha, D. (2011). As práticas educativas parentais em mulheres vítimas e não vítimas de violência conjugal [Parenting practices in women victims and not victims of conjugal violence]. *Psicologia: Teoria e Pesquisa, 27*, 429-437. https://doi.org/10.1590/S0102-37722011000400006.

Sani, A. I., Domingues, H., & Soeiro, C. (2016). Domestic violence in gay, lesbian and bisexual couples. In M. Ortiz (Ed.), *Domestic Violence: Prevalence, Risk Factors and Perspectives* (pp. 95-110). New York: Nova Science Publishers, Inc..

Sani, A. I., & Lopes, A. I. (2018). Police intervention in cases of violence against women and their exposed children. In M. Guggisberg & Henricksen (Eds.), *Violence against women: Global perspectives, challenges and issues of 21st century* (pp. 211-235). New York: Nova Science Publishers, Inc..

Sani, A. I., & Lopes, A. I. (2019). Children's multiple violence exposure: risk assessment, impacts and intervention. In S. Aideen Xu (Ed.), *Violence Exposure: Perspectives, Gender Differences and Outcomes* (pp. 79-99). New York: Nova Science Publishers, Inc..

Sani, A. I., Osório, L., Dinis, A., & Soeiro, C., & 2019). Same sex intimate partner violence: prevalence and characteristics. In S. Aideen Xu (Ed.), *Violence Exposure: Perspectives, Gender Differences and Outcomes* (pp. 19-54). New York: Nova Science Publishers, Inc..

Sani, A. I., Pereira, D., & Dinis, A. (in press). Parenting practices and in the context of domestic violence: the experience of victims. In N. Roman (Eds.), *A Closer Look at Parenting Practices and Styles*. New York: Nova Science Publishers, Inc.

Sarti, C. (2002). *Família e individualidade: um problema moderno. A família Contemporânea em Debate*. São Paulo: EDUC/Cortez.

Siegel, D. J., & Hartzell, M. (2013). *Parenting from the inside out: How a deeper self-understanding can help you raise children who thrive*. New York: Penguin.

Sistema de Segurança Interna (SSI). (2019). *Relatório Anual de Segurança Interna (RASI) 2018*. Gabinete do Secretário-Geral. Retrieved from: https://www.portugal.gov.pt/download-ficheiros/ficheiro.aspx?v=ad5cfe37-0d52-412e-83fb-7f098448dba7.

Walker, L. (2017). *The battered woman syndrome* (4rd ed.). New York: Springer Pub. Co. https://doi.org/10.1891/9780826170996.

Zemp, M., Bodenmann, G., & Cummings, E. M. (2016). The significance of interparental conflict for children: Rationale for couple-focused programs in family therapy *European Psychologist, 21*(2), 99–108. https://doi.org/10.1027/1016-9040/a000245.

In: Victims of Violence
Editor: Mathias L. Knudsen

ISBN: 978-1-53617-140-2
© 2020 Nova Science Publishers, Inc.

Chapter 9

INDONESIAN WOMEN 'BREAKING THE SILENCE' OF DOMESTIC VIOLENCE THROUGH THE DOMESTIC VIOLENCE ACT 2004: BETWEEN THE LAW 'ON THE BOOKS' AND THE LAW 'ON THE GROUND'

Rika Saraswati[*], PhD
School of Law, Faculty of Law and Communication,
Soegijapranata Catholic University, Semarang, Indonesia

ABSTRACT

'Breaking the silence' is necessarily part of women being able to obtain their rights and resolve issues of violence in their lives. The Indonesian government's passage of the Domestic Violence Act in 2004 increased people's awareness of the issue of domestic violence (including women's awareness of domestic violence). The presence of such legislation correlates with the State's serious intention to deal with this

---

[*] Corresponding Author's E-mail: rikasaraswati@unika.ac.id; rikasaras@yahoo.com.

matter; nevertheless, the law 'on the books' (i.e., present in theory) and the law 'on the ground' (i.e., present in fact) differ markedly. This paper will explore the extent to which domestic violence is regulated and the extent to which such regulation is implemented. While the law aims to protect women (and children), in reality the ability of the women victims to assert their rights vary for each woman. This is largely attributable to the varied understandings of the legal officers encountered and their consequent responses.

Keywords: Indonesian women, domestic violence, the law 'on the books,' the law 'on the ground'

INTRODUCTION

Encouraging women experiencing domestic violence to 'break the silence' and supporting them in this action is a necessary part of women being able to obtain their rights and resolve issues of violence in their lives. The experiences of Indonesian women victims of domestic violence have shown that they have often had opportunity to access many resources when they started 'breaking the silence' and reaching out to others (individuals and agencies) in regard to the violence they were suffering (generally at the hands of their husbands), although it must be acknowledged that not all resources were helpful and useful in individual cases (Saraswati 2014, 355-542, also Saraswati 2013, 1-20) However, breaking the silence and disclosing violence within a family is a course not easily undertaken because of values that have been culturally embedded which emphasize the necessity of maintaining family harmony, and as a role often largely assigned to women. Disclosing domestic violence also has consequences for women victims who are affected psychologically, financially, and even physically.

Domestic violence has been an important issue generally among feminists since the 1970s (Radford, Harne and Friedberg 1996, 5), and became an increasing concern of the Indonesian women's movement in the 1990s (Blackburn 2004). The rising number of domestic violence cases was one reason for Indonesian feminists demanding special legislation to protect women victims of domestic violence (Saraswati 2006, 2-3). Responding to

Indonesian Women 'Breaking the Silence' of Domestic Violence ... 181

such demand, the Indonesian government has developed the structure of the legal system and issued relevant legislation. Great difficulties remain on the theoretical and practical levels due to the complexities of domestic violence, for instance in relation to the distinction between 'private' and 'public' law regarding domestic violence and the fragmented system dealing with domestic/family violence (Saraswati 2006, 2-3). Moreover, the long-held tradition of a man's right to discipline his wife has had an impact on society, regarding it as a behaviour that has been widely accepted as part of marital relationships. Also relevant are the cultural expectations for women as wives and mothers, with their primary role seen as to maintain the harmony of family and the husband's/family's name. Hence it is a 'taboo' for a wife to disclose a family's or husband's affairs in public. These expectations have trapped women in situations of domestic violence.

In 2004, the Indonesian government issued Act No 23 of 2004 on the Elimination of Domestic Violence (*Undang-Undang Pengahapusan Kekerasan dalam Rumah Tangga Nomor 34 Tahun 2014* hereinafter 'Domestic Violence Act). The Domestic Violence Act was issued after a seven years long struggle conducted by Indonesian women's movement activists (Saraswati 2013). Its aim was primarily to eliminate all forms of domestic violence, protect the victims of domestic violence, take action against the perpetrators of domestic violence and preserve the unity of harmonious and their prosperity (Elucidation of the Domestic Violence Act 2004, 1; Domestic Violence Act, art 4). The Domestic Violence Act defines such violence very broadly to include any physical, psychological or sexual abuse (including the threat of committing such abuse), as well as economic neglect evidenced by failure to provide for the household or prohibiting women from engaging in paid work (arts 6–9). It also provides fines and imprisonment for up to 15 years (arts 45–55). The scope of a household includes husband, wife, children and domestic servants, and anyone of a blood, marital or adoptive relationship living in a single residence (art 2).

The passage of the Domestic Violence Act in 2004 was an effort to increase women's and people's awareness of domestic violence issues. Through the Act, the State is expected to prevent the occurrence of domestic violence, prosecute perpetrators of domestic violence and protect victims of domestic violence (art 2). In accordance with Elucidation of the Act, every citizen is entitled to safety and freedom from all forms of violence, including violence within the domestic sphere (art 2). The Act insists that all forms of violence within the domestic sphere are an infringement of and crime against human rights. The presence of domestic law in Indonesia correlates with the serious intent of the State to handle these matters; nevertheless, the law 'on the books' (present in theory) and the law 'on the ground' (present in fact) are two different things. This that will be discussed in this paper.

METHODS

The juridical normative approach is used in this research. Collecting data begins from the legal aspect, that is the Domestic Violence Act, and its correlation with the experience of Indonesian women evidenced in domestic violence cases. Collecting data is undertaken through documentary research on academic research/studies and publications on the topic. This research uses an analytical descriptive method in which all secondary data related to the Domestic Violence Act and the experience of women who have experienced domestic violence is analysed comprehensively and then the result are described in a detailed, systematic and comprehensive picture.

THE DOMESTIC VIOLENCE ACT AND THE RIGHTS OF WOMEN AS VICTIMS OF DOMESTIC VIOLENCE

The Domestic Violence Act 2004 defines 'domestic violence' as any conduct by a person (mainly against a woman) that causes a reasonable apprehension of misery or physical (arts 6, 44), sexual (arts 8, 45–48), psychological injury (art 7, 44), or neglect (arts 9, 49); including any threat of such conduct, compelling a person, expropriating the freedom of a person against the law within a household (art 1, also Saraswati 2013). The scope of 'household' in this Act includes: a) husband, wife, and children; b) people whose family relationship with those people (the individual referred to under a) is due to blood relationship, marriage, suckling at the same breast,[1] care, and guardianship, who lives in the household; c) the individual working to assist the household and living in the household shall be considered as family member during the period while living in the household (art 2). The scope of 'victim' is expanded to not only include family members and relatives but also house-keepers because in many cases house-keepers experience violence from their employers, meanwhile there is no regulation provided by government to protect their safety.[2]

The Domestic Violence Act is the first regulation governing the rights of the victims in detail (Saraswati 2013). The rights of the victims of domestic violence in Article 10 include: 1) protection of the family, police, prosecutors, courts, advocates, social institutions, or any other party either temporarily or based on the determination of a court protection order; 2) health services in accordance with medical needs; 3) special handling related to the victim confidentiality; 4) assistance from a social worker and legal assistance at every level of the examination process in accordance with the provisions of legislation; 5) spiritual guidance services (art 10). The police are obliged to immediately provide temporary protection to the victim (that is, within a period of 24 hours). In providing temporary protection, the police may cooperate with a health worker, social worker, companion volunteer, and/or spiritual mentor who can accompany the alleged victim. Temporary protection is to be provided to cover the period 'prior to the issuance of enactment of protection instruction from a court' (art 1.5). (The protection instruction later issued by court order is also referred to as an apprehended

---

[1] This can include a child adopted into the family who has literary been nursed by the same mother as other children (can be a cousin's child and/or no blood relative).

[2] This Act is a breakthrough for the protection of housekeepers since there is no regulations dealing with the employees who work in the domestic sphere because they are considered non-formal workers which are outside regulation by labour law. As a result, this Act only regulates the protection of housekeepers if they are abused, and does not regulate their labour rights (such as the minimum wage, number of hours worked, the type of task done and so on).

violence order. It lasts for up to 12 months and may be extended: art 32.) Various agencies are involved in order to protect the victim and ensure their rights as a victim are upheld (art 1.5). These provisions have also shown the complexity of the treatment of the victims of domestic violence which differs from other crimes.

Then, for the purpose of providing services to women victims, the central and local government provides special units in police offices, also social workers and legal aid; establishes and develops a system and mechanism of networking for the purpose of helping the victim to access such services; and, gives protection to assistants, witnesses, members of the victims' family and their friends. The Act not only gives the responsibility to government to prevent and stop domestic violence, but also involves the role of community (arts 15, 15).

The Act has also regulated the mechanism of the domestic violence order to protect the victim within 24 hours. The police have an obligation to apply for the order before the court, then, investigate the reported complaint. The victim (by her authorisation) family member or someone else can report the violence directly to police. For children exposed to domestic violence, such a report can be made by parents, guardian, or by the children themselves (art 27).

The court within in a specific period (7 days) of the application having been accepted must issue a domestic violence order. The application for the order can be requested by the victim, the victim's family, police, or assistants (social worker, legal aid counsellor, religious personnel). In certain cases, consent from the victim is not needed when the report is requested by a party other than the victim. Based on the request of the applicant, the court makes an apprehended domestic violence orders to protect people from the violence (arts 28-31).

For the purpose of protecting the victim, police are entitled to arrest the perpetrator if the police are convinced that the perpetrator has committed a breach of the apprehended domestic violence order. Any breach of an apprehended domestic violence order can be reported to the court by the victim, police and assistants; the court then investigates the perpetrator. If the court is convinced that the perpetrator has breached the order, the court obliges the perpetrator to make an undertaking that she/he will comply with the undertaking. Any breach of such an undertaking will result in detention for 30 days.

LAW 'ON THE BOOKS' AND 'LAW ON THE GROUND'

Domestic violence experienced by Indonesian women is mostly physical violence, neglect, psychological and sexual violence (Saraswati, 2014). However, the violence they experienceed was sometimes not a single type; some had experienced multiple forms and incidents of violence. Most of them had reported their cases to police. However, the police's response was not always satisfying due to reasons such as tardiness of response, police demands for reconciliation or for the provision of witnesses. Below is the Table of women's experiences in reporting their domestic violence cases to police officer/s and their response.

The research has demonstrated that a major obstacle for Indonesian women bringing a domestic violence case before the court is the police themselves, who often asked the women victim to reconcile with the perpetrator. Reasons for reconciliation supplied by included: the respondents' children (EL), often that such violence was a 'private' or 'household' affairs, in one instance even that a husband's age was too great for him to be imprisoned (GI). Reconciliation through mediation could recommended by police officer because the Elucidation of the Domestic Violence Act states that one of the aims of the passage of Act in 2004 is to preserve household unity, harmony and prosperity. This elucidation seems have led to misinterpretation and misunderstanding on the part of police officers. Reconciliation through mediation was not only implemented in instances of neglect and psychological violence, but also for those involving physical violence. The mediation process in domestic violence is criticised by feminists, due to perpetrator/victim power imbalances and the manifestation of outdated attitudes. A police officer has said that the mediation process would not be undertaken without request from one of parties, and usually the police officer will consider it if the party who

186   *Rika Saraswati*

requested is the woman.[3] The mediation phenomenon worries the Komnas Perempuan because the body has demonstrated that the state, in this case the Indonesian government, tends to prefer to support family harmony through the mediation of mediation process rather than prosecute the perpetrator (Aryani et. all, 2019).

Table 1. Report to Police and the response

Respondent	Report to Police and the Response
MI	Police officer asked her to reconcile with her husband
Y	Police officer asked her to seek witnesses to support her psychological violence report.
GE	Police officer asked her to report her case to another police station
SS	Police officer was reluctant to process her report which had been withdrawn
MR	Police officer was reluctant to process her case due to their anticipation of a pattern of 'report and cancel'
PJ	She had undertaken a *visum et repertum* (examination for doctors statement VeR) but she was reluctant to report the violence
IN	Officer accused her of falsifying marriage documents (which had actually actually been done by her husband)
GI	Police officer was reluctant to process her report because of her husband's age; other officers asked her for a sum of money to process her report about her husband.
EL	Police officer asked her to 'think deeply' (because of the presence of her children) before her husband was taken away (i.e., reconsider her complaint)
NA	Police officer advised her to seek witnesses for psychological violence and neglect. No progress after two years.

Source: Rika Saraswati, 2014.

In the mediation process, the parties make a signed statement and a seal is affixed before a police officer. If the husband violates the agreement, the husband can be reported. However, in fact, the document often fails to function effectively (Saraswati 2014, 416). Police officers usually refuse to process a report that has been submitted by women victims and mediated by police officer. Moreover, police officers can be reluctant to process cases due to their anticipation of a pattern of 'report and cancel' (e.g., MR). This

---

[3] A statement made by a police officer when she was attending a meeting conducted by *Komisi Perlindungan Korban Kekerasan Berbasis Gender dan Anak* (KPK2BGA) [Commission for the Protection of Gender and Child-Based Violence Victims] in Semarang, 2 May 2019.

phenomenon has created a poor image for women domestic violence victims and reduce police cooperation and support; it also reveals the police's lack of awareness of the characteristics of domestic violence cases which differ from those of other crimes due to the very circumstances (familial and societal) in which the violence occurs.

Police officer sometimes based their decisions on their own opinions/biases and refused to process women victims and also cited non-legal factors, such as the perpetrators' age, and/orthe presence of children. Police officers sometimes seemed to make an automatic response, sometimes an expression of their view of what they (the police) think should be the correct outcome for the victim's situation or an outcome that they believed was 'best' for that situation (Saraswati 2014, 416). They failed to consider the safety of women victims (and their children), despite the Domestic Violence Act having provided the option of an apprehended domestic violence order.

Articles 16 the Domestic Violence Act states that within 24 hours of receiving a report of domestic violence from the victim, the duty of police apparatus is to provide a place for temporary protection for victims of domestic violence for up to 7 days. Temporary protection is a protection is provided directly by the police and/or social institutions or other parties, prior to the issuance of a protection order from the court. However, the role of the police in providing temporary protection often occur too slowly and less frequently than desired (Glorianto 2019, 5). A study found that of 132 cases recorded in the Semarang Police Resort in 2014-2018, no more than 20 cases resulted in protection orders. One police officer stated that:

> Not all cases of domestic violence that come in get temporary protection because the weight of the case that comes in is certainly different. There are cases of domestic violence that are very urgent and require protection orders, but in some cases the victim also comes when offered to be given protection, but the victim refuses so the temporary protection process is not given to all victims (Glorianto 2019, 30).

However, according to the Legal Aid-Association Indonesian Women for Justice (LBH APIK) a non-government organisation that is concern with violence against women, police officer are less effective than desired in their handling domestic violence cases, and there seems to be a difference in the handling of cases where an NGO is involved compared to where a victim unassisted seeks redress. When police receive complaints through LBH-APIK the police then follow up that report; however, in generally, if the victims report the violence without LBH-APIK assistance, the police do not respond quickly and do not provide the victim access to shelter. Police must act immediately in response to a victim's report by issuing a letter of investigation and a letter of removal for the victim so that she is able to find shelter and be kept more secure, and help the victim to reduce or eliminate the possibility of continued trauma (Glorianto 2019, 5).

In the research conducted by the author, some women victims did not want to report their husband to police. Reason for that varied. One was fear that their husband would seek revenge for a report having been made. In some cases, women who reported domestic violence cases (in the cases detailed in the author's research, see Table 1, above) have been victimised, or even criminalised by complaints subsequently lodged by their husband. The experience of IN (Table 1 above) demonstrated such a phenomenon and occured because of the power imbalance between a husband and a wife. The power imbalance was caused by various factors, such as: unequal financial sources, different social status, culture, and educational background. Data reported by the National Commission on Violence against Women has revealed phenomenon where many women domestic violence victims had been subsequently reported by their husbands and accused of neglect or defamation. As a result some women victims then become defendant. The National Commission on Violence against Women defines the criminalisation of women victims as an accusation of criminal offence or counter-action or unlawful acts by a party and or by people who have a chain of interest relations against a woman or group of women who are in the process of accessing their rights or the rights of others (in a series of legal facts) (see Aryani et al. 2019, 65). In such instances, a victim's use of the provisins of the Domestic Violence Act has put her in difficult situation (Aryani et al. 2019, 49).

Sexual violence is rarely reported by victims due to their feeling of shame (Saraswati, 2019). However, according to The National Commission on Violence against Women, the number cases involving sexual violence against women and girls in the domestic sphere has rise in 2018 and 2019 (Aryani et al. 2017, 15-17; also Aryani et al. 2019, 3) from 175 to 192 cases; these cases including marital rape and incest. The increasing number of reports have reflected the victims growing awareness that coercion in marital sexual relations in a marriage is rape that can be followed up in the legal process. The incest cases numbered 1,017 in 2018, with 425 perpetrators the biological father, and the remainder stepfathers, uncles, or others who had blood relationship with the victim. The courage to report incest and marital rape to service institutions shows a step forward for women and girls who in the past have tended to keep hidden these harmful acts that happened "behind closed doors" and thereby foster the impunity of perpetrators among family members (aryani et al. 2019, 50).

The Domestic Violence Act still has weaknesses in regard to its protection of women victims of neglect and psychological violence. Gender bias often plays a role. The experience of demonstrated this phenomenon. Women victims of neglect who did not have any job or income are more protected than women victims of neglect who have job or income. Without income a husband's neglect will put her in financial difficulties, and this situation can be understood well by legal apparatus; however, if a woman who has a job or income claimed that she was a victim of neglect, the legal apparatus will have difficulties as a woman may experience diffilcuty in providing the evidence to prove that she experiences financial difficulties because such a woman still has money (from their own efforts as employed or self employed) to fulfil their daily need even though in limited amount of money, but she has striven to fill the gap that her neglectful husband has created for the family. A police officer and the Attorney General Department's officer have demanded (in just such a case) that 'strong' evidence must be provided to convince judges that neglect has made the victim a poor woman – it means that she must give convincing proof that she was in financial difficulties, for example lacking money, lacking daily food and being in very poor circumstances (Saraswati 2016). This demand creates a feeling of frustration for women victims because the elements of Article 9[4] on neglect has fulfilled; however, in fact, providing the evidence that must be provided in order to convince judges is not as simple as the Act states.

Similar difficulties arise in the provision and use of evidence in the event of psychological violence. Police officers argue that processing neglect and psychological violence was not easy because of the lack of witnesses and evidence. Women victims of psychological violence were often asked to look for witnesses. However, looking for witnesses is the duty of police as the legal apparatus. (Saraswati 2014). The role of community in reducing violence is also important. However, many community members are unwilling to be witnesses because of fear of being threatened by perpetrators, fear of interfering in other people's household affairs, or for reasons related to the position, status, wealth of the perpetrator and victim but also fear for the safety of the victim if a complaint is supported (Setiamandani and Suprojo 2018). The willingness of people to become witnesses is very necessary to the needs of the victims in seeking justice either through legal and non-legal channels. The presure to prevent the occurrence or reoccurrence of domestic violence can often come from people close to the victim. Therefore, it is necessary to increase understanding of domestic violence and also of the proper relationship of household members which is a bond of commitment by both parties to form a family of mutual respect in order to avoid violence.

In order to overcome this difficulty in providing evidence for psychological violence, the Indonesian government issued the Government Regulation No. 4 of 2006 on Organization and Cooperation Recovery Victims of Violence in a Household. Article 8 (5) of the Government Regulation states that for the purposes of investigation, the competent health

---

[4] The elements of neglect are satisfied when a husband fails to meet the demands of the legislation, which states that '…according to law and agreements, the [male] person has an obligation to provide basic necessities or to look after family members'. The law mentioned in this Act is the Marriage Act 1974 (*Undang-Undang Perkawinan* 1974) which states that a husband has an obligation to give his wife a living allowance; infringement of this obligation gives the affected party the right to sue (in a civil proceeding) and/or have the negligent party prosecuted (in a criminal proceeding).

personnel must prepare a *visum et repertum* and/or *visum et repertum psychiatricum* or provide a medical certificate. Based on this regulation, the police officer can use the *visum et repertum psychiatricum* as evidence of psychological violence. However, problem remain for any women victim who does not want to undergo the visum because of psychological reasons. As a result, a police officer may be late in receiving result. If the victim has undergone the test it can be used to support the victim's claims. It can provide evidence of the duration of the violence that has occurred. However, even if a visum has been undertaken, the visum is not always useable in court because the distress or psychological trauma cannot be proven as the women victims may have subsequently been healed from the trauma. Nevertheless, revisiting the relationship through an attempt at reconciliation (as often advised by police) could surely cause a relapse. A study has found that legal apparatus argued that the *visum et repertum psychiatricum* is not regulated by the Code of Criminal Procedure, so that legal apparatus tends to ignore this visum when it is provided (Setiawan, Muhadar and Heryani 2018).

This situation becomes worse due to different understandings among police officers about evidence in domestic violence. Article 55 the Domestic Violence Act states that the testimony of a victim witness is sufficient to prove that the perpetrator/accused is guilty if accompanied by one other piece of evidence. This legislation is clearly stated that only one additional piece of evidence is needed to support the testimony given by the victims. Therefore, legal apparatus should not hesitate in processing domestic violence. However, representative of the legal apparatus often argue that one witness and one other evidence is not enough (Setiawan, Muhadar and Heryani 2018, 6). This police attitude becomes an obstacle for women victims in their access justice and has led them to bring their case to the family court to apply for divorce as a solution to their difficulties. However, going to the family court does not provide the perpetrator any punishment and instead acts as a form of impunity for him. Domestic cases remain high, and high compared to other forma of violence against women. In data reported by the National Commission on Violence against Women, there were 5167 and 5114 domestic violence cases in 2018 and 2019 respectively. These numbers remain the highest number when compared to dating violence and violence against women in the public domain (see Aryani et al. 2017, 12–18; also Aryani et al. 2019, 15).

Based on the above, there have been some encouraging outcomes of the passages of the Domestic Violence Act, for example, the increased willingness of victims to seek justice (as evidenced by the increased number of reports of domestic violence) (Aryani et al. 2017, 4–10; Aryani et al. 2019, 13) and the number of institutions established by women's organisations or local government which provide services and support for victims has grown rapidly throughout Indonesia.[5] However, cultural and legal obstacles to the enforcement of the new law remain. Cultural obstacles are derived not only from women victims but also from the legal apparatus; women are reluctant to disclose their cases due to feelings of shame, guilt over the violence that has occurred, fear of blame from family and the local community, and hesitation regarding initiating a complaint or proceeding with a case out of consideration for the family unit. In some cases, the legal apparatus has also the same perspective and sought to encourage the victims to reconcile with the perpetrators when the violence is 'lenient' according to the legal apparatus' view, especially for psychological violence — such a reason is strengthen by the difficulties to provide the evidence (Setiamandani and Suprojo 2018, 38). The aim of the Domestic Violence Act to protect victims has been ignored since the implementation of a protection order is not always undertaken seriously. This is caused by several factors, such as: lack of understanding of the procedure on the part of legal apparatus and the victims; no shelter being provided by local government or, if the shelter is available, it belongs to private persons or members of a non-government organisation; the lack of networking between the legal apparatus and the communityalso affects implementation. This situation will affect the safety of women victims; women victims are often unprotected and must run here and there, hiding in order to avoid the perpetrators of domestic violence (Khusnaeny et al. 2017, 46–47).

---

[5] These institutions include women crisis centres, hospitals, units for services for women and children in police stations, and attorneys' offices. The institutions usually provided eight types of services and supports, namely: hotlines, counselling, support groups, legal aid, shelter, psychological therapy, medical services and economic support.

Temporary protection provisions can include safe shelter other than the person's home and this may be essential for the victim's immediate safety until formal more lasting orders can be made when the complainant appears before the court. Protection orders can involve either the provision of safe shelter other than the domestic home for victims as well an order that the perpetrator cannot come within a certain distance of the victim.

JUDGES' DECISION ON DOMESTIC VIOLENCE CASES

A study on court decisions in domestic violence cases has demonstrated that the implementation of the Act in providing punishment for perpetrator may be more lenient than the legislation was intended to be intended to be (Ramadhan et al. 2018, 21–23). Judges imposed lenient penalties on the perpetrator based on reasons such as an incident being a 'family matter' and the perpetrator the breadwinner, so the judge considers that if the penalties were to be fully applied, this would remove the breadwinner from the family for a longer period, resulting in his family members suffering all the more due to a lack of family income. Such a decision, however, places the family at risk of further physical, sexual and/or psychological harm.

In order to improve judges' performance in cases that involving women, including domestic violence cases, the Indonesian government issued *Peraturan Mahkamah Agung* (Supreme Court Regulation) No. 3 of 2017 on Guidelines for the Prosecution of Women before the Law. This regulation was made on the basis of the Convention on the Elimination of All Forms of Discrimination Against Women (CEDAW) and the aim of the issuing of this regulation was provide a guidelines for judges so that they might adopt a correct gender perspective and apply gender equality and the principles of non-discrimination in court hearings when dealing with cases in which women are involved. In addition, the Supreme Court hopes that through this regulation as well as affirming the court processes, discriminatory practices based on sex and gender stereotypes in the court can be gradually reduced. Hence Supreme Court Regulation No. 3 of 2017 is intended to be a provision in favour of women's rights in court processes(Indonesian Supreme Court

194   *Rika Saraswati*

Women's and Children's Working Group and the Indonesian Judicial Monitoring Society 2018, 2, 10).

Table 2. Verdicts on Domestic Violence Cases

Criminal Act	Number of Free Verdicts	Number of Criminal Sentences)	Average Prison Length (Years)	Minmum prison length (Years)	Maximum Prison Length (Years)
Physical Violence					
Caused injury/pain	-	33	1.0	.1	13
Result in serious injuries	-	7	1.5	.2	4.0
result in death	-	5	8.8	6.0	13.0
Psychological Violence					
Result in fear or psychological pain	-	6	.6	1	2.0
Neglect					
Limit or prohibit	-	9	.5	.2	.8
Not giving a living	1	9	.5	.2	1.5
Resulting in economic dependence	-	5	.5	.3	.7

Source: Ramadhan et al. 2018, 21-23.

According to Rahadianti, Supreme Court Regulation No. 3 of 2017 is ambiguous because on the one hand it upholds the principle of equal treatment which means that women are considered empowered so that it is equal to men (arts 5–8),[6] however, on the other hand women are considered

---

[6] Art 5: In examining women in relation to the law, judges may not: a. Display attitudes or issue statements that demean, blame and/or intimidate women in dealing with the law; justify discrimination against women by using culture, customary rules and other traditional practices as well as using expert interpretations that are gender biased; c. question and/or consider the experience or background sexuality of the victim as a basis for releasing the offender or alleviating the punishment of the offender; and d issue statements or views that are gender stereotyped. Art 6: Judges in adjudicating cases of women dealing with law: a. Considering gender equality and gender stereotypes in statutory regulations and unwritten laws; b. Interpreting legislation and/or unwritten laws that can guarantee Gender Equality; c. Explores the legal values, local wisdom and sense of justice that lives in the community to ensure Gender Equality, equal protection and non-discrimination; d. Consider the application of international conventions and treaties related to ratified gender equality. Art 7: During the hearing, the judge shall prevent and/or reprimand the parties, legal advisors, public prosecutors and/or attorneys who behave or make statements that demean, blame, intimidate and/or use the experience or background sexuality of women dealing with the law. Art 8(1)

powerless because the Perma provides affirmative action for women (art 4[7]). The explanation is as follows: it appears that Article 5 to 8 essentially dictates that judges meet the principle of gender equality, namely equalizing the position of women and men in law and in the court (the principle of equality before the law). However, Article 4 of Supreme Court Regulation No. 3 of 2017 wants to uphold the principle of equality, non-discrimination, and neutrality of the court by assuming women are weak and unequal creatures to men; therefore the Article provides affirmative action in the form of special treatment for women who are dealing with the law by ordering judges to pay attention to the special conditions affecting women, namely inequality in social status between litigants, inequality in legal protection, discrimination, the psychological impact on victims, physical and psychological powerlessness of victims, power relations that result in witnesses/ victims being powerless, and a history of violence by perpetrators against witnesses /victims. Moreover, this regulation is also considered to be able to cause confusion for judges because under the Code of Ethics and the Code of Conduct of Judges (KEPPH) and Article 4 (1) of Judicial Power Act No. 48 of 2009 judges are prohibited from taking aside the parties that have cases with them; they must be fair and consider matters and act "without discriminating against persons."

In addition to fines and the possibility of a range of terms of imprisonment, the Domestic Violence Act provides additional penalties for perpetrators. Article 50 of the Domestic Violence Act states that:

Judges should ask women as victims about losses, the impact of cases and the need for recovery; (2) The judge must notify the victim of their right to merge cases in accordance with Article 98 of the Criminal Procedure Code and/or the usual lawsuit or application for restitution as stipulated in the provisions of the legislation; (3) In the case of recovery of victims or injured parties, the judge shall: a. Consistent with human rights principles and standards b. Free from the view of gender stereotypes; c. Consider the situation and interests of victims from disproportionate loss due to gender inequality.

[7] Article 4: In hearing a case, the judge should consider gender equality and non-discrimination, by identifying the facts of the trial: a. Inequality of social status between parties who litigate; b. Inequality in legal protection that impacts access to justice; c. Discrimination d. Psychic impact experienced by the victim; e. Physical and psychological powerlessness of victims; f. Power relations which results in the victim/witness being helpless; and g. History of violence from the perpetrator towards the victim/witness.

> *In addition to the crimes referred to in this chapter, the Judge may impose additional crimes in the form of: a. limiting the movement of the perpetrators both aimed at keeping the offender from the victim within a certain distance and time, as well as limiting certain rights of the offender; b. the determination of the perpetrators follows a counselling program under the supervision of a particular institution.*

So far, such protection orders mandated by the Domestic Violence Act have never been fully implemented. Use of (a) movement restrictions on perpetrators designed to protect victims and (b) counselling programs for perpetrators do not appear to have eventuated. Indonesian Judge have hardly ever (if at all) issued a protection order the purpose of which is to limit the movement of the perpetrators (in relation to the victim's location, whether home or place of work or schooling, relatives and so on) so that the victim is protected and safe (likewise the dependents or other family or household members). Without such a protection order, perpetrators of domestic violence can encounter or actively seek out the victim/s at any time and perpetrate violence again at any time.

This type of protection order represents a very different approach to the "agreement" or mediation that is often pursued by the police in an effort to cope with instances of domestic violence that have been reported. This approach intends to 'reconcile' the two parties. These peace measures taken and agreements made demonstrate that many within the legal apparatus still holds the concept that domestic violence is essentially a "private" problem between a husband and wife — not a matter where a public court case should be held where both parties would appear, allegations heard, a decision made and any convicted perpetrator punished. Rather, the most desirable outcome is seen to be reconciliation.

This course of action is, however, not recommended because it offers the victims no protection in term of their continued safety, because the perpetrators may, and often do, repeat their violence (Saraswati 2014). If a protection order were issued by the authorities, the perpetrator would perhaps be more likely to rethink his position. He is publically "put on notice" for his behaviour which is identified as unacceptable and, if he violates the protection order, there are sanctions and/or fines applied.

Indonesian Women 'Breaking the Silence' of Domestic Violence ... 197

Unfortunately, the provisions of the Domestic Violence Act have never been applied maximally to provide maximum protection to women who experience domestic violence. In addition to the difficulties outlined above including police reluctance to pursue any course of action other than reconciliation). The process of obtaining a protection order from a judge often takes a long time, so this provision is felt to be less effective by victims.

An active response from law enforcers, one that includes a less frequent dependence on ineffective "reconciliation" attempts to defer possible legal action and an increased use of the to date underutilised protection orders of the Domestic Violence Act, is needed to prevent perpetrators of violence from controlling "justice" which happens because of the power imbalance between the perpetrator and the victim.

Additional penalties in terms of an order for compulsory counselling of the perpetrator, again a provision of the Domestic Violence Act (art 50), also appears not to have been implemented, as neither accredited institutions nor courses appear to currently exist, or if they do, are ignored in sentencing or providing for probation for offenders (see further below). Nevertheless, the elucidation of Article 50(b) states:

> *What is meant by certain institutions are institutions that have been accredited to provide counselling services for the perpetrators. For example hospitals, clinics, counsellor groups, or who have the expertise to provide counselling for perpetrators for a certain period of time. This provision is intended to give freedom to judges to impose probation with the intention to provide guidance to the perpetrators and maintain the integrity of the household.*

The provision for counselling programs in the Domestic Violence Act aims to "break the chain" and prevent a repetition of violence in the household. It recognises that it is not only the victims of domestic violence who need therapy but also the perpetrator. Perpetrators need counselling assistance to overcome their tendency to commit violence. An appointed therapist/counsellor can engage in efforts to raise of the level of awareness of the perpetrators in relation to the unacceptability of his actions, and also coach them on ways to avoid such actions in the future, thus making families safer. Without counselling, a perpetrator may simply return to his existing family and repeat his harmful behaviour or go on to remarry and create a new family that he could abuse.

However, a study on additional penalties in domestic violence cases has revealed that judges prefer to impose a prison sentence rather than additional penalties on perpetrators because imprisonment is a common criminal sanctions and is still considered an adequate means to deal with domestic violence cases (Hayuna 2015). Judges in this study argued that counselling as an additional penalty has never been implemented because there are no guidelines about the institution that that is to provide such a counselling program and that had to be appointed by government. Without the particular institutions that will provide the counselling not yet having been determined, and approved counselling service is not available, nor for that matter, has the cost of counselling been determined, and neither has to whom nor the cost will be charged nor how long the counselling program would be undertaken by perpetrator. Thus both the facilities/infrastructure for any such programs have been provided by the government, nor have the programs themselves been determined. Moreover, the prosecutors in these cases have never asked for the perpetrators to be given additional penalties such as a counselling program; and the judges have not applied an additional penalty in the form of the imposition of counselling for changing behaviour of perpetrators of domestic violence, because the judge in making a decision bases the penalties applied on the demands of the prosecutor for the defendant in the case. Article 50(b) has never been applied to perpetrators in domestic violence cases. Unfortunately, to date there have been no procedures and supervision mechanisms created for the implementation of the application of additional penalties for the perpetrators of domestic violence (Hayuna 2015, 106-108). This situation impacts on women victim who seek to obtain justice.

The government must take action to issue regulation to further support the Domestic Violence Act or parts of the Act that needs new regulations (as revealed above) in order to protect women (and children) victims from ongoing violence, and to guide the legal apparatus in its processing of domestic violence claims/reports and willingness to adopt temporary protection orders, and to guide and support judges in their ability to utilise the provided additional penalties.

CONCLUSION

Indonesian women had experienced domestic violence such as physical, psychological, and/or sexual violence and neglect. The passage of the Domestic Violence Act in 2004 was expected to protect these women victims. However, the existing legal system does not provide adequate protection and services for victims. The formulations in the existing laws and regulations are still discriminatory and are not effective in providing legal access and justice for victims. There are several articles in the Act that have not been implemented adequately (if at all in some instances) by the legal apparatus. These include in the initial phase the provision of in form of safe houses, temporary protection orders, and in the judgement phase the imposition of available additional penalties (counselling of perpetrators) protection orders involving movement restriction for perpetrators in relation to victim/s and apprehended domestic violence orders. Also causing problems are matters related to evidence. The obstacles to implementing the Act come not only from the legislation but also from legal apparatus some of whom still hold a gender biased perspective. As a consequence, women victims who break their silence by reporting to police in order to seek justice and their rights as victims of violence often have to 'take a step back,' and go to family court to apply for divorce as a means of solving their problem of a violent spouse; he then goes largely unpunished and may go on to repeat the offence with another partner.

REFERENCES

Aryani, A. V., A. Mustafainah, A. Khusnaeny, C. Purba, et al. 2019. Korban Bersuara, Data Bicara, Sahkan RUU Penghapusan Kekerasan Seksual

Sebagai Wujud Komitmen Negara Catatan Kekerasan Terhadap Perempuan Tahun 2018 [*Victims Speak Up, Data Talk, Pass the Draft of Sexual Violence as an Government's - A Record of Violence against Women in 2018*]. Jakarta: Komnas Perempuan [Jakarta: National Commission on Violence against Women].

Aryani, A. V., A. Mustafainah, A. Khusnaeny, B. Wahyuni, Choirunnisa, C. Purba, C. Y. Purawati et al. 2018. Tergerusnya Ruang Aman Perempuan dalam Pusaran Politik Populisme - Catatan Tahunan tentang Kekerasan terhadap Perempuan Tahun 2017 [*The crushing of women's safe spaces in the vortex of politics populism - Annual Note on Violence against Women 2017*]. Jakarta: Komnas Perempuan [Jakarta: National Commission on Violence against Women].

Blackburn, Susan. 2004. *Women and the State in Modern Indonesia.* Cambridge, UK: Cambridge University Press.

Glorianto, B. 2019. Peran Polisi Dalam Memberikan Perlindungan Sementara Kepada Korban (Istri) Dari Kekerasan Suami Dalam Rumah Tangga Berdasarkan Undang-Undang Nomor 23 Tahun 2004 Tentang Penghapusan Kekerasan Dalam Rumah Tangga (Studi Kasus di Polrestabes Semarang) [The Role of the Police in Providing Temporary Protection to Victims (Wives) from Husband as Domestic Violence Perpetrator in Households Based on Law Number 23 of 2004 on the Elimination of Domestic Violence (Case Study at Semarang Police Office]. *Draft skripsi* [Draft Thesis Bachelor of Law], Faculty of Law and Communication, Soegijapranata Catholic University.

Hayuna, R. 2015. Konseling Sebagai Sanksi Pidana Tambahan Pada Tindak Pidana Kdrt (Studi Putusan Hakim Pengadilan Negeri Yogyakarta Dan Pengadilan Negeri Bantul Tahun 2010-2014) [Counseling as Additional Criminal Sanctions for the Criminal Act in Domestic Violence Cases (*Study of Judges' Judgment of Yogyakarta District Court and Bantul District Court in 2010-2014*)]. Tesis, Program Magister Ilmu Hukum Program Pascasarjana Fakultas Hukum Universitas Islam Indonesia [Thesis, Master of Law Program, Postgraduate Program, Faculty of Law, Islamic University of Indonesia].

Khusnaeny, A., D. J. Samsoeri, D. Puspitasari, E. Mukarramah, Fatlhurrozi, H. S. Inten, I. Harsono et al. 2017. Membangun Akses ke Keadilan bagi Perempuan Korban Kekerasan: Perkembangan Konsep Sistem Peradilan Pidana Terpadu Penanganan Kasus Kekerasan terhadap Perempuan (SPPT-PKKTP) [Building Access to Justice for Women Victims of Violence: Development of the Integrated Criminal Justice System Concept Handling of Violence against Women Cases (SPPT-PKKTP)]. Cetakan I, November 2017, Komisi Nasional Anti Kekerasan terhadap Perempuan [*National Commission on Violence against Women*, print 1, November], 46–47.

Radford, J., L. Harne, and M. Friedberg. 1996. *Introduction to Women, Violence and Male Power: Feminist Activism, Research, and Practice.* Edited by J. Radford, L. Harne, and M. Friedberg, 5– 24. Buckingham, UK: Open University Press, 1996.

Ramadhan, C. R., D. A. Wicaksana, M. Rizaldi, dA, Primaldhi. 2018. Asesmen Konsistensi Putusan Pengadilan Kasus-Kasus Kekerasan terhadap Perempuan, Kemitraan Australia Indonesia untuk Keadilan [*Assessment of Consistency on Court Decisions Cases of Violence against Women, Australia Indonesia Partnership for Justice*], Badan Penerbit Fakultas Hukum Universitas Indonesia bersama Masyarakat Pemantau Peradilan Indonesia dan Lembaga Bantuan Hukum) [(University of Indonesia, Faculty of Law Publishing Board with the Legal Aid Institute and Australia Indonesia Partnership for Justice)].

Kelompok Kerja Perempuan dan Anak Mahkamah Agung RI dan Masyarakat Pemantau Peradilan Indonesia Fakultas Hukum Universitas Indonesia (MaPPI FHUI) [The Indonesian Supreme Court Women's and Children's Working Group and the Indonesian Judicial Monitoring Society, Faculty of Law, University of Indonesia]. 2018. Pedoman Mengadili Perkara Perempuan Berhadapan dengan Hukum [*Guidelines for Women dealing with the Law*]. Jakarta: Mahkamah Agung Republik Indonesia and Australia Indonesia Partnership for Justice.

Saraswati, R. 2019. "Shame and Indonesian Women Victims of Domestic Violence in Making the Decision to Divorce." *Identities: Global Studies* on Culture and Power, March doi.org/10.1080/1070289X. 2019.1600313.

Saraswati, R. 2016. "Indonesian Women Experiencing Non-physical Violence: Access to Justice through the Legal System." Paper resented to the *Asian Law & Society Association (ALSA) Conference, National University of Singapore*, Singapore, 22–23 September.

Saraswati, R. 2014. *"Public and Private Dichotomy in the Legal System: Indonesian Women's Access to Justice when Dealing with Domestic Violence."* PhD diss., University of Wollongong.

Saraswati, R. 2013. "Justice and the Identities of Women: The Case of Indonesian Women Victims of Domestic Violence who have Access to Family Court." *Forum on Public Policy: A Journal of the Oxford Round Table 1* (1): 1–20.

Saraswati, R. 2006. *Women and the Solution of Domestic Violence.* Bandung: PT. Citra Aditya Bakti.

Setiamandani, E. D. and A. Suprojo. 2018. "Tinjauan Yuridis Terhadap UU Nomor 23 Tahun 2004 tentang Penghapusan Kekerasan Dalam Rumah Tangga" [Juridical Review of the Elimination of Domestic Violence Act No. 23 of 2004]. *Reformasi* 8 (1): 37–46.

Setiawan, D., D. S. Muhadar, and W. Heryani. 2018. "Pembuktian Tindak Pidana Psikis dalam Kasus Kekerasan dalam Rumah Tangga" [The evidence of physical crime in domestic violence cases], *Pagaruyuang Law Journal* 2 (1): 1–23.

BIOGRAPHICAL SKETCH

Rika Saraswati, PhD

Affiliation: Soegijapranata Catholic University

Education: 2014: Graduated from Doctoral Phylosophy program, Faculty of Law, University of Wollongong, New South Wales, Australia.

Business Address: Soegijapranata Catholic University, Jl. Pawiyatan Luhur IV/1, Bendan Dhuwur, Semarang, Indonesia-50234.

Research and Professional Experience:

2019: Anti-hoax movement: Peace Building Initiative through a Service Learning Program, grant from United Board for Christian Higher Education in Asia in 2018 (the fiscal year of 2017-18, Batch: January 2018).

2018: Developing A Bullying Intervention Model In Junior High School (SMP) In Central Java and Klaten (Yayasan Setara, DPPA DALDUK KB Central Java Province, UNICEF Indonesia.

2015-2016: School Rules for Responsive Anti-Violence/Bullying as an Effort to Fulfill the Rights of School Children in Semarang City.

Professional Appointments:

2017-2020: Chair person of Commission for Protection of the victims of gender-based violence and Children, Central Java Province.

Publications from the Last 3 Years:

2019: a. Shame and Indonesian women victims of domestic violence in making the decision to divorce, *Journal Identities: Global Studies on Culture and Power*, (ongoing) https://doi.org/10.1080/10702 89X.2019.1600313 b. The development and pilot testing of an adolescent bullying intervention in Indonesia – the ROOTS Indonesia program, *Journal Global Health Action* Volume 12, issue 1, 2019 https://doi.org/10.1080/16549716.2019.1656905.

2018: Penghargaan Hak Berpendapat Anak di Pengadilan: Studi Kasus di Pengadilan Negeri Semarang [The Right of the Child to be Heard in Court: Case Study in Semarang Court], R Saraswati, V Hadiyono, *Sawwa: Jurnal Studi Gender* 13 (2), 237-260.

2016: Bullying at Schools and Its Prevention through the School Rules (Case Study in Ten Senior High Schools in Semarang, Indonesia), V Hadiyono and Rika Saraswati. *Proceedings of ICWC 2016 Subang Jaya*, Malaysia, 105.

In: Victims of Violence
Editor: Mathias L. Knudsen

ISBN: 978-1-53617-140-2
© 2020 Nova Science Publishers, Inc.

Chapter 10

AN EXAMINATION OF CIRCUMSTANCES RELATED TO FORCED MARRIAGE AMONG CULTURALLY AND LINGUISTICALLY DIVERSE WOMEN IN AUSTRALIA

Marika Guggisberg[1,] and Madalena Grobbelaar[2]*
[1]School of Nursing Midwifery and Social Sciences,
CQUniversity Australia and Queensland Centre for Domestic and
Family Violence Research, Perth, Western Australia
[2]School of Arts and Humanities, Edith Cowan University,
Perth, Western Australia

ABSTRACT

Forced marriage is a form of modern slavery considered a distinct form of sexual violence in Western countries. Forced marriage, which has been identified as the most prevalent form of modern slavery followed by commercial sexual exploitation and labour exploitation, was criminalized in Australia in 2013. Given that Australia's population is highly culturally

---

[*] Corresponding Author's E-mail: m.guggisberg@cqu.edu.au.

diverse, it is unsurprising that increasing concerns are being raised in relation to forced marriage. This chapter examines how the practice of forced marriage arrangements creates vulnerabilities for girls and young women. Accordingly, the chapter presents a discussion concerning differences and similarities between the concepts of arranged and forced marriage, its relationship to sexual trafficking, along with challenges in relation to cultural practices, motivations and barriers for women's help-seeking behaviour. The chapter concludes by offering recommendations for future directions, such as raising awareness of the issue of forced marriage and professional development training for human service providers who are likely to come in contact with victims.

Keywords: arranged marriage, early marriage, forced marriage, sexual trafficking

INTRODUCTION

Modern slavery is an umbrella term for numerous situations that describes how individuals are forced and/or coerced into situations that are illegal and unlawful. The concept encompasses any form of slavery, servitude, debt bondage, sexual exploitation, trafficking, forced labour and forced marriage (Larsen and Renshaw, 2012). Worldwide, an estimated 40 million individuals were victim/survivors of modern slavery in 2017, of which over 13 million were women and girls who were likely deceived, coerced or forced into marrying someone against their will (International Labour Organization, 2017). Australia's population is highly culturally diverse. The Australian Bureau of Statistics (2018) reported that over 29% of individuals currently living in Australia were born overseas. Research and practice evidence have repeatedly identified overseas born women as more vulnerable to becoming victims of sexual and other forms of domestic and family violence (DFV) when compared to their locally born counterparts (Ghafournia and Easteal, 2018).

As a group, culturally and linguistically diverse (CALD) women are particularly vulnerable to intimate partner violence due to differences in culturally embedded barriers to help-seeking as well as social isolation

(Bhandari, 2018). This includes barriers to knowledge about their rights, language differences, and other factors related to cultural and/or religious mismatching between women seeking assistance and service providers (El-Murr, 2018). Furthermore, many CALD women might not recognise being a victim of sexual and other forms of abuse by an intimate partner except when severe physical violence occurs (Kaplanian, 2019).

In Australia, intimate partner violence has been found to be the most common form of any violence in the family home, occurring across all cultural and faith groups (El-Murr, 2018; Multicultural Centre Against Family Violence, 2019). Yet, relatively little is known about experiences of intimate partner violence among women from CALD backgrounds who have immigrated or come to Australia as refugees. However, even though limited research has been conducted todate, empirical evidence suggests that the prevalence of intimate partner violence among women from CALD backgrounds is higher when compared to the general community (Ghafournia aand Easteal, 2018).

It is important to note that women from CALD backgrounds are a diverse group. This diversity applies not only to various countries of origin and faiths, but also among women from the same countries and regions (Ghafournia and Easteal, 2018). It is important to recognize cultural diversity with focus on differences of values, beliefs, experiences, language and political affiliation in addition to the obvious demographics such as family and socio-economic status (Whande, 2019). Additionally, Australia provides regular humanitarian visas in response to conflict in countries such as Iraq, Syria, Myanmar, Congo, and Afghanistan (Department of Home Affairs, 2019). Granting humanitarian visas has been found to be related to modern slavery.

Currently, there is a dearth of research concerning the experiences of individuals who are or have been victim/survivors of varied forms of modern slavery. Thus, this chapter aims to raise awareness of this emerging area of study; as the world is continually more and more globally connected, it is essential that forced marriage as a form of modern slavery and its threat to millions of women and children worldwide is recognized and better understood.

MODERN SLAVERY

Modern slavery is an umbrella term for situations that describe how individuals are forced and/or coerced into illegal and unlawful relationships. Modern slavery encompasses any form of slavery, servitude, debt bondage, sexual exploitation, trafficking, forced labour and forced marriage (Larsen and Renshaw, 2012). In 2013, forced marriage was criminalized in Australia (Multicultural Centre Against Family Violence, 2019). In this regard, it should be noted that Australia is a destination country for modern slavery. Many individuals and children are trafficked and/or exploited in situations around the family home once they arrive in Australia.

There are limited data available on the prevalence of modern slavery (Larsen and Renshaw, 2012). However, estimates provided by the International Labour Organization (2017) indicated that, worldwide, 40 million individuals were victims of modern slavery, of whom 15 million were involved in forced marriage, the vast majority of these being women and children. Importantly, these figures are estimates. They indicate that the actual number of women and children caught up in modern slavery globally and around Australia is unknown, particularly because of the hidden nature of modern slavery (Parliament of Australia, 2018). What is known and undisputed among professionals, is that slavery-like practices do occur in intimate partner and family relationships (Multicultural Centre Against Family Violence, 2019). In fact, forced marriage has been identified as the most prevalent form of modern slavery in Australia followed by commercial sexual exploitation and labour exploitation, which is related to human trafficking.

Human Trafficking

Human trafficking is a form of modern slavery, which is known to pose a so-called 'low-risk, high-return' incentive for traffickers. It is difficult to monitor and control human trafficking, especially given the dramatic increase in the global movement of people and the clandestine nature of the crime (International Labour Organization, 2017). Many countries are affected by human trafficking, which is commonly referred to as a "transnational crime" (Goldsmith, 2012, 276), either as a country of origin, sometimes referred to as "source countries" (Goldsmith, 2012, 288), which is usually the country of birth, "transit countries" (where someone is taken temporarily), or "destination countries" (where someone is trafficked into for the purpose of exploitation). Sometimes a country is a transit and destination location (Roth, 2019). For example, Australia is primarily a destination country for human trafficking. Sometimes, illegal entry into a transit or destination country is voluntary; however, individuals are always vulnerable to exploitation. Jansson (2014) noted that trafficking is not simply a 'crime', but rather it affects the entire democratic fabric of a society as it transgresses the principles of human dignity and integrity. Although not a direct goal, the consequence of trafficking is that human rights are always violated.

Trafficking versus Smuggling

It is important to understand the difference between human trafficking and migrant smuggling, which is often not well understood (Roth, 2019). Goldsmith (2012, 287) explained the increased focus on human trafficking as follows: "By choice or under duress, people are on the move on a global level. Various 'push' and 'pull' factors have caused increased people mobility". Trafficking and migrant smuggling both involve the illegal movement of people. However, they differ in two main aspects, consent and exploitation (Goldsmith, 2012). Smuggled migrants generally give consent to being smuggled to the destination country. By contrast, trafficking victims have not given consent to their transport or the consent is meaningless due to having been obtained under duress.

The phenomena of smuggling and human trafficking are delineated legally, in reality, these situations become blurred (Shelley, 2011). Whilst smuggled migrants usually start off as paying clients, they are vulnerable to human trafficking, especially women and children. Many smuggled migrants may not speak the language of the country they are smuggled in to, they may be told to destroy their identification documents, and they or their families may be in significant debt to their smugglers (Roth, 2019). People may think they are being smuggled into a country, but on arrival might find themselves deceived, coerced or forced into an exploitative situation such as a seemingly arranged marriage, fearing deportation or harm if they do not comply (Roth, 2019).

Australia is not only a destination country for forced marriage, but sometimes children are taken overseas to be forced to marry (Kaplanian, 2019). Child marriage is generally considered to be forced marriage, given that the child cannot give free and informed consent because they cannot grasp what they are consenting to and they do not have the power to decline. The Parliament of Australia (2018) noted its deep concern about the anecdotal evidence suggesting that modern slavery is particularly prevalent among CALD communities. This includes forced marriage, which may be disguised as a culturally accepted practice commonly known as arranged marriage.

FORCED MARRIAGE

The International Labour Organization (2017, 17) defined forced marriage as "situations where persons, regardless of their age, have been forced to marry without their consent". Forced marriage could be either the result of threats, coercion or deception, as well as because victims are "…incapable of understanding the nature and effect of a marriage ceremony, possibly because of their age or mental capacity" (Burn, 2019). It is estimated that worldwide approximately 13 million women and girls have been deceived, coerced or forced into marrying someone against their will. In this regard, it has been noted that forced marriage is an extension of abuse and violence occurring in the privacy of the family home. The Multicultural Centre Against Family Violence (2019, 1) indicated that forced marriage is characterised by "actual and threatened physical and psychological abuse [that] may be used to force a party into the marriage".

Arranged versus Forced Marriage

An arranged marriage generally involves two people being introduced to each other by their respective families. The difference between 'arranged' and 'forced' marriages should be noted, which relates to full and free consent of both parties to be married. In an arranged marriage, parents and extended family usually play a significant role in finding a potential spouse for someone (Kaplanian, 2019). Throughout the process of a modern arranged marriage both individuals' right to accept or refuse the marriage is respected by the families. As an arranged marriage is agreed upon by the families of the individuals to be married, with the people to be married having the right to accept or reject the arrangement, the marriage involves full, free and informed consent (Multicultural Centre Against Family Violence, 2019). However, sometimes these lines are blurred and an arranged marriage can become a forced marriage. Enright (2009) asserted that the task of defining these two concepts in general terms is difficult due to the slippage across the arranged-forced marriage divide.

There are instances where choice is difficult to assess, particularly if there are family interests involved in the marriage (Kaplanian, 2019). In practice, arranged marriages may have varying degrees of choice in relation to full, free and informed consent, suggesting a considerable grey area. Sometimes, a marriage is labelled 'arranged' when in fact there was intense pressure from the families and/or community members (Multicultural Centre Against Family Violence, 2019). Consequently, brides and grooms may not be able to carefully consider the nature and consequences of agreeing to the marriage, which may include time constraints, deception and coercion (Kaplanian, 2019). Sometimes, people that are involved in an arranged marriage face implicit and even explicit threats, which may restrict their choice and decision making process due to feeling compelled to agree to the marriage (Multicultural Centre Against Family Violence, 2019). In extreme cases, they are physically assaulted, locked in a room and otherwise socially isolated until they provide the answer that the families expect. It follows that caution should be exercised if a woman states that her marriage was arranged. In this regard, concern has been raised that distinguishing between arranged and forced marriage may indicate collusion because certain practices associated with 'arranged' marriages may seem to be condoned, particularly if no sexual and/or physical violence was experienced. There are numerous reasons why family and/or community members may use coercion and/or force to press someone into a marriage.

Reasons for Forced Marriage

Several ways of accounting for the practice of forced marriages have been noted in the literature. These include "longstanding cultural practices" (International Labour Organization, 2017, 43), but also for financial reasons (cancellation of debt or a bride price), or to settle family conflict. This may include allowing a rapist to marry the victimised girl (Seff, Williams, Hussain, Landis, Poulton, Falb, & Stark, 2019) "to escape criminal sanctions by marrying the victim, usually with the consent of her family" (International Labour Organization, 2017, 45). It is internationally recognised that once girls or women have been forced to marry, they are at an increased risk of sexual and other forms of violence by their husbands (International Labour Organization, 2017; Lyneham & Bricknell, 2018; Multicultural Centre Against Family Violence, 2019; Seff et al., 2019), which has been associated with unwanted pregnancies and high rates of abortion (Mengesha, Perz, Dune, & Ussher, 2017). In their study, Esthappan, and colleagues (2018) found that the prime reason online respondents identified as being forced to marry was their need to protect their own or their family's reputation. Concurrently, experiencing harm, being threatened with harm or being told that a loved one would engage in self-harm were also common responses.

A forced marriage-like relationship has been defined by Jelenic and Keeley (2013, 7) as a marriage where no registration with state or territory authorities occurs and where there is no full and free consent of at least one partner. This includes the arrangement of a 'promised bride'.

Child Brides

Child marriage has become an issue of particular concern (Jelenic and Keeley, 2013). Funnell (2019) reported that currently over 100 cases of forced marriage of children are investigated by the Australian Federal Police. These include cases of trafficking for sexual purposes but also abduction, kidnapping and threats to kill the child (ren). The International Labour Organization (2017) reported that the youngest girl identified as a forced marriage victim was nine years old at the time of being married off, while Fennell (2019) reported cases in Australia involving children as young as six years old. Jelenic and Keeley (2013, 11) indicated that children subjected to forced marriage endure severe harm as the following excerpt of their report indicates:

> When a child is married she is likely to be forced into sexual activity with her husband. This has severe health consequences where the child is not physically and sexually mature. Child brides are likely to become pregnant at an early age and there is a strong correlation between the age of a mother and maternal mortality. Girls aged 10-14 are five times more likely to die in pregnancy or childbirth than women aged 20-24 and girls aged 15-19 are twice as likely to die. Young mothers face higher risks during pregnancies including complications such as heavy bleeding, obstetric fistula, infection and anaemia, which contribute to higher mortality rates of both mother and child. The age disparity between a child bride and her husband undermines the ability of girls to make and negotiate sexual decisions, including whether or not to engage in sexual activity, and issues relating to the use of contraception.

In Australia, a number of cases that went before the courts highlighted the complexity of forced marriage, particularly if children are involved. For example, Lyneham and Bricknell (2018, 13-14) reported on a case that went before the courts in NSW:

> In 2015 a single case of forced marriage proceeded through the NSW criminal justice system, where a 12-year-old girl was married to a 26-year-

old man in a marriage ceremony that had taken place in 2013. Despite the girl's mother objecting to the union, the ceremony went ahead after the girl's father consented to the marriage on the girl's behalf... The father, husband and cleric were convicted of various criminal offences, including the NSW state offences of procuring a child for sex and persistent sexual abuse of a child, as well as the Commonwealth offence of the solemnisation of a marriage by an unauthorised person under the Marriage Act. The girl's father and the man she was married to were sentenced to eight years and 7½ years imprisonment, respectively. The cleric was fined $500, had his Religious Worker visa cancelled, and was deported from Australia.

The above example illustrates that in Australia, not only is forced marriage a criminal offence (for an overview of specific legislation see Multicultural Centre Against Family Violence, 2019), but the celebrant who solemnises such a marriage can be held criminally accountable. Given that the girl was under the age of 16 years, she was legally presumed to be incapable of understanding the nature of the marriage ceremony in which she participated. The significance of criminalizing forced marriage in Australia was, for stakeholders, clear-cut; it conveyed an absolute message that the practice of forced marriage is not condoned in Australian society and that there is preparedness to take punitive action against those who engage in this practice. Even though research is scarce, some empirical evidence indicated that a substantial number of child marriages had taken place in the US and the UK (Patterson and Zhuo, 2018). A complicating factor in addressing action against forced marriages is the issue of cultural influences. The next section discusses cultural explanations for forced marriage – this examination does by no means condone the practice but sheds light into motivational factors that may result in families deliberately ignoring legislation that criminalizes forced marriage.

Cultural Explanations for Forced Marriage

There is a link between forced marriage and cultural practice or tradition (Lyneham and Bricknell, 2018). Many families wish to preserve their cultural practices and values, even against the pressure of living in a new country with different customs and laws. This creates a particular vulnerability for girls for forced marriage arrangements. Lyneham and Bricknell (2018, 24) stated that "being female mean[s] accepting certain forms of behaviour and doing what [i]s expected, even if that mean[s] not having (or not recognising the existence of having) a choice".

It is important to note that CALD women experience considerable distress, having to live "between two cultures" (Pangas et al., 2019, 31). While immigrant and refugee women try to maintain their cultural identity, they have to also assimilate and adapt to a new context in the country of residence, which can create a cultural conflict.

Major Risk Factors for Forced Marriage

Kaplanian (2019) identified additional risk factors for forced marriage including when a girl's or boy's sexual preference or sexual behavior is at odds with parental or community norms. For example, if the teenage girl is perceived to, or actually engages in promiscuous sexual activity, this may be a major risk factor for forced marriage. Similarly, whether perceived or real, if someone engaged in same-sexual behaviors, the community response tends to be an imposed marriage to preserve family honour and maintain cultural norms. This is so important that even sexual assault does not deter families to force girls to marry their perpetrators (Lyneham and Bricknell, 2018; Seff et al., 2019). Lyneham and Bricknell (2018) reported that one of their study participants was sexually assaulted by a man at the age of 14 years. She was made to marry the perpetrator.

Forced marriage has been described as a form of sexual violence (Lyneham and Bricknell, 2018) and frequent sexual victimization is reported by victims of forced marriage as some evidence suggests. This includes actual sexual assault, but also forced exposure to pornography and being made to re-enact the viewed scenes, and forced impregnation. Lyneham and Bricknell's (2018, 44) study found that most commonly, perpetrators were the women's husbands, but sometimes also their fathers in law and other male relatives of the women's husbands:

> One victim/survivor described how she did not realise that being married would require her to have a sexual relationship with her husband and how, because she expressed that she did not want to be married and have sex, her husband would sexually assault her as punishment.

Forced marriage is also used as a means of protecting girls from the perceived promiscuity of others (Kaplanian, 2019). Some fathers believe that marrying off their daughters will guard them from sexual violence of promiscuous men. Understanding the role of the extended family is essential when discussing the issues of arranged/forced marriage. Further research is required to examine the motivation of families who wish to protect their children from sexual violence by arranging an early marriage. Researchers who had explored the role of extended family members found that in marriages that had been arranged, the husband's family could have a considerable impact on the couple's relationship (Ali, O'Cathain and Croot, 2018).

Boys as Victims of Forced Marriage

While research consistently confirms that forced marriage most often affects girls, some boys are also forced into marriage (International Labour Organization, 2017; Kaplanian, 2019; Lyneham and Bricknell, 2018; Multicultural Centre Against Family Violence, 2019; Seff et al., 2019). For example, the International Labour Organization (2017) reported that a limited number of victims of forced marriage are males although the vast majority (88%) are female, with half of them having been forced to marry before they reached 15 years of age.

Similarly, Lyneham and Bricknell's (2018) study found that some males become victim/survivors of forced marriage. One case involved the brother of a woman who was forcibly married and he too was going to be forced into marriage by their father. In this regard, Lyneham and Bricknell (2018) noted that some third-generation children, those who were raised in Australia, and have adopted a Western lifestyle, are at an increased risk of forced marriage.

By contrast, Esthappan and colleagues (2018) found that more men than women reported having had experiences of forced marriage. This study suffered limitations including methodological issues and selection bias, which may explain the unexpected findings. It further underscores the need for research in this area. It is likely that gender roles and expectations are central to the occurrence of forced marriage, with females and males both facing different risk factors.

As identified by Esthappan et al. (2018), research on forced marriage is beset with the same methodological challenges that other research investigating sensitive topics faces, which can contribute to underreporting and consequently difficulty in estimating the scope of the problem. Given the complexity of the issues discussed above, it is unsurprising that most women and men will not actively seek assistance for being forced into a marriage but rather for other issues such as violence against women (Multicultural Centre Against Family Violence, 2019).

BARRIERS FOR HELP SEEKING

Women from CALD backgrounds face many barriers to accessing support services when they seek help for sexual and other forms of intimate partner violence (Multicultural Centre Against Family Violence, 2019). These include limited English capabilities, family/community factors, belief in karma and fear of retribution, immigration status, cultural silencing, and fear of authorities (Bhandari, 2018; Vaughan et al., 2015). For example, lack of English proficiency has been identified as particularly dangerous for women as abusive partners, family members or community representatives may offer to act as interpreters. Consequently, women's fears about compromised confidentiality are of particular concern (Vaughan et al., 2015). Such risks impact severely on victims' willingness to report their experiences of forced marriage and intimate partner violence victimisation.

Other factors include victim/survivors not being able to discern whether or not they have been forced into marriage as they are not aware of their rights (Baker, 2015). Still others cannot distinguish between persuasion and coercion and many believe that they have no choice.

Karma and Fear of Retribution

Some victims are reluctant to seek help because they are pressured by family members and friends in their community to stay in the marital relationship. Other women reported that due to religious beliefs, they perceive their experiences of sexual and other forms of intimate partner violence as normal and as a form of karma or destiny. Karma has been defined as "the actions in this birth and previous births will determine the current fate" (Bhandari, 2018, 67). Consequently, these experiences, according to the belief of karma, are inescapable.

Sometimes, victims are exposed to intimidation such as, threats of deportation, being ostracised from the community, and even honour-based homicide (Kaplanian, 2019). For example, being threatened with an honor killing if a woman refuses the marriage or she wishes to separate from her husband, has been identified as a serious and life-threatening issue (Kaplanian, 2019; Lyneham and Bricknell, 2018). Similarly, Shah (2018) reported a case of a 28-year-old Pakistani woman who was raped and murdered by her first husband and his father in 2016. The families had arranged her marriage to a cousin four years earlier. The men's motivation for the murder was their belief that the woman brought shame to their family because she fell in love with another man and divorced her first husband. However, the first husband's family did not recognise the second marriage and committed an honor killing. Consequently, to protect themselves, women often feel compelled to stay silent and endure sexual and other forms of intimate partner violence (Lyneham and Bricknell, 2018).

Visa Issues

Experiences of sexual and other forms of intimate partner violence among CALD women who are victims of forced marriage can be particularly complex for those on insecure visa arrangements such as being on a temporary visa that is linked to the abusive partner. These women may be disproportionately vulnerable to violence and at the same time be isolated and unable to access informal and formal support because perpetrators often use their vulnerability in relation to visa entitlements coercively (Multicultural Centre Against Family Violence, 2019). Immigrant women affected by sexual and other forms of intimate partner violence often report abuse tactics that are specific to their immigrant status. Threats of reporting the women to immigration authorities, having them deported and taking away the children are commonly used by perpetrators. Women on humanitarian visas often experience additional barriers due to their immigration status. Research found that these women are less likely to seek assistance from support services because perpetrators "wield power and control over women, including through [the use of] threats of deportation, threats to family living overseas and threats that women would lose access to their children" (Vaughan et al., 2015, 31).

Cultural Silencing

Faith and culture are extrinsically linked and are factors that may affect women's help-seeking behaviour. Sometimes, because women from CALD backgrounds have a strong culture of silence around sexual and other forms of intimate partner violence victimisation, may believe that it is their destiny to find themselves in the situation they are in (Kaplanian, 2019). They may also fear that their disclosure of the violence will break up the family (Bhandari, 2018). Many women fear ostracism from their family and community, which greatly influences their decision to not seek help. The threat of losing their sense of belonging is a powerful silencer and drives the women into social isolation because of the status of community among many

CALD women. In this regard, Vanaghan and colleagues (2015, 32) stated "perpetrators used isolation as a deliberate strategy to control women and ensure they were unable to leave".

Social isolation is exacerbated when women live in rural or remote areas (Ragusa, 2017). CALD women who live outside of metropolitan areas have limited access to services, which has been found to negatively influence their help-seeking decision. However, El-Murr (2018) indicated that the impact of geographic location is unknown, thus research on this is sorely needed. Some evidence suggests that there is a lack of opportunities for victims along with an increased risk of social stigma and confidentiality concerns in small communities for CALD women. This is of particular concern, given that the Commonwealth government plans to increase regional settlement of families from CALD backgrounds (El-Murr, 2018).

Fear of Authorities

It has been recognized in the literature that women who have been victim/survivors of forced marriage are fearful of authorities (Lyneham, Dowling and Bricknell, 2019). This may influence not only their help-seeking behaviours, but also their willingness to engage with support services. Fear and distrust of authorities have been found to be exploited by abusive men and the women's extended family (Kaplanian, 2019). Consequently, CALD women are particularly at risk of social isolation, which impacts their willingness to reach out and seek help with support services.

FUTURE DIRECTIONS

Baker (2015) suggested that interventions need to focus on education and early intervention to address the range of motives for forced marriage. For example, developing public awareness campaigns and education initiatives in the local community, which focus on the violation of human rights for those individuals who find themselves in a forced marriage. Similarly, it is important to include forced marriage in definitions of sexual and other forms of domestic and family violence. Such measures will grant victims increased access to services already in place.

Based on this analysis, we offer suggestions for future practice. These include considerations for culturally informed practice, establishing safety for vulnerable individuals, and reporting sexual exploitation. We argue that further research is needed to develop effective guidelines and policies for effective service provision.

Culturally Informed Practice

Service providers face numerous challenges when attempting to provide culturally safe services. This includes knowledge and awareness of multiculturalism and the recognition of cultural diversity and consideration of close collaboration with members of the various communities. An increased understanding of the context of CALD women's experiences is needed for practitioners to safely engage with clients from diverse backgrounds and provide culturally safe interventions to victims of forced marriage (Multicultural Centre Against Family Violence, 2019).

Furthermore, it is important to identify potential victims of forced marriage, given CALD women's reluctance of seeking support from human service providers. In this regard, Jelenic and Keeley (2013) recommended that asking simple questions at the beginning of an encounter may be helpful. For example, having guidelines for routine enquiries about the meaning of marriage and asking every CALD woman, who had made decisions on the marriage in the client's family, may provide valuable information, and assist in the assessment of whether or not forced marriage may be an issue. A risk assessment tool, which identifies characteristics common to forced marriages, as well as ways of dealing with a relevant situation, would also be helpful (Baker, 2015).

Providing a culturally safe environment for clients requires increasing staff knowledge about sexual and other forms of intimate partner violence that occur in CALD communities (Multicultural Centre Against Family Violence, 2019). When providing services for CALD women, it is important to note that male partners and other family members may exert pressure on the women if they are allowed to act as interpreters (Kaplanian, 2019; Mengesha et al., 2017). Often, male partners would not allow women to use an independent interpreter, which is a major challenge for service providers (Mengesha et al., 2017). To reduce risk of re-victimization, the provision of culturally safe services may include careful screening of interpreters before they are employed by the organization. Ideally, eligible interpreters do not know the women and are unrelated to their communities.

Safety Planning

Creating a safety plan may be important when working with CALD clients who were victims of forced marriage and/or sexual trafficking. A safety plan may assist clients to protect themselves from further victimization and contribute to safe help-seeking. A safety plan should be collaboratively developed taking into account idiosyncratic information for each woman. This may include an outline of how and where to find safety, how to communicate to family and friends safely and how to respond appropriately in unsafe situations.

In this regard, it is critically important to keep confidentiality and be careful when sharing personal information about the client, which should only occur after informed consent has been obtained. While this is a principle of universal application, confidentiality may be particularly important in relation to CALD women's safety considerations as they may need to rely on other people due to a language barrier, which may place them at risk of further victimization. Additionally, information should not be revealed that may result in clients being identified to the public.

Reporting Child Sexual Exploitation

If a practitioner suspects that a child has experienced or is at risk of slavery or slavery-like practices such as forced marriage, authorities should always be contacted immediately. In Australia, this is either State and Territory based law enforcement or the Australian Federal Police. This is important because a child under the age of 16 years cannot, in any circumstance, consent to marriage. In Australia, practitioners do not require informed consent from the child or a parent to contact authorities because child trafficking is a specific offence in the *Criminal Code Act 1995*(Cth). Similarly, in the UK, referrals should be made through the National Referral Mechanism (NRM) to safeguard children according to the Modern Slavery Act 2015 (Home Office, 2019).

In the US, *Polaris*, a not-for-profit non-government organization is dedicated to raise awareness and assist victims of modern slavery. It is one of the largest anti-trafficking organisations, which offers 24/7 reporting through the National Human Trafficking Hotline. Suspected victims can seek assistance as well as individuals wishing to support someone can make referrals by calling 1-888-373-7888 or contact *Polaris* BeFree Textline for a live chat by texting the number 233733 (BeFree) (US Department of State, 2019).

It has been recognised that a global effort is required to combat child sexual exploitation and other forms of modern slavery (US Department of State, 2019). The Counter-Trafficking Data Collaborative (CTDC) was launched in November 2017, which is an initiative of the International Organization for Migration in Switzerland. It brings together government and non-government organizations from all over the world, including *Polaris*, to collect international data on human trafficking and share information to assist global anti-trafficking efforts. The CTDC has identified 172 countries of exploitations with 91,416 victims of human trafficking at the date of accessing the database by late July 2019.

Further Research

A lack of knowledge on the issues of forced marriage and its complex interaction with intimate partner violence has been noted in the literature (Multicultural Centre Against Family Violence, 2019). Indeed, further research is urgently needed, which is not restricted to the issues discussed in this chapter. Placing focus of attention on evidence-based practice to ensure that CALD women receive comprehensive and competent assistance and support requires research that informs policy development. In this regard, we argue that bi-cultural practitioners can be important assets in the design and development of specific policies along with the evaluation of existing guidelines, tools and practices.

CONCLUSION

This chapter discussed specific issues related to CALD women as a vulnerable group for sexual exploitation and victimisation in the family home, which includes forced marriage. Forced marriage has been acknowledged as forming a prevalent part of modern slavery, which was criminalised in Australia in 2013. Given that Australia's population is highly culturally diverse, it is unsurprising that increasing concerns are being raised in relation to forced marriage for girls and young women. Differences and similarities between sexual trafficking and the concepts of arranged versus forced marriage were examined. Cultural explanations and risk factors inherent in forced marriage situations were presented prior to a discussion regarding the barriers for seeking assistance from support service providers experienced by CALD women. In this regard, we highlighted that CALD women's help seeking may be complicated by an accumulation and intersection of risk factors such as language barriers, a lack of social ties in Australia, and culturally specific community and family pressures to avoid tainting the reputation of the relevant migrant community by disclosing sexual and other forms of victimisation by an intimate partner. The chapter offered considerations for service provision and future directions, which included professional development training to ensure culturally sensitive and effective service provision along with an identified need for future research.

We hope that independent and rigorous empirical enquiry into forced marriage as part of modern slavery and sexual trafficking will generate scholarly interest to improve the lives of vulnerable girls and women from CALD backgrounds living in Australia and elsewhere. This includes countries assuming leadership by promoting a culture of change, which includes raising awareness and implementing policies that encourage reporting and rigorous service provision on national and international levels.

REFERENCES

Ali, Parveen Azam., Alicia, O'Cathain. & Elizabeth, Croot. (2018). 'Influences of Extended Family on Intimate Partner Violence: Perceptions of Pakistanis in Pakistan and the United Kingdom'. *Journal of Interpersonal Violence*. Accessed July 28, 2019. doi:10.1177/0886260518785378.

Australian Bureau of Statistics. (2018*). 'Migration, Australia 2016 – 17'. 3412.0. Canberra, ACT.* Accessed May 26, 2019. https://www.abs.gov.au/AUSSTATS/abs@.nsf/mf/3412.0.

Baker, Joanne. (2015). *'Forced Marriage – A Review of the Literature'. Ending Violence Association of British Columbia.* Accessed July 28, 2019. http://www.endforcedmarriages.ca/wp-content/uploads/2015/03/FORCED-MARRIAGE-lit-review-11-March-2015-2.pdf.

Bhandari, Shreya. (2018). 'South Asian Domestic Violence and Karma'. In *Violence Against Women in the 21st Century: Challenges and Future Directions*, edited by Marika Guggisberg, and Jessamy Henricksen, 57 – 85. New York, NY: Nova Science Publishers.

Borg Jansson, Dominika. (2014). Modern Slavery: A Comparative Study of the Definition of Trafficking in Persons. *Brill: International Studies in Human Rights*. Vol. *110*. https://brill.com/view/title/26730.

Burn, Jennifer. (2019). 'Human Trafficking and Slavery Still Happen in Australia. This Comic Explains How'. *The Conversation*, June 12. Accessed June 28. https://theconversation.com/human-trafficking-and-slavery-still-happen-in-australia-this-comic-explains-how-112294.

Counter Trafficking Data Collaborative. (2018). Accessed July 25, 2019. https://www.ctdatacollaborative.org.

Department of Home Affairs. (2019). *'Discussion Paper: Australia's Humanitarian Program 2019-20'. Canberra, ACT.* Accessed July 25, 2019. https://www.homeaffairs.gov.au/reports-and-pubs/files/2019-20-discussion-paper.pdf.

El-Murr, Alissar. (2018). *'Intimate Partner Violence in Australian Refugee Communities: Scoping Review of Issues and Service Responses', CFCA Paper No. 50.* South Bank, VIC: Australian Institute of Family Studies. Accessed May 26, 2019. https://aifs.gov.au/cfca/ publications/ cfca-paper/intimate-partner-violence-australian-refugee-communities.

Enright, Mairead. (2009). 'Choice, Culture and the Politics of Belonging. The Emerging Law of Forced and Arranged Marriage'. *The Modern Law Review, 72,* 331-359. Accessed July 28, 2019. https://doi.org/ 10.1111/j.1468-2230.2009.00747.x.

Esthappan, Sino., Sara, Bastomski., Janine, Zweig., Meredith, Dank. & Hanna, Love. (2018). 'Understanding Forced Marriage in the United States: Developing Measures, Examining its nature, and Assessing Gender Disparities'. *Journal of Interpersonal Violence.* Accessed July 28, 2019. https://doi.org/10.1177/0886260518801935.

Funnell, Nina. (2019). *'Shocking Reality for Australia's Victims of Forced Marriage'.* News.com.au, February 11. Accessed May 27, 2019. https://www.news.com.au/lifestyle/real-life/news-life/shocking-reality-for-australias-victims-of-forced-marriage/news-story/4f8ef092237c2606d845f1ecf7b45df9.

Ghafournia, Nafiseh. & Patricia, Easteal. (2018). 'Are Immigrant Women Visible in Australian Domestic Violence Reports that Potentially Influence Policy?' *Laws, 7,* 1 – 16. Accessed May 25, 2019. https:// doi.org/10.3390/laws7040032.

Goldsmith, Andrew. (2012). 'Crimes Across Borders'. In *Crime and Justice: A Guide to* Criminology, edited by Marinella Marmo, Willem de Lint, and Darren Palmer, (4th ed.), 275 – 301. Pyrmont, NSW: Thomson Reuters.

Home Office. (2019). *'Child Exploitation Disruption Toolkit'*. London, UK. Accessed July 25, 2019. https://assets.publishing.service.gov.uk/government/uploads/system/uploads/attachment_data/file/794554/6.51 20_Child_exploitation_disruption_toolkit.pdf.

Ilana, Seff, Williams, Anaise, Hussain Farah, Landis, Debbie, Poulton, Catherine, Falb, Kathryn, & Stark, Lindsay (2019). 'Forced Sex and Early Marriage: Understanding the Linkages and Norms in a Humanitarian Setting'. *Violence Against Women*. Accessed July 17, 2019. https://doi.org/10.1177/1077801219845523.

International Labour Organization. (2017). *'Global Estimates of Modern Slavery: Forced Labour and Forced marriage'*. Geneva, Switzerland. Accessed May 15, 2019. http://www.ilo.org/global/publications/books/WCMS_575479/lang--en/index.htm.

Jelenic, Tina. & Matthew, Keeley. (2013). *'End Child Marriage: Report on the Forced Marriage of Children in Australia'*. Sydney, NSW: National Children's and Youth Law Centre, University of New South Wales. Accessed May 26, 2019. https://yla.org.au/wp-content/uploads/2019/01/End-Child-Marriage-NCYLC-Research-Report.pdf.

Kaplanian, Carol. (2019). 'Understanding and Responding to Forced Marriage'. Paper presented at *the Protection and Prevention: WA Inaugural Forced Marriage Conference*, Newman Siena Centre, Perth, WA, 12 March.

Larsen, Jaqueline J. & Lauren, Renshaw. (2012). 'People Trafficking in Australia'. *Trends & Issues in Crime and Criminal Justice*, No. 441. Canberra, ACT: Australian Institute of Criminology. Accessed May 13, 2019. https://aic.gov.au/publications/tandi/tandi441.

Lyneham, Samantha, Christopher, Dowling, & Samantha, Bricknell. (2019). 'Estimating the Dark Figure on Human Trafficking and Slavery Victimisation in Australia'. *Statistical Bulletin, 16.* Canberra, ACT:

Australian Institute of Criminology. Accessed July 25, 2019. https://aic.gov.au/publications/sb/sb16.

Mengesha, Zelalem B., Jeanette, Perz., Tinashe, Dune. & Jane, Ussher. (2017). 'Refugee and Migrant Women's Engagement with Sexual and Reproductive Health Care in Australia: A Socio-Ecological Analysis of Health Care Professional Perspectives'. *PLoS ONE, 12,* e0181421. Accessed July 28, 2019. https://doi.org/10.1371/journal.pone.0181421.

Multicultural Centre Against Family Violence. (2019). *'Research Brief: Forced Marriage in Australia'. Melbourne,* VIC: Monash Gender and Family Violence Prevention Centre. Accessed May 25, 2019. https://intouch.org.au/wp-content/uploads/2019/03/ MonashResearchBrief_ForcedMarriageInAustralia.pdf.

Pangas, Jacqueline., Olayide, Ogunsiji., Rakime, Elmir., Shanti, Raman., Pranee, Liamputtong., Elaine, Burns., Hannah, G. & Virginia, Schmied. (2019). 'Refugee Women's Experiences Negotiating Motherhood and Maternity Care in a New Country: A Meta-Ethnographic Review'. *International Journal of Nursing Studies, 90,* 31 – 45. Accessed June 04, 2019. https://doi.org/10.1016/ j.ijnurstu.2018.10.005.

Parliament of Australia. (2018). 'A Modern Slavery Act for Australia?' Canberra, ACT. Accessed, May 26, 2019. https://aph.gov.au/ Parliamentary_Business/Committees/Joint/Foreign_Affairs_Defence_a nd_Trade/ModernSlavery/Final_report.

Patterson, Orlando. & Xiaolin, Zhuo. (2018). 'Modern Trafficking, Slavery, and other Forms of Servitude'. *Annual Review of Sociology, 44,* 407 – 439. Accessed July 28, 2019. https://doi.org/10.1146/ annurev-soc-073117-041147.

Ragusa, Angela. T. (2017). 'Rurality's Influence on Women's Intimate Partner Violence Experiences and Support Needed for Escape and Healing in Australia'. *Journal of Social Service Research, 43,* 270 – 295. Accessed June 04, 2019. https://doi.org/10.1080/01488376.2016. 1248267.

Roth, Carolyn. A. (2019). 'Human Trafficking vs. Migrant Smuggling: Exploring the Differences'. *PolitiChick.,* March 22. Accessed May 27,

2019. https://politichicks.com/2019/03/human-trafficking-vs-migrant-smuggling-exploring-the-differences/.

Shah, Naz. (2018). 'There is No Honour in 'Honour Killings', Only Male Shame'. *The Guardian*, 21 July. Accessed May 26, 2019. https://www.theguardian.com/commentisfree/2018/jul/20/honour-killings-male-shame-violence-fgm-forced-marriage.

Shelley, Louise. (2011). 'Human Trafficking: A Global Perspective'. *European Journal on Criminal Policy and Research*, 17, 349 – 352. Accessed July 28, 2019. https://doi.org/10.1007/s10610-011-9145-z.

US Department of State. (2019). *'Trafficking in Persons Report'*. Accessed July 26, 2019. https://www.state.gov/wp-content/uploads/2019/06/2019-Trafficking-in-Persons-Report.pdf.

Vaughan, Cathy, Erin, Davis, Adele, Murdolo, Jasmin, Chen, Linda, Murray, Karen, Block, Regina, Quiazon. & Deb, Warr. (2015). *'Promoting Community-Led Responses to Violence Against Immigrant and Refugee Women in Metropolitan and Regional Australia: The ASPIRE Project'*. *Research Report*. Sydney, NSW: ANROWS. Accessed July 28, 2019. https://d2rn9gno7zhxqg.cloudfront.net/wp-content/uploads/2019/02/19024843/12_1.2-Landscapes-ASPIRE-web.pdf.

Whande, Fazi (2019). *'Beyond Cultural Diversity'*. Masterclass. Western Australia Family Law Pathways Network: Perth, Western Australia.

In: Victims of Violence
Editor: Mathias L. Knudsen

ISBN: 978-1-53617-140-2
© 2020 Nova Science Publishers, Inc.

Chapter 11

CYBER DATING ABUSE VICTIMIZATION AND ASSOCIATION WITH OFFLINE DATING VIOLENCE

Sónia Caridade[1,2,3,], Isa Ataíde[1] and Maria Alzira Pimenta Dinis[1,2,4]*

[1]University Fernando Pessoa (UFP), Porto, Portugal
[2]Permanent Observatory Violence and Crime (OPVC),
University Fernando Pessoa (UFP), Porto, Portugal
[3]Behaviour and Social Sciences Research Center (FP-B2S),
University Fernando Pessoa (UFP), Porto, Portugal
[4]UFP Energy, Environment and Health Research Unit (FP-ENAS),
University Fernando Pessoa (UFP), Porto, Portugal

ABSTRACT

Despite the positive effects associated with information and communication technologies (ICTs) on youth socialization process (e.g., ability to exercise self-control, to promote tolerance and respect for others,

---

[*] Corresponding Author's E-mail: soniac@ufp.edu.pt.

232   *Sónia Caridade, Isa Ataíde and Maria Alzira Pimenta Dinis*

to adequately express feelings, to exercise critical thinking, and to make decisions), negative effects have also been documented (e.g., cyberbullying or online risk behaviour), including cyber dating abuse (CDA). Some studies have been documenting that CDA is an extension of offline dating violence (ODV). Accordingly, this chapter summarizes the findings when analysing the association between CDA and ODV in a sample of 145 Portuguese adolescents and young adults, mostly female (89%), with a mean age of 23.54 years and standard deviation (SD) of 4.01 years. Results show that CDA and ODV are very prevalent among Portuguese youth involved in dating relationships and that both types of abuse are positively associated in terms of victimization and perpetration. The co-occurrence of CDA and ODV signals the importance of finding additional strategies to encourage a more cautious use of ICTs in order to prevent specific situations between dating partners, able to trigger abusive behaviour.

Keywords: Cyber Dating Abuse (CDA), Offline Dating Violence (ODV), victimization, dating relationships

INTRODUCTION

The use of a wide variety of information and communication technologies (ICTs) as digital tools, i.e., text messages, emails, messages through different social networks, etc., has exponentially increased, playing a crucial role in the social developmental of young people. Cyber space acts as a very flexible and attractive context in the establishment of new interpersonal relations, such as dating relationships. However, the same environment will also be able to encourage the occurrence of multiple victimization experiences such as sexting, cyberstalking, cyberbullying and or cyber dating abuse (CDA) (Borrajo, Gamez-Guadix, Pereda, & Calvete, 2015), considering the greater interpersonal intrusiveness underlying the use of these digital tools.

It is possible to find a vast number of constructs in literature to designate and further define victimization and perpetration of violence through digital tools in dating relationships. Examples are Digital Dating Abuse (Reed, Tolman, & Ward, 2016), Electronic Aggression (Bennett, Gumar, Ramos,

& Margolin, 2011), Electronic Dating Violence (Hindusa & Patchin, 2011) and Intimate Partner Cyber Aggression (Marganski & Melander, 2016; Schnurr, Mahatmya, & Basche, 2013). The association of CDA with offline dating violence (ODV) will be discussed in this chapter.

CDA has been defined as a form of control and harassment by the loving partner, using ICTs and the media (Zweig, Lachman, Yahner, & Dank, 2014). It has been described as a multidimensional construct, that can involve multiple abusive behaviours through digital interaction (e.g., daily control and surveillance of the dating or ex-dating partner; sending/posting offensive or humiliating comments to/of the dating partner; sending emails or messages containing different threats; posting photos) (Bennett et al., 2011; Burke et al., 2011) and integrates different typologies of abuse which include cyber psychological abuse, cyber harassment, cyber psychological and verbal aggression, or cyber sexual abuse (e.g., Gámez-Guadix, Borrajo, & Calvete, 2018).

In terms of CDA prevalence, it has been documented that victimization among adolescents may range from 22.2% (Temple, Choi, Brem et al., 2016) to 26.3% (Zweig et al., 2013). Even more worrying data was reported by Stonard, Bowen, Walker and Price (2017) in a review of twenty-one studies analysing this type of digital dating abuse. Depending on the type of instruments used, the same authors found that victimization ranged from 12 to 56% and the perpetration between 12 and 54%. Peskin et al. (2017) also found that 15% of the participants had already perpetrated some kind of abuse using social networks throughout their lives. A critical review of CDA measures by Brown and Hegarty (2018) found perpetration rates among youth ranging from 6 to 91%.

In addition to the high indicators of victimization and perpetration, literature has also documented the existence of reciprocity of CDA, i.e., associations between victimization and perpetration (e.g., Leisring & Giumetti, 2014; Morelli, Bianchi, Chirumbolo, & Baiocco, 2017; Watkins, Maldonado, & DiLillo, 2016; Reed, Tolman & Ward, 2017; Villora, Yubero, & Navarro, 2019), associations also found in face-to-face violence (Straus, 2008).

ODV is usually defined as aggressive behaviour perpetrated by the boyfriend/girlfriend against his/her dating partner (Hamby & Turner, 2013). It may involve the use or threat of different typologies of violence, either physical, emotional/psychological or sexual (Caridade, 2016), and may occur in both heterosexual and homosexual, i.e., lesbian, gay, relationships (Dank, Lachman, Zweig, & Yahner, 2014).

Different international (e.g., Hamby & Turner, 2013; Haynie, Farhat, Brooks-Russell, Wang, Barbieri, & Iannotti, 2013; Jennings et al., 2017; Straus, 2004) and Portuguese (e.g., Machado, Caridade, & Martins, 2010; Neves, Cameira, Machado, Duarte, & Machado, 2016; Santos & Caridade, 2017; Santos, Caridade, & Cardoso, 2019) studies have demonstrated that ODV is a prevalent problem. In United States (US), the Center for Disease Control and Prevention (2016) estimated that one in five women and one in seven men experienced some kind of intimate violence between 11 and 17 years of age. A systematic review developed by Jennings et al. (2017), involving 169 studies, conducted with young people aged 15-30 years, found lower prevalence estimates among younger (<10%) compared to older persons (between 20 and 30%), and women reported high indicators of victimization.

In Portugal, as in other European countries (FRA, 2014), studies have documented high rates of dating violence among adolescents (e.g., Neves et al., 2016; Santos & Caridade, 2017; Santos et al., 2019). One of the first studies conducted in Portugal involving a large sample of young people (n = 4,665) (Machado et al., 2010), found that one in four subjects in the sample revealed to have experienced at least a lifelong ODV episode. In another study by Guerreiro et al. (2017) carried out with a sample of 2,500 young people aged 12 to 18 years, 7% admitted having suffered ODV at least once. As in the previous study of Machado et al. (2010), psychological violence emerged as the most prevalent (8.5%), followed by physical violence (5%) and by sexual violence (4.5%).

CDA was frequently associated, or cooccurring, with ODV (Borrajo et al., 2015; Borrajo, Gámex-Guadix, & Calvete, 2015a; Marganski & Melander, 2015; Temple et al., 2016; Yahner et al., 2015; Zapor et al., 2017; Zweig et al., 2013) and other forms of violence such as cyberbullying

(Borrajo et al., 2015), bullying (Ouytsel, Ponnet, & Walrave, 2017) or cyberstalking (Strawhun et al., 2013). Some international evidence has documented the co-occurrence of CDA and ODV in dating relationships of adolescents and young people. In a study using a large sample of 3,745 youth in the north-eastern US, Zweig et al. (2013) found that CDA often cooccurs with other forms of dating violence, in particular with sexual violence. More concretely, the study shows that half of the victims of sexual CDA were also victims of physical violence, and nearly all of both types of CDA victims, i.e., victims of sexual and physical violence, also experienced other abusive psychological experiences.

Dating violence, either online or offline, is an extremely important social problem, and although both forms may be related, they differ in many aspects (e.g., it is more difficult for a victim to escape from online abuse; some abusers may suffer less inhibitions against abuse), thus justifying greater investment in this area of study (Ouytsel, Ponnet, & Walrave, 2016). The increase of ICTs originates new tools and opportunities for those involved in ODV to abuse and control their partners. Little is known about the nature of CDA on Portuguese context, specifically how often youth experience it or how CDA is connected to ODV. In this sense, CDA is a problem that needs to be properly detected, perceived, understood and addressed, aiming to break the progressive cycle of violence. With this study, it is intended to describe the prevalence of CDA and ODV, as well as to analyse the association between both forms of violence in a sample of Portuguese youth.

METHODS

Participants

This study included a sample of 145 Portuguese adolescents and young adults, mostly female (89%), mainly college students (64.2%) and with a mean age of 23.54 years and a standard deviation (*SD*) of 4.01 years. In terms of education, a significant percentage of participants were attending

236   *Sónia Caridade, Isa Ataíde and Maria Alzira Pimenta Dinis*

the 1st cycle of studies (49.7%), with 12.4% in the 2nd cycle of studies, and postgraduate attendance (1.4%). 35.9% of the participants reported other non-tertiary education. When completing the questionnaire, and regarding the relational situation, 75.2% of the participants revealed that they were involved in a romantic relationship in the last year, with the remaining 27.8% reporting that the dating relationship was already over. The average duration of the romantic relationship was 5.20 months (SD = 2.76 months).

Instruments

Three questionnaires were used for the data collection:

1. *Sociodemographic Questionnaire*: This included a series of questions about age, sex, whether the participant has or had a relationship, and the duration of it in months;
2. *Cyber Dating Abuse Questionnaire* (CDAQ, Borrajo et al., 2015), version translated and validated to the Portuguese population by Caridade and Braga (CibAN – Cyber Abuse in Dating, 2019) to assess CDA occurring within the scope of dating relationships, by investigating reciprocity in terms of victimization and perpetration. CibAN is a self-report measure consisting of 20 items about various types of CDA, such as threats, identity theft, control, and humiliation. Each item consists of two parallel items: one for victimization and another one for perpetration (e.g., "My partner or former partner made a comment on a wall of a social network to insult or humiliate me" and "I wrote a comment on the wall of a social network to insult or humiliate my partner or former partner"). The response scale used was a 6-point Likert scale: 1 (never), 2 (not in the last year, but before); 3 (1 or 2 times); 4 (3 to 10 times); 5 (10 to 20 times); and 6 (more than 20 times). The questionnaire integrates two factors: Direct aggression (e.g., "I threatened my partner or former partner using new technologies to physically hurt her/him") and control (e.g., "Using mobile applications, I controlled

the hour of the last connection with my partner or former partner). Measured through Cronbach's alpha (α), the reliability of the scale for this sample was α = .91 for victimization of direct aggression and α = .95 for victimization of control; α = .45 for perpetration of direct aggression and α = .85 for perpetration of control;

3. *Abusive Dating Experiences Questionnaire* (QVAA, Santos & Caridade, 2016). In the present study, only section 4 of the instrument on the characterization of abusive dating experiences was used. Initially, the participants had to answer two questions, indicating whether they had experienced any kind of dating violence within their romantic relationship and/or if they had used any type of violence within their dating relationship. If they answered yes to some of the above questions, participants had to identify from a list of 19 abusive behaviours (cf. Table 2) how often they experienced and/or perpetrated any of these behaviours towards their dating partner. The reliability of the scale for this sample was α = .91 for ODV victimization and α = .81 for ODV perpetration.

Procedures

The study was approved by the institutional ethics committee. The questionnaire was initially made available on Google Docs online platform. The URL with the questionnaires was later disseminated through social networks and contacts were established with different Universities. Before asking the participants to complete the questionnaire, a brief description of the study was presented regarding the objectives, the inclusion criterion (i.e., being involved in romantic relationships in the last year), the confidentiality and anonymity of the data, the voluntary nature of response and the absence of any compensatory economic participation. The informed consent was also presented, and the participants could only advance in the completion of the instruments after indicating (obligatory completion item) their agreement to participate in the study. The questionnaires were available online between January and March 2019, and the process was completed in April 2019.

RESULTS

Prevalence of CDA and ODV

Of all participants who stated having been engaged in dating relationships in the last year, 26.2% reported having experienced at least some type of CDA and 29% assumed to have perpetrated at least one act of CDA (cf. Table 1).

Analysing the different typologies of CDA measured by the instrument, and presented in Table 1, it can be observed that most participants assumed to have had suffered (25.5%) and practiced some type of intimate control (28.3%) through the use of ICTs. With regard to direct aggression, lower prevalence indicators were found in terms of victimization (5.5%) and perpetration (11.7%), although still worrying.

Concerning ODV prevalence, 37.2% of the participants reported to have been subjected to some kind of abuse in their dating relationship and 15.9% admitted using some form of violence in their dating relationships (cf. Table 2). According to Table 2, the analysis of abusive behaviours received/suffered shows a preponderance of minor violence such as insults (22.8%), prevent from having or talking to friends (17.2%), blackmail (15.2%), control email and/or social networks (15.2%), search the phone and/or backpack (11.7%) and shout out (10.3%). Although behaviours associated with victimization by severe violence are less expressive, non-trivial prevalence indicators are identified, specifically to press to have sex (9%) and to force to have sexual acts (5.5%) (cf. Table 2).

Table 1. Prevalence of CDA typologies

	CDA	*n*	%
Victimization	Control	37	25.5
	Direct Aggression	8	5.5
	Total	38	26.2
Perpetration	Control	41	28.3
	Direct Aggression	17	11.7
	Total	42	29.0

Table 2. Global prevalence of ODV and its abusive behaviours

	Victimization (%)	Perpetration (%)
Global prevalence	37.2	15.9
QVAA abusive behaviours		
Insult	22.8	15.2
Control email and/or social networks	14.5	15.2
Search the phone and/or backpack	11.7	11.7
Shout out	13.1	10.3
Push	8.3	6.9
Prevent from having or talking to friends	17.2	5.5
Prevent from hanging out with friends	13.1	4.1
Blackmail	15.2	4.8
Threaten (use of violence)	7.6	2.1
Chasing and watching dating partner's movements	9.0	4.8
Throw objects	6.9	3.4
Slap	5.5	2.8
Tighten the neck	2.1	2.8
Pull hair	2.1	2.1
Prevent wearing certain clothes	11.0	1.4
Kick	1.4	1.4
Force kiss	3.4	1.4
Press to have sex	9.0	0.7
Force to have unwanted sexual acts	5.5	0.7

Analysing the perpetration of different abusive behaviours in Table 2, there is also a greater preponderance of milder forms of violence. Thus, as with victimization, respondents admitted to having practiced more insults (15.2%) and control email and/or social networks (15.2%), search the phone and/or backpack (12.7%) and shout out (10.3%). Similarly, perpetration also involved the use of more serious behaviours within dating relationships, namely to pull hair (2.1%), kick (1.4%), press to have sex (0.7%) and force to unwilling sexual acts (0.2%).

Association between CDA and ODV

To analyse the association between CDA and ODV victimization the Pearson's chi-squared test (χ^2) was used (cf. Table 3). Statistically significant results were found with the total CDA [$\chi^2(1) = 25.18$; $p = .000$] as in the control factor of CDA [$\chi^2 (1) = 23.19$; $p = .000$]. Fifteen percent of ODV victims also report victimization by CDA and a majority of victims by control CDA (48.1%) admitted having suffered ODV. ODV victimization also showed a statistically significant association with total CDA perpetration [$\chi^2(1) = 11.42$; $p = .001$] and its abusive typologies: control [$\chi^2(1) = 10.02$; $p = .002$] and direct aggression [$\chi^2(1) = 28.77$; $p= .000$] perpetration. Between the group of victims who assumed having experienced ODV, 46.3% also assume perpetrating total CDA, 31.5% direct aggression and 44.4% control CDA.

Table 3. Association between CDA and ODV victimization

ODV Victimization			No	Yes	χ^2
CDA Victimization	Total	No	87.9	50.0	25.18***
		Yes	12.1	50.0	
	Direct Aggression	No	96.7	90.7	2.31
		Yes	3.3	9.3	
	Control	No	87.9	51.9	23.19***
		Yes	12.1	48.1	
CDA Perpetration	Total	No	80.2	53.7	11.42***
		Yes	19.8	46.3	
	Direct Aggression	No	98.9	68.5	28.77***
		Yes	1.1	31.5	
	Control	No	80.2	55.6	10.02**
		Yes	19.8	44.4	

$**p < .01$; $***p < .001$.

Using the same Pearson's chi-squared test (χ^2) in Table 4, only a statistically significant association between ODV perpetration and total CDA victimization [$\chi^2(1) = 4.21$; $p = .04$] was found, with 43.5% of aggressors by ODV also assuming to have suffered total CDA victimization.

In turn, ODV perpetration showed a statistically significant correlation with total CDA perpetration [$\chi^2(1)$ = 20.87; p = .000], and control CDA perpetration [$\chi^2(1)$ = 21.90; p = .000], i.e., within the group of ODV aggressors, the majority also assume perpetrating total CDA (69.6%) and control CDA (69.6%).

Table 4. Association between CDA and ODV perpetration

ODV Perpetration			No	Yes	χ^2
CDA Victimization	Total	No	77.0	56.5	4.21*
		Yes	23.0	43.5	
	Direct Aggression	No	95.9	87.0	2.97
		Yes	4.1	13.0	
	Control	No	77.0	60.9	2.66
		Yes	23.0	39.1	
CDA Perpetration	Total	No	77.9	30.4	20.87***
		Yes	22.1	69.6	
	Direct Aggression	No	88.5	82.6	.62
		Yes	11.5	17.4	
	Control	No	78.7	30.4	21.90***
		Yes	21.3	69.6	

*p < .05; **p < .01; ***p < .001.

DISCUSSION AND CONCLUSION

The main objective of the present study was to analyse the association between CDA and ODV, still less studied in the Portuguese context. Accordingly, this chapter intends to make a relevant contribution to the understanding of this phenomenon and to contribute to the development of other studies in this area.

High indicators were found in terms of CDA victimization (26.2%) and perpetration (29%), corroborating those found in other international studies (e.g., Ouytsel et al., 2016; Stonard et al., 2017) and in a Portuguese study by Caridade and Braga (2019). However, the indicators in this study are lower than those found in other research that used the same instrument, CibAN, with Portuguese population, in terms of victimization (59.2%) and perpetration (66.9%) (Caridade & Braga, 2019),

Regarding the different typologies of CDA, and as found by Borrajo et al. (2015), victimization and aggression for control CDA (25.5% vs. 28.3%) were higher compared to victimization and direct aggression (5.5% vs. 11.7%). However, and once again, these indicators are lower than those found in the Portuguese study by Caridade and Braga (2019), in respect to victimization and aggression for control (58.8% vs. 62.3%) and victimization and direct aggression (18% vs. 14.7%). However, the indicators of victimization and perpetration of control CDA are consistent with other international studies (e.g., Burke et al., 2011; Hindusa & Patchin, 2011; Zweig et al., 2013) reporting rates below 50%. The increase of CDA control compared to direct aggression may be explained by the fact that it is a cyberabuse typology that includes abusive behaviours (e.g., persistent messaging, partner surveillance), being less explicit and therefore more acceptable by young people and sometimes even perceived as a sign of love or jealousy (Ameral, Palm Reed, & Hines, 2017). It has been documented that the use of ICTs and networking tends to trigger control and jealous behaviours (Baker & Carreño, 2015).

The present study corroborates the existence of high indicators of ODV, similarly to other Portuguese (e.g., Machado et al., 2010; Neves et al., 2016; Santos & Caridade, 2017; Santos et al., 2019) and international (Haynie et al., 2013; Jennings et al., 2017; Straus, 2004) studies. Also, as in other international (e.g., Fernández-Fuertes & Fuertes, 2010; Sears & Byers, 2010) and Portuguese (e.g., Guerreiro et al., 2017; Machado et al., 2010; Santos et al., 2019) studies, in the present study, the abusive behaviours associated with minor violence were the most admitted by the participants, either in terms of perpetration as in terms of victimization. Nonetheless, these data are of concern and should not at all lead to a devaluation of the problem of violence in dating context.

Consistent with previous international studies (e.g., Borrajo et al., 2015; Borrajo et al., 2015a; Marganski & Melander, 2015; Temple et al., 2016; Zapor et al., 2017; Zweig et al., 2013), in the present study CDA victimization and perpetration were positively related to ODV victimization and perpetration. Effectively, the literature has been conceptualizing CDA either as a form of psychological abuse, frequently related to face-to-face intimate violence (Schnurr et al., 2013), or as an extension of ODV (Korchmaros, Ybarra, Langhinrichsen-Rohling, Boyd, & Lenhart, 2013). A longitudinal study developed by Temple et al. (2016) also show that the CDA experiences tend to coincide with ODV involvements, concluding that adolescents and young people who are victims in one context (e.g., physical-to-face abuse) have a higher risk of victimization in the other context (e.g., using ICTs), with detrimental implications for adolescent psychosocial adjustment and developmental pathways.

This study contains some limitations that should be considered to better interpret the results. It is an exploratory study, using self-report and retrospective instruments and with a mostly female participation (89%), which does not allow to generalize the results to the entire Portuguese population. The sample is small. It is therefore important that future studies in this field ensure a larger number of participants, gender balance and sample representativeness. Additional longitudinal research is needed in Portuguese context, to elucidate whether CDA is a distinct form of abuse, or if it constitutes an extension of ODV. Longitudinal studies are also important to better understand predictors of CDA perpetration and victimization. Finally, it is also important to identify and perceive the effects of ODV versus CDA to better understand its potential and possible differential impact, or if the cumulative abuse of both CDA and ODV results in greater harm to the victim.

The co-occurrence of CDA and ODV signals the importance of additional strategies to encourage a more cautious use of ICTs, aiming to prevent specific situations between dating partners, able to trigger abusive behaviours. Prevention efforts should focus on promoting healthy relationships, either through face-to-face interactions or when involving the use of ICTs.

REFERENCES

Ameral, V., Palm Reed, K. M., & Hines, D. A. (2017). An analysis of help-seeking patterns among college students victims of sexual assault, dating violence, and stalking. *Journal of Interpersonal Violence, 00*, 1-25. https://doi.org/10.1177/0886260517721169.

Baker, C., & Carreno, P. (2015). Understanding the role of technology in adolescent dating and dating violence. *Journal Child Family Studies, 25*, 308-320. https://doi.org/10.1007/s10826-015-0196-5.

Bennett, D. C., Guran, E. L., Ramos, M. C., & Margolin, G. (2011). College students' electronic victimization in friendships and dating relationships: Anticipated distress and associations with risky behaviors. *Violence and Victims, 26*, 410-429. https://doi.org/10.1891/0886-6708.26.4.410.

Borrajo, R., Gámex-Guadix, M., & Calvete, E. (2015a). Cyber dating abuse: Prevalence, context, and relationships with offline dating aggression. *Psychological Reports: Relationships & Communications, 116*(2), 566-585. https://doi.org/10.2466/21.16.PR0.116k22w4.

Borrajo, R., Gámex-Guadix, M., Pereda, N., & Calvete, E. (2015). The development and validation of the cyber dating abuse questionnaire among young couples. *Computers in Human Behavior, 48*, 358-365. https://doi.org/10.1016/j.chb.2015.01.063.

Borrajo, R., Gámex-Guadix, M., Pereda, N., & Calvete, E. (2015). The development and validation of the cyber dating abuse questionnaire among young couples. *Computers in Human Behavior, 48*, 358 – 365. https://doi.org/10.1016/j.chb.2015.01.063.

Brown, C., & Hegarty, K. (2018). Digital dating abuse measures: A critical review. *Aggression and Violent Behavior, 40*, 44-59. https://doi.org/10.1016/j.avb.2018.03.003.

Burke, S. C., Wallen, M., Vail-Smith, K., & Knox, D. (2011). Using technology to control intimate partners: an exploratory study of college undergraduates. *Computers in Human Behavior, 27*, 1162 - 1167. https://doi.org/10.1016/j.chb.2010.12.010.

Caridade S. & Braga, T. (2019). Versão portuguesa do Cyber Dating Abuse Questionaire (CDAQ) – Questionário sobre Ciberabuso no Namoro (CibAN): Adaptação e propriedades psicométricas [Portuguese Version of Cyber Dating Abuse Questionnaire (CDAQ) - Dating Cyberabuse Questionnaire (CibAN): Adaptation and Psychometric Properties]. *Análise Psicológica, 1*(XXXVII), 93-105. https://doi.org/10.14417/ap.1543.

Caridade, S. (2018). Violência no namoro: Contextualização teórica e empírica [Dating violence: Theoretical and empirical contextualization]. In S. Neves & A. Correia (Orgs.). *Violências no namoro [Dating violence]* (pp.9-40). Maia: Edições ISMAI.

Caridade, S., (2016). Violência no namoro [Dating violence]. In R. Maia, L. Nunes et al. (Ed.,), *Dicionário Crime, Justiça e Sociedade [Ditionary Crime, Justice and Society]*, pp. 527-529. Lisboa: Sílabo.

Centers for Disease Control and Prevention (CDC) (2016). *Teen dating violence.* Retrieved on 10 April 2019 from http://www.cdc.gov/violenceprevention/intimatepartnerviolence/teen_dating_violence.html

Dank, M., Lachman, P., Zweig, J., & Yahner, J. (2014). Dating violence experiences of lesbian, gay, bisexual, and transgender youth. *Journal of Youth and Adolescence, 43*(5), 846-57. https://doi.org/10.1007/s10964-013-9975-8.

Fernández-Fuertes, A., & Fuertes, A. (2010). Physical and psychological aggression in dating relationships of Spanish adolescents: Motives and consequences. *Child Abuse & Neglect, 34*, 183-191. https://doi.org/10.1016/j.chiabu.2010.01.002.

FRA - European Union Agency for Fundamental Rights (2014). *Violence against women: An EU-wide survey.* Austria: FRA – European Union. Agency for Fundamental Rights.

Gámez-Guadix, M., Borrajo, E., & Calvete, E. (2018). Abuso, control y violencia en la pareja através de internet y los smartphones: Características, evaluación y prevención [Partner abuse, control and violence through internet and smartphones: characteristics, evaluation and prevention]. *Papeles del Psicólogo, 39*(3), 218-227. https://doi.org/10.23923/pap.psicol2018.2874.

246 *Sónia Caridade, Isa Ataíde and Maria Alzira Pimenta Dinis*

Guerreiro, A., Teixeira, M., Dias, T., Pontedeira, C., Cordeiro, J., Magalhães, M. J., Silva, M., Ribeiro, P. & Mendes, T. (2017). Violência no namoro: Resultados nacionais apontam a gravidade do Problemas [*Dating Violence: National Results Point to Severity of Problems*]. *UMAR - União de Mulheres Alternativa e Reposta,* Porto.

Hamby, S., & Turner, H. (2013). Measuring teen dating violence in males and females: Insights from the national survey of children's exposure to violence. *Psychology of Violence, 4,* 323-339. https://doi.org/ 10.1037/a002970.

Haynie, D. L., Farhat, T., Brooks-Russell, A., Wang, J., Barbieri, B., & Iannotti, R. J. (2013). Dating violence perpetration and victimization among US adolescents: Prevalence, patterns, and associations with health complaints and substance use. *Journal of Adolescent Health, 53*(2), 194-20. https://doi.org/10.1016/j.jadohealth.2013.02.008.

Korchmaros, J. D., Ybarra, M. L., Langhinrichsen-Rohling, J., Boyd, J., & Lenhart, A. (2013). Perpetration of teen dating violence in a networked society. *Cyberpsychology, Behavior, Networking, 16*(8), 561-567. https://doi.org/10.1089/cyber.2012.0627.

Leisring, P., & Giumetti, G. (2014). Sticks and stones may break my bones, but abusive text messages also hurt: Development and validation of the cyber psychological abuse scale. Partner Abuse, 5(3), 323-341. https://doi.org/10.1891/1946-6560.5.3.323.

Machado, C., Caridade, S., & Martins, C. (2010). Violence in juvenile dating relationships self-reported prevalence and attitudes in a Portuguese sample. *Journal of Family Violence,* 25, 43-52. https://doi.org/10.1007/s10896-009-9268-x.

Marganski, A. & Melander, L. (2016). Intimate partner violence victimization in the cyber and real world: Examining the extent of cyber aggression experiences and its association with in-person dating violence. *Journal of Interpersonal Violence,* 1-25. https://doi.org/10.1177/0886260515614283.

Morelli, M., Bianchi, D., Chirumbolo, A., & Baiocco, R. (2017). The cyber dating violence inventory. Validation of a new scale for online perpetration and victimization among dating partners. *European*

Journal of Developmental Psychology, 1-8. https://doi.org/10.1080/17405629.2017.1305885.

Neves, S., Cameira, M., Machado, M., Duarte, V., & Machado, F. (2016). Beliefs on marital violence and self-reported dating violence: A comparative study of Cape Verdean and Portuguese adolescents. *Journal of Child and Adolescent Trauma,* 1-8. https://doi.org/10.1007/s40653-016-0099-7.

Ouytsel, J., Ponnet, K., & Walrave, M. (2016). Cyber dating abuse victimization among secondary school students from a lifestyle-routine activities theory perspective. *Journal of Interpersonal Violence,* 1-10. https://doi.org/10.1177/0886260516629390.

Ouytsel, J., Ponnet, K., & Walrave, M. (2017). Cyber dating abuse: Investigating digital monitoring behaviors among adolescents from a social learning perspective. *Journal of Interpersonal Violence,* 1-22. https://doi.org/10.1177/0886260517719538.

Peskin, M., Marklam, C., Shegogl, R., Temple, J., Baumler, E., Addy, R., Hernandez, B., Cuccaro, P., Gabay, E., Thiel, M., & Emery, S. (2017). Prevalence and correlates of the perpetration of cyber dating abuse among early adolescents. *Journal Youth Adolescence, 46,* 358–375. https://doi.org/10.1007/s10964-016-0568-1.

Reed, L., Tolman, R., & Ward, M. (2016). Snooping and sexting: Digital media as a context for dating aggression and abuse among college students. *Violence Against Women, 22*(13) 1556-1576. https://doi.org/10.1177/1077801216630143.

Reed, L., Tolman, R., & Ward, M. (2017). Gender matters: Experiences and consequences of digital dating abuse victimization in adolescent dating relationships. *Journal of Adolescence, 59,* 79-89. https://doi.org/10.1016/j.adolescence.2017.05.015.

Santos, R., & Caridade, S. (2017). Vivências amorosas em adolescentes: das dinâmicas abusivas ao (des)ajustamento psicossocial [Adolescents intimate relationships: from abusive dynamics to (de) psychosocial adjustment]. *Revista Psique, 13,* 18-39.

Santos, A., Caridade, S., & Cardoso, J. (2019). Violência nas relações íntimas juvenis: (Des)ajustamento psicossocial e estratégias de coping

[Dating violence in young people: Psychosocial adjustment and coping strategies]. *Contextos Clínicos, 12*(1) 1-25. https://doi.org/10.4013/ctc.2019.121.01.

Schnurr, M., Mahatmya, D., Basche, R. (2013). The role of dominance, cyber aggression perpetration, and gender on emerging adults' perpetration of intimate partner violence. *Psychology of Violence, 3*(1), 70-83. https://doi.org/10.1037/a0030601.

Sears, H. A., & Byers, E. A. (2010). Adolescent girls' and boys' experiences of psychologically, physically, and sexually aggressive behaviors in their dating relationships: co-occurrence and emotional reaction. *Journal of Aggression, Maltreatment & Trauma, 19*, 517-539. https://doi.org/10.1080/10926771.2010.495035.

Stonard, K. E., Bowen, E., Walker, K., & Price, S. A. (2017). "They'll always find a way to get to you": Technology use in adolescent romantic relationships and its role in dating violence and abuse. *Journal of Interpersonal Violence, 32*(14), 2083-2117. https://doi.org/10.1177/0886260515590787.

Straus, M. (2004). Prevalence of violence against dating partners by males and female university students worldwide. *Violence Against Women, 10*, 790-811. https://doi.org/10.1177/1077801204265552.

Straus, M. (2008). Dominance and symmetry in partner violence by male and female university students in 32 nations. *Children and Youth Services Review, 30*, 252-275. https://doi.org/10.1016/j.childyouth.2007.10.004.

Temple, J. R., Choi, H. J., Brem, M., Wolford-Clevenger, C., Stuart, G. L., & Peskin, M. F., et al. (2016). The temporal association between traditional and cyber dating abuse among adolescents. *Journal of Youth and Adolescence, 45*, 340–349. https://doi.org/10.1007/s10964-015-0380-3.

Villora, B., Yuberro, S., & Navarro, R. (2019). Cyber Dating Abuse and masculine gender norms in a sample of male adults. *Future Internet, 11*, 84. https://doi.org/10.3390/fi11040084.

Watkins, L., Maldonado, R., & DiLillo, D. (2016). The cyber aggression in relationships scale: A new multidimensional measure of technology-based intimate partner aggression. *Assessment,* 1-19. https://doi.org/10.1177/1073191116665696.

Yahner, J., Dank, M., Zweig, J. M., & Lachman, P. (2015). The co-occurrence of physical and cyber dating violence and bullying among teens. *Journal of Interpersonal Violence, 30,* 1079–1089. https://doi.org/10.1177/0886260514540324.

Zapor, H., Wolford-Clevenger, C., Elmquist, J., Febres, J., Shorey, R. C., Brasfield, H., Leisring, P., & Stuart, G. (2017). Psychological aggression committed through technology: A study with dating college student. *Partner Abuse, 8*(2), 127-145. https://doi.org/10.1891/1946-6560.8.2.127.

Zweig, J. M., Dank, M., Yahner, & Lachman, P. (2013). The rate of cyber dating abuse among teens and how it relates to other forms of teen dating violence. *Journal of Youth Adolescence, 42,* 1063–1077. https://doi.org/10.1007/s10964-013-9922.

Zweig, J. M., Dank, M., Yahner, & Lachman, P. (2013). The rate of cyber dating abuse among teens and how it relates to other forms of teen dating violence. *Journal of Youth Adolescence, 42,* 1063–1077. https://doi.org/10.1007/s10964-013-9922.

Zweig, J., Lachman, P., Dank, J., Yahner & M., (2014). Correlates of cyber dating abuse among teens. *Journal of Youth Adolescence, 43,* 1306–1321. https://doi.org/10.1007/s10964-013-0047-x.

In: Victims of Violence
Editor: Mathias L. Knudsen

ISBN: 978-1-53617-140-2
© 2020 Nova Science Publishers, Inc.

Chapter 12

MULTIPLE VICTIMIZATION OF CHILDREN AND ADOLESCENTS: DEVELOPMENTAL IMPACT AND PSYCHOLOGICAL INTERVENTION

Ana Sani[1,2,3,], Daniela Bastos[1] and Maria Alzira Pimenta Dinis[1,2,4]*

[1]University Fernando Pessoa (UFP), Porto, Portugal
[2]Permanent Observatory Violence and Crime (OPVC),
University Fernando Pessoa (UFP), Porto, Portugal
[3]Research Center on Child Studies (CIEC),
University of Minho (UM), Braga, Portugal
[4]UFP Energy, Environment and Health Research Unit (FP-ENAS),
University Fernando Pessoa (UFP), Porto, Portugal

---

* Corresponding Author's E-mail: anasani@ufp.edu.pt.

ABSTRACT

Children and adolescents are exposed to violence every day and in various contexts, either in the family, at school or in the community. Child and youth victimization is considered a serious public health problem. The lack of knowledge and understanding about it has serious consequences for the individual and for the society. International scientific literature has shown that in addition to life-long victimization, children and young people tend to experience multiple forms of victimization, so an evaluative and interventive approach focused on a single type of violence may be ineffective and inefficient. The study of the phenomenon of multiple victimization is crucial to understand the impact on the adjustment of children and adolescents, as well as for the development of intervention strategies better suited to the needs assessed in this population. In this chapter, a review of the literature on the phenomenon of child and youth multiple victimization will be carried out, addressing the main risk factors, the implications for the development of children and young people, and subsequently suggesting guidelines for intervention. Awareness of the phenomenon of child and youth multiple victimization is of particular importance for the prevention of violence at all developmental stages.

Keywords: multiple victimization, polyvictimization, risk factors, psychological intervention, children and adolescents

INTRODUCTION

The phenomenon of child and youth victimization is a global social, public health and human rights problem that has severe, high-impact and lasting consequences (Gracia, López-Quílez, Marco, & Lila, 2017). Child and youth victimization results from an interpersonal process through which a child or adolescent suffers physical and psychological consequences caused by another person, which is contrary to social norms (De Jorge, 1998). More recently (Pina, 2016), victimization has been defined as a "complex concept" of negative connotation, presupposing "the idea of an undesirable event, or an event with undesirable consequences, caused by an external source, or by an individual, group or organization" (p. 534).

Multiple Victimization of Children and Adolescents 253

Studies by the international scientific community on the co-occurrence of multiple forms of victimization in children and young people have raised empirical interest in developmental victimology. According to the literature, the occurrence of singular victimization predicts the possibility of other lifelong victimization (e.g., Finkelhor, 2013; Finkelhor, Ormrod, & Turner, 2007b).

Multiple victimization is defined as the simultaneous experience of different specific forms of violence (e.g., exposure to domestic/interparental violence, child maltreatment, sexual assault/abuse, bullying, stalking, sexual violence, dating violence), and there are different expressions to refer to this problem, (e.g., multiple victimization, repeated victimization, polyvictimization) (Matos, 2016). According to the studies of Finkelhor, Ormrod, Turner and Hamby (2005), the singular experience of a single type of victimization is rare, and as such, the authors proposed the concept of polyvictimization, so that it was possible to characterize the experience of four or more forms of victimization. These two concepts differ in that "multiple victimization" refers to two or more forms of victimization (Hope, Brian, Trickett, & Osborn, 2001), while "polyvictimization" is characterized by the experience of four or more types of victimization (Finkelhor et al., 2007a). Both concepts have implied that increased victimization is associated with greater psychological maladjustment (Finkelhor et al., 2005).

Multiple victimization and polyvictimization should be distinguished from the terms "chronic victimization" and "revictimization," as these imply the experience of more than one episode of the same type of violence over a given period of time (Finkelhor et al., 2007a). It should also be considered that children and young people who experience extremely high levels of victimization (i.e., four or more types of violence), and from multiple sources, are classified as polyvictims (Finkelhor et al., 2005; Finkelhor et al., 2007a; Finkelhor, 2013), distinguishing themselves from other victims who are less exposed to violence because of the nature of their victimizations being more severe, the greater number of victimizations they experience and the excessive representation among certain demographic groups (Finkelhor, Turner, Hamby, & Ormrod, 2011).

Child and youth victimization is a major public health problem, but the lack of understanding of its serious life-long consequences and its implications for society make prevention programs for this problem difficult to accomplish (Norman, Byambaa, Butchart, Scott, & Vos, 2012). To understand the etiology of these phenomena, it is important to consider that there is no single cause for the occurrence of the symptoms, as there are multiple and interactive factors at individual, family, community and social levels contributing to the existence of child and youth victimization (Dong et al., 2004).

Thus, in this chapter the risk factors for child and youth multiple victimization will be discussed, aiming to help to understand the potential effects of this experience on the development of children, youth and adults. Considering the importance of understanding this problem for the prevention of violence, some proposals for intervention in the phenomenon of child and youth multiple victimization are debated at the end.

RISK FACTORS FOR MULTIPLE CHILD AND YOUTH VICTIMIZATION

Whether at home, at school or in the community, children and young people are exposed to violence every day. Exposure of children and/or young people to violence can cause significant physical, mental and emotional damage, with long-term effects that may last into adulthood (Turner et al., 2017). Focusing on a single type of victimization may contribute to overestimate the impact of hiding the effect of another type of victimization suffered by a child or adolescent (Finkelhor, 2013; Soler, Forns, Kirchner, & Segura, 2015). It is important to consider that exposure to multiple forms of victimization is relatively common, with literature on the subject reporting that when a person is exposed to a violence category, that person is likely to fall victim to additional categories as well (Elliott, Alexander, Pierce, Aspelmeier, & Richmond, 2009; Finkelhor et al., 2007a). This means that child and youth victimization is a risk factor for maladaptive

Multiple Victimization of Children and Adolescents   255

outcomes (Elliott et al., 2009), particularly for those who are polyvictims because they are at even greater risk of continuing to experience repeated victimization throughout their lives (Finkelhor, 2013; Finkelhor et al., 2007b; Musicaro et al., 2017). This is because polyvictimization is associated with a reduction in social and personal resources (Turner, Shattuck, Finkelhor, & Hamby, 2015). The effects and adversities often accumulate over time (Turnet, Finkelhor, & Ormrod, 2010) and, after a certain threshold of victimization, this will make child or youth coping strategies generalized to all other interpersonal contexts in which they are inserted (Finkelhor et al., 2007a). Overall, children and youth experiencing significant trauma and who have experienced a wide range of interpersonal and relationship difficulties are more likely to have developed into dysfunctional families (Elliot et al., 2009) or families more vulnerable to crime (Finkelhor et al., 2011).

Children and young people exposed to parental abuse are more likely than non-parental victims to experience peer, or other abuse throughout their lives (Finkelhor, 2013). This is because environmental, family and community circumstances may increase the risk of varying victimization (Finkelhor et al., 2007a). That is, the "place" where the child and young person resides is crucial to understand the variations in prevalence and inequalities in the risk of child and youth victimization, and exposure to victimization can generally be considered to occur within a dysfunctional context of social deprivation and other environmental stressors that are also associated with psychological problems (Gracia et al., 2017). In this sense, child and youth victimization becomes a marker of family problems and both situations can lead to the development of psychological problems (Norman et al., 2012).

The studies by Finkelhor (2013) thus corroborate that although additional victimization occurs, parental abuse is an important indicator up to 17 years of age. When young people are faced with unexpected relational scenarios, ruled by violent behaviour and other forms of imposition, they may be led to adopt a position of legitimacy, conceiving such practices as manifestation of love and/or hate (Caridade & Machado, 2006). A period considered as vulnerable is when children and adolescents move into a new school environment (Finkelhor et al., 2011). Accordingly, maintaining healthy relationships is crucial to the proper development of physical, emotional, social, behavioural and intellectual abilities (Turner et al., 2017). The number of friends that the child or young person has is related to the risk of victimization, since having few friends is considered a factor of vulnerability or, on the contrary, making friends becomes a factor of protection (Finkelhor et al., 2007b).

The family plays a very important role in the development of the child's socialization, and both parents and other caregivers are the privileged reference model that shape the child's attitudes and behaviours for the future (Sani, 2017). Thus, early exposure to violent, abusive and/or neglectful environments can disrupt the development of healthy emotional regulation and social skills of the child or adolescent (Peh et al., 2017). Also, the fact that victimization occurs in one context increases the probability of occurring in a different context, so children and adolescents may have been victimized in various places, suffering a decline in support levels in distinct areas of life, such as family or peers (Finkelhor, 2013; Turner et al., 2015). When a child or young person is victimized in various places, the number of "safe havens" available to the youth decreases, i.e., contexts where there is no victimization are reduced (Wright, Fagan, & Pinchevsky, 2013). Decreasing these safety havens may be one of the reasons why polyvictims lives experience greater trauma than victims of a single type of victimization (Jackson-Hollis, Joseph, & Browne, 2017). It can also be considered that suffering from multiple victimization may be an indicator that children or young people are poorly supervised or socially isolated and thus unprotected, as well as having poor social interaction skills or a variety of pre-existing psychological problems (Finkelhor et al., 2007a). It can thus be stated that the risk of victimization is increased by the environmental condition of the individual (Finkelhor, 2013).

Children and young people with multiple sources of risk, who have no relationship components or safe, stable and stimulating environments, should be identified as intervention targets (Turner et al., 2017). Victims are often flagged with multiple diagnoses that are not specific to trauma symptoms, which may diminish the role of trauma exposure in manifesting

Multiple Victimization of Children and Adolescents 257

their symptomatic profile, leading to a diagnosis that is neither accurate nor specific (Musicaro et al., 2017). Children and young people may not, for various reasons, disclose all of their exhibitions, and parents or caregivers in particular may have an incentive to cover up their children's exhibitions (Finkelhor, Turner, Shattuck, & Hamby, 2013). Not only is violence one of the most damaging experiences among these children and young people, but co-occurrence with other risk factors seriously complicates the prevention and minimization of the negative effects of exposure on healthy development (Nurius, Russell, Herting, Hooven, & Tompson, 2009).

It is known that children and young people who suffer multiple victimization usually report significantly high risk factors, such as stress, suicide risk, risk behaviours, and consequently have lower protective factors, such as social support, school involvement and family structure, than children and/or youth who are exposed to one or no type of victimization (Nurius et al., 2009). Some children or young people suffer several different types of victimization in a short period of time, which may expose them to a particularly high risk of lasting impairment of their physical, mental and emotional health (Finkelhor et al., 2011). Thus, given the complexity of the epidemiology of victimization, it is important to consider that several types of victimization can occur in a single episode, i.e., in a single event, multiple victimization can be identified (Finkelhor et al., 2005).

According to Finkelhor, Ormrod, Turner and Holt (2009), children and young people make individual decisions that may leave them vulnerable to the phenomenon of multiple victimization and polyvictimization, and may consider vulnerabilities such as: (a) living in a family experiencing considerable violence and conflict; (b) have a family affected by economic, employment and substance abuse problems that may compromise a child's supervision or create emotional needs; (c) reside or move to a dangerous community; and (d) being a child or young person with pre-existing emotional problems that increase risky behaviour, generate antagonism and compromise the ability to protect oneself. If victimization occurs cumulatively, the risk may increase and in the long run an individual may appeal to substance abuse to counter present negative emotions (Norman et al., 2012).

As for gender, it has been linked to certain types of victimization. Forns et al. (2015) state that females are approximately twice as likely to report relational and sexual child victimization than males. According to the same authors, these gender-related differences are still associated with general psychopathological impairment.

IMPACT OF MULTIPLE VICTIMIZATION ON CHILD AND YOUTH DEVELOPMENT

Child and youth victimization have been associated with negative health outcomes at different stages of development, and if multiple forms of victimization are experienced, this may be associated with a higher risk of health problems (Springer, Sheridan, Kuo, & Carnes, 2007). Multiple lifelong exposures are associated with psychological functioning and resilience in adulthood (Elliot et al., 2009; Guerra, Inostroza, Villegas, Villalobos, & Pinto-Cortez, 2017). An individual with a history of childhood victimization may be predisposed to react more strongly to subsequent adverse events, even those of minor impact, than if that individual had no history of any type of traumatic experience (Elliot et al., 2009).

The normative development of children and adolescents can be altered, particularly if occurring at an early age, as it negatively affects the physical, cognitive, emotional and social growth of the child, leading to psychological, behavioural and lifelong learning problems (Finkelhor et al., 2005). In addition, polyvictimization increases with age (Finkelhor et al., 2007a), as it also tends to persist over time, with especially intense and lasting effects that occur when problems aggregate, usually in childhood, and thus a higher risk for developing trauma symptoms exists (Finkelhor et al., 2011).

Guerra et al. (2017) point out that the consequences of multiple victimization are more severe than those of exposure to a single type of victimization. Children and/or young victims of a single type of victimization seem to be able to overcome this more easily, compared to victims of multiple types with multiple sources (Finkelhor, 2013). Chan (2013) claims that polyvictimization has a more negative impact on victims' physical and mental health than any individual form of victimization, concluding that polyvictims are more prone to posttraumatic stress, depressive symptoms, suicidal ideation and self-harm.

Exposure to violence in multiple forms has been linked to poorer functioning of mental health and increased stress on life for non-victimized young people, and even for young people with repeated episodes of the same type of victimization (Finkelhor et al., 2007a; Finkelhor et al., 2011). Young people with multiple exposures, i.e., those with the highest levels of cumulative exposure, are considered to exhibit more vulnerable development, as well as greater life adversity, less social support, and negative mental health (Finkelhor et al., 2005). In the study by Turner et al. (2016), it was concluded that a group of young people exposed to abuse in the housing context also had high school victimization rates, and also, that when occurring in more than one context, polyvictimization is strongly associated with worse results at school. Thus, the risk of developing psychological and emotional difficulties resulting from negative experiences may last into adulthood and may or may not exhibit adaptive functioning, despite a history of adversity in childhood and adolescence (Gonzalez-Mendez, Ramírez-Santana, & Hamby, 2018).

The victimization picture reveals that many young people are entangled in a web of violence, suffering victimization in multiple contexts and by multiple perpetrators (Hamby et al., 2018). The characteristics of polyvictims will differ significantly from those of other young people, as their exposure to violence, crime and abuse is much more serious and chronic, accounting for a disproportionate share of the most serious victimizations, having, therefore, relatively few safety areas, which may explain the increasing distress and vulnerability to further victimization (Finkelhor et al., 2007a; Finkelhor et al., 2011).

Multiple victimization and polyvictimization should be controlled or exploited without forgetting the impact of individual forms of victimization, considering that polyvictims are more likely to suffer victimization involving the use of weapons, injury and/or a sexual element than non-victims of violence (Finkelhor, Turner, Shattuck, Hamby, & Kracke, 2015). Thus, polyvictims are probably prevalent among those experiencing the most severe and interpersonal forms of victimization, and their presence is likely to influence the results of any exploration of the impact of these types of victimization if left uncontrolled (Jackson-Hollis et al., 2017).

It is important to note that children and young people are not all equally affected by exposure to violence. Some may have high symptomatology and some may have little or no symptomatology, depending on the individual characteristics of the child or young person, as well as situational-contextual variables (McGloin & Widom, 2001; Soares & Sani, 2015). Thus, despite facing considerable adversity or even childhood trauma, these children and/or young people may not exhibit problematic behaviours and may still have stable cognitive and behavioural patterns, even high, helping the child to achieve resilience, which will or will not be taken into adolescence and consequently into adulthood, depending on their individual, environmental and social characteristics (DuMont, Widom, & Czaja, 2007). Thus, some individuals seem to be able to manifest a positive adaptation and not follow a negative developmental line, i.e., they can function quite positively throughout their lives (McGloin & Widom, 2001). Variations in prevalence and impact in different countries can be attributed, among others, to the influence of cultural factors on the understanding of the concept of violence (Pinto-Cortez, Gutiérrez-Echegoyen, & Henríquez, 2018). Each individual has his own characteristics, and as such, failing in one domain does not necessarily mean that will be failing in another (McGloin & Widom, 2001).

As noted earlier, the polyvictimization model is a good predictor of mental health problems with traumatic symptomatology (Finkelhor et al., 2005; Finkelhor et al., 2007a), such as post-traumatic stress disorder, depressive disorders, substance abuse, anxiety and anger/aversion (Cyr, Clément, & Chamberland, 2014; Le, Hotlon, Nguyen, Wolf, & Fisher, 2016; Wrigth et al., 2013). According to studies by Le et al. (2016), polyvictims were more likely to report suicidal thoughts and plans in the 12 months after victimization, in both sexes.

Multiple Victimization of Children and Adolescents   261

Polyvictimization is highly predictive of trauma symptoms and, when taken into account, tends to considerably lessen or eliminate the association between individual victims and symptomatology. This means that polyvictimization experiences are associated with more severe symptoms than single-type victimization, even if prolonged over time. When other types of victimization are considered, the effects of individual victimizations are reduced or even eliminated (Finkelhor et al., 2007a; Sabri, Hong, Campbell, & Cho, 2013). Polyvictims were more symptomatic than children and young people with only repeated episodes of the same type of victimization (Finkelhor et al., 2007b). It is then considered that some exposures, particularly occurring at a later time than the present, may be forgotten or may have occurred before the memory capacity of some victims is well structured (Finkelhor et al., 2013).

The severity of the type of victimization suffered is one of the strongest predictors for the analysis of the history of victimization (Clemmons, Walsh, DiLillo, & Messman-Moore, 2007) and it should be considered that the older victims are, the more victimization accumulations they have, given that they lived longer (Finkelhor et al., 2011). Exposure to multiple types of trauma, particularly in childhood, is associated with clinically significant difficulties in regulating emotion and severe emotional and behavioural problems (Musicaro et al., 2017). When a child or adolescent resort to self-mutilation behaviours, these behaviours can be seen as maladaptive attempts to deal with the emotional deregulation resulting from the victimization (Peh et al., 2017).

In order to assess the impact of various forms of victimization in childhood and adolescence, and in how to relate it to trauma symptoms, Finkelhor et al. (2007b) named and grouped five categories of child and youth victimization: conventional crime, maltreatment, peer victimization, sexual victimization, and exposure to violence. It is known that polyvictimization is associated with symptoms of high trauma, revictimization in subsequent years, internalizing and externalizing symptoms and problems of social behaviour (Forns et al., 2015). Thus, exposure to multiple victimizations is associated with an increased risk of a wide range of psychological and behavioural problems including depression, substance abuse, low self-esteem, anxiety and other disorders (Norman et al., 2012).

Although an individual has suffered multiple victimization, some can demonstrate positive adaptation and continue to develop in a healthy way (Go, Chu, Barlas, & Chng, 2017). According to Hamby et al. (2018), most people can be resilient, as nearly everyone has been exposed to some form of victimization or other adversity during their lives. However, victimizations experiences are more likely to trigger significant symptomatology as they accumulate, which may lead to post-traumatic discomfort or other clinically significant distress (Hamby et al., 2018). Resilience of these individuals will require consideration of criteria such as employment, homelessness, education, social activity, psychological disturbance, substance abuse and an assessment of their criminal behaviour, while knowing that women will be most resilient throughout their lives (McGloin & Widom, 2001; DuMont et al., 2007).

The initiation of victimization experiences and their consequent permanence has direct effects on the development of social, adaptive skills and coping strategies for children and/or young people (Finkelhor et al., 2009). Without these components, they may not be able to protect themselves or recognize danger signs in their daily lives, thus becoming more vulnerable to other types of victimization (Herman, 1992, as cited in Obsuth, Johnson, Murray, Ribeaud, & Eisner, 2017). Multiple victimization and polyvictimization also weaken some psychological resources that are associated with an individual's self-efficacy, such as self-esteem and self-confidence, as both constructs mediate part of the effect of multiple victimization and polyvictimization on psychological stress, i.e., the higher these phenomena, the lower the self-efficacy and, consequently, more symptoms (Turner et al., 2015). When considered unresolved, multiple victimization and polyvictimization can cause the life of the child or young person to be plagued by the negative consequences of poor school performance, involvement in criminal activity, psychological distress, and likely physical illness (Musicaro et al., 2017).

The consequences can be diverse, such as the impact on physical or mental health, on personality development, potentiating delinquency development, behavioural or educational problems, and it should be noted that these are in fact avoidable problems, as risk factors can be detected and directed to preventive interventions (Finkelhor, 2013; Gracia et al., 2017). Thus, the consequences are great for children and young people, diverting them from the normative and healthy developmental trajectories (Finkelhor, 2013). Regardless of the role of psychosocial resources, exposure to multiple forms of victimization is detrimental to youth well-being (Sabri et al., 2013; Turner et al., 2015), and this may be due, for example, to high levels of emotional arousal, such as fear or anger resulting from suffered victimization, which asserts that multiple victimization and polyvictimization appear to represent a highly consequential set of adverse life experiences, even in the short-term. Therefore, experiencing multiple types of victimization has a powerful effect on self-confidence-related personal resources by negatively impacting adolescents' perceptions of themselves (Turnet et al., 2015). It is this erosion of social and personal resources that will represent an important part of the chain of risk factors that arise from multiple victimization and contribute to a cycle of mental health and revictimization problems over time.

Children and young people exposed to multiple forms of victimization, particularly those with a higher cumulative exposure, report lower social support and consequent higher levels of peer contact, which often serve as supportive resources, involving them in considered high risk behaviours, expressing higher externalizing symptoms (Nurius et al., 2009; Segura, Pereda, Guilera, & Hamby, 2017).

Particular attention should be paid to the identity of the perpetrator, as aggression by caregivers or intimate partners is likely to have a greater negative impact (Grych, Banyard, & Hamby, 2015). It is also very important to realize that witnessing violence, particularly from family members or other loved ones, has mental health effects that are similar to experiencing violence directly (Turner et al., 2010). This is why positive peer relationships have been linked to psychological well-being, while rejection and low peer support in adolescence are associated with distress (Turner et al., 2015).

Intervention with Child and Youth Experiencing Multiple Victimization

Developmental victimology is a field designed to help foster interest and understanding of the wide range of victimizations that children and young people suffer (Finkelhor, 2013). This field of knowledge contributes to the discussion of the psychological and social effects of multiple victimization during childhood and adolescence (Pinto-Cortez et al., 2018). Either the school, the family, and the environment where the child and/or young person are inserted have a direct impact on the long-term resilience the child will have (DuMont et al., 2007). According to studies on the phenomenon, it is concluded that children and young people who develop in stable environments tend to be more resilient than those placed in foster homes and constantly changing, as well as individual and contextual poverty are associated with the risk of being subjected to stressors and psychological distress, as well as a reduction in resources and strategies to deal with these factors (DuMont et al., 2007; Banyard, Hamby, & Grych, 2017). Therefore, the context in which the child and/or young person are inserted will have a direct impact on the stability and resilience it will present in their adult life, and therefore deserves greater attention to prepare professionals to deal with and assess all types of situations (Hamby & Finkelhor, 2001). On the other hand, the extra-family context in which the child or adolescent fits in must also be considered, so as to have a more holistic perception of previous experiences, which may also be contributing to the symptoms presented (Jackson-Hollis et al., 2017). Both social interactions and the environmental contexts associated with family and care relationships represent a crucial part of the social support needed for healthy development (Turner, Shattuck, Finkelhor, & Hamby, 2016).

Conflicts in children are known to be experienced quite intensively, which may lead them to develop non-adaptive behaviours that may persist in the short, medium and long-term (DuMont et al., 2007; Sani, 2017; Turner et al., 2017). Therefore, a succession of factors, often not clearly evident, must be considered for impact analysis. In the assessment to be made, it is

Multiple Victimization of Children and Adolescents 265

necessary to take into account not only what is evident but also other factors associated with children or young people, their families and context. These factors can be functional, not only to increase the risk but also acting as protective mediators of a more negative impact (Sani, 2017).

It is crucial to reduce child and adolescent victimization to accurately and comprehensively measure this experience. These assessments help child and youth welfare professionals to identify and provide services to children and adolescents and victims of violence, as well as their families, also providing programs to educate subjects at-risk and families, as those who work with the risk of violence (Finkelhor et al., 2015). When violence against children or youth is perpetrated by an intimate or family member, better screening protocols are necessary to be used in the various contexts where victims are inserted, as they need more and better prevention programs, and based on evidence and interventions to reduce the harm this type of violence causes (Hamby, Finkelhor, Turner, & Ormrod, 2011). Greater efforts are necessary to coordinate the services needed to keep children, youth and adults safe at home (Hamby et al., 2011).

When faced with a victimized child and/or young person, both clinicians and other professionals dealing with them may refer pessimistic thinking to make expectations about their development. These children and young people should not be regarded as resilient just because at some point in their life they have not been diagnosed with any psychological disturbance, because in doing so an incomplete picture of the individual's life may be created (McGloin & Widom, 2001). People who intervene with victimized children or young people should stress the importance that a significant, non-abusive, person in their life builds a positive and supportive relationship with them, since when this happens, the child tends to show more likely to be competent in the face of adversity (DuMont et al., 2007).

As part of treatment for victims of violence, crime and abuse in various domains, professionals dealing with these children and young people need to provide support to help them reduce their vulnerability to further victimization and to break down the pathways they face that could lead to these adversities (Hamby et al., 2011). This is because children may be resilient to a certain threshold, but when they experience violence over time, or across multiple contexts of their lives, the accumulation of these victimizations can become difficult to overcome and lead to misfit, internalizing and externalizing the problems (Finkelhor et al., 2007a). Thus, professionals dealing with child and juvenile victims should work in both prevention and treatment, working from school prevention programs to therapies for traumatized children (Hamby & Finkelhor, 2001). It must be emphasized the extreme importance for professionals to identify children experiencing multiple victimization/polyvictimization, with priority attention to polyvictims, with high traumatic symptomatology, but also to be aware that when children and/or young people do not respond as well to an intervention, that may be due to facing a higher victimization burden (Finkelhor et al., 2007a; Hamby et al., 2018).

In the case of children, coping strategies can be developed as problem-focused strategies concentrating on the existing problem, or emotion-focused strategies, oriented to lessen the stress experienced (Soares & Sani, 2015). They may also have difficulty remembering certain events as a protection mechanism, but when involved in a healthy and close relationship, tend to be more resilient in adulthood than children who do not have any kind of relationship (Dong et al., 2004). In the case of adolescents at-risk, multiple assets may be considered, such as individual protective factors, competence and effectiveness, and access to multiple resources such as context, environment, family support and community services that will help them to achieve better results (Go et al., 2017).

When positive changes occur in the life of the child and young person, and if they can remain cognitively and contextually stable, they will be able to bring these changes into their future (DuMont et al., 2007). Children and young people who experience these adversities survive and in fact can thrive throughout their lives (Elliott et al., 2009). Working with the strengths of a child and adolescent can be a good predictor, as understanding and applying these strengths to the individual can be as important as having them (Go et al., 2017). It is important for the individual to recognize these strengths in order to be able to apply and develop them in a healthy way and to solve problems, for example through social support, which protects against the negative consequences of adversity and victimization (Finkelhor et al., 2007b; Go et al., 2017).

According to Jackson-Hollis et al. (2017), professionals who come into contact with children victim of violence and are aware of their victimization, should also be aware that they are more likely to develop trauma symptoms and have a greater need for monitoring and intervention. Correctly identifying children and young people at-risk and developing interventions to protect them from violence is extremely important, as all forms of victimization should be considered as part of the set of risk factors for interpersonal violence in future assessments (Norman et al., 2012).

At the clinical level, questioning only about a particular type of victimization can result in a failure to identify children who experience other, even more serious types of victimization (Finkelhor et al., 2007a). It may also result in focusing more on a type of victimization, which is not necessarily the most important, or at least losing a considerable part of the full clinical picture, and failing to identify the most at-risk children or young people, chronically victimized (Finkelhor et al., 2005; Finkelhor, 2013). It is crucial to consider that these young people are systematically exposed to various forms of violence and often in more than one context, and that such exposure can trigger long-term problems, including the onset of substance abuse (Wright et al., 2013). Intelligence, or high cognitive ability, also proves to be a protective variable for the victimized child and/or young person, as it may play a direct or mediating role in other factors such as school performance or problem-solving skills, which in turn may prove beneficial in their future (Frodi & Smetana, 1984, as cited in DuMont et al., 2007).

With regard to multiple victimization and polyvictimization, it is necessary to build broad risk profiles, because while particular forms of victimization cause serious psychological consequences, e.g., sexual abuse, neglect and severe physical abuse, other types of victimization that affect significantly individuals during childhood cannot be ignored when drawing a more complete and reliable picture of the mental health of young adults (Finkelhor et al., 2007; Finkelhor, 2013; Pinto-Cortez et al., 2018; Turner et al., 2015). The protective factors in this regard are the individual and/or environmental resources that are found to contribute to positive adaptation and/or alleviate the effects of risk factors, so that children or young people are able to adapt more successfully. Similar variables such as social support, positive family functioning, positive self-esteem, perceived self-efficacy, problem-solving confrontation, and decision-making appear to protect or mitigate the risk effects on youth exposed to violence (Nurius et al., 2009). Increased emotional awareness can contribute to reducing vulnerability and avoiding revival (Gonzalez-Mendez et al., 2018).

A practitioner working with victimized children and youth should consider the concept and predictors of resilience in developing both prevention and intervention strategies, always bearing in mind the possibility that a child or young person will not only suffer a single type of victimization and consequently, not only the child and/or young person who suffers the victimization must be involved, but also the context must be taken into consideration (DuMont et al., 2007; Gracia et al., 2017). The experiences of the child should not be considered as isolated events in their life, since suffering victimization does not exclude another event of a completely different type (Dong et al., 2004). Resilience means not only maintaining psychological health after an experience of victimization, but also broadening one's perspective, developing confrontational strategies, and strengthening social relationships after negative experiences (Feeney & Collins, 2015). Focusing on working with resilience represents a shift from looking at-risk factors leading to psychosocial problems, identifying strengths in past negative experiences (Gonzalez-Mendez et al., 2018).

It is crucial to go beyond simple classifications of victim or non-victim and to consider different characteristics such as frequency, duration, nature of acts and use of force, as, cumulatively, these factors are indicators of the severity of the victimization suffered by children or young people (Clemmons et al., 2007). Taking a person-centred and strengths-based approach will further improve the effectiveness of interventions and also improve outcomes for abused adolescents living in residential care (Go et al., 2017). It is important to understand the ways to improve anger management and increase emotional regulation, also taking into account the entire family history, as early on comes the congruence that on an individual

Multiple Victimization of Children and Adolescents 269

level, a child or young person who has the opportunity to engage in sport, art, music or some pastime, has better functioning and well-being during adolescence. If children or young people maintain safe, nutritional and stable relationships, this will be a significant aspect for the social and physical environments that protect children and promote their healthy development (Turner et al., 2015). On the contrary, an unpredictable and chaotic home environment may diminish the child's perception of a trustworthy and fair world (Turner et al., 2017). Continuing to focus on the prevalence and incidence of children relating violence, can help those working with children and their families to better understand what can be effective in preventing violence and improving safety (Finkelhor et al., 2015).

Therefore, interventions should ensure that these children and young people receive assistance in the form of increasing positive confrontation skills and decreasing the likelihood of using negative confrontation skills when dealing with violence, victimization or negative emotions associated with such exposure (Wright et al., 2013). Formally less therapeutic programs, including engaging in extracurricular activities rather than spending time with only other victimized children or youth, can have positive effects on protective factors (Segura et al., 2017). Effective school-based prevention programs, such as promoting alternative thinking strategies and skills training are also important. They can be used to improve the behavioural and emotional competence of children or young people by providing them with coping skills, deal with anxiety and to recognize and respond appropriately to negative emotions, when exposed to victimization (Wright et al., 2013). Adaptive regulation of emotions has been broadly conceptualized to include awareness and identification of emotions, recognition and acceptance of emotions, tolerance for suffering, impulse control or emotional reactivity, and the ability to use goal-directed regulatory strategies to shape emotions and/or to influence behaviours. Interventions aimed at developing and/or improving the skills of healthy emotional regulation among maltreated children and adolescents may also contribute to the prevention of self-injury (Peh et al., 2017).

One of the strategies known to be effective is the resilience portfolio model, which is a strength-based framework designed to provide a holistic understanding of the protective factors and processes that promote resilience in children and youth people exposed to violence, which proposes that the density and diversity of resources and assets available to individuals shape their responses to violence, thus identifying three functional categories of high-order forces considered to be particularly relevant to resilience: regulatory, interpersonal and meaning forces. The resilience portfolio model proposes that the psychological health of individuals after exposure to violence is a product of the characteristics of adversity, the assets and resources available to them, and their behaviour or response to the problem (Grych et al., 2015). Personality factors such as self-esteem, easy temperament, and the fundamental role of interpersonal relationships, especially family relationships, are important to one's resilience (Banyard, Hamby, & Grych, 2017). Thus, building strengths can help not only to alleviate symptoms and increase well-being, but also help in the ability to better cope with new adversity in the future, i.e., intervention must go beyond the symptom's relief (Grych et al., 2015). Individuals with strong emotional regulation skills are less likely to develop risky behaviours, and meaning-making practices can help one reshape adversity by practicing stress reduction and relieving pressure on the emotional regulation system (Banyard et al. al., 2017).

The poly-strengths capture the number of resources and assets that children and their families can use to help isolate young people from violence, i.e., prevention, or to help confront and promote well-being after victimization, i.e., intervention. Well-being can be treated directly with interventions related to positive psychology, such as mindfulness, relaxation and social involvement (Hamby et al., 2018). It is important not to forget that at all stages of development, the involvement of parents or carers in the intervention process can be crucial to success, as interventions focused on their involvement were more effective in reducing child self-reporting than interventions that did not focus directly in parental involvement (Musicaro et al., 2017).

Clinicians, social workers and other practitioners related to these phenomena should consider the triad made up of a history of victimization experiences, protective factors and mental health problems, so that efforts

Multiple Victimization of Children and Adolescents 271

are directed to ensuring that wherever children and young people live, they can be free from the factor of violence (Segura et al., 2017).

CONCLUSION

It is crucial to understand and signal the phenomenon of multiple victimization or polyvictimization that may be experienced by child and young people in different contexts and throughout life. Within a wide spectrum of victimization experineces, it is not possible to consider single victimization alone, because the impact suffered by a child or adolescent, may be overestimated, increasing the risk of perpetuating the victimization throughout life, not offering the more accurate intervention to respond to the problem. In fact, one victimization experience may predict other forms of violence that may co-occur, and that information is important because it allows a correct assessment of the victimization experience in terms of frequency, duration, severity, context and type of the aggression, determining subsequent intervention.

Multiple victimization and polyvictimization have short, medium and long-term consequences. A lack of understanding of both the phenomenon and the serious consequences of life-long victimization has hampered prevention programs in this area. In certain cases, the intervention plan may be directed towards symptom relief, but it is important to consider that there is not always associated symptomatology.

In addition to working with the child, it is important to consider the entire context and to assess the need to direct the intervention to it as well. Such an action requires a coordinated strategy, which may involve the mobilization of poly-forces exhibited by the child and family. Such factors may help to prevent or confront violence, as well as to promote the well-being of children and young people in the face of one or more experiences of victimization.

It is necessary to raise awareness to this phenomenon, particularly among professionals dealing with this specific population, so that they are adequately flagged. This makes it possible to better assess the problem of

272   *Ana Sani, Daniela Bastos and Maria Alzira Pimenta Dinis*

child or adolescent victimization and, consequently, to better target intervention strategies for each case.

ACKNOWLEDGMENTS

This work is funded by National Funds through the FCT - Foundation for Science and Technology within the framework of the CIEC (Research Center for Child Studies of the University of Minho) project under the reference UID/CED/00317/2019.

REFERENCES

Banyard, V., Hamby, S., & Grych, J. (2017). Health effects of adverse childhood events: identifying promising protective factors at the intersection of mental and physical well-being. *Child Abuse & Neglect, 65,* 88-98. https://doi.org/10.1016/j.chiabu.2017.01.011.

Caridade, S., & Machado, C. (2006). Violência na intimidade juvenil: da vitimação à perpetuação [Violence in juvenile intimacy: from victimization to perpetuation]. *Análise Psicológica, 4*(XXIV), 485-493. https://doi.org/10.14417/ap.541.

Chan, K. L. (2013). Victimization and poly-victimization among school-aged chinese adolescents: Prevalence and associations with health. *Preventive Medicine, 56,* 207-210. https://doi.org/10.1016/j.ypmed. 2012.12.018.

Clemmons, J. C., Walsh, K., DiLillo, D. K., & Messman-Moore, T. L. (2007). Unique and combined contributions of multiple child abuse types and abuse severity to adult trauma symptomatology. *Child Maltreatment, 12*(2), 172-181. https://doi.org/10.1177/ 1077559506298248.

Cyr, K., Clément, M. È., & Chamberland, C. (2014). Lifetime prevalence of multiple victimizations and its impact on children's mental health.

Multiple Victimization of Children and Adolescents 273

Journal of Interpersonal Violence, 29, 616-634. https://doi.org/10. 1177/0886260513505220.

De Jorge, L. (1998). *Victims and criminal process.* España: Fondo de Población de Naciones Unidas (PNUD).

Dong, M., Anda, R. F., Felitti, V. J., Dube, S. R., Williamson, D. F., Thompson T. J., ... Giles W. H. (2004). The interrelatedness of multiple forms of childhood abuse, neglect, and household dysfunction. *Child abuse & neglect, 28,* 771-784. https://doi.org/10. 1016/j.chiabu.2004.01.008.

DuMont, K. A., Widom, C. S., & Czaja, S. J. (2007). Predictors of resilience in abused and neglected children grown-up: The role of individual and neighborhood characteristics. *Child Abuse & Neglect, 3,* 255–274. https://doi.org/10.1016/j.chiabu.2005.11.015.

Elliott, A. N., Alexander, A. A., Pierce, T. W., Aspelmeier, J. E., & Richmond, J. M. (2009). Childhood victimization, poly-victimization, and adjustment to college in women. *Child Maltreatment, 14*(4), 330-343. https://doi.org/10.1177/1077559509332262.

Feeney, B. C., & Collins, N. L. (2015). A new look at social support: A theoretical perspective on thriving through relationships. *Personality and Social Psychology Review, 19,* 113-147. https://doi.org/10.1177/ 1088868314544222.

Finkelhor, D. (2013). Developmental victimology: The comprehensive study of childhood victimization. In R. C. Davis, A. J. Lurigio, & S. Herman (Eds.), *Victims of crime* (Fourth Edition, pp. 75–106). Thousand Oaks, CA: Sage.

Finkelhor, D., Ormrod, R. K., & Turner, H. A. (2007a). Poly-victimization: A neglected component in child victimization. *Child Abuse & Neglect, 31,* 7–26. https://doi.org/10.1016/j.chiabu.2006.06.008.

Finkelhor, D., Ormrod, R. K., & Turner, A. (2007b). Re-victimization patterns in a National longitudinal sample of children and youth. *Child Abuse & Neglect, 31,* 479-502. https://doi.org/10.1016/j.chiabu. 2006.03.012.

Finkelhor, D., Ormrod, R. K., Turner, H. A., & Hamby, S. L. (2005). The victimization of children and youth: a comprehensive, national survey.

Child maltreatment, 10, 5-25. Sage. https://doi.org/10.1177/1077559504271287.

Finkelhor, D., Ormrod, R. K., Turner, H. A., & Holt, M. (2009). Pathways to poly-victimization. *Child Maltreatment, 14,* 316–329. https://doi.org/10.1177/1077559509347012.

Finkelhor, D., Turner, H. A., Hamby, S. L., & Ormrod, R. (2011). *Polyvictimization: Children's exposure to multiple types of violence, crime, and abuse.* Office of Juvenile Justice and Delinquency Prevention Bulletin NCJ235504. Washington, DC: U.S. Government Printing Office.

Finkelhor, D., Turner, H. A., Shattuck, A., & Hamby, S. L. (2013). Violence, crime, and abuse exposure in a national sample of children and youth: an update. *Jama Pediatrics, 167*(7), 614-621. https://doi.org/10.1001/jamapediatrics.2013.42.

Finkelhor, D., Turner, H., Shattuck, A., Hamby. S., & Kracke, K. (2015). Children exposure to violence, crime, and abuse: an update. *JAMA Pediatrics, 167*(7), 614–621. https://doi.org/10.1001/jamapediatrics.2013.42.

Forns, M., Kirchner, T., Gómez-Maqueo, E. L., Landgrave, Soler, L., Caterina, C., & Magallón-Neri, E. (2015). The ability of multi-type maltreatment and poly-victimization approaches to reflect psychopathological impairment of victimization in Spanish community adolescents. *Child & Adolescent Behavior, 3,* 187.

Go, M., Chu, C. M., Barlas, J., & Chng, G. S. (2017). The role of strengths in anger and conduct problems in maltreated adolescents. *Child Abuse & Neglect, 67,* 22-31. https://doi.org/10.1016/j.chiabu.2017.01.028.

Gonzalez-Mendez, R., Ramírez-Santana, G., & Hamby, S. (2018). Analyzing Spanish adolescentes through the lens of the resilience portfolio model. *Journal of interpersonal violence,* 1-18. https://doi.org/10.1177/0886260518790600.

Gracia, E., López-Quìlez, A., Marco, M., & Lila, M. (2017). Mapping child maltreatment risk: a 12-year spatio-temporal analysis of neighborhood influences. International *Journal of Health Geographics,* 1-12. https://doi.org/10.1186/s12942-017-0111-y.

Grych, J., Banyard, V., & Hamby, S. (2015). Resilience portfolio model: understanding healthy adaptation in victims of violence. *Psychology of violence, 5*(4), 343-354. https://doi.org/10.1037/a0039671.

Guerra, C., Inostroza, R., Villegas, J., Villalobos, L., & Pinto-Cortez, C. (2017). Polivistimización y sintomatologia postraumática: el rol del apoyo social y la autoeficácia [Polyvictimization and post-traumatic symptomatology: the role of social support and self-efficacy]. *Revista de psicologia, 26*(2), 1-10.

Hamby, S. L., & Finkelhor, D. (2001). Choosing and using child victimization questionnaires. *Juvenile Justice Bulletin* - NCJ186027 (pp. 1-15). Washington, DC: US Government Printing Office. https://doi.org/10.1037/e317972004-001.

Hamby, S., Taylor, E., Jones, L., Mitchell, L. J., Turner, H. A., & Newlin, C. (2018). From poly-victimization to poly-strengths: understanding the web of violence can transform research on youth violence and illuminate the path to prevention and resilience. *Jounal of interpersonal violence, 33*(5), 719-739. https://doi.org/10.1177/0886260517744847.

Hamby, S. L., Finkelhor, D., Turner, H. A., & Ormrod, R. K. (2011). *Children's exposure to intimate partner violence and other family violence*. Bulletin. Washington, DC: U.S. Department of Justice, Office of Justice Programs, Office of Juvenile Justice and Delinquency Prevention.

Hope, T., Bryan, J., Trickett, A., & Osborn, D. R. (2001). The phenomena of multiple victimization. *The British Journal of Criminology, 41,* 595-617. https://doi.org/10.1093/bjc/41.4.595.

Jackson-Hollis, V., Joseph, S., & Browne, K. (2017). The impact of extrafamilial victimization and poly-victimization on the psychological well-being of English young people. *Child Abuse & Neglect, 67,* 349-36. https://doi.org/10.1016/j.chiabu.2017.03.004.

Le, M. T. H., Hotlon, S., Nguyen, H. T., Wolf, R., & Fisher, J. (2016). Poly-victimisation and health risk behaviours, symptoms of mental health problems and suicidal thoughts and plans among adolescents in

Vietnam. *International Journal of Mental Health Systems, 10*(66). https://doi.org/10.1186/s13033-016-0099-x.

Matos, M. (2016). Vitimação múltipla [Multiple victimization]. In R. Maia, L. Nunes, S. Caridade, A. Sani, A., R. Estrada, C. Nogueira, H. Fernandes, & L. Afonso (Coord.), *Dicionário - Crime, Justiça e Sociedade* (pp. 538 – 540). Lisboa: Edições Sílabo.

McGloin, J. M., & Widom, C.S. (2001). Resilience among abused and neglected children grown up. *Development and Psychopathology, 13*, 1021–1038. https://doi.org/10.1017/S095457940100414X.

Musicaro, R. M., Spinazzola, J., Arvidson, J., Swaroop, S.R., Grace, L. G., Yarrow, A., … Ford, J. D. (2017). The complexity of adaptation to childhood polyvictimization in youth and young adults: recommendations for multidisciplinary responders. *Trauma, Violence, & Abuse,* 1-18. Sage. https://doi.org/10.1177/1524838017692365.

Norman, R. E., Byambaa, M., De, R., Butchart, A., Scott, J., & Vos, T. (2012). The long-term health consequences of child physical abuse, emotional abuse, and neglect: a systematic review and meta-analysis. *PLOS Medicine, 9*(11), e1001249. https://doi.org/10.1371/journal.pmed.1001349.

Nurius, P. S., Russel, P. L., Herting, J. H., Hooven, C., & Tompson, E. A. (2009). Risk and protective profiles among never exposed, single form, and multiple form violence exposed youth. *Journal of Child & Adolescent Trauma, 2,* 106-123. https://doi.org/10.1080/193615 20902880798.

Obsuth, I., Johnson, K. M., Murray, A. L., Ribeaud, D., & Eisner, M. (2017). Violent poly-victimization: the longitudinal patterns of physical and emotional victimization throughout adolescence (11-17 years). *Journal of research on adolescence,* 1-21. https://doi.org/10. 1111/jora.12365.

Peh, C. X., Shahwan, S., Fauziana, R., Mahesh, M. V., Sambasivam, R., … Subramaniama, M. (2017). Emotion dysregulation as a mechanism linking child maltreatment exposure and self-harm behaviors in adolescents. *Child abuse & neglect, 67,* 383-390. https://doi.org/10.1016/j.chiabu.2017.03.013.

Multiple Victimization of Children and Adolescents 277

Pina, M. (2016). Vitimação [Victimization]. In R. Maia, L. Nunes, S. Caridade, A. Sani, A., R. Estrada, C. Nogueira, H. Fernandes, & L. Afonso (Coord.), *Dicionário - Crime, Justiça e Sociedade* (pp. 534-536). Lisboa: Edições Sílabo.

Pinto-Cortez, C., Gutiérrez-Echegoyen, P., & Henríquez, D. (2018). Child victimization and polyvictimization among young adults in northern Chile. *Journal of interpersonal Violence*, 1-23. https://doi.org/10.1177/0886260518759058.

Sabri, B., Hong, J. S., Campbell, J. C., & Cho, H. (2013). Understanding children and adolescents' victimizations at multiple levels: an ecological review of the literature. *Journal of Social Service Research, 39*, 322-334. https://doi.org/10.1080/01488376.2013.769835.

Sani, A. I. (2017). Psychological expertise in cases of interparental conflict: recommendations for practice. *Trends in Psychology, 25*(2), 437-445. doi: 10.9788/TP2017.2-20En.

Segura, A., Pereda, N., Guilera, G., & Hamby, S. (2017). Resilience and psychopathology among victimized youth in residential care. *Child Abuse & Neglect, 72*, 301-311. https://doi.org/10.1016/j.chiabu.2017.08.019.

Soares, L., & Sani, A. I. (2015). O impacto da exposição à violência interparental nas crenças [The impact of exposure to interparental violence on beliefs]. *Revista de Psicologia da Criança e do Adolescente, 6*(2), 155-169.

Soler, L., Forns, M., Kirchner, T., & Segura, A. (2015). Relationship between particular areas of victimization and mental health in the context of multiple victimizations in Spanish adolescents. *European Child and Adolescent Psychiatry, 24*, 417–425. https://doi.org/10.1007/s00787-014-0591-2.

Springer, K.W., Sheridan, J., Kuo, D., & Carnes, M. (2007). Long-term physical and mental health consequences of childhood physical abuse: Results from a large population-based sample of men and women. *Child Abuse & Neglect, 31*(5), 517-530. https://doi.org/10.1016/j.chiabu.2007.01.003.

Turner, H. A., Finkelhor, D., & Ormrod, R. (2010). Poly-victimization in a national sample of children and youth. *American Journal of Preventive Medicine, 38*(3), 323-330. https://doi.org/10.1016/j.amepre. 2009.11.012.

Turner, H. A., Merrick, M. T., Finkelhor, D., Hamby, S., Shattuck, A., & Henly, M. (2017). *The prevalence of safe, stable, nurturing relationships among children and adolescents.* National survey of children's exposure to violence. U.S. Department of Justice.

Turner, H. A., Shattuck, A., Finkelhor, D., & Hamby, S. (2015). Effects of poly-victimization on adolescent social support, self-concept, and psychological distress. *Journal of Interpersonal Violence, 32*(5), 755-780. https://doi.org/10.1177/0886260515586376.

Turner, H. A., Shattuck, A., Finkelhor, D., & Hamby, S. (2016). Polyvictimization and youth violence exposure across contexts. *Journal of Adolescent Health, 58*(2), 208–214. https://doi.org/10.1016/ j.jadohealth.2015.09.021.

Wright, E. M., Fagan, A. A., & Pinchevsky, G. M. (2013). The effects of exposure to violence and victimization across life domains on adolescent substance use. *Child Abuse & Neglect, 37,* 899-909. https://doi.org/10.1016/j.chiabu.2013.04.010.

In: Victims of Violence
Editor: Mathias L. Knudsen

ISBN: 978-1-53617-140-2
© 2020 Nova Science Publishers, Inc.

Chapter 13

YOUTH VICTIMS OF COMMUNITY VIOLENCE: DEVELOPMENTAL OUTCOMES AND PREVENTION CHALLENGES

Sónia Caridade[1,2,3,], Ana Sani[1,2,4], Laura M. Nunes[1,2,3] and Maria Alzira Pimenta Dinis[1,2,5]*

[1]University Fernando Pessoa (UFP), Porto, Portugal
[2]Permanent Observatory Violence and Crime (OPVC),
University Fernando Pessoa (UFP), Porto, Portugal
[3]Behaviour and Social Sciences Research Center (FP-B2S),
University Fernando Pessoa (UFP), Porto, Portugal
[4]Research Center on Child Studies (CIEC),
University of Minho (UM), Braga, Portugal
[5]UFP Energy, Environment and Health Research Unit (FP-ENAS),
University Fernando Pessoa (UFP), Porto, Portugal

ABSTRACT

Community violence (CV) is recognized as a complex problem, with multiple origins and expressed in variable ways, encompassing different

---

[*] Corresponding Author's E-mail: soniac@ufp.edu.pt.

types of violence and crimes (e.g., assault, rape, robbery), as a result of circumstances that are related to the characteristics of the environment. Due to socialization and independence processes that are part of youth developmental pathways, young people tend to spend more time away from home and on the street, becoming more exposed to violence and thus also contributing to repeated victimization processes. Different studies have shown that distinct situations may promote numerous victimization processes, with a particular impact on the developmental outcomes of youth and causing great suffering. It has been reported that exposure to violence in the community is associated with mental health issues, i.e., post-traumatic stress disorder (PTSD), anxiety, depression, poor academic performance, aggressive and antisocial behaviours, alcohol and substance abuse, along with multiple adverse health risk behaviours, suicidal ideation, and also resulting in subsequent homelessness in adulthood. With this review chapter, it is intended to analyse and discuss the impact that CV exposure has on youth, accompanied with practical proposals to prevent it. The concept of CV and the different types of violence and crimes that could be involved are examined, mapping the prevalence of youth affected by this form of violence, analysing the effects of exposure to CV, and concluding with initiatives aimed to contribute to the prevention against this sort of violence, and to minimize the consequences and suffering involved.

Keywords: youth victims, community violence (CV), developmental outcomes, prevention challenges

INTRODUCTION

According the World Health Organization (WHO) (2002, p. 5) violence involves the "use of physical force or power, whether in threat or in practice, resulting in or may result in suffering, death, psychological harm, poor development or deprivation." Based on this definition, WHO (2002) proposes the existence of 3 types of violence: i) self-inflicted violence, which includes suicidal behaviour or intentions to self-harm; ii) collective violence, addressed to a group or community, in order to achieve certain political, economic or social goals (e.g., hate crimes or terrorist acts committed by organized groups); and iii) interpersonal violence, involving violence between individuals, and which can be subdivided into partner and

Youth Victims of Community Violence 281

family violence, often manifested, although not exclusively, between members of the same family or intimate partners, in the domestic context (e.g., child abuse, elder abuse, intimate partner violence), and community violence (CV), which is developed among people who are not family-related, who can know one another or not (e.g., youth violence, occasional violence, sexual violence or rape by unknown persons), generally taking place outside the home, and occurring between unrelated individuals, either known or unknown (WHO 2002).

Given the socialization and independence processes that are part of youth developmental pathways, young people tend to spend more time away from home and on the street or other public spaces of social and recreational interactions, becoming more exposed to violence and thus also contributing to repeated victimization processes (Walklate, 2017). Victimization may also be explained by the routine activity theory as being a consequence of whom people associate with, where they live, and where people spend their time (Cohen & Felson, 1979).

Youth may be exposed to CV through various ways, i.e., as offenders, through victimization, witnessing, and hearing about or vicarious exposure (Buka, Stichick, Birdthistle, & Earls, 2001). In this review chapter, the focus will only be on youth as victims or witnesses of CV and the impact that this phenomenon has on youth will be analysed and discussed, along with practical proposals to prevent it. The chapter starts by mapping the prevalence of youth affected by this type of violence and then the effects of CV exposure are analysed and discussed, concluding with initiatives aimed to contribute to the prevention against CV and to minimize the consequences and suffering involved.

YOUTH VICTIMS OF COMMUNITY VIOLENCE AND DEVELOPMENTAL OUTCOMES

The literature has been documenting a high prevalence of CV exposure among adolescents and youth (e.g., Barroso, Peters, Kelder, Conroy,

Murray, & Orpinas, 2008; Finkelhor, Turner, Shattuck, & Hamby, 2015; Kilpatrick, Ruggiero, Acierno, Saunders, Resnick, & Best, 2003). Data of the National Survey of Adolescents (Kilpatrick et al., 2003) show that 39% of the 12-17 years of age range were exposed to CV. Also, in the National Survey of Children's Exposure to Violence (NatSCEV II), Finkelhor and collaborators (2015) found that the rate of exposure to violence throughout life (69.7% as a victim and 71.5% as witness of violence) was high among young people between 14 and 17 years of age.

In Portugal, a study by Nunes, Sani, Caridade, Sousa, & Dinis (2018) developed with 307 university students, reported that 15% of young people admitted having experienced victimization, mostly on the street (71.7%). The majority of respondents acknowledged crimes by students involving theft, robbery, damage to public equipment and drug trafficking. Some neighbourhoods attract some types of crime because they offer opportunities for offending, as there is an appropriate victim (Sammons & Putwain, 2019) with specific activities and routines.

Young men have an increased risk of experiencing all forms of criminal victimization, particularly violent crime, both on the street and in public spaces (see Davies, 2018). It has also been documented that men are at increased risk of violence by other men involving firearms or other weapons, while women are at higher risk of being sexually assaulted by men (Davies, 2018; Mathews et al., 2010).

Different victimization studies (e.g., Barroso et al., 2008; Copeland-Linder, Lambert, & Ialongo, 2010; Gurrola-Pena, Balcazar-Nava, Villar, Luis, & Almanza-Avendano, 2018) have shown that distinct situations may promote numerous victimization processes, with a particularly impact on the developmental outcomes of youth, thus causing great suffering. In this sense, it has been reported that CV exposure, either as a victim or as witness, is associated with diverse internalizing and emotional problems (e.g., post-traumatic stress disorder (PTSD), anxiety, depression) (Chen, Corvo, Lee, Hahm, 2017; Goldner, Gross, Richards, & Ragsdale, 2016; Mrug & Windle, 2010; Sammons & Putwain, 2019), externalizing problems (e.g., aggressive and delinquency behaviours) (Goldner et al., 2016; Mrug & Windle, 2010), alcohol and substance abuse, along with multiple adverse health risk behaviours (Barroso et al., 2008) and poor academic performance (Kliewer & Lepore, 2015). A longitudinal study carried out by Chen et al. (2017) with 8,947 adolescents show that those witnessing CV were more likely to experience depressive symptoms during adolescence, but not during their young adulthood. The same study also reports that the direct exposure to violence during adolescence predict depressive symptoms in adulthood only. A meta-analysis developed by Fowler et al. (2009) aiming to examine the impact of CV exposure on the psychological well-being of children and adolescents found a great association between CV exposure and PTSD symptoms and with externalizing problems, although not as large as the effect of PTSD symptoms. In the same meta-analysis, the age of the sample moderated the effects of CV on internalizing and externalizing problems, i.e., younger children exposed to CV reported more internalizing symptoms, but fewer externalizing symptoms, than adolescents did.

Because exposure to different types of CV may impact youth differently, Goldner et al. (2016), conducted a study in a nonclinical community sample of urban African American young adolescents, examining how exposure to different types and levels of CV was related to emotional and behavioural difficulties. The authors found that moderate victimization was related to all the measures of emotional distress. Both moderate victimization and severe witnessing were associated with symptoms of PTSD child report and every type and severity level of exposure to violence was related to youth report of delinquency. In addition, another study from Barroso et al. (2008), conducted with a sample of urban and ethnically diverse adolescents (n = 8,259) show that students' CV exposure is very frequent and is associated with engagement in aggressive and other risk behaviours, such as to carry a handgun, to be involved in a gang, to use marijuana, compulsive drinking, and to be injured as a result of fighting. These associations between CV exposure and risk behaviours appear to be stronger for girls than boys (Barroso et al., 2008). However, when examining the independent and interactive effects of violence exposure across three different contexts, i.e., home, school, and community, on youth adjustment, Mrug and Windle (2010) found that CV exposure has reduced incremental effects on the problems of internalization and externalization, besides the effects found in the exposure to violence in other contexts.

CV exposure could also impact on the family system, namely on family relationships, family's ability to function and family systems' cope (Vincent, 2009). More specifically, in a qualitative study with 38 low-income urban African American families, Vincent (2009) found distinct problems adversely affecting family relationships and functioning, i.e., communication problems, manifested through the inability or unwillingness of family members to share the most traumatic aspects of their experiences; family conflict as a consequence of CV exposure; caregiver distress and caregiver unavailability, significantly interfering with the caregiver's ability to protect the family. CV exposure also results in increased family isolation, safety concerns among family members, loss of financial resources, and chronically violent neighbourhoods (Vincent, 2009).

Shapland and Hall (2017 as cited by Sammons & Putwain, 2019) identify a range of effects that results of being victimised, as loss of faith in society, i.e., guilty for not being able to avoid victimization, financial loss, avoiding certain places or activities or increased fear of victimization. The media contributes to increase the fear of crime when focusing on sensational events or exaggerating certain incidents.

All this evidence has greatly contributed to the recognition of CV as an important public health problem, impacting the lives of youth, and requiring urgent and coordinated responses.

YOUTH VICTIMS OF COMMUNITY VIOLENCE AND PREVENTION CHALLENGES

CV control should involve recognition of the importance of violence prevention, considering the development of several strategies aimed at eliminating risks and promoting protection against violence in the social environment (Chen & Corvo, 2011). Accordingly, the literature documents the need and benefits in adopting structural measures that mobilize a network of entities to reduce the risk of violence exposure. Therefore, and according to Sani et al. (2019), a close and continuous coordination among academics, police, victim support agencies, social reintegration services and strategies and policies designed to prevent criminal activity, is necessary. Other authors, such as Barroso et al. (2008), have also suggested the need to move from individual-centred behavioural science approaches, to more inclusive broad-based community and ecological approaches, aiming violence prevention. The ecological transactional model has been characterized within a broader theoretical context, supporting both the risk and resilience perspectives. The latter attributes the vulnerability of the adolescent to the compromising health outcomes and to the nature and number of stressors, as well as to the presence of protective factors, able to mitigate the impact of those stressors (Chen & Corvo, 2010).

From the point of view of social recognition approach, the local diagnoses analysing criminal occurrences and encompassing the feelings of the target relevant populations regarding (in)security, are an important resource for the necessary visibility towards victimization. Thus, the development of awareness-raising actions incorporating a primary preventive character and targeting the population identified by Diagnosis of Local Security (DLS) in particularly vulnerable communities may benefit global policy makers in CV risk management (Sani, Nunes, & Caridade, 2019).

Accordingly, in this CV multidisciplinary approach, a perspective focused on the Crime Prevention Through Environmental Design (CPTED) programs (Jeffery, 1971) can enrich the community assessment, aiming CV prevention. Effectively, crime prevention models as CPTED understand environmental spatial conditions as impact factors on behaviours involving CV, since the planned and strategic manipulation of spaces can greatly contribute to the prevention of violent conducts (Nunes & Trindade, 2015).

Given the significant impacts that CV exposure has on youth's family systems, the need to implement a family system intervention model, able to mitigate the problems experienced by a family exposed to CV (Vincent, 2009), is also suggested.

Finally, an important prevention challenge involves considering factors or resources, i.e., individual, family and social characteristics, that could contribute to protect young people from the development of psychopathological symptoms, as stated by Gurrola-Pena et al. (2018). The knowledge of these distinct protective factors is extremely important for the promotion and development of effective CV prevention programs.

CONCLUSION

This chapter intends to document the high prevalence of CV exposure among adolescents and youth, as well as the impact it has on the developmental outcomes of youth, discussing the diverse mental health implications (e.g., PTSD, anxiety, depression, poor academic performance), behavioural problems (e.g., aggressive and antisocial behaviours, alcohol and substance abuse, adverse health risk behaviours, suicidal ideation, also resulting in subsequent homelessness in adulthood), and the impacts on family system.

Despite the limitations of criminal statistics, the prevalence studies indicate that young people are relatively familiarized with crime, either as offenders or as victims. Young people are one of the most vulnerable targets of CV because of their lifestyle, routines or sense of invulnerability. Criminal victimization is one of the most powerful experiences affecting people's lives and, in some cases, PTSD can be developed after trauma. Reducing the risk of victimization and supporting the victims are two important and complementary tasks that must involve the participation of the entire community. Crime prevention implies interrelated and coordinated approaches, implying to move from individual to social intervention levels. CV, in particular, can benefit from an extensive and coordinated work with local control entities that are responsible for the security of population. DLS is an effective tool to recognise the most important needs of the population, thus being able to contribute to crime prevention. When accompanied by spatial observations allowing the observance of physical changes to more pacifying and non-violent conditions, such as CPTED, DLS can make the difference in the work to be developed by the local authorities who have the power of decision on modern urban planning.

ACKNOWLEDGMENTS

This work was financed by National Funds through FCT (Foundation for Science and Technology) under the project LookCrim - Looking at Crime: Communities and Physical Spaces - PTDC/DIR-DCP/28120/2017 and within the framework of the CIEC (Research Center for Child Studies of the University of Minho) project under the reference UID/CED/00317/2019.

REFERENCES

Barroso, C. S., & Peter, R. J., Kelder, S., Conroy, J., Murray, N., & Orpinas, P., (2008). Youth exposure to community violence: Association with aggression, victimization, and risk behaviors. *Journal of Aggression, Maltreatment & Trauma, 17*(2). https://doi:10.1080/10926770802374916.

Buka, S. L., Stichick, T. L., Birdthistle, I., & Earls, F. J. (2001). Youth exposure to violence: Prevalence, risks and consequences. *The American Journal of Orthopsychiatry, 71*(3), 298-310. https://doi.org/10.1037//0002-9432.71.3.298.

Chen, W., & Corvo, K. (2011). Community violence. In Roger J. R. Levesque (Ed.), *Encyclopedia of Adolescence*. USA: Springer. https://doi.org/10.1007/978-1-4419-1695-2.

Chen, W., Corvo, K., Lee, Y., & Hahm, H. C. (2017). Longitudinal trajectory of adolescent exposure to community violence and depressive symptoms among adolescents and young adults: Understanding the effect of mental health service usage. *Community Men Health, 50,* 39-52. https://doi.org/10.1007/s10597-016-0031-5.

Cohen, L. E., & Felson, M. (1979). Social change and crime rate trends: A routine activity approach. *American Sociological Review, 44,* 588-608. https://doi.org/10.2307/2094589.

Copeland-Linder, N., Lambert, S., & Ialongo, N. (2010). Community violence, protective factors, and adolescent mental health: A profile analysis. *Journal Clinical Child Adolescence Psychological, 39*(2), 176-186. https://doi.org/10.1080/15374410903532601.

Davies, P. (2018). Feminist voices, gender and victimizations. In S. Walker (Org.), *Handbook of victims and victimology* (pp. 107-123, 2nd edition). London and New York: Routledge Taylor & Francis Group. https://doi.org/10.4324/9781315712871-8.

Finkelhor, D., Turner, H. A., Shattuck, A., & Hamby, S. L. (2015). Prevalence of childhood exposure to violence, crime, and abuse: Results from the National Survey of Children's exposure to violence. *JAMA Pediatrics, 169*(8), 746-754. https://doi.org/10.1001/jamapediatrics.2015.0676.

Fowler, P. J., Tompsett, C. J., Braciszewski, J. M., Jacques-Tiura, A. J., & Baltes, B. B. (2009). Community violence: A meta-analysis on the effect of exposure and mental health outcomes of children and adolescents. *Development and Psychopathology, 21*(1), 227-259. http://dx.doi.org/10.1017/S0954579409000145.

Goldman-Mellor, S., Margerison-Zilko, C., Allen, K., & Cerda, M. (2016). Perceived and objetively-measured neighborhood violence and adolescent psychological distress. *Journal of Urban Health, 93*(5), 758-769. https://doi.org/10.1007/s11524-016-0079-0.

Goldner, J., Gross, I. M., Richards, M. H., & Ragsdale, B. L. (2015). The relation of severity and type of community violence exposure to emotional distress and problem behaviors among urban African American adolescents. *Violence and Victims, 30*(3), 432-449. https://doi.org/10.1891/0886-6708.vv-d-13-00129.

Gurrola-Pena, G., Balcazar-Nava, P., Villar, O., Luis, A. & Almanza-Avendano, M. (2018). Protective factors for the development of psychopathological symptoms in young victims of community violence. *International Journal of Emergency Mental Health and Human Resilience, 20*(1), 1-9. https://doi.org/10.4172/1522-4821. 1000389.

Jeffery, C. (1971). *Crime prevention through environmental design.* Beverly Hills: Sage Publications.

Kilpatrick, G., Ruggiero, K., Acierno, R., Saunders, B., Resnick, H., Best, C. (2003). Violence and risk of PTSD, major depression, substance abuse/dependence, and comorbidity: Results from the national survey of adolescents. *Journal of Consulting and Clinical Psychology, 71*(4), 692-700. https://doi.org/10.1037/0022-006X.71.4.692.

Kliewer, W., & Lepore, S. J. (2015). Exposure to violence, social cognitive processing and sleep problems in urban adolescents. *Journal of Youth Adolescence, 44*, 507-517. https://doi.org/10.1007/s10964-014-0184-x.

Mathews, S., Outwater, A., Kilonzo, N., Mutto, M., Butchart, A., Odhiambo, A., & Matzopoulos, R. (2010). Community violence. In WHO (Ed.), *Violence and health in the WHO African Region* (pp. 55-77). Brazzaville, WHO.

Mrug, S., & Windle, M. (2010). Prospective effects of violence exposure across multiple contexts on early adolescents' internalizing and externalizing problems. *Journal Child Psychology Psychiatry, 51*(8), 953-61. https://doi.org/10.1111/j.1469-7610.2010.02222.x.

Nunes, L., & Trindade, J. (2015). *Delinquência - Percursos criminais. Desenvolvimento, controle, espaço físico e desorganização social [Delinquency - Criminal Paths. Development, control, physical space and social disorganization].* Porto Alegre: Livraria do Advogado.

Nunes, L., Sani, A., Caridade, S., Sousa, H., Dinis, A. (2018). Segurança e vitimação entre estudantes universitários na cidade do Porto [Security and victimization of university students in the city of Oporto]. *Análise Psicológica, 36*(2), 169-183. https://doi.org/10.14417/ap.13950.

Sani, A., Nunes, L., & Caridade, D. (2019). Exposure to violence in the community: differential vulnerability, diagnoses and interventions. InS. Xu (Ed.), *Violence exposure: Perspectives, gender differences and outcomes (pp. 1-18).* Nova Publishers.

Sammons, A., & Putwain, D. (2019). *Psychology and Crime*. (2nd Edition). London: Routledge. https://doi.org/10.4324/9781351252140.

Vincent, N. (2009). Exposure to community violence and the family: Disruptions in functioning and relationships. *Families in Society: The Journal of Contemporary Social Services, 90*(2), 137-142. https://doi.org/10.1606/1044-3894.3865.

Walklate, S. (2017). Defining victims and victimization. In P. Davies, P. Francis, & C. Greer (Eds.), *Victims, crime and society: An introduction* (pp. 30-46, 2nd Ed). United Kingdom: Sage Publications.

World Health Organization (WHO) (2002). *World report on violence and health*. World Health Organization.

In: Victims of Violence
Editor: Mathias L. Knudsen

ISBN: 978-1-53617-140-2
© 2020 Nova Science Publishers, Inc.

Chapter 14

VIOLENCE IN URBAN COMMUNITY: DIAGNOSIS OF LOCAL SECURITY AND VICTIMIZATION

Ana Sani[1,2,3,], Laura M. Nunes[1,2,4], Sónia Caridade[1,2,4] and Vanessa Azevedo[1,2]*
[1]University Fernando Pessoa (UFP), Porto, Portugal
[2]Permanent Observatory Violence and Crime (OPVC),
University Fernando Pessoa (UFP), Porto, Portugal
[3]Research Center on Child Studies (CIEC),
University of Minho (UM), Braga, Portugal
[4]Behaviour and Social Sciences Research Center (FP-B2S),
University Fernando Pessoa (UFP), Porto, Portugal

ABSTRACT

Community violence is one of the phenomena that most affects perceptions of security. Moreover, when it is associated with violent or criminal victimization (both direct and indirect), it can deeply impact a

---

[*] Corresponding Author's E-mail: anasani@ufp.edu.pt.

population's level of security and fear of crime within a specific geographical context. Accordingly, to develop appropriate helpful responses to victims of violence and crime, it is particularly relevant to assess people's perceptions, to be aware of their victimization experiences and to identify their needs. The Diagnosis of Local Security (DLS) is a community assessment measure that allows for not only the gathering of information about criminal occurrences in a specific geographical area but also the collection of data on experiences of victimization and feelings of (in)security. The DLS became an internationally well-known procedure that empirically supports the development of community interventions. In this regard, based on a study that we are conducting through the community project "LookCrim," in this chapter, we propose to analyze the DLS's potential to assess perceptions of (in)security with respect to the experience of victimization to discuss the challenges of and the responses to the phenomenon of community violence.

Keywords: community violence, victimization, diagnosis of local security

INTRODUCTION

"Life in cities has become an experience full of insecurity, embracing the uncertainty of the world where they are. Crime and antisocial behavior seem to follow the zigzag of the urban environment and its multidimensional flutters, excitement, speed, and confused actions." (Trindade 2017, 193)

Community violence is one of the major challenges of the 21st century, crossing all countries and being particularly prominent for cities and urban contexts (e.g., Muggah 2012; Nunes et al. 2017). Indeed, this type of violence is one of the phenomena that most affects people's perception of (in)security and can deeply impact their daily routines and lifestyles. According to the Global Peace Index 2019, "the Safety and Security domain improved on average, with 85 countries improving and 74 deteriorating. (...) Despite the overall improvement in the Safety and Security domain, there were a number of indicators that deteriorated, including the perceptions of criminality and incarceration rate indicators" (Institute for Economics & Peace 2019, 6). Concomitantly, topics such as crime, violence and

Violence in Urban Community 293

victimization are continuously and avidly widespread by the media – and more recently by social media, which also seem to contribute to the fear of crime and perceptions of (un)safety (Intravia et al. 2017). However, information and empirical data on violence and crime are often presented in a noncontextualized manner, covering extensive and unspecific areas that are socially unconnected, which compromises not only a deeper understanding and knowledge of the phenomena but also the development of proper preventive and intervention strategies. Therefore, it is essential to perform research that is geographically delimited and joins together efforts by academics and stakeholders. An intervention that is geographically focused will clearly promote community development, with consideration given to the needs of the different social groups present in that specific area, for instance, taking into account domains such as age, gender, or social conditions (Sani, Nunes, and Caridade 2019).

In this chapter, we will present a research project named "LookCrim - Looking at Crime: Communities and Physical Spaces," and in more detail, we will describe an empirical study about community violence that is part of this project. Assuming that a community intervention will benefit (i.e., be more effective) when the community itself is involved in the actions of improvement of its geographic area (Silva 2010), one aim of the Project "LookCrim" was to perform a diagnosis of a specific geographic area, namely, the historic center of Porto (HCP), with a focus on urban (in)security issues. More specifically, through the implementation of a Diagnosis of Local Security (DLS) based on the community of the historic center of Porto, we will address the following questions: What are the feelings of (in)security experienced by this urban community? Are the most prevalent crimes similar to those that the population most fears? What is the extent of the victimization reported by the population? Providing answers to these questions will allow for the identification of key points of intervention that can promote increased levels of safety and well-being in the community.

Considering our proposed goals, we structured this chapter into five separate sections. More specifically, in the first section, we briefly address urban communities as spaces of violence, (in)security, and victimization and present the Project "LookCrim." To contextualize the empirical study, we stress the DLS as an evaluation tool and revisit some sociodemographic, territorial and criminal markers from the area under analysis. Then, we present the empirical study, describing its methodological issues (Section 2) and some results (Section 3), organized according to the questions previously defined. Later, those same results will be discussed (Section 4), and the chapter ends with some implications and general comments about crime, violence, and victimization (Section 5).

URBAN COMMUNITIES: SPACES FOR VIOLENCE, INSECURITY AND VICTIMIZATION

Based on World Urbanization Prospects 2018 (United Nations - DESA/POPULATION DIVISION 2019), since 2017, the majority of the world population is concentrated in cities, accounting for 3.5 billion people. Nevertheless, in Europe, that figure was achieved in 1950, and despite this milestone being achieved slightly later in Portugal, it was established during the 20th century, specifically in 1994. Moreover, in 2050, it is estimated that the proportion of the total population living in cities globally, in Europe, and in Portugal will be 68.4%, 83.7%, and 79.3%, respectively. Given these forecasts, the United Nations included "sustainable cities and communities" in the Global Goals for Sustainable Development, stressing the importance of safety across different contexts (e.g., home, public spaces).

As several authors have noted (e.g., Muggah 2012), urbanization (which includes not only the territory but also the associated lifestyle) has not only advantages but also disadvantages; in other words, the city presents itself as a space for opportunity and risk simultaneously. Indeed, "in rapidly growing cities, more people need food, housing, water supply, sanitation and employment to generate incomes to buy basic services. This demand, in turn, generates many opportunities for productive as well as criminal responses to ever more stimulating and demanding social environments" (United Nations Humans Settlements Programme 2007, 3).

Urban violence thus presents as a central topic not only for those who live in the city but also for researchers studying this issue and for the different professionals and stakeholders (e.g., police, policymakers) who address this issue. Although the relevance of the phenomenon is widespread, its definition (and operationalization) is far from achieving consensus. As claimed by Lourenço (2010[a], 4), "there is no single definition" and the distinct subjects, especially from the fields of the social sciences, adopt divergent meanings. For instance, Pavoni and Tulumello (2018) reviewed the available definitions and organized them around four typologies: i) Psychiatry views urban violence as a complex set of experiences, emphasizing physical violence; ii) the positivist and legalistic criminological perspective adds to this component deviant behavior; iii) humanitarian perspective includes other forms of violence, such as psychological violence; and finally, iv) ethnographic studies introduce media representations of crime. According to Muggah (2012), despite obvious conceptual idiosyncrasies, academics seem to agree on some aspects, such as differential impacts (direct costs *vs.* indirect costs), the intensity continuum ("acute," "endemic," and "chronic" *vs.* "everyday," "common" and "petty"), a focus on systems (e.g., self-directed, relational, communal, and structural), variation in intentionality by perpetrators (e.g., social, economic, ethnic, political) and contextual diversity (e.g., war, elections, crime, or terrorism).

Accordingly, urban violence encompasses a wide and diverse set of crimes legally typified (e.g., property crimes, crimes against people), but other incidents—for example, Lourenço (2010a)—also include other behaviors that are not punished by law but that are likely to affect community perceptions of safety and quality of life, such as incivilities. In this context, Grangeia and Cruz (2013) argued that "the feeling of unsafety can be even more harmful than the criminal act itself, considering that it erodes confidence levels and affects the well-being of the populations and societies, which become vulnerable and more easily manipulated." Although a city fully free of crime and violence sounds utopian (Ponce 2016), and despite the fact that Portugal occupies the third position on the Global Peace Index 2019 (Institute for Economics & Peace 2019) and the ninth position in the Safety and Security domain, according to the European Social Survey (European Commission 2013), the Portuguese seem to be very concerned about violent crime. Indeed, they rank sixth on a list of twenty-seven countries. Moreover, based on the same study, the countries in Southern Europe, which includes Portugal, seem to show particular effects of the fear of crime on well-being, and people who report that the fear of crime deeply impacts their quality of life also tend to report less confidence and less satisfaction with policing. Regardless of whether the fear of crime in the city was previously personified in the images of "the tramp, the outcast, the burdger, the whore, the ordinary crimes offender, the insane offender, the child that roves around the area and steals" (Fernandes and Rêgo 2011, 169), currently fear "is materialized in the 'drug user,' the 'illegal immigrant,' the 'homeless,' the 'illegal car usher,' the 'street prostitute,' the 'juvenile delinquent' " (Fernandes and Rêgo 2017, 78), changes that reproduce the "dynamic and evolving character of the [urban violence] phenomenon" (Muggah 2012, 19).

In addition to crime and violence, victimization represents the third phenomenon under consideration in this chapter. Regarding this topic, we highlight a recent study by Maia and Estrada (2017), which is entitled "Population, Territory and Crime: An Overview of Official Statistics". This study analyzed data from Statistics Portugal (INE) and the Portuguese Directorate-General for Justice Policy (DGPJ), with consideration given to the urban-rural dichotomy in three different territorial sets. Authors found that the crime rate was higher in urban contexts, concluding that "they seem more capable, simultaneously, of generating and attracting crime: they are more affected by inequalities and by the concentration of segregated ghettos, and, on the other hand, they are appealing for those subgroups that are less protected, more dependent, and consequently, more exposed to conditions that drive them to the practice of illegal behaviors" (145). It should be noted, however, that these results are based on officially recorded crimes, excluding the so-called dark figures. Finally, despite crime and (in)security concerns being collectively shared by all cities (Ponce 2016; Sani and Nunes 2016; Nunes et al. 2017), current knowledge about violence, (in)security, and victimization in urban contexts remains quite limited, being concentrated in some geographic areas. For instance, major cities in America, mainly the USA and Latin America, were presented as paradigmatic cases (e.g., United Nations Humans Settlements Programme 2007). In contrast, urban violence in cities perceived as small (Bolger and Bolger 2018) or with low crime rates (Valera and Guàrdia 2014) tend to be neglected. Assuming that urban violence comprises a heterogeneous range of experiences that vary over time and space, it is urgent to address urban violence from a micro approach (Muggah 2012); in our case, a community project was designed and will be presented below.

LOOKCRIM: A COMMUNITY PROJECT AT THE HISTORIC CENTER OF PORTO

Considering previous research experience in other areas of the city of Porto – among those, a study conducted in the geographical area of the campus of Asprela, where the population is mostly composed of students (Nunes et al. 2018), we designed a new project focused on community assessment. In an effort to analyze crime from a holistic perspective and attending to its multifaceted and multisystemic features, the Project "LookCrim | Looking at Crime: Communities and Physical Spaces" aims to gather data from different sources (e.g., official statistics, self-report surveys and spatial observation), which will be further explored through triangulation, thus providing a comprehensive portrait of community violence in the HCP.

The project, supported by the Foundation for Science and Technology— PTDC/DIR-DCP/28120/2017, involves a multidisciplinary team of researchers from different fields, such as criminology, sociology, psychology, law, literature, earth sciences, computer engineering and agronomical engineering. Briefly, the project has four main purposes: i) to characterize official crimes (e.g., type of crime, geographical/spatial location, seasonality); ii) to obtain access to nonreported crimes; iii) to identify risk factors for crime in the school context; and iv) to identify/map the conditions of physical spaces that may promote crime.

Conceptualizing crime as simultaneously a multifaceted phenomenon (since it comprises a complex and interconnected net of facets) and a multisystemic phenomenon (because it implies not only different contexts, systems, and social actors but also different communities, populations and physical spaces), the Project "LookCrim" initially examines official statistics of crime. Then, assuming that not all criminal incidents are reported to the police, we will collect information about nonreported crime through a self-report survey targeted to individuals from the HCP community. Additionally, we will also enlist professionals from the school community to gather complementary data, to recognize vulnerabilities and to identify community risk factors for criminality and violence. A third major purpose is devoted to the observation and assessment, through a mobile app, of physical spaces of the HCP and the identification of those features that promote or restrain crime according to Crime Prevention Through Environmental Design principles.

As a research project about community violence, the Project "LookCrim" is strongly committed to social responsibility through the public presentation of findings, the development (and dissemination) of guidelines for crime prevention, and strategies that will potentially improve feelings of security among citizens from the HCP. Additional and detailed information about the project (e.g., research team, scientific outputs, news/events or contacts) can be found at the following website: http://lookcrim.com/.

DIAGNOSIS OF LOCAL SECURITY

The Diagnosis of Local Security (DLS) is an empirically validated community assessment that aims to collect various indicators, both objective and subjective, such as crime, incivilities, victimization, (in)security, or formal social control, among others (Direcção Geral de Administração Interna [DGAI] 2009; Sani and Nunes 2013). Based on this assessment, contextualized analyses will be produced and then used in the development of interventions, which will promote development and security in specific assessed spaces.

Therefore, a DLS constitutes an essential tool for gathering knowledge about selected geographical areas, being particularly interesting if the assessment follows a multidisciplinary approach that focuses on different dimensions of the actual experiences and perceptions of the population. This approach can be realized through multidisciplinary teams or through partnerships with local authorities (e.g., police). In this case, the partnerships would allow for a better definition of the intervention strategies by organizations of formal social control to guarantee security in spaces used by the citizens (Nunes and Sani 2014; Sani and Nunes 2017). It is this kind of commitment, which is aimed to reduce and prevent crime, that will generate significant results and impacts (DGAI 2009), given the challenges associated with contemporary cities (Nunes et al. 2017).

HISTORIC CENTER OF PORTO: BACKGROUND

The historic center of Porto (HCP) is a downtown geographical area in this northern city of Portugal that joins the parishes of Cedofeita, Santo Ildefonso, Sé, Miragaia, São Nicolau and Vitória and extends over an area of 5.43 km2. According to Census 2011 (Statistics Portugal, n. d.), there are 40,400 individuals living in the HCP, and the population density is 7447.5/km2. In addition to inhabitants, this busy urban area is also populated by many workers and students. It should also be mentioned that in 1996, the HCP was classified as a World Heritage Site by UNESCO, and recently (i.e., 2012, 2014 and 2017), Porto was considered the best European destination. These designations help explain the strong presence of (inter)national tourists.

Currently, there are no available data (e.g., official statistics, surveys) on criminality and violence in the HCP, which cannot be properly characterized. Nevertheless, the Portuguese Directorate-General for Justice Policy (DGPJ) publishes some annual indicators about the Metropolitan

Area of Porto, which includes the HCP. More specifically, the Metropolitan Area of Porto is marked by high daily movement, as it has the second-highest number of crime occurrences in the country, only surpassed by the capital (Lisbon). Indeed, in 2018, the crime rate was 15.6% (Sistema de Segurança Interna [SSI] 2019), and 58,765 criminal incidents were reported to the police, especially general crimes against property, which were quite prevalent, such as theft. In addition, several cases of crimes against people were also reported, including simple and voluntary offenses to physical integrity ($n = 4274$) and domestic violence toward intimates ($n = 4003$). Despite the undeniable value of these data, given that the data are aggregated from different areas, it becomes unfeasible to perform community analysis; consequently, it is relevant to promote a Diagnosis of Local Security in the HCP.

METHODS

Design

The current study, being exploratory and descriptive, relied on a cross-sectional and observational design based on self-reports from citizens. Participants, measures and procedures will be described in detail below.

Participants

Individuals of both sexes from the community who were aged 18 years and above were included in this convenience sample. More specifically, 359 participants were assessed, including inhabitants, workers and students from the HCP.

Workers represented 34.1% of the sample, while residents accounted for 30.5% and students accounted for 11.0%; the remaining 4.3% comprised individuals with a double condition (i.e., resident and student or worker). Most participants (55.2%) were female, and 44.6% were male. It should be noted that the average age was 44.38 years (SD = 18.89), ranging from 18 to 96 years.

Regarding marital status, participants were mainly "single" (42.6%), followed by "married" (39.3%). The "divorced" participants represented 13.9% of the sample, while the "widowed" participants corresponded to 4.2%. The sample predominantly had qualifications above the 10th grade level, namely, secondary education (35.9%), followed by higher education (33.4%). In addition, 20.1% had qualifications between the 5th- and 9th-grade levels, and 10.3% had only elementary education; the remaining 0.3% had other qualifications.

Measure: The Diagnosis of Local Security Questionnaire

As previously mentioned, this chapter presents an exploratory, descriptive, cross-sectional, and observational study based on self-reports using the survey technique.

The Diagnosis of Local Security Questionnaire (Sani and Nunes 2013) differs from other measures by including closed- and open-ended questions, allowing for both quantitative and qualitative coding; consequently, it allows for the collection of objective and subjective data. Briefly, the questionnaire comprises 61 items organized into five sections: i) sociodemographic information; ii) perception of security/insecurity; iii) victimization; iv) formal social control; and v) community participation.

The questionnaire is validated among the Portuguese population (Sani and Nunes 2013) and has been widely used, even with other populations (e.g., Sani and Nunes 2012; Sani and Nunes 2016; Sani and Nunes 2017).

Procedures and Data Analysis

After the approval of the Internal Review Board, the study was approved by the Council of the Union of Parishes from the HCP, which was also asked to cooperate with data collection efforts. The project was also supported by Porto City Hall.

Prior to data collection, participants were asked to sign an informed consent form, which presented, in detail, the aims of the study as well as its procedures and conditions (e.g., anonymity, confidentiality).

Data were collected using the Diagnosis of Local Security Questionnaire, which was administered through interviews performed by properly trained researchers. Interviews were conducted between June 2018 and July 2019 in public and private places visited by inhabitants, workers and students from the HCP.

Then, the data were analyzed using the *Statistical Package for Social Sciences (SPSS) Software - Version 25*. Qualitative data were initially coded based on a system of categories (cf. Bardin 2004); next, they were analyzed as nominal variables through a quantitative approach.

FINDINGS

With respect to the aims of this chapter and to the research questions previously outlined, we present the most relevant results below.

What Is the Feeling of (In)Security in This Urban Community?

Initially, it is crucial to understand how (un)safe individuals who live, work or study in the historic center of Porto feel. Accordingly, we found that 73.8% of respondents evaluated this urban area as safe, presenting several reasons to justify their perception. Nevertheless, the most frequent explanations were previous positive experiences or an absence of knowledge about crime incidents (68.3%) and the presence of formal social control (13.2%).

Notwithstanding, for 23.7% of participants, the HCP was an unsafe area; their perceptions were explained by the "presence of crime/danger" (31.8%), the "predominance of night insecurity" (24.7%), or the "limitations on

Violence in Urban Community 303

policing" (14.1%). Finally, despite the low value, it should be noted that 2.5% of the sample did not evaluate Sin the HCP.

Are the Most Prevalent Crimes Similar to Those That the Population Fears Most?

Next, we presented a list of criminal categories to participants and asked them to identify those they considered most common in the HCP. Figure 1 depicted that "theft" was the crime most reported by participants (66.0%), followed by "robbery" (49.7%), "drug traffic" (46.8%) and "burglary—commercial property" (38.7%). Conversely, "arms traffic" was a crime that was less frequently reported (3.3%). Moreover, the crimes of "domestic violence against children and against elderly adults" presented low values—4.2% and 6.4%, respectively—which suggests that they were perceived as uncommon in the HCP. Criminal categories such as "vandalism," "physical assault" and "fraud" were reported as frequent by a significant number of participants; more specifically, frequencies ranged from 30-37%.

In addition to the perception of occurrence, participants were asked to identify the most feared crimes in the HCP. In this sense, "robbery" (64.3%), "theft" (54.3%) and "physical aggression" (48.5%) were the crimes that were most feared by the citizens. In contrast, "domestic violence" involving intimates, elderly adults or children was the least feared crime. More specifically, only 6.4% feared "domestic violence against children," 8.6% feared "domestic violence against intimates," and 8.4% feared "domestic violence against elderly adults."

Crimes of "burglary—residence," "burglary—commercial property," "fraud" and "sexual offense" provoked fear among 30 to 42% of the participants.

As shown in Figure 1, when we compared perceptions of occurrence and fear, two distinct patterns emerged. On the one hand, there was a group of crimes perceived as common, but they did not generate significant fear among citizens, such as "drug traffic," "road traffic crime," "vandalism," "domestic violence against intimates," "burglary—commercial property," and "theft." For instance, 46.8% of the participants reported "drug traffic" as common in the HCP, but only 17.5% feared it, and 36.5% of the participants claimed that "vandalism" was frequent, but it was feared by only 14.2%. On the other hand, there was a second group of crimes for which fear overcame the perception of occurrence. These crimes included "physical assault," "theft," "fraud," "arms traffic," "domestic violence against elderly adults," "sexual offense," and "burglary—residence." For instance, differences between fear and perception of occurrence are particularly evident for "burglary—residence" (42.3% feared *vs.* 25.1% occurred), "physical assault" (48.5% feared *vs.* 31.5% occurred) and "sexual offense" (30.6% feared *vs.* 15% occurred).

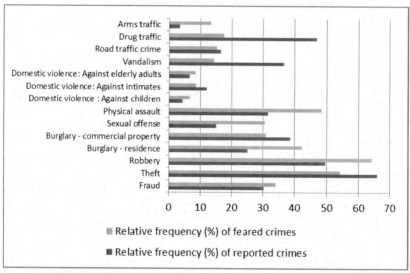

Source: OPVC – LookCrim.

Figure 1. Most reported crimes vs. most feared crimes.

What Is the Extension of the Victimization Reported by the Population?

In an effort to further explore the potential relationship between fear and crime in the HCP, we asked participants about their own experiences as victims of any kind of crime in the last five years. For those individuals who reported being victims, additional information (e.g., type of crime, impact) was also collected.

Overall, 18.9% of the participants were victims of crime, while 80.2% did not report any criminal victimization experience. When asked to identify the crime that they experienced, victims (n = 68) reported "theft" (41.2%), "robbery" (20.6%), "burglary—commercial property" (14.7%), "burglary—residence" (8.8%), "physical assault" (5.9%), "domestic violence against intimates" (2.9%), "fraud" (2.9%), "threat" (1.5%) and "sexual offense" (1.5%).

The impact caused by victimization was an additional key point that deserved attention. Indeed, only 4.4% of the victims reported no impact at all, while 82.4% presented only one type of damage. In accordance with the identified types of crime, "economical damage" was mentioned by 83.8% of victims, followed by "psychological damage" with 14.7% and "physical damage" reported by 10.5% of individuals.

Finally, it was also essential to explore victims' reactions, especially the involvement (or lack thereof) of the formal authorities. Indeed, the majority of victims (63.2%) sought the support of the police due to insurance requirements (38.1%), feelings of worth (33.3%), trust (14.3%), or other reasons (14.3%). Among the 36.8% of the victims who decided not to seek police support, the main explanatory reasons were the perception that it would be worthless (68%), a lack of confidence (12%) or another reason (16%).

DISCUSSION

This study relied on a sample of inhabitants/workers/students who visited the HCP, where a Diagnosis of Local Security was performed—included in the Project "LookCrim" —to provide input for a potential community intervention designed to promote security and quality of life among citizens. As an exploratory analysis, data were collected in a sample of 359 individuals that was heterogenous with respect to age and gender.

Despite the strong feelings of security reported by our participants, approximately a quarter of the sample (23.7%) felt unsafe in the HCP, which is easily understandable if we consider the rapid growth of contemporary societies (Nunes et al. 2017), which can impact concerns about security at individual and community levels (Agra, Quintas, and Fonseca 2001). Several factors may underlie the feelings of security /insecurity; among them, the time of the day seems to play a crucial role. In the current study, insecurity was closely related to the nighttime, as well as the occurrence of incidents perceived as criminal or dangerous. These results are in line with those observed by Valera and Guàrdia (2014), who investigated the fear of crime and the perception of insecurity in the city of Barcelona.

Based on the participants' responses, there are several crimes perceived as common in the HCP, especially property crimes and theft. The occurrence of this type of criminality, which is well known in urban and touristic areas, is also documented by official statistics (cf. SSI 2019), affects people's perceptions of crime and, consequently, impacts their sense of insecurity. In some studies, the city is described as a vulnerable space due to its constant change (Ramíres 2000); moreover, its growth may be associated with negative consequences, such as the weakness of social ties, social disorganization, poverty and conflicts, which are factors that may promote increases in crime (Lourenço 2010a). Indeed, it is the minor and major crimes, the news of which is spread via rumors, which strengthen feelings of insecurity and fear among the individuals who live, work or study in the HCP (Fernandes and Rêgo 2011).

Our results also suggest that the feeling of insecurity is not the result of a formula in which more common and more serious crimes generate more fear because we observed that the most feared crimes were not necessarily the most common or those that are included in the category of violent crime (e.g., traffic). In the current study, the most feared crimes are related to incidents of interpersonal violence (e.g., physical assault, sexual offense), which participants tended to perceive as uncommon crimes.

Physical proximity of an incident and the associated violence are factors that together influence citizens' feelings of security. This would explain why some crimes perceived as frequent (e.g., drug traffic) were not reported as the most feared by individuals. As suggested by other studies (Sani and Nunes 2012; Sani and Nunes 2016), in some areas, people develop their own security strategies (e.g., through the definition of no-go spaces, staying at home at night) and eventually become resilient to crime. In contrast, incidents that involve a high risk to physical integrity, which remained mostly underreported (e.g., due to the offender-victim relationship), may generate more fear in the individuals. Therefore, performing a DLS in a community becomes quite relevant, since it allows for the collection of both objective and subjective indicators of (in)security focused on a specific area (DGAI 2009; Sani and Nunes 2013). Our results revealed that 18.9% of the sample was victimized; specifically, at least one in five participants was victim of crime in the last five years, particularly street crime. Crimes against property seem to be especially prevalent; nonetheless, there were also claims about crimes against people, traditionally omitted in victimization surveys and official statistics (SSI 2019). It is also important to note that victimization is not an equally reported phenomenon; indeed, as we observed in this study, some crimes tended to be underreported—which is crucial to understanding the underlying reasons, such as minimization, avoidance of public exposure, and lack of confidence and trust in the judicial system—while others are easily reported (e.g., due to their severity, the perception of civil duty, or the expectation to recover personal belongings). In this sense, crimes against property—particularly associated with economic damage—tended to be more frequently reported to the police.

Finally, it should be noted that although we are presenting an exploratory study with an acceptable sample size, the assessment of the community is not yet fully representative and, as a consequence, should be further extended. Additionally, the results should be comprehensively analyzed by the multidisciplinary team involved in the project, as well as by national and international consultants, in an effort to reach a grounded and holistic representation of the issue that is capable of providing useful recommendations and proposals for HCP stakeholders.

CONCLUSION

Contemporary cities offer great opportunities for development at different levels, but they also constitute a vulnerable space for the emergence of unwanted phenomena such as crime and violence. Indeed, these events are symptomatic of society's functioning: they represent phenomena that should be combated but through an empirically supported and strategic approach. Therefore, collecting information through the DLS about objective and subjective indicators that can help us improve knowledge about feelings of (in)security in a population from a specific community represents an essential step in the process of defining strategies and mechanics to promote safer communities. We truly believe that the best intervention will be one that meets the specific needs of citizens and victims from an identified urban area. Therefore, given its crucialness to the recognition and understanding of the perceptions of the population, in this chapter, we presented an empirical study focused on the security of the HCP.

The impact of crime and violence is currently widely known in the international context, although to the best of our knowledge, the topic remains understudied in Portugal. In general, the impact can be direct (i.e., victim) or indirect (i.e., community) and may be scattered across different domains, such as the psychological, physical, economic, professional, and social domains (Lourenço 2010b). Wickramasekera et al. (2015) performed a systematic review of the direct, indirect and intangible estimated costs of crime, analyzing data from developed countries and including both crimes against property and crimes against people. Researchers found that the total cost of crime ranged from $9 billion to $35 billion in Australia, from $36 billion to $60 billion in the United Kingdom, and from $450 billion to $3200 billion in the United States. In addition to these short- to medium-term costs, there is also evidence that suggests that the impact of crime may last for years. For instance, Sharkey and Torrats-Espinosa (2017) compared economic mobility in urban communities with different crime rates and concluded that the violent crime and homicide rates in the areas where participants lived as children were significant predictors of their income rank in adulthood. More specifically, children who lived in areas with high rates of violent crime and homicide tended to earn lower incomes as adults. In sum, "crime actively contributes to reducing economical resources that are essential for the development and wealth of countries and for the citizens' well-being—either through illegal appropriation or through the funds required to prevent and combat it, criminality and its associated feeling of unsafety have a strong negative impact on democracy" (Lourenço 2010, 55).

In addition to the focus on the individual and the territory (Ponce 2016), we think that a successful community intervention should consider two assumptions:

1. The inclusion of objective indicators, either static or dynamic, in the community security solution. For instance, in the current study, two variables—namely, social control (e.g., policing) and spatiotemporal features (e.g., luminosity *vs.* darkness, crime hotspots)—were identified and should be addressed; and
2. the inclusion of subjective indicators experienced by citizens in a community. In our study, we gathered data about three distinct variables, namely, feelings of (in)security, occurrences *vs.* impacts of violence and crime, and direct victimization, which should guide the definition of goals and the prioritization of actions centered on security promotion.

In conclusion, considering the absence of universal or one-size-fits-all solutions for reducing crime and violence and increasing the sense of security in the urban context, we agree that "failure to engage local communities in the past has stopped many ideas that in their own right may well have been good ones from reaching their full potential. Community engagement is central to initiatives in this field, since community members are the ultimate beneficiaries of such initiatives. This being the case, the basic principle here which derives from people's rights as citizens is that initiatives should be 'done with' them rather than 'done to' them" (United Nations Humans Settlements Programme 2007, 105).

ACKNOWLEDGMENTS

This work was financed by National Funds through FCT (Foundation for Science and Technology) under the project LookCrim - Looking at Crime: Communities and Physical Spaces - PTDC/DIR-DCP/28120/2017 and within the framework of the CIEC (Research Center for Child Studies of the University of Minho) project under the reference UID/CED/00317/2019.

REFERENCES

Agra, Cândido, Jorge Quintas, and Ernesto Fonseca. 2001. "De La Sécurité Démocratique à La Démocratie de Sécurité: Le Cas Portugais." ["From democratic safety to the Safety Democracy: The Portuguese Case."] *Déviance et Société* 4 (25): 499–513.

Bardin, Laurence. 2004. *Análise de Conteúdo. [Content Analysis].* 3rd ed. Lisboa: Edições 70.

Bolger, Michelle A., and P. Colin Bolger. 2018. "Predicting Fear of Crime: Results from a Community Survey of a Small City." *American Journal of Criminal Justice*, 334–51. https://doi.org/10.1007/s12103-018-9450-x.

Direcção Geral de Administração Interna [DGAI]. 2009. *Manual de Diagnósticos Locais de Segurança [Guidance on Local Safety Audits. A Compendium of International Practice].* Lisboa: Ministério da Administração Interna http://www.dgai.mai.gov.pt/cms/files/conteudos/Manual%20Diagnosticos%20Locais%20de%20Seguranca.pdf.

European Comission. 2013. *"European Social Survey: Exploring Public Attitudes, Informing Public Policy."* Acessed August 22, 2019. https://www.europeansocialsurvey.org/docs/findings/ESS1-3_findings_booklet.pdf.

Violence in Urban Community

Fernandes, Luís, and Ximene Rêgo. 2011. "Por Onde Anda o Sentimento de Insegurança? Problematizações Sociais e Científicas Do Medo à Cidade." ["Where is the feeling of insafety? Social and scientific questions concerning the fear of the city."] *Etnográfica* 15 (1): 167–81. https://doi.org/10.4000/etnografica.869

———. 2017. "Da Hipótese Predatória à Cidade Exposta: Metamorfoses Da Insegurança Urbana." ["From Predatory Hypothesis to the Exposed City: Metamorphoses of urban Insafety."] In *Crime and Safety in Contemporary Cities*, edited by Laura M. Nunes, Ana Sani, Rui Estrada, Fernanda Viana, Sónia Caridade, and Rui Leandro Maia, 73–87. Porto: Fronteir do Caos Editores.

Grangeia, Helena, and Olga F. Cruz. 2013. "Inseguranças Urbanas e Vitimações Coletivas." ["Urban Insecurities and Collective Victimizations."] *Plataforma Barómetro Social.* 2013. Acessed August 14, 2019. http://www.barometro.com.pt/2013/12/12/insegurancas-urbanas-e-vitimacoes-coletivas/.

Institute for Economics & Peace 2019. *"Global Peace Index 2019. Measuring Peace in a Complex World."* Sidney. http://visionof humanity.org/reports.

Instituto Nacional de Estatística. n. d. *"Censos 2011."* ["Census 2011."] Acessed August 1, 2019. https://censos.ine.pt/xportal/xmain? xpid=CENSOS&xpgid=censos2011_apresentacao.

Intravia, Jonathan, Kevin T. Wolff, Rocio Paez, and Benjamin R. Gibbs. 2017. "Investigating the Relationship between Social Media Consumption and Fear of Crime: A Partial Analysis of Mostly Young Adults." *Computers in Human Behavior* 77: 158–68. https://doi.org/ 10.1016/j.chb.2017.08.047.

Lourenço, Nelson. 2010a. "Cidades e Sentimento de Insegurança: Violência Urbana Ou Insegurança Urbana?" [Cities and Feelings of Insafety: Urban Violence or Urban Insafety?"] *Um Toque de Qualidade. Eficiência e Qualidade Na Gestão Da Defesa Social*, 15–39. http://www.fd.unl.pt/Anexos/3841.pdf.

312   Ana Sani, Laura M. Nunes, Sónia Caridade et al.

————. 2010b. "O custo social e económico do crime." *Pela Lei e Pela Grei*. ["Social and economic costs of crime." *Pela Lei e Pela Grei*]. *Revista Da Guarda Nacional Republicana* XXII (88): 50–55.

Maia, Rui Leandro, and Rui Estrada. 2017. "População, Território e Crime: Um Olhar Pelas Estatísticas Oficiais." [Population territory, and crime: An Overview of Official Statistics."] In *Crime and Safety in Contemporary Cities*, edited by Laura M. Nunes, Ana Sani, Rui Estrada, Fernanda Viana, Sónia Caridade, and Rui Leandro Maia, 139–56. Porto: Fronteira do Caos Editores.

Muggah, Robert. 2012. "Researching the Urban Dilemma: Urbanization, Poverty and Violence." *Ottawa: Centro Internacional de Investigaciones Para* ..., 1–118. http://www.iadb.org/intal/intalcdi/PE/2012/12203.pdf.

Nunes, Laura M., and Ana I. Sani. 2014. "Avaliação de Uma Comunidade Urbana. Diagnóstico Local de Segurança e Soluções de Policiamento." ["Evaluation of an urban community - diagnosis of local security, and policing solutions."] *Direito e Democracia–Revista de Ciências Jurídica* 15 (1): 4–17.

Nunes, Laura M., Ana Sani, Rui Estrada, Fernanda Viana, Sónia Caridade, and Rui Leandro Maia. 2017. *Crime e Segurança Nas Cidades Contemporâneas* [*Crime and Safety in Contemporary Cities*]. Porto: Fronteira do Caos Editores.

Nunes, Laura M., Ana Isabel Sani, Maria Alzira Pimenta Dinis, Hélder Fernando Sousa, and Sónia Maria Caridade. 2018. "Segurança e Vitimação Entre Estudantes Universitários Na Cidade Do Porto." ["Safety and victimization among university students in the city of Porto."] *Análise Psicológica* 36 (2): 169–83). https://doi.org/10.14417/ap.1395.

Pavoni, Andrea, and Simone Tulumello. 2018. "What Is Urban Violence?" *Progress in Human Geography*. https://doi.org/10.1177/030913251 8810432.

Ponce, Jorge. 2016. "La Inseguridad Ciudadana Como Proceso de 'Territorialización': Aproximación Conceptual y Teórica." *Desafios* 28 (2): 145–76. ["Citizen Insafety as a Process of "Territorialization":

Conceptual and Theoretical Approach."] *Desafios* 28 (2): 145–76. https://doi.org/10.12804/desafios28.2.2016.04.

Ramíres, B. Fernández. 2000. "El Medio Urbano." ["The Urban Enviroment."] In *Psicologia Ambiental*, edited by J. Araganés, 259–80. Madrid: Psicogia Pirâmide.

Sani, Ana I., and Laura M. Nunes. 2017. *Insegurança e Vitimação - A Importância Do Diagnóstico Local* [Insecurity and Victimization. The Importance of Local Diagnosis." Saarbrücken: NEA: Novas Edições Acadêmicas].

Sani, Ana I., Laura M. Nunes, and Sónia Caridade. 2019. "Violence Exposure: Perspectives, Gender Differences and Outcomes." In *Exposure to Violence in the Community: Differential Vulnerability, Diagnoses and Interventions*, edited by S. Aideen Xu, 1–18. New York: Nova Science Publishers, Inc.

Sani, Ana Isabel, and Laura M. Nunes. 2013. "Questionário de Diagnóstico Local de Segurança: Estudo Numa Comunidade Urbana." ["Diagnosis of Local safety Questionnaire: Study in an urban community."] *Análise Psicológica* 31 (2): 185–95. https://doi.org/10.14417/ap.609.

Sani, Ana Isabel, and Laura M Nunes. 2012. "Relatório Do Inquérito Diagnóstico Local de Segurança Na Freguesia Da Sé (Porto)." ["Diagnosis of Local Security at the Parish of Sé (Porto) Report."] Porto: Universidade Fernando Pessoa. http://bdigital.ufp.pt/handle/10284/3313.

Sani, Ana, and Laura M. Nunes. 2016. "Diagnóstico de Seguridad/Inseguridad. Un Estudio Exploratorio En Una Comunidad Urbana." ["Diagnosis of Security/Insecurity. An exploratory study in an urban community."] *Anuario de Psicología Jurídica* 26: 102–6]. https://doi.org/10.1016/j.apj.2016.03.001.

Sharkey, Patrick, and Gerard Torrats-Espinosa. 2017. "The Effect of Violent Crime on Economic Mobility." *Journal of Urban Economics* 102: 22–33. https://doi.org/10.1016/j.jue.2017.07.001.

Silva, Nuno. 2010. "Cidadania e Segurança: Uma Análise Prospetiva." ["Citizenship and Security: A Prospective Analysis."] In *I Congresso Nacional de Segurança e Defesa. Para Uma Estratégia de Segurança*

314   *Ana Sani, Laura M. Nunes, Sónia Caridade et al.*

Nacional., 1–20. Lisboa. http://icnsd.afceaportugal.pt/conteudo/congresso/ICNSD_4H_texto_pdf_nuno_parreira_silva.pdf.

Sistema de Segurança Interna [SSI]. 2019. "Relatório Anual de Segurança Interna 2018." ["Homeland Security - Annual Report 2018."] *Relatório Anual de Segurança Interna – Ano*, 254. Acessed August 1, 2019. http://www.ansr.pt/InstrumentosDeGestao/Documents/RelatórioAnual deSegurançaInterna(RASI)/RASI2016.pdf.

Trindade, Jorge. 2017. "Posfácio." ["Afterword."] In *Crime e Segurança Nas Cidades Contemporâneas*, edited by Laura M. Nunes, Ana Sani, Rui Estrada, Fernanda Viana, Sónia Caridade, and Rui Leandro Maia, 191–96. Porto: Fronteira do Caos Editores].

United Nations - DESA/POPULATION DIVISION. n. d. *"World Urbanization Prospects 2018."* Accessed August 22, 2019. https:/population.un.org/wup/.

United Nations Humans Settlements Programme. 2007. *"Enhancing Urban Safety and Security. Global Report on Human Settlements 2007."* London.

Valera, Sergi, and Joan Guàrdia. 2014. "Perceived Insecurity and Fear of Crime in a City with Low-Crime Rates." *Journal of Environmental Psychology* 38: 195–205. https://doi.org/10.1016/j.jenvp.2014.02.002.

Wickramasekera, Nyantara, Judy Wright, Helen Elsey, Jenni Murray, and Sandy Tubeuf. 2015. "Cost of Crime: A Systematic Review." *Journal of Criminal Justice* 43 (3): 218–28. https://doi.org/10.1016/j.jcrimjus.2015.04.009.

In: Victims of Violence
Editor: Mathias L. Knudsen

ISBN: 978-1-53617-140-2
© 2020 Nova Science Publishers, Inc.

Chapter 15

SAFETY AND ISLAND LIFE

Lori K. Sudderth, PhD
Criminal Justice Program, Quinnipiac University,
Hamden, CT, US

ABSTRACT

Island communities in the Caribbean experience high levels of gender-based violence and low levels of reporting. Victim advocates in these settings assist survivors within a complicated context of individual and structural violence that includes high levels of poverty and marginalization in communities with little anonymity and limited options for escape. The geographic isolation of islands demands both a creative and informed response from the criminal justice system and an intentional campaign to carve out safe space for survivors of intimate violence; moreover, it is important to invest in prevention campaigns to create communities that not only support victims, but no longer tolerate intimate violence within their boundaries. Using Saint Lucia as an example, this chapter illustrates some of the challenges of supporting victims of intimate violence on an island and discusses innovative policies and practices to best support victims in this context.

INTRODUCTION

Saint Lucia, like many islands in the Caribbean, is a place where people tend to know each other. Like a small town, there is comfort in the familiarity that lies around every corner. But for survivors of gender-based violence, that familiarity can either guarantee the support they need or exacerbate the challenges typical of surviving this type of violence. In addition, there are conditions unique to life on an island, particularly in the Caribbean, that present multiple challenges to survivors of gender-based violence. This chapter discusses some of these challenges and ends with suggestions for responding to them.

In the Caribbean, one fourth to over a third of women experience some type of intimate violence, including physical, emotional, and sexual violence; the risk for violent victimization increases when childhood experience includes witnessing violence or being targeted for violence, being economically dependent upon a partner, lower educational attainment, and younger age at marriage (Morrison et al., 2007; UNDP, 2016). A report by the United Nations Office of Drugs and Crime and the World Bank indicated that the rate of rape in some Caribbean countries was significantly higher than the average internationally (UN Women, 2019). In some places, sexual coercion is so pervasive that the assumption is that girls' first sexual experience will be forced (e.g., Curtis, 2009).

Information and communication technologies (ICTs) have expanded the ways in which women and girls can be exploited and victimized, including online stalking, harassment, and verbal abuse, as well as the nonconsensual sharing of private images (Kee, 2005; Thakur, 2018). Woodlock (2017) found that perpetrators used technology (e.g., Facebook, mobile tracking devices) to intimidate and punish victims, to isolate them, and to convince them they could not escape the perpetrator. Thakur (2018) noted in a Jamaican study that abusive male partners often used ICTs to monitor and control their female partners or to embarrass them publicly by inappropriately sharing pictures on social media.

The majority of survivors of gender-based violence worldwide, however, do not report to authorities, and the Caribbean context is no exception (Thompson et al., 2007; UNWomen, 2019). Underreporting exacerbates the challenges of providing services to survivors, because so few are identified through official channels. For example, the St. Lucia Crisis Centre reported in 2008 that less than 2% of clients requested counseling due to sexual assault (Department of Gender Relations, 2010).

In the literature on disclosure of gender-based violence, the majority of survivors of sexual assault and intimate partner violence disclose to someone, even if they do not report to authorities (Ahrens, Cabral, & Abeling, 2009; Evens et al., 2019). Studies suggest that reactions to disclosure of sexual assault can be positive and supportive or negative and disabling (Ahrens, Cabral, & Abeling, 2009; Evens et al., 2019; Hakimi et al., 2018; Sudderth, 1998). Negative social reactions, in fact, exacerbate the impact of sexual assault in the form of PTSD, substance use, and depression, and this happens regardless of race, but the severity of the symptoms are worse for African American women as compared to white women because African American women rely on the African American community and an extended kin network to cope with the stress (Budescu, Taylor, & McGill, 2011; Hakimi et al., 2018). If that network of support is the source of negative social reactions to a sexual assault disclosure, African American women experience more symptoms of PTSD and depression than white women (Bryant-Davis et al., 2011). Reactions to disclosure may vary by relationship to the survivor, and supportive reactions of friends and counselors are described as the most beneficial, while romantic partners were less supportive or helpful; frontline responders, including police, medical personnel, and counselors, are most likely to give tangible aid, but they are not necessarily described as supportive by research participants (Ahrens, Cabral, & Abeling, 2009). In summary, in addition to the psychological impact of disclosure, there are sociological factors that shed light on rates of disclosure of gender-based violence across cultural contexts.

UNIQUE CONTEXT OF GENDER-BASED VIOLENCE IN THE CARIBBEAN

In the Caribbean, there is evidence that disclosure of gender-based violence is hindered by several factors, including victim-blaming, the lack of anonymity, the persistence of gender inequality, and systemic gaps in support for survivors. First, victim-blaming in Caribbean culture not only stigmatizes the victim but the victim's family as well, discouraging survivors from reporting to authorities (Rivas, Kelly, & Feder, 2013). Disclosure alone brings on the risk of being blamed (Curtis, 2009). For example, according to a needs assessment conducted in St. Lucia in 2013, in traditional St. Lucian culture, "what happens in the family stays in the family" (Sudderth, 2013). In other words, if the victim were to report the sexual violence or intimate partner violence to the police, it would bring dishonor to the family. Curtis' (2009) study of girls' sexuality on Nevis suggested "Not only do many of the girls have a difficult time telling pieces of their stories, but once they do, they run the risk of being blamed for whatever might have happened..." (Curtis, 2009: 112). Rivas, Kelly, & Feder (2013) interviewed Caribbean, African, and white British women about their experiences of psychological abuse and found that all of the women were concerned about "community reactions," that is, "damaging their family's and their own reputation if they went against community values and expectations" (Rivas et al., 2013: 114). For the Caribbean women, the concern was for their "reputation," and this had a depressing effect on disclosure, leaving the survivor to feel alone, and reinforcing the cultural norm to keep family troubles private, out of view of the community. The interviews also revealed varying boundaries of "acceptable" levels of abusive behavior from an intimate partner. Caribbean women were more likely to seek social support from a family member as opposed to friends.

Moreover, in St. Lucian culture, the connection to community and family is strong, making it difficult for victims to leave the island or leave their community to escape abuse (Sudderth, 2013). Similarly, studies from other parts of the Caribbean suggest that victims of intimate partner violence maintain social ties despite the isolation typical of abusive relationships. In one study, women used active strategies to continue their relationships with their abusive partners, including emotional detachment and purposefully relying on traditional gender roles or empowerment to reduce abuse and maintain the relationship; but disclosure of abusive behavior was avoided to keep from embarrassing their family (Rivas, Kelly & Feder, 2013). Nevertheless, there are challenges to finding both formal and informal support because of the stigma attached to victimization, fear of the perpetrators, and the inadequacy of social services (Hadeed & El-Bassel, 2006). For some survivors, like GLBTI individuals who experience intimate violence, families are, in fact, key to getting them to seek services (Evens et al., 2019).

Second, the stigma of victim-blaming is exacerbated by the lack of anonymity, particularly in smaller island cultures (Curtis, 2009). In St. Lucia, for example, which is 616 square kilometers, participants in a 2013 needs assessment pointed out that "everybody knows everybody," so it is extremely difficult to report a rape or intimate partner violence anonymously (Sudderth, 2013). The lack of anonymity exacerbates the pressure to keep quiet about sexual violence or intimate partner violence, not only to avoid stigmatization, but to avoid possible retaliation by the perpetrator. Curtis (2009) similarly noted the reluctance of women on Nevis to buy condoms or discuss birth control with a doctor out of feat that even professionals would tell someone on the island. "The absence of anonymity resulting from the size of the population and the island's geography provides Nevisians with fewer opportunities to be discreet when it comes to breaches of moral sexual codes" (Curtis, 2009: 67). But it also means that reporting a crime by an intimate partner or an acquaintance to the police or to the hospital may expose the survivor to rumor and innuendo.

Third, systemic inequalities in the Caribbean not only underscore gender-based violence, but they interfere with linkages between services and survivors. Although there has been improvement in legal equality for women in the Caribbean, the reality of equality is somewhat illusory (Essayag, 2017; Vassell, 2017). Despite the increase in women's educational gains in the Caribbean, women still make about 68% of what men make, and are responsible for the majority of housework and childcare (Bailey, 2003; Baksh, 2016). Compared to other regions of the world, women in the Caribbean have been more likely to be in the labor force albeit in low-skilled, low-wage jobs; nevertheless, compared to Caribbean men, they have a higher unemployment rate (Baksh, 2016; United Nations Statistics Division, 2015).

Moreover, the persistence of patriarchal belief patterns inhibits the disclosure of gender-based violence. Caribbean masculinity is often associated with aggression and violence which tends to be normalized (DeShong, 2015; Kempadoo, 2009). Curtis (2009) found a double standard of sexuality in Nevis in that men who bought condoms were considered responsible, but women who bought condoms were considered promiscuous. Part of the sexual script she found was that women and girls were to be sexually available to men, and men were to be in control sexually (Curtis, 2009). These patterns contribute to societal attitudes about abusive and sexually exploitive relationships as normative, and they are consistent with traditional gender prescriptions.

In many Caribbean countries, gender-based violence, then, is taken less seriously than other violent crimes and seldom receives the government support necessary to provide adequate resources to address the problem. Mutri & Donald (2006) point out, for example, that despite the fact that Jamaica ratified the Convention on the Elimination of All Forms of Discrimination against Women (CEDAW), the government has taken little action to ensure compliance. Indeed, the implementation of laws advancing women's status in the Caribbean are, for the most part, left to lower level government officials (Essayag, 2017). "Such laxity is associated with the failure to consider the seriousness of the crime, compared to other crimes and problems facing the countries, as in the case of Jamaica, as well as inadequate resources devoted to combat it. Both of these factors apply in the Jamaican situation where the bulk of work is left to the local non-governmental and community-based organizations to address violence against women, with support from the international community" (Mutri & Donald, 2006: 90).

Fourth, the lack of support from government leadership, financial infrastructure, and frontline workers complicates the provision of services for survivors of gender-based violence. Governments in the Caribbean rely heavily on under-resourced NGOs to address violence against women (Essayag, 2017). Similarly, the same report suggested that the inertia behind implementing many policies advancing the status of women in the Caribbean was that low-level administrators were in charge of execution of the policies (Essayag, 2017). In addition, getting services to survivors of gender-based violence is challenging due to the lack of resources and the lack of coordination of services, as well as the "indifferent" attitudes of police and service workers (CADRES, 2009). Curtis (2009) commented that the lenient treatment of sex offenses in Nevis added to the overall trivialization of sexual violence, hindering disclosure by survivors. Moreover, a 2015 study by UN Women suggested that the criminal justice system in five Caribbean countries described sexual offense cases as being unnecessarily delayed, poorly investigated, lacking coordination between agencies, and short of resources (see Judicial Reform and Institutional Strengthening Project [JURIST], 2017).

Moreover, the infrastructure is impacted by natural disaster and climate change, that is, rising temperatures and sea levels, increased drought in some areas, as well as the possibility of more extreme hurricanes and tropical storms (UNDP, 2019). Hurricanes, for example, may destroy the infrastructure of an island, devastating roads, schools, and hospitals. Sources of water may be compromised or limited, leading residents to try to find enough water to sustain their families, sometimes under desperate circumstances (see Bermudez et al., 2019). While all island residents are impacted by the force of hurricanes, women and girls are at increased risk of gender-based violence in the aftermath of disaster (CDC, 2014; Inter-Agency Standing Committee, 2015), making gender-responsive recovery policies imperative (Jacobs, 2017). The disruption of commerce and the economic stress of natural disasters impacts the abilities of men to provide for their families, exacerbating other correlates of interpersonal violence, such as intergenerational normalization of intimate partner violence, substance use, and adherence to traditional gender beliefs; in addition, there

322   *Lori K. Sudderth*

is a loss of control in the aftermath of disasters that can trigger interpersonal violence (Bermudez et al., 2019).

All of these cultural factors intensify the difficulty of reporting gender-based violence in the Caribbean to the police or to other official agencies, exacerbating the tenuous connection between survivors and services. The following section discusses some recommendations for improving the response to gender-based violence in the Caribbean.

Policy Implications

Like many other places in the world, Caribbean nations suffer from unacceptably high levels of gender-based violence. In order to reduce the violence, policymakers and practitioners must take into account what is known from evidence-based practice as well as the unique context of life in the Caribbean. Recent improvements have focused on enhancing the criminal justice response to gender-based violence. In 2018, for example, Barbados became the first country to adopt the Model Guidelines for Sexual Offences in the Caribbean Region, with the goals of improving the way the justice system responds to reports of sexual violence by holding offenders accountable, providing more support for survivors, more training for criminal justice personnel, and increasing the efficiency of the process (Judicial Reform and Institutional Strengthening [JURIST] Project, 2017). The hope is to improve the capacity of judges as well as other criminal justice personnel to respond sympathetically to rape survivors, using a collaborative model to reduce delays in investigation and to reduce minimalization of sexual offenses. The new guidelines aim to hold offenders accountable and support survivors as they move through the system (Rajnauth-Lee, 2019). But in order to be most effective, survivors have to feel more comfortable disclosing to authorities in the first place. Therefore, the following are additional recommendations:

Recommendation 1.

Education to reduce myths about gender-based violence, increase support for survivors, and hold offenders accountable. Since survivors rarely report to authorities, it is important to provide widespread education about survivors' experiences, rape myths, and best practices for support to the public so that whoever they disclose to will be able to be supportive and/or link that survivor to services (Hakimi et al., 2018). Victim-blaming serves to minimize the effects of sexual coercion on the victims. "In part, when girls are held responsible for the sexual trauma that men inflict, it serves to downplay the trauma, to make it less significant than what it might have been, particularly in the eyes of others" (Curtis, 2009:112). Curtis (2009) argues that this trivialization of sexual violence means that girls don't recognize and acknowledge their experiences as trauma, but rather as a normal part of a woman's life. In fact, there is an expectation that "...violence is unavoidable, regardless of what the girls do,...Indeed, due to the reluctance to view certain forms of sexuality as exploitive, sexual coercion and violence remain, if not socially acceptable, then at the very least, accepted as inevitable by a society that tolerates it" (Curtis, 2009: 114).

UN Women recommends educating the public with the intention of transforming "patriarchal cultural patterns and sexist stereotypes" which includes mass media campaigns to prevent violence against women, raise awareness about the connections between the social construction of gender and violence (Essayag, 2017). Ahrens et al., (2009) recommended training people in the legal field to offer more support to survivors in addition to practical assistance. But in this setting, it is important to expand the idea of education to include other professionals as well—health care professionals, law enforcement, social workers, policymakers, and any frontline workers who could come in contact with survivors of gender-based violence—as well as the wider public, including programming that targets men. One goal of this type of campaign is to reduce the chances that survivors who do disclose will encounter negative reactions. This is especially true for populations who rely heavily on their community to cope with structural violence (Budescu, Taylor, & McGill, 2011).

Thakur (2018) points out that although ICTs have exacerbated the exploitation of girls and women, they can also been used for networking and emotional support of victims, providing avenues for reaching out to other survivors as well as getting information that would be otherwise unavailable to isolated or intimidated victims of gender-based violence. Thakur (2018) further suggests a "national campaign to help raise awareness of the issues" (279), "Take Back the Tech!" which is a global campaign to raise awareness, and "workshops that can educate users on gender-based violence and ICTs, the potential of ICTs to empower women and realise gender equality, and the risks associated with ICTs linked to both online and offline gender-based violence" (Thakur, 2018: 279). Trainings targeting both women and girls, men and boys, churches, judges, lawyers, and other professionals could include how to practice safer online behaviors, strategies to combat abuse and harassment, controlling behavior of abusive partners, how to use ICTs as evidence, and the harm associated with sharing objectionable videos and photos with others.

Recommendation 2.

Services for survivors should be coordinated and collaborative, including where possible "one-stop" centers. The lack of leadership on women's issues and budgetary support for initiatives to address violence against women impacts the abilities of NGOs to provide training and coordination (Essayag, 2017). Some of the gaps in services for survivors of gender-based violence in many Caribbean nations are related to the lack of coordination between frontline services as well as inconsistent training of frontline personnel. For example, in one Caribbean study, "…only one-third of participants reported ever being asked by a healthcare provider about GBV, and slightly less than this shared their experiences with providers" (Evens et al., 2019: 8), but over half said they would like for health care providers to ask these questions—questions that could be included in training frontline workers in the healthcare field. When participants did seek services, the majority said "the services did not meet their needs, or they were further victimized by service providers" (Evens et al., 2019: 9). It is essential that law enforcement, the judicial system, health care, local community members, the private sector, victim services, and mental health services present a united front to address the needs of survivors, hold offenders accountable, and promote the "de-normalization" of gender-based violence (Bermudez et al., 2019). Given their role in Caribbean culture, a collaborative effort that included faith communities would allow for maximum exposure to cross-training and dialogue to demystify the causes and correlates of gender-based violence. The goals of any collaborative effort should include training for frontline personnel and streamlining the processing of cases of gender-based violence so that re-traumatization of survivors is minimized while offenders are less likely to escape justice. This is especially important in the context of low anonymity and minimal government support.

An example of this level of coordination was recently developed in Antigua and Barbuda. In 2017, Antigua and Barbuda created a 24/7 one-stop center to serve survivors of gender-based violence. The Support and Referral Centre provides intake, counseling, medical exams, a child-friendly room, shower facilities, legal services, and there is a police unit (special victims unit) on site (Directorate of Gender Affairs, 2017; Jacobs, 2017). The Centre includes a courtroom for vulnerable persons, collaborative relationships between agencies that serve survivors, training for community organizations, including police, medical personnel, and shelter managers (Jacobs, 2017). Victim advocates are available to accompany survivors throughout the medical and legal process; in addition, there is a monitoring oversight committee that is responsible for evaluation of client services (Jacobs, 2017).

Mutri & Donald (2006) evaluated an interagency collaboration to address violence against women and girls in Jamaica over a two-year period (1998-2000). The collaboration included local, regional, and international agencies coordinated by the Association of Women's Organizations in Jamaica (AWOJA). The aims of the campaign included gender and gender-based violence sensitivity training, increasing information about gender-based violence available to the public through the media, and mobilizing the public to support the campaign (Mutri & Donald, 2006). The collaboration targeted specific populations for increased awareness and sensitivity, including workers in the health and justice fields, inner-city and rural communities, and schools. While there was no reduction in violence against women during this time, the evaluation suggested the importance of responding to violence against women collaboratively. This requires clarification of the role and responsibilities of each agency as well as conflict resolution skills. The evaluation also suggested the value of mobilizing the media, taking advantage of academic/practitioner relationships to facilitate research, and systematically involving men in the campaign (Mutri & Donald, 2006).

Recommendation 3.

Reduce gender inequality through gender mainstreaming policies and implementing policies that promote gender equality. Essayag (2017) recommends intervening in patriarchal cultural patterns, while Bermudez et al., (2019) suggest "gender transformative programming" to specifically take the pressure off of men to be "providers," while meeting basic needs in terms of recovery, employment, etc. Programming should include workshops aimed at reducing gender inequality and intervening in beliefs about gender, such as the social construction of masculinity, economic empowerment of women, egalitarian relationship practices, and best practice responses to disclosures of gender-based violence experiences. Workshops should be designed for survivors, for both women and men, for judges, attorneys, other frontline workers, and policymakers as well. "Examining the ways in which violence can be a key part of the gendered experience of life should sharpen the understanding of the root causes and consequences of all forms of violence and allow for the development of a broader array of interventions" (UNIFEM/ECLAC, 2005: 76). These interventions should include reducing gender disparities to ensure that women and girls, men and boys have the same opportunities to education, work, healthcare, family life, and political expression (Kabeer, 2003).

In conclusion, the challenges of providing services to survivors of gender-based violence in Caribbean nations include victim-blaming and concerns about shaming family, lack of anonymity, gender inequality and stereotyping, and lack of support from government sources. The

Safety and Island Life 327

transformation of policy and practice should involve educational initiatives that challenge patriarchal assumptions and clarify appropriate responses to disclosure of experiences of gender-based violence. Services that respond to survivors should be coordinated to streamline the reporting process, and governments should prioritize the reduction of gender inequality through targeted training and interventions that increase opportunities for all citizens regardless of gender. It is imperative that Caribbean justice systems respond to gender-based violence more rigorously so that offenders are held accountable for their actions, but it is also important that Caribbean island societies respond more senstively to gender-based violence so that survivors are able to disclose to get the help they need.

REFERENCES

Ahrens, Courtney E., Giannina Cabral, & Samantha Abeling. 2009. "Healing or hurtful: Sexual assault survivors' interpretations of social reactions from support providers." *Psychology of Women Quarterly* 33(1): 81-94.

Bailey, Barbara. 2003. "The search for gender equity and empowerment of Caribbean women: The role of education." In Gemma Tang-Nain & B. Bailey (eds.). *Gender Equality in the Caribbean: Reality or Illusion.* Kingston, Jamaica, Ian Randle Publishers, p. 136.

Baksh, Rawwida. 2016. *"Country Gender Assessments: Synthesis Report."* Caribbean Development Bank.

Bermudez, Laura Gauer, Lindsay Stark, Cyril Bennouna, Celina Jensen, Alina Potts, Inah Fatoumata Kaloga, Ricardo Tilus, Jean Emmanuel Buteau, Mendy Marsh, Anna Hoover, Megan Laughlin Williams. 2019. "Converging drivers of interpersonal violence: Findings from a qualitative study in post-hurricane Haiti." *Child Abuse & Neglect* 89: 178-191.

Bryant-Davis, Thema, Sarah E. Ullman, Yuying Tsong, and Robyn Gobin. 2011. "Surviving the storm: The role of social support and religious coping in sexual assault recovery of African American women." *Violence Against Women* 17(12): 1601-1618.

Budescu, Mia, Ronald D. Taylor, Rebecca Kang McGill. 2011. "Stress and African American Women's Smoking/Drinking to Cope: Moderating Effects of Kin Social Support." *Journal of Black Psychology* 37(4): 452-484.

Caribbean Development Research Services Inc. (CADRES). 2009. "Domestic violence in Barbados: Report on a national study designed to determine the prevalence and characteristics of domestic violence in Barbados."

Center for Disease Control and Prevention (CDC). 2014. *Violence against Children in Haiti: Findings from a National Survey*. Retrieved 12 Aug. 2019 at https://www.cdc.gov/violenceprevention/pdf/violence-haiti.pdf.

Curtis, Debra. 2009. *Pleasures and Perils: Girls' Sexuality in a Caribbean Consumer Culture*. New Brunswick, NJ: Rutgers University Press.

Department of Gender Relations. 2010. "Women's Support Centre: Statistics on Client Intake and Crisis Calls 2001-2013." Ministry of Wellness, Family Relations, and Gender. Castries, St. Lucia.

DeShong, Halimah A. F. 2015. "Policing Femininity, Affirming Masculinity: Relationship Violence, Control and Spatial Limitation." *Journal of Gender Studies* 24 (1): 85-103.

Directorate of Gender Affairs. 2017. "DoGA launches its Support and Referral Centre." Retrieved 26 July 2019 at https://genderaffairs. gov.ag/news/14985742306697.

Essayag, Sebastian. 2017. "From Commitment to Action: Policies to End Violence Against Women in Latin America and the Caribbean." UNDP and UN Women. Retrieved 2 Oct. 2019 at https//www2.unwomen.org/-/media/field%20office%20americas/documentos/publicaciones/2017/1 1/fromcommitmenttoactionengcompressed.pef?la=en&vs=3922.

Evens, Emily, Michele Lanham, Karin Santi, Kathleen Ridgway, Giuliana Morales, Caleb Parker, Claire Brennan, Marjan de Bruin, Pavel Chladni Desrosiers, Xenia Diaz, Marta Drago, Roger Mclean, Modesto Mendizabal, Dirk Davis, Rebecca B. Hershow, and Robyn Dayton. 2019. "Experiences of gender-based violence among female sex workers, men who have sex with men, and transgender women in Latin America and the Caribbean: A qualitative study to inform HIV programming." *BMC International Health and Human Rights* 19(9): 1-14.

Hadeed, Linda F. & Nabila El-Bassel. 2006. "Social support among Afro-Trinidadian women experiencing intimate partner violence." *Violence Against Women* 12(8): 740-760.

Hakimi, Dehnad, Thema Bryant-Davis, Sarah E. Ullman, and Robyn Latrice Gobin. 2018. "Relationship Between Negative Social Reactions to Sexual Assault Disclosure and Mental Health Outcomes of Black and White Female Survivors." *Psychological Trauma* 10(3): 270-275.

Inter-Agency Standing Committee. 2015. *Guidelines for Integrating Gender-Based Violence Interventions in Humanitarian Action: Reducing Risk, Promoting Resilience and Aiding Recovery.* Global Protection Cluster. Retrieved at www.gbvguidelines.org.

Jacobs, Farmala. 2017. "From where I stand: Leaving no one behind in Barbuda." *From Where I Stand....Editorial Series.* Retrieved 26 July 2019 at www.unwomen.org/en/news/stories/2017/12/from-where-i-stand-famala-jacobs.

Judicial Reform and Institutional Strengthening [JURIST] Project. 2017. "Model Guidelines for Sexual Offence Cases in the Caribbean Region." Retrieved 30 July 2019 at https://www.juristproject.org/images/publications/model_guidelines/Model_Guidelines_for_Sexual_Offence_Cases_in_the_Caribbean_Region_-_For_website.compressed.pdf.

Kabeer, Naila. 2003. *Gender Mainstreaming in Poverty Eradication and the Millennium Development Goals: A Handbook for Policymakers and Other Stakeholders.* London: The Commonwealth Secretariat.

Kee, Jac. S. M. 2005. *Cultivating Violence Through Technology?* Association for Progressive Communications Women's Networking Support Programme. Retrieved 19 Aug. 2019 at http://www.apc.org/en/system/files/VAW_ICTG_EN.pdf.

Kempadoo, Kamala. 2009. "Caribbean Sexuality: Mapping the Field." *Caribbean Review of Gender Studies* 3: 1-24.

Morrison, Andrew, Mary Ellsberg and Sarah Bott. 2007. "Addressing gender-based violence: A critical review of interventions." *The World Bank Research Observer*. 22(1): 25-51.

Mutri, Nancy & Patricia Donald. 2006. "Violence against women and girls in the Caribbean: An intervention and lessons learned from Jamaica." *Caribbean Quarterly* 52(2-3): 83-103.

Rajnauth-Lee, Maureen. 2019. "Beyond Bias: Access to Justice and Social Protection in the Caribbean." Presentation to UN Commission on the Status of Women, 15 March.

Rivas, Carol, Moira Kelly, & Gene Feder. 2013. "Drawing the line: How African, Caribbean and White British women live out psychologically abusive experiences." *Violence Against Women* 19(9): 1104-1132.

Sudderth, Lori K. 1998. "'It'll Come Right Back to Me': The Interactional Context of Discussing Rape with Significant Others" *Violence Against Women*, 4(5): 572-595.

Sudderth, Lori K. 2013. "Services for Survivors of Sexual Assault in St. Lucia." Unpublished report for PROSAF, Castries, St. Lucia.

Thakur, Dhanaraj. 2018. "How Do ICTs Mediate Gender-based Violence in Jamaica?" *Gender & Development* 26(2): 267-282.

Thompson, Martie, Dylan Sitterle, George Clay, & Jeffrey Kingree. 2007. "Reasons for Not Reporting Victimizations to the Police: Do They Vary for Physical and Sexual Incidents?" Journal of American College Health 55(5): 277-282.

UNIFEM/ECLAC. 2005. *Eliminating Gender-based Violence, Ensuring Equality*. Regional Assessment Actions to End Violence Against Women in the Caribbean. Christ Church, Barbados: United National Devopment Fund for Women Caribbean Office.

United Nations Development Program [UNDP]. 2016. *Caribbean Human Development Report—Multidimensional Progress: Human Resilience Beyond Income*. Retrieved 19 Aug. 2019 at https://www.un.org/documents/ga/res/48/a48r104.htm.

United Nations Development Program. 2019. *"Caribbean: Climate Vulnerability."* Retrieved 2 Oct 2019 at https://www.adaptation-undp.org/explore/caribbean.

Safety and Island Life

United Nations Statistics Division. 2015. *"The World's Women 2015: Trends and Statistics."* New York City: United Nations.

UN Women. 2019. *"Advocacy Brief—Ending Violence Against Women."* Retrieved Oct. 2, 2019 at https://caribbean.unwomen.org/en/our-work/ending-violence-against-women/advocacy-brief.

Vassell, Linnette. 2017. "Bringing the broader context home: Gender, human rights and governance in the Caribbean." *Caribbean Quarterly* 52(2/3): 51-65.

Wilets, Jim. 2010. "Divergence between LGBTI Legal, Political, and Social Progress in the Caribbean and Latin America." Pp. 349-357 in *The Politics of Sexuality in Latin American: A Reader on Lesbian, Gay, Bisexual, and Transgender Rights* ed. By Javier Corrales & Mario Pecheny. Pittsburgh, PA: University of Pittsburgh Press.

Woodlock, Delanie. 2017. "The abuse of technology in domestic violence and stalking." *Violence Against Women* 23(5): 584-602.

INDEX

#

20th century, 294
21st century, 20, 128, 174, 175, 176, 292

A

abduction, 213
abortion, 212
academic performance, xviii, 280, 283, 286
adolescents, x, xvii, 19, 55, 56, 232, 233, 234, 235, 243, 245, 246, 247, 248, 252, 255, 256, 258, 263, 265, 266, 268, 269, 272, 274, 275, 276, 277, 278, 281, 283, 286, 287, 288, 289
adulthood, xviii, 53, 254, 258, 259, 260, 266, 280, 283, 286, 308
adults, 41, 76, 84, 108, 143, 168, 248, 254, 265, 303, 304, 309
advocacy, xv, 91, 131, 135, 143, 144, 148, 331
affirmative action, 195
African American women, 317, 328
African-American, 147

agencies, 2, 43, 47, 102, 180, 184, 285, 321, 322, 325
aggression, 5, 6, 7, 21, 27, 28, 32, 43, 55, 57, 76, 77, 102, 172, 233, 236, 238, 240, 242, 244, 245, 246, 247, 248, 249, 263, 271, 287, 320
aggressive behavior, 248
AIDS, 97
alcohol abuse, 8
alcohol consumption, 7, 10
anger, 68, 110, 113, 114, 117, 119, 137, 260, 263, 268, 274
animal assisted, 132, 133, 135, 136, 147, 153, 155
animal assisted activities, 132, 136
animal assisted therapy, 132, 133, 135, 136, 147, 153, 155
anonymity, xix, 45, 46, 47, 237, 302, 315, 318, 319, 325, 326
anxiety, xviii, 63, 64, 68, 70, 71, 72, 73, 74, 76, 77, 85, 107, 108, 110, 112, 113, 114, 117, 119, 132, 260, 262, 269, 280, 282, 286
arranged marriage, 206, 210, 211, 226

334 *Index*

assault, xiii, xiv, xviii, 7, 14, 43, 45, 50, 56, 57, 79, 80, 81, 82, 83, 84, 87, 89, 90, 91, 95, 96, 97, 98, 144, 215, 216, 244, 253, 280, 303, 304, 305, 306, 317, 327, 328

assessment, xi, xii, xviii, 2, 3, 4, 14, 15, 16, 18, 24, 26, 29, 43, 55, 57, 59, 72, 73, 76, 82, 83, 94, 111, 221, 262, 264, 271, 285, 292, 297, 298, 299, 307, 318, 319

assessment questionnaire (POLICE DV), v, xii, 23, 24, 26, 29

Association of Women's Organizations in Jamaica (AWOJA), 325

attachment theory, 105, 108, 124, 125

attitudes toward DV, 29

B

Barbados, 322, 328, 330

barriers, xvi, 58, 103, 206, 217, 219, 224

barriers to help-seeking, 206

bounds, 139, 146, 149

boys, 216, 248, 283, 324, 326

brides, 211, 213

bullying, 203, 235, 249, 253

C

campus climate, 50, 56

canine advocates, x, xv, 132, 137, 139, 144, 145, 147, 154, 155

canine therapist, 132, 137, 139, 140, 141, 142, 150, 151

Caribbean, xix, 315, 316, 317, 318, 319, 320, 321, 322, 324, 326, 327, 328, 329, 330, 331

Caribbean countries, 316, 320, 321

Caribbean nations, 322, 324, 326

Catholic Church, 134

CCN, 132, 133, 135, 136, 137, 138, 139, 140, 141, 142, 143, 144, 145, 146, 147, 148, 151, 152, 153, 154, 155, 157

child maltreatment, 253, 274, 276

child marriage, 214, 227

child protection, 35, 175

children and adolescents, xvii, 252, 255, 256, 258, 265, 269, 277, 278, 283, 288

choice, 138, 141, 209, 211, 215, 218, 226

coerced, 114, 206, 208, 210

coercion, xiii, 79, 81, 90, 172, 189, 210, 211, 218, 316, 323

cognitive ability, 267

cognitive process, 289

cognitive processing, 289

cognitive psychology, 105

commercial sexual exploitation, xvi, 205, 208

community violence (CV), vii, xviii, 115, 279, 280, 281, 282, 283, 284, 285, 286

consent, 69, 83, 84, 85, 88, 95, 166, 184, 209, 210, 211, 212, 222, 223, 237, 302

counseling, 40, 132, 136, 139, 140, 141, 142, 143, 144, 147, 149, 150, 151, 157, 317, 325

criminal activity, 262, 285

criminal justice system, xix, 213, 315, 321

criminality, 292, 298, 299, 306, 309

Crisis Center North, vi, 131, 132, 138, 141, 147, 156, 157

cultural conflict, 215

cultural identity, 215

cultural influences, 214

cultural practices, xvi, 206, 212, 215

cultural silencing, 217, 219

culture, 111, 188, 194, 219, 225, 318, 325

CV exposure, xviii, 280, 281, 282, 283, 284, 285, 286

cyber dating abuse (CDA), vi, x, xvii, 231, 232, 233, 234, 235, 236, 238, 240, 241, 242, 243, 244, 245, 247, 248, 249

cyberbullying, xvii, 158, 232, 234

Index

335

D

dating relationships, xvii, 232, 235, 236, 238, 239, 244, 245, 246, 247, 248

dating violence, 34, 56, 57, 192, 231, 233, 234, 235, 237, 244, 245, 246, 247, 248, 249, 253

debt bondage, 206, 208

deceived, 206, 210

deportation, 210, 218, 219

depression, xviii, 50, 56, 63, 64, 68, 71, 72, 74, 75, 76, 262, 280, 282, 286, 317

depressive symptomatology, 9, 71, 78

depressive symptoms, 74, 259, 283, 287

deprivation, 25, 65, 81, 255, 280

developmental outcomes, vii, xviii, 279, 280, 281, 282, 286

diagnosis of local security, 292, 312

domestic and family violence, 129, 206, 221

Domestic Violence Risk (RVD), xi, 2, 3, 4

duress, 209

E

early marriage, 206, 216, 227

education, 17, 54, 56, 67, 81, 94, 102, 125, 127, 153, 156, 157, 159, 165, 170, 172, 202, 203, 220, 235, 262, 301, 323, 326, 327

evidence collection, x, xiv, 80, 81, 82, 84, 87, 92

excess alcohol/drugs, 10

exploitation, xvi, 205, 206, 208, 209, 221, 223, 224, 227, 324

extended family, 211, 216, 220, 225

F

faith, 207, 284, 325

family conflict, 212, 284

family environment, 94

family functioning, 172, 268

family relationships, 208, 270, 284

family violence, 96, 121, 129, 175, 181, 206, 221, 275, 281

firearms access, 6

forced, vi, x, xi, xvi, 2, 57, 144, 205, 206, 207, 208, 210, 211, 212, 213, 214, 215, 216, 217, 219, 220, 221, 222, 223, 224, 225, 226, 227, 228, 229, 316

forced impregnation, 215

forced marriage, vi, x, xvi, 205, 206, 207, 208, 210, 211, 212, 213, 214, 215, 216, 217, 219, 220, 221, 222, 223, 224, 225, 226, 227, 228

formal, xii, 2, 17, 24, 25, 29, 40, 43, 47, 49, 51, 52, 53, 133, 149, 165, 183, 193, 219, 298, 299, 301, 302, 305, 319

formal help, xii, 40, 43, 47, 49, 51, 53

Freud, Sigmund, 133

frontline workers, 321, 323, 324, 326

functional model of parenting, 163

G

gender, ix, xi, xix, 19, 23, 26, 28, 29, 30, 31, 32, 34, 35, 36, 40, 42, 44, 48, 49, 50, 51, 52, 53, 54, 56, 57, 58, 80, 88, 93, 101, 111, 112, 126, 159, 173, 176, 186, 189, 193, 194, 195, 199, 203, 217, 226, 228, 243, 247, 248, 258, 288, 289, 293, 305, 313, 315, 316, 317, 318, 319, 320, 321, 322, 323, 324, 325, 326, 327, 328, 329, 330, 331

gender differences, 42, 49, 50, 53, 54, 56, 57, 176, 289, 313

gender equality, 193, 194, 195, 324, 326

gender equity, 327

gender inequality, 195, 318, 326

gender role, 26, 28, 217

Index

gender stereotypes, ix, xi, 23, 26, 28, 29, 30, 31, 193, 194
gender violence, 80
gender-based violence, xix, 203, 315, 316, 317, 318, 319, 320, 321, 322, 323, 324, 325, 326, 328, 329, 330
girls, x, xvi, 58, 140, 141, 142, 189, 206, 210, 212, 213, 215, 216, 224, 225, 248, 283, 316, 318, 320, 321, 323, 324, 325, 326, 328, 330
government leadership, 321
grooms, 211
guidelines, x, xvii, 82, 83, 87, 193, 198, 221, 224, 252, 298, 322, 329

H

Haiti, 327, 328
health care, 82, 83, 88, 92, 93, 94, 96, 98, 323, 324
health care professionals, 82, 92, 94, 98, 323
health care system, 94, 96
health personnel, xiii, 80, 81, 90, 91, 92, 191
health problems, 258
health services, 29, 47, 82, 88, 92, 93, 183
health status, 50, 89
healthcare professional training, 80
helplessness, 113, 116, 118
help-seeking, v, ix, xii, xvi, 34, 39, 40, 44, 45, 47, 48, 49, 51, 52, 53, 54, 102, 103, 206, 219, 220, 222, 244
homelessness, xviii, 262, 280, 286
homicide, 3, 4, 5, 6, 7, 8, 9, 10, 11, 12, 14, 17, 19, 20, 21, 151, 174, 218, 308
homicide rates, 308
honor killing, 218
hostility, 63, 68, 71, 113
human animal bond, vi, 131, 132, 138

human rights, 25, 81, 162, 182, 195, 209, 221, 252, 331
human service providers, xvi, 206, 221

I

illegal, 206, 208, 209, 296, 309
illegal movement of people, 209
Indonesia, x, 179, 182, 192, 200, 201, 203
Indonesian women, vi, 179, 180, 181, 182, 185, 187, 199, 201, 202, 203
inferences, 106
informal, 17, 25, 40, 43, 47, 49, 51, 52, 53, 219, 319
informal help, 43, 47, 49, 51, 53
information and communication technologies (ICTs), xvi, 231, 232, 233, 235, 238, 242, 243, 316, 324, 330
informed consent, 69, 83, 84, 85, 88, 166, 210, 211, 222, 223, 237, 302
insecurity, 25, 107, 113, 124, 292, 301, 302, 306
intervention, ix, x, xii, xiii, xiv, xvii, 20, 24, 26, 28, 30, 33, 35, 72, 80, 82, 88, 92, 94, 96, 99, 103, 118, 119, 175, 176, 203, 220, 252, 254, 256, 266, 267, 268, 270, 271, 272, 285, 286, 293, 299, 305, 308, 309, 330
intervention strategies, xvii, 26, 252, 268, 272, 293, 299
intimate partner violence (IPV), v, vi, ix, x, xii, xiv, 1, 5, 7, 11, 15, 16, 18, 20, 21, 24, 29, 33, 34, 35, 36, 39, 40, 41, 42, 43, 44, 45, 46, 47, 48, 49, 50, 51, 52, 53, 54, 56, 57, 59, 61, 62, 63, 64, 65, 67, 72, 74, 75, 76, 77, 78, 98, 99, 100, 101, 102, 103, 108, 110, 111, 113, 115, 116, 118, 119, 120, 121, 122, 123, 124, 126, 128, 137, 166, 176, 206, 207, 217, 218, 219, 221, 224, 225, 226, 228, 248, 275, 281, 317, 318, 319, 321, 329

Index

intimate violence, xi, xix, 13, 154, 155, 234, 243, 315, 316, 319

intuitive training, 132, 145, 146, 149

IPV victimization and consequences, 46

J

juvenile delinquency, 33

K

karma, 217, 218, 225

kidnapping, 213

L

Latin America, 297, 328, 329, 331

law, vi, xvi, 2, 3, 15, 17, 29, 32, 35, 36, 37, 86, 102, 125, 126, 127, 179, 180, 181, 182, 183, 185, 190, 192, 193, 194, 195, 197, 200, 201, 202, 216, 223, 226, 227, 229, 295, 297, 323, 324

M

Malaysia, 76, 203

maltreatment, 261, 274

marriage, x, xvi, 123, 183, 186, 189, 205, 206, 207, 208, 210, 211, 212, 213, 214, 215, 216, 217, 218, 219, 220, 221, 222, 223, 224, 225, 226, 227, 229, 316

medical and forensic examination, 83, 89

mental disorders, 9, 13, 62

mental health, xviii, 4, 11, 41, 44, 55, 63, 64, 73, 74, 75, 76, 77, 93, 97, 111, 125, 163, 175, 259, 260, 262, 263, 267, 270, 272, 275, 277, 280, 286, 288, 325

mental health problems, 4, 9, 11, 64, 111, 125, 260, 270, 275

Model Guidelines for Sexual Offences in the Caribbean Region, 322

modern slavery, xvi, 205, 206, 207, 208, 210, 223, 224, 225, 227, 228

mothers, x, xv, 161, 162, 163, 164, 167, 168, 169, 170, 171, 172, 173, 174, 181, 213

multiple victimization, vi, xvii, 232, 251, 252, 253, 254, 256, 257, 258, 261, 262, 263, 264, 266, 267, 271, 272, 275, 277

N

norms, 111, 168, 215, 227, 248, 252

O

Office of Justice Programs, 57, 152, 275

offline dating violence (ODV), vi, x, xvii, 232, 233, 234, 235, 237, 238, 239, 240, 241, 242, 243

ostracism, 219

P

parenting, vi, x, xv, 125, 129, 161, 162, 163, 164, 168, 170, 171, 172, 173, 174, 175, 176

parenting of the victim, 172

parenting practices of the victim, 163

Paws for Empowerment, 131, 132, 133, 135, 139, 143, 144, 146, 148, 149, 152, 153, 154, 155, 157

perpetrators, 10, 17, 30, 51, 86, 87, 92, 95, 115, 124, 125, 181, 187, 189, 190, 192, 195, 196, 197, 198, 199, 215, 219, 220, 259, 295, 316, 319

physical abuse, 24, 173, 267, 276, 277

physical aggression, 43, 76, 303

physical environment, 269

physical well-being, xiii, 62, 272
police, v, ix, xi, 1, 2, 3, 6, 13, 14, 20, 23, 24, 25, 27, 28, 29, 30, 31, 32, 33, 34, 35, 36, 37, 40, 43, 47, 51, 57, 66, 84, 162, 176, 183, 184, 185, 186, 187, 188, 189, 190, 191, 192, 196, 197, 199, 200, 213, 223, 285, 295, 298, 299, 300, 305, 307, 317, 318, 319, 321, 322, 325, 330
police attitudes, v, ix, xii, 23, 24, 26, 28, 29, 31
POLICE DV, xii, 24, 29, 30
police interventions, 27
police officers, xi, 2, 3, 24, 25, 27, 28, 29, 30, 31, 32, 33, 35, 185, 186, 191
polyvictimization, 252, 253, 255, 257, 258, 259, 260, 261, 262, 263, 266, 267, 271, 274, 275, 276, 277, 278
pornography, 215
Portugal, 1, 2, 3, 23, 61, 64, 65, 66, 67, 70, 75, 161, 162, 165, 231, 234, 251, 279, 282, 291, 294, 295, 296, 299, 308
prevalence, x, xii, xviii, 16, 25, 36, 40, 41, 42, 44, 45, 48, 49, 50, 51, 53, 54, 55, 56, 57, 59, 64, 76, 100, 123, 176, 207, 208, 233, 234, 235, 238, 239, 244, 246, 247, 248, 255, 260, 269, 272, 278, 280, 281, 286, 287, 288, 328
prevention challenge, vii, 279, 280, 284, 286
prevention challenges, vii, 279, 280, 284
promiscuity, 216
promised bride, 212
protection, xi, xii, 2, 17, 24, 29, 103, 105, 169, 171, 172, 183, 184, 187, 189, 192, 194, 196, 197, 199, 256, 266, 284
protective factors, 257, 266, 267, 269, 270, 272, 285, 286, 288
psychoanalysis, 105, 124
psychological distress, 262, 264, 278, 288
psychological health, 55, 72, 268, 270
psychological intervention, vi, 164, 251, 252

psychological well-being, 56, 74, 263, 275, 283
psychopathological symptomatology, v, ix, xii, 61, 62, 63, 64, 65, 69, 70, 71, 72, 73
psychopathological symptoms, 68, 75, 286
psychopathology, 10, 62, 64, 72, 76, 77, 111, 127, 276, 277, 288

Q

quality of life, 33, 295, 305
questionnaire, xii, xiii, 24, 26, 29, 30, 51, 62, 69, 166, 236, 237, 244, 301

R

rape, xviii, 41, 55, 87, 92, 97, 189, 280, 281, 316, 319, 322, 323, 330
reporting to authorities, 27, 318
resources, 44, 45, 143, 171, 180, 255, 263, 264, 266, 270, 286, 309, 320, 321
risk assessment, v, xi, xiii, 1, 2, 3, 4, 5, 6, 7, 11, 13, 14, 15, 18, 19, 20, 26, 62, 73, 176, 221

S

safe haven, 109, 256
safety, 13, 25, 31, 33, 40, 103, 105, 119, 128, 135, 138, 144, 145, 173, 182, 183, 187, 190, 192, 196, 221, 222, 256, 259, 269, 284, 293, 294, 295, 310, 313
sanctions, 20, 32, 196, 198, 212
security, xi, xii, xviii, 2, 11, 24, 27, 29, 108, 126, 156, 169, 170, 285, 286, 291, 292, 293, 296, 298, 299, 301, 305, 306, 308, 309, 312
security forces, xi, 2, 27
seek help, xii, 24, 25, 27, 28, 29, 40, 49, 52, 53, 217, 218, 219, 220

Index

separation/attempted separation/divorce, 11, 13

service, xii, 28, 30, 40, 43, 46, 54, 55, 58, 59, 92, 97, 102, 123, 139, 152, 153, 158, 189, 198, 203, 207, 221, 222, 224, 225, 226, 227, 228, 277, 288, 321, 324

service provider, xii, xvi, 40, 44, 46, 54, 139, 206, 207, 221, 222, 224, 324

services for survivors, 321, 324

servitude, 206, 208, 228

sex, ix, xi, xiii, xiv, 2, 23, 24, 26, 27, 28, 30, 32, 36, 37, 74, 79, 80, 86, 162, 176, 193, 214, 216, 236, 238, 239, 321, 328

sexism, 30, 35

sexual abuse, 35, 82, 89, 94, 151, 181, 214, 233, 267

sexual activity, xiii, 79, 213, 215

sexual assault, xiii, xiv, 43, 45, 50, 56, 57, 79, 80, 81, 82, 83, 84, 87, 89, 90, 91, 95, 96, 97, 98, 215, 244, 253, 317, 328, 329, 330

sexual exploitation, 206, 208, 221, 223, 224

sexual orientation, 24, 27, 30, 88

sexual trafficking, x, xvi, 206, 222, 224, 225

sexual violence, v, xvi, 5, 6, 11, 41, 45, 47, 48, 50, 55, 59, 65, 79, 80, 81, 82, 83, 88, 92, 93, 96, 97, 98, 101, 120, 122, 153, 185, 189, 199, 200, 205, 215, 216, 234, 235, 253, 281, 316, 318, 319, 321, 322, 323

sexuality, 81, 129, 194, 318, 320, 323

sexually transmitted diseases, 82

shame, 25, 51, 53, 103, 110, 112, 117, 189, 192, 218, 229

shelter, x, xv, 47, 132, 137, 138, 143, 148, 154, 155, 157, 158, 188, 192, 325

smuggling, 209, 229

social isolation, 8, 25, 27, 206, 219, 220

social media, 293, 311, 316

social network, 232, 233, 236, 237, 238, 239

social support, 74, 78, 257, 259, 263, 264, 266, 268, 273, 275, 278, 318, 327

social workers, 27, 123, 184, 270, 323

society, xvii, 24, 27, 181, 209, 214, 246, 252, 254, 284, 290, 308, 323

stress, xiv, 8, 11, 64, 73, 74, 85, 93, 94, 100, 106, 118, 119, 122, 123, 126, 127, 132, 147, 149, 150, 167, 257, 259, 265, 266, 270, 294, 317, 321

substance abuse, xi, xviii, 2, 8, 18, 257, 260, 262, 267, 280, 282, 286, 289

substance use, 10, 32, 46, 58, 125, 246, 278, 317, 321

suicidal ideation, xviii, 63, 259, 280, 286

suicide, 6, 10, 21, 63, 64, 77, 140, 257

suicide attempts, 63, 64

survivors, ix, x, xii, xiv, xv, xix, 34, 39, 40, 41, 43, 44, 51, 54, 81, 88, 96, 99, 100, 101, 102, 103, 110, 113, 120, 121, 125, 127, 131, 143, 206, 207, 216, 218, 220, 315, 316, 317, 318, 319, 321, 322, 323, 324, 325, 326, 327

symptoms, 55, 62, 63, 64, 68, 70, 74, 75, 76, 77, 85, 93, 118, 123, 254, 256, 258, 261, 262, 263, 264, 267, 270, 275, 283, 286, 289, 317

systemic inequalities, 319

T

the law 'on the books,' the law 'on the ground', xvi, 180, 182

therapeutic process, xiv, 100, 120, 141

therapeutic relationship, 104

therapist, xiv, 100, 104, 109, 113, 116, 117, 118, 119, 123, 128, 132, 137, 139, 140, 141, 142, 150, 151, 197

therapy, xiv, 36, 74, 100, 104, 109, 110, 111, 112, 113, 115, 116, 119, 120, 121, 122, 123, 124, 125, 126, 127, 128, 132, 133, 135, 136, 137, 139, 141, 147, 149, 156, 158, 159, 177, 192, 197

340   *Index*

threats, 6, 8, 11, 12, 27, 46, 47, 50, 105, 210, 211, 213, 218, 219, 233, 236
tradition, 134, 181, 214
traditional beliefs, xii, 24, 26, 29, 31
traditional gender role, 319
trafficking, x, xvi, 206, 208, 209, 213, 222, 223, 224, 225, 226, 229
training, x, xv, xvi, 2, 3, 31, 54, 80, 92, 96, 100, 119, 123, 132, 135, 138, 142, 145, 146, 148, 149, 150, 153, 154, 157, 206, 225, 322, 323, 324, 325, 327
transference, xiv, 100, 109, 110, 111, 116, 120
transference and countertransference, xiv, 100, 109, 111
transnational crime, 209
types of violence, x, xviii, 12, 42, 48, 49, 50, 253, 274, 280

U

unwanted pregnancies, 212

V

values, 69, 103, 168, 171, 180, 194, 207, 215, 303, 318
vicarious trauma, xiv, 100, 118, 119, 126, 127
victim-blaming, 29, 102, 318, 319, 326
victims/survivors, vi, x, 99, 100, 110, 113, 120, 121

violence prevention, ix, 2, 158, 228, 284
violent crime, 29, 282, 296, 306, 308, 320
visa, 214, 219
vulnerability, 73, 114, 116, 169, 215, 219, 256, 259, 265, 268, 285, 289

W

witness, 191, 195, 282
women victims of domestic violence, 164, 180
World Health Organization (WHO), 24, 80, 280, 290

Y

young adults, x, xvii, 50, 232, 235, 267, 276, 277, 287
young people, x, xvii, xviii, 232, 234, 235, 242, 243, 248, 252, 253, 254, 255, 256, 257, 259, 260, 261, 262, 263, 264, 265, 266, 267, 268, 269, 270, 271, 275, 280, 281, 282, 286
youth, vii, x, xvi, xvii, xviii, 53, 57, 227, 231, 233, 235, 245, 247, 248, 249, 252, 254, 255, 256, 257, 258, 261, 263, 264, 265, 268, 269, 270, 273, 274, 275, 276, 277, 278, 279, 280, 281, 282, 283, 284, 285, 286, 287, 289
youth victims, vii, 279, 280, 281, 284

Related Nova Publications

Occupational Stress: Risk Factors, Prevention and Management Strategies

Editors: Nicola Mucci, MD, PhD, Gabriele Giorgi, PhD, Francesco Sderci, MD, and Giulio Arcangeli, MD

Series: Safety and Risk in Society

Book Description: Related work stress also generate significant costs, both direct and indirect, for companies. A budgeted economic investment will be use

Hardcover ISBN: 978-1-53615-404-7
Retail Price: $160

Indicators of School Crime and Safety

Author: Liam Shephard

Series: Safety and Risk in Society

Book Description: The report included in this book is the seventeenth in a series of annual publications produced jointly by the National Center for Education Statistics (NCES), Institute of Education Sciences (IES), in the U.S. Department of Education, and the Bureau of Justice Statistics (BJS) in the U.S. Department of Justice. This report presents the most recent data available on school crime and student safety.

Hardcover ISBN: 978-1-53613-680-7
Retail Price: $250

To see a complete list of Nova publications, please visit our website at www.novapublishers.com

Related Nova Publications

PUBLIC AND SCHOOL SAFETY: RISK ASSESSMENT, PERCEPTIONS AND MANAGEMENT STRATEGIES

EDITOR: Jarrett Conaway

SERIES: Safety and Risk in Society

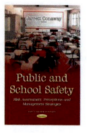

BOOK DESCRIPTION: This book discusses the EDURISC self-assessment questionnaire used for the assessment of integral safety in schools; provides insight on school indoor quality; and examines integration of chemical safety education into the preschool curriculum.

SOFTCOVER ISBN: 978-1-63117-223-6
RETAIL PRICE: $82

SAFETY CULTURE: PROGRESS, TRENDS AND CHALLENGES

EDITOR: Michel Sacré

SERIES: Safety and Risk in Society

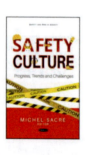

BOOK DESCRIPTION: In this compilation, the authors first analyze three components of safety culture: safety climate, safety values, and culture of prevention. The analysis includes both new empirical results and a review of earlier studies.

HARDCOVER ISBN: 978-1-53616-289-9
RETAIL PRICE: $230

To see a complete list of Nova publications, please visit our website at www.novapublishers.com